« DARK SCENES F

Dark Scenes
from
Damaged Earth

The Gothic Anthropocene

JUSTIN D. EDWARDS, RUNE GRAULUND, AND
JOHAN HÖGLUND EDITORS

University of Minnesota Press
Minneapolis
London

The University of Minnesota Press gratefully acknowledges support for the open-access edition of this book from Linnaeus University, Sweden and the University of Southern Denmark.

Published by the University of Minnesota Press
111 Third Avenue South, Suite 290
Minneapolis, MN 55401-2520
http://www.upress.umn.edu

◼ Available as a Manifold edition at manifold.umn.edu

ISBN 978-1-5179-1122-5 (hc)
ISBN 978-1-5179-1123-2 (pb)

A Cataloging-in-Publication record for this book is available from the Library of Congress.

Printed in the United States of America on acid-free paper

The University of Minnesota is an equal-opportunity educator and employer.

UMP BmB 2022

Contents

Acknowledgments

A project of this scope cannot be accomplished without the support of a number of hardworking and generous friends, scholars, administrators, and family members. Among the many to whom we extend our gratitude, we need to mention, in particular, David Ellison, who helped organize the Gothic Extremities workshop where this collection got started, and the International Gothic Association for permitting us to organize conference panels on Gothic in the Anthropocene in Manchester (2018) and Romeoville (2019). At these conferences, we presented some of our early ideas on the subject, and we received valuable feedback that helped and inspired us to push forward with this book. We also want to give our warmest thanks to the Swedish foundation Riksbankens Jubileumsfond for its generous funding of the Gothic in the Anthropocene workshop held at Linnaeus University in 2019, where the first drafts of this collection were presented and discussed, and to the Linnaeus University Centre for Concurrences in Colonial and Postcolonial Studies, which funded editorial meetings along the way. We owe special thanks to Rebecca Duncan, who commented generously on the Introduction, and to the good people at the University of Minnesota Press, who gave this collection the best possible home. We are also very grateful to Linnaeus University and to the University of Southern Denmark for the funding that made it possible to make this book Open Access on the excellent Manifold system. Finally, we thank the contributors whose chapters make up its content and who helped provide essential feedback on early drafts as well as collaborator Esthie Hugo for her assistance when preparing the manuscript for publication. On a personal note, Johan Höglund thanks his colleagues in Concurrences for comments and support and David, Agnes, Edith, Hilda, and Cissi for giving his life joy and meaning outside the confines of the computer screen.

Introduction

Gothic in the Anthropocene

We live in gothic times. This has become a cliché in the critical literature. But in a new epoch overflowing with narratives of excess, exploitation, death, self-destruction, tipping points, and apocalypse, it is more than a mere platitude. Gothic forms are as useful as they are pervasive: they can conjure dark terrains layered by plantation slavery and petro-economic cultures like in the television series *True Detective* (2014–19); they can imagine apocalyptic landscapes ravaged by environmental destruction and consumed by zombification like in the novel *The Girl with All the Gifts* (2014); they can reflect the tortured bodies of nonhuman animals within the destructive economies of animal agriculture like in the film *Raw* (2014); they can depict the brutalized bodies of human animals when nonhuman animals bite back like in the film *Crawl* (2019). The realities of planetary destruction are disseminated in gothic fictions. In the Anthropocene, in other words, gothic has the potential to present us with a "realer," if darker, reality wherein we can imagine a future world based on what we have done in the past, whether it be excessive consumption, exploitation of resources, murder, or other kinds of transgression. For in gothic, as in the Anthropocene, we will claim, the "boundaries between fiction and reality blur, to the extent that each interpenetrates and shapes the other, dismantling conventional patterns of differentiation."[1]

We call this study *Dark Scenes from Damaged Earth: The Gothic Anthropocene* despite being deeply aware of the latter concept's inability to make plain the long material history of the violence that has brought on a notably unequal climate crisis. This is an awareness that has prompted us to structure this collection with the help of three additional denominations: Capitalocene, Plantationocene, Chthulucene. As discussed in more detail later in this Introduction, these recognize crucial histories and biological entanglements that the Anthropocene, as a concept, is often perceived to evade. Still, we hold on to the Anthropocene because the historical and scientific provenance of the term makes sense in ways that, from the perspective of the gothic at least, are eerily familiar. As a term first proposed in geology, the Anthropocene has a natural affinity with temporalities that reach far beyond the human, as of course with the chthonic[2] elements of all that which lies below. Indeed, as Tobias Menely and Jesse Oak Taylor suggest in *Anthropocene Reading: Literary History in Geologic Times* (2017), we might usefully begin "to read the Anthropocene as a literary object and at the same time to recognize the Anthropocene as a geohistorical event that may unsettle our inherited practices of reading."[3]

Yet what if we read the Anthropocene not just as a geohistorical event but as a gothic geohistorical event? As any reader of gothic tales will know, the desire to upend and unearth is generally speaking one that should be left alone, a maxim that seems to be doubled down on in the Anthropocene. Digging in the dirt is a hazardous pursuit, whether it is for the extraction of oil, minerals, and precious stones or the reverse activity of depositing plastics, spent nuclear fuel, and other toxic materials that have already caused irreparable ecological destruction in the Global South and that are now beginning to haunt also the Global North with a vengeance. Digging in the dirt is of course but one of the many upendings and disruptions instigated by anthropogenic change on a planetary scale. In our release of fossil fuels from the bowels of the earth to fuel the bright lights of modernity, for instance, it is important to recall that "fossil" fuels do in fact come from dead matter, but also that the dormant organic matter of fossilized remains of what was once alive is given new life as it has been released into the atmosphere. Rotting plants and decaying corpses, over time turning into amorphous masses of gas, coal, and oil, have after millions of years entombed once again seen daylight, only to be turned into the fire and smoke that have for the past couple of centuries been heating up the world's climate, in turn playing a key role in the sixth mass extinction that is currently killing fish, animals, and plant life in the oceans, in and on the ground, and in the sky at a rate not seen for hundreds of millions of years. Viewed in this way, the Anthropocene does not denote simply a present in which we recognize that humans have become "geological agents," as proposed by Chakrabarty, but a time when the Anthropos must conduct the introspective, abject historical work in which gothic has always engaged its audience.

Genre and the Anthropocene

While the dangers to planetary life that anthropogenic climate change brings with it have been discussed in fiction for a long time, an increasing number of authors and filmmakers have turned their attention to the climate crisis since the beginning of the millennium. The work they have produced has been theorized by Adam Trexler, Adeline Johns-Putra, Timothy Clark, and Amitav Ghosh into the distinct genre of climate fiction (cli-fi).[4] These critics point to the fact that conventional realism has struggled to imagine the crises of the Anthropocene. As Ghosh described, realism can be said to have grown out of the assumption "in both fiction and geology, that Nature was moderate and orderly."[5] Thus the realist novel "has never been forced to confront the centrality of the improbable."[6] Now when, as Ghosh argues, "the Anthropocene has already disrupted many assumptions that were founded on the relative stability of the Holocene . . . the very gestures with which it [realist fiction] conjures up reality are actually a concealment of the real."[7] To properly represent the improbable catastrophes of the Anthropocene, authors have to inhabit what Ghosh calls "the humbler dwellings that surround the manor house—those generic out-houses that were once known by names such as the gothic, the romance or the melodrama, and have now come to be called fantasy, horror and science fiction."[8] Ghosh's observation that it is primarily speculative genres that have investigated catastrophic climate change is important, as it suggests that gothic and horror are able to say things about the climate crisis that conventional, realistic modes cannot.[9]

Among speculative genres, we argue, gothic's profound interest in "transgression, excess and monstrosity"[10] makes it a supremely suitable chronicler of the violence of climate change and of the human being's tentacular connection to all uncanny, damaged life on this planet. To live in the Anthropocene is to recognize that transgression, excess, and monstrosity are no longer anomalies in human life but inextricable parts of it.[11] Gothic has the power to unsettle readers more than most other literary or cultural forms because it dwells on widespread anxieties, dread, the horrific, the repellent, and achieves a *frisson* that other mimetic modes of representation can barely render. Gothic is one of the most impulsive and adaptive of forms; it can split and reform the cells of texts in other categories, routinely combining with dystopias and apocalyptic narratives, science fiction and cli-fi, weird fiction and the new weird, noir and detective fiction, and so on. And gothic has no predictable setting or abode: it flourishes in the Arctic in Mary Shelley's *Frankenstein* (1818), in the tropics in the computer game *Dead Island* (2011), on the South Sea in Edgar Allan Poe's novella *Narrative of Arthur Gordon Pym* (1838), in the Global North in Bram Stokers's *Dracula* (1897), in the Global South in Lauren Beukes's *Zoo City* (2010), on the battlefields of the Middle East in Ahmed Saadawi's *Frankenstein in Baghdad* (2013), and in outer space as in Ridley Scott's film *Alien* (1979). It seeps into places where it ought not to be, and therein lies the vitality of gothic: it is malleable and unpredictable, refusing to be contained or clearly mapped.

This malleability allows gothic texts to merge with other forms. This should not be surprising, as gothic has a long history of hybridity, migration, cross-pollination infection, and contamination. In *Gothic Science Fiction 1818 to the Present* (2015), Sian MacArthur charts how two centuries of gothic, which is often read as reimagining the past, meshes with science fiction, a form celebrated for its futuristic imagination and its freedom to explore unique subjects and themes. Mad scientists, grotesque operations, chemical experiments, alien monsters, and other tropes speak to a form that MacArthur identifies as "Gothic science fiction."[12] Central to our discussion of the intersection of science fiction with gothic and the Anthropocene, as of the novel language we may hope to construct in the process, is the notion of the human itself. For, just as science fiction has provided us with a wide range of speculative scenarios in which the planet has either been nearly destroyed (as is typically the case in postapocalyptic fiction) or decimated in some form or other (as is typically the case in dystopian fiction and certainly so in climate fiction), science fiction has also provided us with an overabundance of ideas of how the human, the transhuman, the posthuman, and the nonhuman intersect, yet also of how they can abolish and haunt each other.

Questions of genre and form also relate to gothic and a genre that has been labeled the weird. In *Weird Fiction in Britain 1880–1939*

(2018), James Machin charts a literary history in which the weird of Machen, Blackwood, M. R. James, and Onions merges with gothic, uncanny, supernatural, horror, strange, and so on. "Acknowledging that 'weird' is," he writes, "a suggestive adjective and a mode rather than a genre also entails accepting that its subsequent slipperiness means that any attempt at rigidly differentiating it from what is now discussed as the Gothic would be both self-contradictory and counterproductive."[13] In a weird American context, Lovecraft owes much to gothic writers from England and Scotland—such as Horace Walpole and Walter Scott—who often invoke tropes of ancestral terror and anxieties about breakdowns in the borders that divide racial, national, and class differences. The fears of class upheavals in Walpole and Scott are replicated in Lovecraft's white supremacist celebration of a primordial race purity and his anxieties about a racial mixing that would engender what he envisioned as an impure Anglo-American civilization.

Within the trajectory of this literary history, there are thus tentacular lines that connect the fiction of E. T. A. Hoffmann to Charles Brocken Brown to Edgar Allan Poe to Lovecraft to China Miéville to Jeff VanderMeer to Caitlín R. Kiernan to Lauren Beukes, even as later authors resist the racist undercurrent that informs many of the early weird writers. Since the 1980s, the expression "new weird" has been used to describe slipstream fiction that meshes gothic, horror, fantasy, and science fiction. For VanderMeer, a noteworthy author of new weird fiction, the gothic tropes of haunting and the uncanny are significant for any reflections on contemporary ecology: "in the Anthropocene," he writes, "hauntings and similar manifestations become emissaries or transition points between the human sense of time and the geological sense of time."[14] Global warming is, he continues, an example of a "hyperobject"[15] that haunts us every day through repetitions of cause and effect; it cannot always be seen, but it is always there in a liminal and uncanny presence. This haunting is conceptual and corporeal: it dislocates and relocates the mind and the body not through a scientific understanding of climate change but through a reimagining of an ecological condition that includes the totalities of breakdown and disintegration. The return of the environmentally repressed does not only have the potential to inspire fear and anxiety; the ecological uncanny can also be embraced to change the cultural practices that contribute to environmental crises.

While exciting work has been done on the role of speculative fiction in general and science fiction in particular, and in the representation of ecology and of nonhuman animals, the space that ecology fills in gothic warrants a thorough investigation in any reconfiguration of our relationship with the environment, albeit always with an eye on the future and not just the past, which is the usual terrain of the gothic. Indeed, while there is merit in the claim that "the Anthropocene itself can usefully be understood as a Science Fiction trope,"[16] there is something inherently uncanny, dark, and haunting about an era defined by a "dark ecology"[17] of rising temperatures and seas, microplastics and extreme weather, the decline of the Arctic and the spread of the Great Pacific Garbage Patch, and the sixth mass extinction. Formerly envisioned as a sublime entity that no one could hope to master, or that any words supposedly fully describe, nature in the Anthropocene is rapidly drifting beyond our control in ways that are far more complex— yet at the same time also frighteningly literal—than ever before. As former conceptions of the divide between human and environment, culture and nature, artificial and natural, local and global, and past, present, and future continue to erode, we are left in the paradoxical position of having a greater impact on nature than ever before, while at the same time experiencing a profound sense of loss and agency when it comes to its continued existence.

To date, the important research on gothic and ecology has been largely limited to thematic studies of "eco-gothic," including Andrew Smith and William Hughes's *Ecogothic* (2013), Katarina Gregersdotter, Johan Höglund, and Nicklas Hållén's *Animal Horror Cinema: Genre, History, and Criticism* (2015), Dawn Keetley and Angela Tenga's *Plant Horror: Approaches to the Monstrous Vegetal in Fiction and Film* (2016), Keetley and Sivils's *Ecogothic in Nineteenth-Century American Literature* (2017), Elizabeth Parker's *The Forest and the EcoGothic: The Deep Dark Woods in the Popular Imagination* (2020), and Sladja Blazan's *Haunted Nature: The Cultural Work of Environmental Haunting* (2021). These books are significant for reflecting on gothic and environmentalism, but overall, they do not consistently engage with the important work in the humanities and social sciences that has recently been done on the Anthropocene. The present study attempts to fill that gap and, we hope, inspire further research into the field.

Gothic Methodologies in the World of the (Post)Human

To realize that we live in the Anthropocene is to recognize that the border that has separated the Anthropos from nature was always an illusion. As a range of thinkers from Bruno Latour to Timothy Morton and Bill McKibben and on to Dipesh Chakrabarty have pointed out,[18] it has become increasingly clear, as Jason W. Moore argues in *Capitalism in the Web of Life: Ecology and the Accumulation of Capital* (2015), that "the old language—Nature/Society—has become obsolete."[19] Accordingly, there is a need to develop "new methodological procedures, *narrative strategies*, and conceptual language" that will replace "the breakdown of the strategies and relationships that have sustained capital accumulation over the past five centuries."[20] It is the second of Moore's three subjects that is the focus of this volume, namely, developing novel narrative strategies for the Anthropocene, strategies that are necessarily speculative, and often dark, in nature.

If the Anthropocene is a geohistorical event that can be understood only in relation to ancient and deep history, any meaningful conceptualization of the term must, however, also look to the future. As David Farrier remarks in *Anthropocene Poetics: Deep Times, Sacrifice Zones, and Extinction* (2019), the Anthropocene

> represents a quickening in deep time, an uncanny coincidence of ancient resources, rapid change, and long consequence. Our intervention in the carbon cycle, excavating vast quantities of geological material and displacing it into the atmosphere, shows how this newly apparent immediacy of deep time is evident both in the material and immaterial evidence we leave behind. . . . The peculiar intimacy of the Anthropocene is that, in this moment thickened by contradictory temporalities and velocities, the ground has shifted.[21]

On such shifting grounds, the Anthropocene therefore presents a special chapter in the history of humankind in that our former experiences, predictive models, and narratives are no longer effective because we are witnessing, as Moore argues, "not a crisis of capitalism and nature but of modernity-in-nature."[22] *Dark Scenes from Damaged Earth* thus interrogates preconceived notions not only of time but also of space and investigates the breaking down of the borders of human worlds and bodies. In the gothic horror film *Crawl* (2019), a category 5 hurricane lets Florida alligators invade human dwellings. Human spaces are suddenly haunted by monstrous creatures who insist, by their very presence inside human dwellings, that transgression is the new normal, that the very notion of a sacred human space is meaningless, and that hiding from nature is pointless.

As exemplified by the Covid-19 pandemic that began spreading across the world in 2019 and is now so thoroughly seared into almost everything we do, nature transgresses into the world of the Anthropos also in more subtle, but equally dramatic, ways. When Rachel Carson in her influential *Silent Spring* (1962) warned of the effects that pesticides may have on the (human) animal, she tacitly recognized that the Anthropos is not a being bounded by his or her inviolate individuality but a porous vessel into which metals, chemicals, and plastics can flow, changing and deteriorating the body from within.[23] Since then, evolutionary microbiologists, such as Lynn Margulis and Margareth McFall-Ngai, have further revised our understanding of *Homo sapiens,* showing it to be a multispecies ecosystem that has coevolved with a host of other beings and that is inhabiting a fundamentally permeable body.[24] Covid-19 is one of many viruses that first formed in nonhuman wild animals and spread into humans and then across the world due to human activity. As O'Callaghan-Gordo and Antó argued, viruses like Covid-19 "appear and spread in circumstances that denote the effects of an economic and commercial practices that destroys [*sic*] natural habitats and animal populations, including those of humans living there."[25] In this way, the Covid-19 pandemic must be understood as part of the Anthropocene era; it may not have been intentionally produced in a human lab, as some conspiracists claim, but it emerged out of regions where human activity has disrupted "earth's natural habitats and ecosystems by intensely altering the patterns and mechanisms of interactions between species,"[26] and it then took advantage of countless pandemic pathways constituted by, for instance, global air travel and human megacities.

Gothic has for a long time recognized this permeable state of the (human) animal body and, in countless narratives, speculated on the transformative and often, but not invariably, catastrophic effects that occur when it is entered and transformed by foreign species. In *Dark Scenes from Damaged Earth,* these species are frequently anthropogenic; viruses, bacteria, or fungi made in labs in the interest of the military–industrial complex. In the South Korean zombie film *Train to Busan* (2016) and in Ling Ma's novel *Severance* (2018), (human) animal bodies are invaded and transformed by an anthropogenically engineered virus so that houses are haunted not by alligators but by humans transformed into carriers of Anthropocene plagues. Again, the separation between the Anthropos and nature was always an Enlightenment rhetoric. Hungry alligators in the flooded living room marks but one of the moments when this rhetoric collapses; anthropogenically engineered viruses turning humans into zombies is another.

This turn away from anthropocentrism has been critically examined by a range of recent theoretical formations, including animal studies, critical plant studies, new materialism, ecocriticism, object-oriented ontology, thing studies, and critical posthumanism. All these fields share a critical stance on "the human," and on anthropocentric ways of knowing and ordering the world, instead advocating a nonhierarchical relationship to the (multispecies) beings that inhabit it. Such skeptical angles on the human and humanism are important in any approach to the Anthropocene, but are doubly so in an investigation of the gothic and the Anthropocene. For, just as we need to interrogate what is and is not in focus when we choose the "Anthropos" of the human over other competing terms, so we need to take care when defining "the human" in the first place. As an entity that has always been under threat, always questioned, by the gothic, the human takes up an endangered position in the Anthropocene too. "At the start of it all there is He: the classical ideal of 'Man,'"[27] Rosi Braidotti remarks, a supposedly universal ideal of "the human" that has time and again proven to be "in fact a historical construct and as such contingent as to values and locations."[28] Approaching the same Enlightenment epistemologies from the perspective of race, Zakiyyah Iman Jackson observes in *Becoming Human: Matter and Meaning in an Antiblack World* (2020) that the exclusion of Black people from a humanity understood as white and male rendered the Black or Brown body into an "infinitely malleable and lexical and biological matter" for science, philosophy, and the arts.[29]

If it is true that "humanism is the idea by which constant identification with a quasi-mythical universal human 'nature' produces great cultural achievements,"[30] we must also acknowledge how "humanism deconstructs itself whenever 'the human' is observed not as a unity but as an assemblage."[31] Indeed, Jackson poses African diasporic fiction as texts that "critique and depose prevailing conceptions of 'the human' found in Western science and philosophy."[32] We propose that gothic, some of it emerging precisely out of the key African American or African texts, similarly explores alternative and radical modes of humanity. Gothic constantly places the human in duress, either physically, as in horror movies; existentially, as in postapocalyptic fiction and extinction narratives; but also conceptually, as in the human–machine–animal assemblages that tend to populate the gothic science fiction of the new weird, biopunk, or steampunk. Contributions to this collection thus explore how a clinging to such ideals, as to the notion of the universal subject of "the human," is at heart a nostalgic longing for a state of being that never was. At the same time, these chapters reveal how a critical posthumanism exemplified in a range of gothic texts dares point another way.

Transhumanist visions in particular, refusing "to see the human as a construct enmeshed with other forms of life and [seeing] technology as a means of 'adding' to already existing human qualities and of filling a lack in the human,"[33] are invariably tied to science fiction tropes: whether they are of partial cyborg replacement parts, or of a full displacement of the original human form through robotic or organic physical forms, or of eschewing the physical altogether to become pure data, the utopian and techno-fetishistic beliefs of transhumanism in endless human progress sit squarely with science fiction rather than with the gothic. The posthuman and the nonhuman, in comparison, are more ambiguous, as are their allegiances in terms of genre. The transhuman may, like the posthuman, seem to indicate a willful distance from the human. But proponents of the transhuman in fact do the opposite in that they "rely on, and in fact reinforce, a humanist conception of the subject."[34] In this they "believe in the Enlightenment ideals of the human/animal divide,"[35] a brightly optimistic and anthropocentric focus that looks solely to the (science fiction) future, while refusing to delve into the murkier, messier (gothic) territory of matter, the animal, and the nonhuman.

While gothic is thus a mode that takes up and turns into narrative the intellectual challenge that much new critical theory and methodology voice, it operates also through affect. Through affect, gothic is capable of informing and structuring a more general experience and understanding of the Anthropocene as it occurs in disparate social and geographical spaces. In one of the first attempts to define the affective impact of gothic, Ann Radcliff influentially argued that "Terror and Horror are so far opposite that the first expands the soul, and awakens the faculties to a high degree of life; the other contracts, freezes and nearly annihilates them."[36] Botting concurs, arguing that terror "marks the uplifting thrill" like "the dilation of the pupil in moments of excitement and fear," while "horror distinguishes a contraction at the imminence and unavoidability of the threat."[37] Of course, gothic texts frequently treat audiences to both of these affects, where terror precedes horror. Before *Alien* (1979) becomes a vehicle of annihilating body horror, it is a classic gothic narrative of dread, excitement, and fear. Before the alien itself becomes a horrific physical monstrosity in front of the audience, it is a ghost haunting the foreign ship in which its primal larval form hides, then the human body this larval form has invaded, then the corridors of the human spaceship.

These two basic affects by which gothic and horror narratives operate also inform two very different relationships to the Anthropocene. The concepts of terror, haunting, horror, and monstrosity can thus be used to describe the crucial temporal, geographical, and financial displacement that creates two very different experiences of the Anthropocene. As Rob Nixon has observed, there is a tremendous difference between how poor communities and affluent communities experience the climate crisis. It can be argued that affluent communities, most located in the Global North, encounter the Anthropocene not as physical violence but as a haunting, uncanny presence, a ghost that rises out of the global landscape. The Anthropocene haunts everyday objects and practices: cars, air-conditioned houses, gardens, airplanes, dinners, trips to the beach. The moment when the (wealthy) Anthropos grasps first that the Anthropocene is real in the sense that it produces dramatic and catastrophic climate change, and that it is precisely the affluent section of humanity—the benefactors of capitalism—who have engineered this era through the mass production of these cars, houses, and holidays, is also the moment when these objects and practices become haunted and uncanny. The plastic bag drifting in the shallows on the beach is not simply a lost, single-use container but ghostly evidence of a global environmental problem, the haunting and menacing hyperobject of a collapsing climate. Leaving the beach, or picking up the bag, will not solve the problem. Similarly, to return to a point made earlier, the bodies of the affluent are also haunted through "radiological and chemical violence" that "is driven inward, somatized into cellular dramas of mutation."[38] As observed by a multitude of medical and microbiological research, this indirect violence causes a range of illnesses,[39] but the medical complexes of the Global North can often eradicate or delay the effects of these, making their plight livable. Again, the suppressed presence of these ill effects makes the (human) animal body of the wealthy appear as uncanny and haunted, but not necessarily as monstrous. In this way, and in this moment in time, the Anthropocene remains a prophesy, a promise of future violence, and thus a ghostly, haunting presence, for most inhabiting the affluent Global North.

By contrast, to large communities of the world's poor, most located in the Global South, the Anthropocene is not an uncanny, ghostly presence but already a horror: an immanent and unavoidable threat and a prophesy fulfilled. As Nixon notes, it is the world's poor populations that are the principal casualties of the most direct and violent manifestations of the Anthropocene.[40] The "thawing cryosphere, toxic drift, biomagnification, deforestation, the radioactive aftermaths of wars, acidifying oceans, and a host of other slowly unfolding environmental catastrophes"[41] that are some of the most adverse results of living in the Anthropocene have a direct and daily influence on the lives of the poor.[42] Deforestation, desertification, flooding, overfishing, and pollution are making life impossible in places, causing death and destruction to communities that lack the financial means for escape or that are driven into diasporas just as monstrous and hopeless as the life from which they escaped. The radiological and chemical violences that haunt rather than destroy the affluent "remain largely unobserved, undiagnosed, and untreated" in "the bodies of the poor."[43] As Kathryn Yusoff argues in *A Billion Black Anthropocenes or None* (2018), this corporeal and geological violence is not new, as it may appear to wealthy communities decrying what they perceive as a coming crisis but has been practiced on Black and Brown bodies since the early days of extractive colonialism.[44] In this way, the world's poor, whether living in Indonesia or in New Orleans, have long experienced the various material consequences of the Anthropocene not as a ghostly haunting but as monstrous horror, as an inexorable, ongoing apocalypse. Today, this apocalypse rises out of land made unlivable by climate change–accelerated drought or flooding, out of the fallout from nuclear testing, out of precarious work conditions and wars fought over natural resources, and out of a global viral pandemic where those located outside of the privileging category of whiteness suffer both the medical and economic consequences of the plague much more severely than those placed inside. With this in mind, political movements like Black Lives Matter are reactions not just to the violent policing of Black and Brown bodies—although they are certainly this too—but to the centuries-long entangled colonial and environmental history that has produced the climate crisis.

When considering the uneven nature of the Anthropocene as apocalypse, it is necessary also to recognize the violence perpetrated on nonhuman lives. A general tendency accelerated enormously by industrialized human society is that nonhuman species are either domesticated by the meat and dairy industries or slowly being wiped out of existence in what has been termed the sixth mass extinction of species.[45] Cows, elephants, tigers, and the northern bald ibis; insects like bees or bumblebees; marine invertebrates like coral; plants like the mountain lobelia; and microbes like the oxygen-producing phytoplankton suffer from anthropogenic change, many disappearing from the planet forever. As contributions to this collection show, gothic imaginaries investigate the industrialized slaughter of animals and the extinction of non-domesticated species. These investigations test the borders that liberal Enlightenment humanism has established between the human and the nonhuman, and some radical gothic is involved in a programmatic critique of the human–animal distinction and of the routine violence done to nonhuman animal bodies. Such texts participate in the furthering of what Braidotti has termed a material vitalism that dislocates "difference from binaries to rhizomatics, from sex-gender or nature-culture to processes of differing that take life itself, or the vitality of matter, as the main subject."[46] Even conservative gothic that insists on absolute borders between the human and an animality imagined as monstrous draw attention to the entwined nature of these categories and the porousness of this imagined border.

The Thousand Names of the Anthropocene

Noting that the concept Anthropocene vies with a number of other -cenes, McKenzie Wark exclaims that we should "have a thousand names for the Anthropocene. . . . Anything of this scale and complexity, not least emotional complexity, needs a whole poetics of its own."[47] As a term, the *Anthropocene* has been heavily critiqued and is contested by a great number of competing terms, such as *Capitalocene, Plaintainocene, Gynecene, Homogenocene,* and *Plasticene.* These alternative terms stress a variety of environmentally destructive phenomena, such as capital, colonization, slavery, and the plantation system; patriarchal domination; monoculture; or plastics, thus putting the focus on other contributing or perhaps even more dominant factors than "the human" in explaining the increasingly poor environmental state of the planet. Indeed, as T. J. Demos observes in *Against the Anthropocene* (2017), the concept of "the Anthropocene itself is far from neutral."[48] As Astrida Neimanis noted in *Bodies of Water: Posthuman Feminist Phenomenology* (2017), this lack of neutrality arises from the concept's inability to decentralize humanity, turning it into "less a plea for curbing the Human, and more an insistence that we do matter, and always will."[49] Ecosocialists Andreas Malm and Alf Hornborg are similarly suspicious of the concept, arguing that it "occludes the historical origins of global warming and sinks the fossil economy into unalterable conditions."[50] In other words, by foregrounding the "anthropos" of our current "cene" (era), we are in danger of erasing and smoothing out not just important links between cause and effect but also responsibility and culpability. Indeed, letting capitalism (and by implication the Global North) off the hook by pointing to "the human"—and human history as a whole—can be disastrous in terms of future action, as in a reckoning of the mistakes of the past by pointing at the wrong culprit.

This book does not attempt to mediate in this particular debate. Instead, it recognizes that the many -cenes that have been proposed have merit and highlight particular histories and aspects that need to be considered. As Pieter Vermeulen has pointed out, "for the proponents of these alternative names, [the Anthropocene] is not only a misnomer, but also serves as a kind of disingenuous *disclaimer* that dissolves accountability," something of which we must at all times be vigilant, but also perhaps the very infelicity of the term is useful precisely if "we accept that it is inevitably a misnomer [that] covers a makeshift assemblage of discourses, terms, protocols, and experiments that never fully hit home."[51] Thus we seek to open up various understandings of how gothic narrates the climate crisis in ways that are necessarily mushy, imprecise, and transgressive.

While it is impossible to give room to the thousand names envisioned by Wark, or indeed the billions demanded by Yusoff, we do however want to highlight four -cenes that are of particular importance to gothic: Anthropocene, Plantationocene, Capitalocene, and Chthulucene. Accordingly, this book consists of four parts that use these -cenes as titles. This structure, we hope, is an opportunity to explore four concepts central to the debate and to consider how gothic interrogates particular aspects of the geological age of man, of the warming climate, of extinction, and of the rethinking of the place of the Anthropos on this world. We do not mean to suggest that these particular -cenes are "better" than the other alternatives, yet we do believe they make for critically useful perspectives on gothic and anthropogenic planetary change. Moreover, and importantly, this structure is not an effort to compartmentalize the individual contributions that follow the part heading. Rather, the structure, and the contributions themselves, takes the opportunity to note how these four concepts connect and inform each other. The contributions, like gothic itself, and like the unequal ecological emergency that forms the starting point for the readings of the contributions, thus refuse simple categories. They move in and out of concepts and narratives; they are transgressive, excessive, and monstrous, and they mean to help change our understanding of this planet and of the Anthropos's relationship to it. For a description of the contributions that the individual chapters make to this collection, the reader should turn to these parts.

NOTES

1. Fred Botting, *Limits of Horror* (Manchester, U.K.: Manchester University Press, 2013), 5.
2. *Chthonic* coming from the Greek *khthon*, meaning "earth," but often referring to the subterranean and often implying deities and spirits.
3. Tobias Menely and Jesse Oak, *Anthropocene Reading: Literary History in Geologic Times* (University Park: Penn State University Press, 2017), 5.

4. See Adam Trexler and Adeline Johns-Putra, "Climate Change in Literature and Literary Criticism," *Wiley Interdisciplinary Reviews: Climate Change* 2, no. 2 (2011): 185–200; Trexler, *Anthropocene Fictions: The Novel in a Time of Climate Change* (Charlottesville: University of Virginia Press, 2015); Timothy Clark, *Ecocriticism on the Edge: The Anthropocene as a Threshold Concept* (London: Bloomsbury, 2015); and Amitav Ghosh, *The Great Derangement: Climate Change and the Unknowable* (Chicago: University of Chicago Press, 2016).

5. Ghosh, *Great Derangement*, 22.

6. Ghosh, 23.

7. Ghosh, 21, 23.

8. Ghosh, 24.

9. A similar argument is forwarded in the Warwick Research Collective's coauthored study *Combined and Uneven Development: Towards a New Theory of World-Literature* (Liverpool, U.K.: Liverpool University Press, 2015). This publication emphasizes the potential of what the Collective terms "irrealism" to describe the lived experience of people marginalized by poverty and to challenge dominant systems of power.

10. Fred Botting, *Gothic* (London: Routledge, 1996), 8.

11. The metaphor that Ghosh employs to describe the inability of realism to address climate change is therefore very apt in a way that goes beyond the discussion of genre only. In a time of melting ice caps and floating islands of plastic waste, the citizens of the Global North can no longer afford the conspicuous consumption of the manor house. Displacements from home are inevitable: climate refugees from rising sea levels or migrants from increased desertification cannot be ignored.

12. Sian MacArthur, *Gothic Science Fiction: 1818 to the Present* (Basingstoke, U.K.: Palgrave Macmillan, 2015), 2.

13. James Machin, *Weird Fiction in Britain 1880–1939* (Basingstoke, U.K.: Palgrave Macmillan, 2018), 16.

14. Jeff VanderMeer, "Hauntings in the Anthropocene: An Initial Exploration," *Environmental Critique*, July 7, 2016, https://environmental.critique.wordpress.com/2016/07/07/hauntings-in-the-anthropocene/.

15. VanderMeer is here referring to Timothy Morton, *Hyperobjects: Philosophy and Ecology after the End of the World* (Minneapolis: University of Minnesota Press, 2013).

16. Ursula Heise, *Imagining Extinction: The Cultural Meanings of Endangered Species* (Chicago: University of Chicago Press, 2016), 18.

17. Timothy Morton, *Dark Ecology: For a Logic of Future Coexistence* (New York: Columbia University Press, 2016).

18. Bruno Latour, *Politics of Nature: How to Bring the Sciences into Democracy* (Cambridge, Mass.: Harvard University Press, 2004); Timothy Morton, *Ecology without Nature: Rethinking Environmental Aesthetics*

(Cambridge, Mass.: Harvard University Press, 2007); Bill McKibben, *Eaarth: Making a Life on a Tough New Planet* (New York: Henry Holt, 2010); and on to Dipesh Chakrabarty, "Humanities in the Anthropocene: The Crisis of an Enduring Kantian Fable," *New Literary History* 47, no. 2/3 (2016): 377–97.

19. Jason W. Moore, *Capitalism in the Web of Life: Ecology and the Accumulation of Capital* (London: Verso, 2015), 5.

20. Moore, 4–5, emphasis added.

21. David Farrier, *Anthropocene Poetics: Deep Times, Sacrifice Zones, and Extinction* (Minneapolis: University of Minnesota Press, 2019), 16.

22. Moore, *Capitalism,* 4.

23. See Rachel Carson, *Silent Spring* (Boston: Houghton Mifflin, 1962).

24. See, e.g., Lynn Margulis, *The Symbiotic Planet: A New Look at Evolution* (London: Weidenfeld and Nicolson, 1998), and Margareth McFall-Ngai, Michael G. Hadfield, Thomas C. G. Bosch, Hannah V. Carey, Tomislav Domazet-Lošo, Angela E. Douglas, Nicole Dubilier et al., "Animals in a Bacterial World, a New Imperative for the Life Sciences," *Proceedings of the National Academy of Sciences of the United States of America,* 110, no. 9 (2013): 3229–36.

25. Cristina O'Callaghan-Gordo and Josep M. Antó, "COVID-19: The Disease of the Anthropocene," *Environmental Research* 187 (2020): 1.

26. O'Callaghan-Gordo and Antó.

27. Rosi Braidotti, *The Posthuman* (Cambridge: Polity Press, 2013), 13.

28. Braidotti, 24.

29. Zakiyyah Iman Jackson, *Becoming Human: Matter and Meaning in an Antiblack World* (New York: New York University Press, 2020), 3.

30. Stefan Herbrechter, *Posthumanism: A Critical Analysis* (London: Bloomsbury, 2013), 12.

31. Bruce Clark, "The Nonhuman," in *The Cambridge Companion to Literature and the Posthuman,* ed. Bruce Clarke and Manuela Rossini (Cambridge: Cambridge University Press, 2017), 141.

32. Jackson, *Becoming Human,* 1.

33. Pramod K. Nayar, *Posthumanism* (Cambridge: Polity Press, 2014), 6.

34. R. L. Rutsky, "Technologies," in Clark and Rossini, *Cambridge Companion to Literature and the Posthuman,* 190.

35. Nayar, *Posthumanism,* 7.

36. Anne Radcliffe, "On the Supernatural in Poetry," *New Monthly Magazine* 16 (1826): 149.

37. Botting, *Gothic,* 10.

38. Rob Nixon, *Slow Violence and the Environmentalism of the Poor* (Cambridge, Mass.: Harvard University Press, 2011), 6.

39. See Ed Yong, *I Contain Multitudes: The Microbes within Us and a Grander View of Life* (New York: HarperCollins, 2016), for a review of some of this research.

40. For a discussion of how horror and terror can be used to understand differences between how the Global South and the Global North experience the climate crisis, see Johan Höglund, "Alligators in the Living Room: Terror and Horror in the Capitalocene," in *Haunted Nature*, ed. Sladja Blazan (Basingstoke, U.K.: Palgrave Macmillan, 2021).

41. Nixon, *Slow Violence*, 2.

42. While most of the world's poor are located in the Global South, most nations are today multiscalar so that the Global North contains regions and sections of cities inhabited by communities vulnerable to the (slow) violence of climate change. See Dorceta Taylor, *Toxic Communities: Environmental Racism, Industrial Pollution, and Residental Mobilities* (New York: New York University Press, 2014), and Ingrid R. G. Waldron, *There's Something in the Water: Environmental Racism in Indigenous and Black Communities* (Nova Scotia: Fernwood, 2018), for discussions of the impact of pollution and the climate crisis in the United States and Canada.

43. Nixon, *Slow Violence*, 6.

44. Kathryn Yusoff, *A Billion Black Anthropocene or None* (Minneapolis: University of Minnesota Press, 2018).

45. See Elizabeth Kolbert, *The Sixth Extinction: An Unnatural History* (New York: Henry Holt, 2014), for a discussion of the ongoing mass extinction of species.

46. Rosi Braidotti, "Four Theses on Posthuman Feminism," in *Anthropocene Feminism,* ed. Richard Grusin (Minneapolis: University of Minnesota Press, 2017), 34.

47. Wark McKenzie, "On the Obsolescence of the Bourgeois Novel in the Anthropocene," *Verso* (blog), August 16, 2017, https://www.versobooks.com/blogs/3356-on-the-obsolescence-of-the-bourgeois-novel-in-the-anthropocene.

48. T. J. Demos, *Against the Anthropocene* (Berlin: Sternberg Press, 2017), 81.

49. Astrida Neimanis, *Bodies of Water: Posthuman Feminist Phenomenology* (London: Bloomsbury Press, 2017), 11.

50. Andreas Malm and Alf Hornborg, "The Geology of Mankind? A Critique of the Anthropocene Narrative," *Anthropocene Review* 1, no. 1 (2014): 67.

51. Pieter Vermeulen, *Literature and the Anthropocene* (London: Routledge, 2020), 7–9.

Part I
ANTHROPOCENE

As a term, *Anthropocene* has made a rapid transition from geology on to the rest of the sciences and the humanities. Coined in its current form in 2000 by the atmospheric chemist Paul J. Crutzen, the term has in the past two decades seen an explosive rise in popularity in a range of disciplines outside the sciences, including but not limited to philosophy, literary studies, cinema studies, architecture, anthropology, sociology, politics, and law.[1] It is inarguably the most common denominator of the era that we have entered, a notion that "has gained an almost viral popularity,"[2] and it clearly identifies the entity that it understands as the cause: the Anthropos.

Geologists, much like practitioners of their sibling disciplines of paleontology and archaeology, are interested in phenomena that stretch over thousands, millions, and sometimes billions of years. While distinct in their areas of specialization (minerals and stone, dinosaurs, humans) and time scales (billions and millions of years vs. thousands of years), geologists, paleontologists, and archaeologists all share a preoccupation with the past, one that is motivated through a way of chthonic reading dependent on the unearthing and disturbing of that which was once hidden. Looking to the past, geologists, paleontologists, and archaeologists make sense of the present by charting shifts that have occurred over thousands of generations as well as cosmic temporalities in which the human registers as barely a blip. Thus it is not strange that scientists from this discipline should take the relatively long history of the Anthropos in mind, rather than just the past 250 years. As will be discussed, it is certainly true that while most of the damage done to the planet has been done since industrialization, the invention of the steam engine, and the proliferation of capitalism, the Anthropos has had a significant impact on the planet for a very long time. Before Columbus arrived in what is today known as America,

the number of societies practicing agriculture and animal husbandry on this continent was so significant that they had begun a
small but noticeable warming of Earth's climate.[3] In this way, the
Anthropocene in fact predates the invention of the steam engine
and the industrialization that Crutzen proposes as the beginning
of this epoch, even if it is not until the introduction of what Andreas Malm refers to as fossil capital that it begins to have a truly
significant effect on ecology.[4]

As the first term to recognize that human societies have long
had an impact on planetary ecology, it remains a useful umbrella
term. It is via this concept that humans, as Dipesh Chakrabarty
puts it, recognize that they have, through sheer numbers and reliance on the fossil fuel economy, "become a geological agent on
the planet."[5] In this way, as observed by Jason W. Moore, the "Anthropocene sounds the alarm—and what an alarm it is!"[6] Moore,
as will be discussed in the part on Capitalocene, is one of many
to have taken issue with the concept, but even critics of the concept do recognize the important role it has played for the sciences
and in critical humanities and social sciences scholarship. As the
most widely used denominator, it has made an entire generation
aware of the price the planet is paying for the comforts generated
by modernity. Because of its impact, even resistance to the term
must necessarily engage with it at length, simply because of its
by now pervasive influence. As T. J. Demos admits, albeit reluc-
tantly, "the term Anthropocene is likely here to stay."[7] Also, while
it is true that the generic nature of the Anthropocene can be misleading, it does, however, for those very same reasons, also allow
for a wider range of subjects to be discussed under the heading of
anthropogenic change that competing -cenes in their focus on one
or the other may leave out. As Elizabeth DeLoughrey has argued,
even while critiquing it for its supposed blindness to questions of
empire and the Global South, "the Anthropocene is both forward-
looking and a future retrospective, characterized by 'anticipatory
logics' and anticipatory mourning . . . [which] is constituted by a
deep geological sense of the *longue durée,* as well as disjunctive special relations between the enormity of the planet and the experience of local place."[8] Thus DeLoughrey continues to find the term
useful precisely because "the Anthropocene dictates that we need
multiscalar theorizing of the human."[9]

The essays included in this part address this problem both

through theoretical discussions of the concept as such and via interrogations of gothic and horror texts where Anthropocene is the structuring concept. In the part's opening chapter, titled "The ~~Anthropocene~~," Jeffrey Andrew Weinstock observes that gothic has become a privileged mode in the critical and cultural attempt to understand not just concerns about the climate crisis but the concept of the Anthropocene as such. Weinstock shows how three gothic master tropes—spectrality, monstrosity, and apocalypse—have become central to theoretical paradigms that struggle to understand both the ongoing, global, and increasingly catastrophic transformation of the Earth's ecosystem and the complicity of the human in this development.

Michael Fuchs's chapter "De-extinction: A Gothic Masternarrative for the Anthropocene" examines various de-extinction projects and the discourses surrounding them to explore visions of resurrection science as they have been reimagined in popular culture and vice versa. Fuchs argues that de-extinction epitomizes the Anthropocene in that the potential for the creation of Anthropocene specters of once-extinct animals promises (and threatens) to unlock a future in which the undead will literally walk the Earth again. In this, Fuchs suggests, we see an evocative merger of the gothic and the Anthropocene in "necrofaunal revenants" like once-extinct animals, such as the mammoth, resurrected, but he also asks poignant questions about the manner in which de-extinction as ideology can be seen to perpetuate human technological imperialism while also seeking to atone for it.

In "Lovecraft vs. VanderMeer: Posthuman Horror (and Hope?) in the Zone of Exception," Rune Graulund argues that while the Anthropocene is often portrayed as unfolding in a state of emergency and exception, it can also be construed as the opposite. For, while the Anthropocene may seem to present a potentially horrifying new normal in which humans have gained a catastrophic upper hand over nature, the supposed dominance of the human species is in fact anything but. In an analysis of the cosmic horror of H. P. Lovecraft's "The Colour out of Space" (1927), Graulund juxtaposes the terror of the nonhuman in weird fiction with the far more acceptant approach to the monstrous, the bestial, and the vegetative as seen in the fiction of Jeff VanderMeer's novel *Annihilation* (2014). Reading these two texts in the light of the exception zone, Graulund suggests that they exemplify two very different kinds of strategies for dealing with anthropogenic change, one of them dystopian, the other utopian.

In her chapter "Monstrous Megalodons of the Anthropocene: Extinction and Adaptation in Prehistoric Shark Fiction, 1974–2018," Jennifer Schell examines the gothic representations of monstrous sharks and marine science and argues that these creatures rarely engage with the subversive potential of monstrosity; rather, they are foils for showcasing the power of white American masculinity, which triumphs over these massive predators by overcoming them and brutally slaughtering them. Within this narrative trajectory, man exerts supreme power over his environment and conquers threats posed by the environment in which he finds himself. In megalodon narratives, she asserts, gothic tropes are appropriated for reactionary political ends and are rarely used to espouse environmentalist agendas or progressive politics.

In the final chapter of this part, "A Violence 'Just below the Skin': Atmospheric Terror and Racial Ecologies from the African Anthropocene," Esthie Hugo examines what she terms atmospheric racism. Reflecting on the broader problem of a world suffocating in literal as well as figurative terms—gasping for air on a planet suffering from air pollution, rising temperatures, and pandemics like Covid-19 targeting the respiratory system—Hugo's chapter queries the politics and aesthetics of racial toxicity of atmospheric terror. Reading Nigerian author Ben Okri alongside the artistic portraits of Beninese photographer Fabrice Monteiro, Hugo lays bare the racialized experience of deathly atmospheric vulnerability as it is experienced through the "slow violence" of poisoned air, water, and land.

NOTES

1. Joanna Zylinska, *Minimal Ethics for the Anthropocene* (Ann Arbor, Mich.: Open Humanities Press, 2014); Christophe Bonneuil and Jean-Baptiste Fressoz, *The Shock of the Anthropocene* (London: Verso, 2016); McKenzie Wark, *Molecular Red: Theory for the Anthropocene* (London: Verso, 2016); Jedediah Purdy, *After Nature: A Politics for the Anthropocene* (Cambridge, Mass.: Harvard University Press, 2015); Etienne Turpin, ed., *Architecture in the Anthropocene: Encounters among Design, Deep Time, Science and Philosophy* (Ann Arbor, Mich.: Open Humanities Press, 2014); Anna Tsing, Heather Swanson, Elain Gan, and Nils Bubandt, eds., *Arts of Living on a Damaged Planet* (Minneapolis: Uni-

versity of Minnesota Press, 2017); Jennifer Fay, *Inhospitable World: Cinema in the Time of the Anthropocene* (Oxford: Oxford University Press, 2018); Kathryn Yusoff, *A Billion Black Anthropocenes or None* (Minneapolis: University of Minnesota Press, 2018).

2. Pieter Vermeulen, *Literature and the Anthropocene* (London: Routledge, 2020), 1.

3. Alexander Koch, Chris Brierley, Mark Maslin, and Simon Lewis, "Earth System Impacts of the European Arrival and Great Dying in the Americas after 1492," *Quaternary Science Reviews* 207 (2019): 13–36.

4. Andreas Malm, *Fossil Capital: The Rise of Steam Power and the Roots of Global Warming* (London: Verso, 2016).

5. Dipesh Chakrabary, "The Climate of History: Four Theses," *Critical Inquiry* 35, no. 2 (2009): 209.

6. Jason W. Moore, "Introduction: Anthropocene or Capitalocene? Nature, History, and the Crisis of Capitalism," in *Anthropocene or Capitalocene? Nature, History, and the Crisis of Capitalism,* ed. Jason W. Moore (Oakland, Calif.: PM Press, 2016), 5.

7. T. J. Demos, *Against the Anthropocene: Visual Culture and Environment Today* (Berlin: Sternberg Press, 2017), 85.

8. Elizabeth M. DeLoughrey, *Allegories of the Anthropocene* (Durham, N.C.: Duke University Press, 2019), 4–5.

9. DeLoughrey, 15.

« 1 »

The ~~Anthropocene~~

JEFFREY ANDREW WEINSTOCK

The Anthropocene is uniquely haunted by the prospect of its own undoing.

Indeed, the Anthropocene is doubly haunted: first, by the nagging suspicion that we Anthropos are not quite the masters of the planet the name "Anthropocene" supposes and, second, that, as a consequence of ignorance and recklessness, we are sowing the seeds of our own destruction. Geologic epochs are human inventions of course, marked by changing climate, and they have come and gone. What distinguishes the Anthropocene, however, is not just an implicit awareness that it will be succeeded by something else but the active complicity of Anthropos in its end. Call it Anthropocenic irony: what defines the era we name after ourselves is our implication in its conclusion and, indeed, our uncertainty if the name even fits in the first place. The Anthropocene thus insistently calls into question not just its own persistence but indeed its very existence—the name should perhaps more fittingly be rendered under erasure: not Anthropocene but ~~Anthropocene~~.

The prevailing structure of feeling of the twenty-first century may well be what we might refer to as Anthropocenic anxiety as both critical discourse and popular culture draw repeatedly upon the gothic as a means through which to express concerns about human impotence, hubris, and our future disappearance. In the critical literature, particularly that group of approaches categorized by Richard Grusin as the "nonhuman turn," including Latourean actor-network theory, affect theory, animal studies, new materialism, and speculative realism, gothic figures and tropes abound as humans become things, things acquire uncanny animacy, and we brush shoulders with Lovecraftian monsters, serial killers, zombies, and other weird (or eerie) creatures.[1] In popular culture, Anthropocenic anxiety is expressed more directly through gothic narratives of human decentering and apocalypse. This is particularly evident when considering the mainstreaming of speculative literature and media featuring narratives in which human autonomy and presumptions of mastery are challenged or the human race is threatened with extinction. Such narratives take many forms and range from Lovecraftian tales of cosmic dread to eco-catastrophe stories to wish-fulfillment superhero narratives in which only the intervention of secularized deities saves the world from some otherwise unstoppable force.

This chapter accordingly will explore not gothic tales in the Anthropocene but rather <u>Anthropocene *as* gothic metanarrative</u> and will focus on the rhetorical clustering of gothic tropes and analogies that proliferate across contemporary theoretical paradigms that together express a twenty-first-century structure of feeling undergirded by anxiety over the fate of the human. This survey will pivot around three master tropes of gothicized Anthropocentric discourse: spectrality, monstrosity, and apocalypse. Spectrality encompasses the weird, eerie, and outside of things; monstrosity addresses the in-/posthuman; and apocalypse concerns anxieties over the fate of the human when confronted by potentially cataclysmic events and effects: climate change, global pandemics, nuclear annihilation, and so on. Despite the frequent attempt to spin or repurpose these tropes as ethical provocations to live more justly, gently, and deliberately, their proliferation and overlap in critical discourse and popular culture express the irony of the Anthropocene: the anxiety that the pinnacle of human achievement has been the creation of the conditions of our destruction.

Spectrality (*Geist* as *Zeitgeist*)

The first of the three master tropes of Anthropocenic gothic discourse to be considered here is the one that has been most fully addressed from a metacritical perspective: spectrality, together with the associated concept of haunting. Taken broadly, spectrality can be considered as that which does not materialize fully; haunting is what the spectral does. Writ large, both have to do with incompleteness. As María del Pilar Blanco and Esther Peeren address in the Introduction to their *The Spectralities Reader: Ghosts and Haunt-*

ings in *Contemporary Cultural Theory* (2013), the publication in 1993 of Jacques Derrida's *Specters of Marx* is typically considered the catalyst for the so-called "spectral turn" of critical and cultural theory.[2] Long before the concept of spectrality ironically crystalized with *Specters*, however, spectrality had emerged as the organizing premise of both psychoanalysis and deconstruction. Fundamental to psychoanalysis is, of course, the idea of the return of the repressed, while Derridean deconstruction focused on the idea that concepts must be understood in relation to their opposites and that meaning is nowhere present but rather consistently deferred. As I wrote regarding the spectral turn in 2004:

> because ghosts are unstable interstitial figures that problematize dichotomous thinking, it perhaps should come as no surprise that phantoms have become a privileged poststructuralist academic trope. Neither living nor dead, present nor absent, the ghost functions as the paradigmatic deconstructive gesture, the "shadowy third" or trace of an absence that undermines the fixedness of such binary oppositions. As an entity out of place in time, as something from the past that emerges into the present, the phantom calls into question the linearity of history. And as, in philosopher Jacques Derrida's words in his *Specters of Marx,* the *"plus d'un,"* simultaneously the "no more one" and the "more than one," the ghost suggests the complex relationship between the constitution of individual subjectivity and the larger social collective.[3]

In divisions ranging from "spectral media" to "spectral places" to "haunted historiographies," Pilar Blanco and Peeren's 2013 anthology collects together selections testifying to the pervasiveness of the concept of spectrality in late twentieth- and early twenty-first-century cultural theory, and the prevailing critical framework—the mode of haunting—is largely the uncanny: the emergence of the strange within the familiar. Reason is haunted by its opposite, science by the occult, familiar places by traumatic histories that refuse to lie quietly, and so on. And it is fair to say that, early into the third decade of the twenty-first century, critical and cultural theory continues to emphasize the linked concepts of the ghost and hauntings, albeit often with a more eco-critical orientation. A case in point is the ambitious two-part collection *Arts of Living on a Damaged Planet* (2017), edited by Anna Tsing, Heather Swanson, Elaine Gan, and Nils Bubandt. Organized around the themes of ghosts and monsters, the essays assert that "entangled histories, situated narratives, and thick descriptions offer urgent 'arts of living' . . . for survival in a more-than-human Anthropocene."[4] In "Introduction: Haunted Landscapes of the Anthropocene," which opens the "Ghosts on a Damaged Planet" section, the editors emphasize the "Holocene entanglements" of the human and nonhuman as our present is haunted by the past, which in turn directs our possible futures. "Every landscape is haunted by past ways of life," they write. "We see this clearly in the presence of plants whose animal seed-dispersers are no longer with us. Some plants have seeds so big that only big animals can carry them to new places to germinate. When these animals became extinct, their plants could continue without them, but they have been unable to disperse their seeds very well. Their distribution is curtailed; their population dwindles. This is an example of what we call haunting."[5] The essays that follow in this section then address the consequences of human influence on the environment with emphases ranging from radiation to wetlands to lichens and stones.

"Ghosts on a Damaged Planet" offers an illustration of the assertion that our narration of the Anthropocene is as a gothic tale. That the contributors span multiple disciplines from biology to ecology to philosophy to anthropology suggests the transdisciplinary entrenchment of this narrative. The essays included in the ghosts section utilize a more capacious framework for thinking spectrality than earlier models rigidly focused on human history. It is now the planet that is haunted by the intermingling of human and nonhuman pasts.

Despite the familiar framework of haunting as uncanny—the strange within the familiar—the "Ghosts on a Damaged Planet" assertions of a haunted planet nevertheless start to exert torque on the spectral turn, twisting it in a different direction away from the uncanny and toward the modes to which Mark Fisher refers as the weird and the eerie. Both ghosts and haunting are forms of what Fisher in his final book, *The Weird and the Eerie* (2016), would consider the strange. As opposed to the horrific, the strange has to do with "a fascination for the outside, for that which lies beyond standard perception, cognition, and experience."[6] Fisher then divides the strange into three categories: the uncanny, the weird, and the eerie. The uncanny, as discussed earlier, is "about the strange *within* the familiar, the strangely familiar, the familiar as strange— about the way in which the domestic world does not coincide with itself."[7] The weird and the eerie, in contrast, are not about the familiar but, as Fisher describes it, the "outside."[8] The weird "brings to the familiar something which ordinarily lies beyond it, and which cannot be reconciled with the 'homely' (even as its negation)."[9] The weird is associated with a "sense of *wrongness* . . . the conviction that *this does not belong.*"[10] The weird is marked by "the irruption into *this* world of something from outside."[11] The eerie, in contrast, is marked either by a "*failure of absence* or by a *failure of presence.*"[12] "The sensation of the eerie," continues Fisher, "occurs either when there is something present where there should be nothing, or [when] there is nothing present when there should be something."[13] The eerie concerns the unknown: "There must be . . . a sense of alterity, a feeling that the enigma might involve forms of knowledge, subjectivity and sensation that lie beyond common experience."[14] Ultimately, Fisher connects eeriness with questions of agency—the "forces that govern our lives and the world."[15] Put concisely, the uncanny emerges from within, while the weird and the eerie intrude from without. The uncanny is strangely familiar; the weird and eerie are disconcertingly foreign.

The twenty-first-century twist to the spectral turn, the one perhaps signaled by *The Art of Living on a Damaged Planet*'s roomier articulation of haunting, is one that shifts the spectral turn away from psychoanalysis and deconstruction and instills it instead at the heart of our interactions with objects: in our twenty-first-century narrativization of the Anthropocene, we move from uncanny ghosts to weird spectrality. One place to start to consider this shift is with Graham Harman and the school of philosophy with which he is associated: object-oriented ontology. Object-oriented ontology, or OOO (triple-O), is a twenty-first-century school of thought that rejects "correlationalism," the perspective that, as Ian Bogost explains, "being exists only as a correlate between mind and world" or, put differently, that "if things exist, they do so only *for us.*"[16] OOO maintains instead that objects exist independently of human perception and are not exhausted in their interactions with us and other objects. In Harman's 2011 *The Quadruple Object* and elsewhere, he differentiates between "sensual" qualities and objects and "real" qualities and objects. Our perceptions of things are not their truth. The real is that which exists outside of our sensual apprehension of something—it is that which withdraws from knowing. As Harman puts it in *The Quadruple Object*, "when I stare at a river, wolf, government, machine, or army, I do not grasp the whole of their reality. This reality slips from view into a perpetually veiled underworld, leaving me with only the most frivolous simulacra of these entities. In short, the phenomenal reality of things for consciousness does not use up their being."[17]

Already here we have shifted into the language of ghosts, haunting, and radical uncertainty. We never encounter real objects directly; these withdraw into a "veiled underworld." Instead, we encounter only "frivolous simulacra"—essentially ghosts of real objects. Harman is associated with the philosophical movement known as "speculative realism"—a general rubric encompassing a variety of different philosophical perspectives united most immediately by their rejection of correlationalism. As usefully summarized by Steven Shaviro:

> Speculative Realism insists upon the independence of the world, and of things in the world, from our own conceptualizations of them. . . . Reality is far *weirder* than we are able to imagine. Things never conform to the ideas that we have about them; there is always something more to them than what we are able to grasp. The world does not fit into our own cognitive paradigms and narrative modes of explanation. "Man" is *not* the measure of all things. This is why speculation is necessary. We *must* speculate, to escape from our inveterate anthropocentrism and take seriously the existence of a fundamentally alien, non-human world.[18]

Shaviro's word "weird" in his overview is also Harman's word—and in both cases, the use resonates with Fisher's meditations. Harman uses the word several times in *The Quadruple Object* to refer to the strangeness of a universe of things that we don't encounter directly, but then makes it central to his 2012 *Weird Realism: Lovecraft and Philosophy*. For Harman, the fiction of H. P. Lovecraft offers useful illustrations of the principles of OOO: "The major topic of object-oriented philosophy is the dual polarization that occurs in the world: one between the real and the sensual, the other between objects and their qualities. . . . Lovecraft's constant exploitation of these very gaps automatically makes him as great a hero to object-oriented thought as Hölderlin was to Heidegger."[19] That Harman turns to horror fiction for examples to help illustrate his philosophical assertions is part and parcel of the gothic narrative that is the Anthropocene: in the twenty-first century, reality is weird, things in themselves are unknowable, and human beings, as we shall see, are objects among other objects.

The twenty-first-century twist to more conventional gothic discourse relating specters to repression and the uncanny is that speculative realism's specters are weird—they are, as Fisher remarks of Lovecraft's gods and monsters, irruptions *"into* this world from outside."[20] The "outside" for the speculative realists is what Quentin Meillassoux in *After Finitude* (2008) refers to as "the Great Outdoors"—*le Grand Dehors* in the French—"the *absolute* outside . . . that outside which [is] not relative to us . . . existing in itself regardless of whether we are thinking of it or not."[21] The specters of speculative realism are thus glimpses of another universe—they are, as suggested by the title of Ian Bogost's *Alien Phenomenology; or, What It's Like to Be a Thing* (2012)—aliens. The narrative of the Anthropocene as told by the speculative realists is thus a weird one indeed, as it is one in which we are surrounded by alien ghosts irrupting from the absolute outside and highlighting the limitations on what we can truly know.

Connected to the speculative realism school, but coming at the hauntedness of the planet from a somewhat different direction, is Timothy Morton, whose influential concept of "hyperobjects" has catalyzed a substantial amount of intellectual inquiry since the publication of *Hyperobjects: Philosophy and Ecology after the End of the World* in 2013. For the speculative realists, all objects are ultimately unknowable, withdrawing into themselves and hiding their real qualities. Hyperobjects, however, are a special class of unknowable objects defined by their enormous spatial and temporal dimensions. The term *hyperobject* refers to "things that are massively distributed in time and space relative to humans"[22] and encompasses things like black holes, climate change, and the "whirring machinery of capitalism."[23] Importantly, we never encounter these objects directly even when they influence, touch, or penetrate us. The local manifestation of the hyperobject is not the object itself—an unusually hot day or a megastorm is not global warming, which "cannot be directly seen, but it can be thought and computed."[24] Hyperobjects are, in Morton's terminology, "phased": "they occupy a high-dimensional *phase space* that makes them impossible to see as a whole on a regular three-dimensional human-scale basis."[25] This means "we can only see pieces of hyperobjects at a time."[26]

What hyperobjects do is "humiliate"[27] us, bring us low, highlighting as they do our physical, temporal, and intellectual limitations as well as our fragility. Where they are massive, we are tiny indeed, and they are weird in every sense. In keeping with Fisher's definition, hyperobjects intrude from without rather than irrupt from within and, in doing so, reveal our conceptions of things to be inadequate. In keeping with Harman, they highlight the gap between sensual qualities of things and the things themselves, and in keeping with Harman's OOO muse, Lovecraft, hyperobjects excite in us a "profound sense of dread, and of contact with unknown spheres and powers," as Lovecraft characterizes the weird tale.[28] Our entanglement with them even invokes the older concept of *wyrd*, fate, as they influence human destiny on the planet. Our experience of them is inevitably incomplete—we only ever encounter spectral glimpses of them even as they haunt our experience. Recycling an idea present in Carl Sagan's 1985 science fiction novel *Contact* and its 1997 film adaptation, the third season of the science fiction series *The Expanse* (2018) has an alien intelligence manifesting before a protagonist in the form of a ghost. The alien civilization is the hyperobject, the ghost a local manifestation of it that our minds can grasp—both metonymy (connected to the alien intelligence) and metaphor (intelligible form of expression). What Morton discusses as the spectral nature of hyperobjects in particular corresponds with what speculative realists assert as the nature of reality in general. We only ever encounter the piecemeal ghosts of things, not the things themselves. Hyperobjects, one must note, are certainly not all new—planetary forces of course predate the Anthropocene; what is new is our awareness of them and our abilities to chart and calculate and speculate on their qualities—and it is our awareness of them and their implications for the human species that, as we shall see, structure the gothic Anthropocene master narrative of apocalypse. Knowledge of our own limitations when confronted with deep time and cosmic forces highlights the precarity of the human situation.

My reference to *Contact* and *The Expanse* was an analogy suggested by one final piece that I will briefly consider here before moving on: author and scholar Jeff VanderMeer's 2016 piece "Hauntings in the Anthropocene." In this article, VanderMeer—the popular author of weird fiction notable in particular for his Southern Reach trilogy and its first novel, *Annihilation,* which was adapted for film in 2018—relates Morton's notion of hyperobjects to his own fiction. Hyperobjects in general, and global warming in particular, according to VanderMeer, should be understood as "hauntings" that not only "make a mockery of what our five senses can perceive" but challenge conventional understandings of the fixed laws of nature.[29] In particular, these hyperobject hauntings foreground the entanglement of the human with inhuman forces and time scales. "In the Anthropocene," writes VanderMeer, "hauntings and similar manifestations become emissaries or transition points between the human sense of time and the geologic sense of time."[30] The spectral acts as a kind of hinge, pivoting us toward the inaccessible real. In the Anthropocene, the age of hyperobjects, *"the uncanny has infiltrated the real,"* concludes VanderMeer, *"and in some sense that boundary is forever compromised."*[31] Weird fiction's contemporary popularity is explained then, at least in part, by its reflection of weird reality. Its defamiliarizations function as analogies for incomprehensible yet lived experience. The weird gives shape to the amorphous irruptions of the outside that puncture the Anthropocene.

Examples can proliferate here. No doubt there are many other directions one could take and paths to consider when exploring the ubiquity of spectral metaphors within twenty-first-century critical discourse, and indeed, that is precisely the point: spectrality, along with monstrosity and apocalypse, has become an organizing conceit of how we narrate our experience of the Anthropocene. When we tell the story of the Anthropocene, whether it focuses on what the human species has done to the world or on how we interact with it, the story seems "naturally" to become a kind of ghost story, a tale of haunting—haunted selves, haunted landscapes, haunted planet.

Monstrosity (from Monster to "Monster")

If the planet is haunted in twenty-first-century critical and popular culture discourse, it is also overrun by monsters ranging from antagonistic angels to flesh-eating zombies. And, like spectrality, monstrosity has received considerable attention from late twentieth- and twenty-first-century cultural critics who deploy the term in various ways, often ironically turning it back on itself to challenge the human–nonhuman binary opposition it frequently signifies. As master trope of Anthropocenic discourse, the monster is frequently rendered as "monster," calling attention to monstrosity as social construction and relational rather than ontological. The concept functions most centrally in twenty-first-century discourse to trouble humanist understandings of identity as singular and autonomous. This is where the irony of the Anthropocene becomes most obvious: in the Anthropocene, we are all "monsters"—not discrete, independent actors but things enmeshed with other things in various constantly shifting networks. The human is always entangled with the nonhuman; indeed, what makes us human is that we are not fully human.

If Derrida's *Specters of Marx* catalyzed the spectral turn, then Jeffrey Jerome Cohen's "Monster Culture (Seven Theses)," the Introduction to his 1996 edited collection *Monster Theory: Reading Culture,* arguably touched off the "monster turn" of critical and cultural studies. In this Introduction, Cohen develops seven theses concerning what monsters are and how they function: (1) they are "pure culture"[32] reflecting the culturally specific understandings of normalcy and deviance; (2) they "always escape" both because the anxieties and desires they express are difficult to contain and because the same monster can shift over time to reflect different sets of concerns and desires; (3) they reflect categorical confusion; (4) they give shape to anxieties concerning differences of all types; (5) they warn against transgression of cultural expectations—violate the rules, and you are in danger of either being eaten by the monster or becoming one; (6) they reflect tabooed desires as well as anxieties—monsters are powerful and do not concern themselves with being polite and abiding by social expectations; and (7) they can metacritically prompt us to reflect on our own assumptions, biases, and expectations.

Cohen's essay has served as a touchstone essay for "monster theory" because of its concise and insightful formulations of what monsters are and what they do, and subsequent cultural criticism related to monsters, directed by Cohen's essay, has followed two main channels: explications of how monsters function as metaphors for particular anxieties and desires in specific contexts, and appropriations/deconstructions of monstrosity in the name of social and, more recently, ecological justice. While individual readings of particular monsters as canny reflections of contemporary anxieties and desires (say, zombies as giving shape to anxieties concerning global pandemics; vampire heroes as reflecting capitalist demands to consume to stay youthful) and even more ambitious explications of monsters as overdetermined "meaning machines" that "can represent gender, race, nationality, class, and sexuality in one body"[33] are certainly useful and often compelling, the more interesting thread of monster theory to pursue in our articulation of the Anthropocene as gothic tale is what we could refer to as the "hopeful monster" theme.

What Cohen expresses through his seven theses is that the idea of monstrosity is a social construction dependent on one's perspective but that the label of "monster" has functioned as a powerful tool of social control (here Cohen channels the work of Michel Foucault). This understanding of the political deployment of monstrosity as part of a program to maintain an exclusionary status quo and license abuse and domination has led to attempts first to invert and then to displace the normal–abnormal binary opposition as forms of political resistance. Central to the inversion step in cultural criticism has been Donna Haraway, who, particularly in her 1985 "A Cyborg Manifesto"[34] and her 1992 "The Promises of Monsters: A Regenerative Politics for Inappropriate/d Others,"[35] offers an ironic reappropriation of the label of monster as a gesture of sociopolitical liberation. Adopting a strategy similar to the reclamation of the word *queer* in the late 1980s, Haraway essentially reclaims the word *monster* as a form of resistance to the discriminatory logic of social expectation: monstrosity as refusal.

Haraway's reclamation of the label "monster" in general and, famously, "cyborg" in particular reflects a broad cultural shift in which the label "monster" is ironically turned back on those who affix the label in the first place as a strategy of control and domination. While there are still zombies that eat brains and giant resurrected dinosaurs that rampage and destroy, in progressive twenty-first-century discourse, both popular and critical, the recurring lessons are (1) monsters are not intrinsically bad, just misunderstood, and (2) human beings—most often white guys in positions of power—are the *true monsters*. This is the inversion step reflective of a system of values that now privileges diversity and free expression of individuality (the ironic "we're all nonconformists here!"). The monsters are not those who look different or act quirky but those who attempt to bend others to their will in the pursuit of power or profit (typically foiled by a gruff but actually goodhearted ogre or a bunch of meddling kids). The logic often boils down to embracing the term *monster*, on one hand, as a rejection of constraints on the free expression of individuality while, on the other, ironically characterizing those who deploy the rhetoric of monstrosity to further their own designs as the true monsters.

Twenty-first-century cultural theory, however, has taken the next step in the deconstruction of the human–nonhuman (monster) binary, which is to displace the opposition entirely through the notion of the posthuman. The logic here shifts to "we are all monsters/none of us is a monster." This notion, too, can be traced back to Haraway and her celebration of the cyborg, which she characterizes as a third term that undoes many of the defining oppositions of Western culture, including nature–culture, organic–inorganic, and man–woman. Haraway's cyborg has come to function as an iconic avatar of posthumanism, that branch of cultural inquiry critical of humanist assumptions about "the human" and "human nature" (assumptions that have often been central to determining who is or is not construed as monstrous).

Twenty-first-century cultural theory, taking its cues from Haraway and others, utilizes the rhetoric of monstrosity to highlight the ways human beings are not independent and autonomous but "entangled" or "enmeshed" in networks of human and nonhuman actants. Here again, Tsing, Swanson, Gan, and Bubandt's *Arts of Living on a Damaged Planet* is instructive. The monsters section, titled "Monsters and the Arts of Living" (which, indeed, includes an essay from Haraway), begins with an Introduction titled "Bodies Tumbled into Bodies" that frames monstrosity as multiplicity. The editors essentially agree with Cohen's thesis that monstrosity is associated with "category crisis" but then foreground the fact that categorical confusion is the nature of existence, prompting the need to rethink the idea of discrete categories altogether: "Against the conceit of the Individual, monsters highlight symbiosis, the enfolding of bodies within bodies in evolution and in every ecological niche. In dialectical fashion, ghosts and monsters unsettle Anthropos, the Greek term for 'human,' from its presumed center stage in the Anthropocene by highlighting the webs of histories and bodies from which all life, including human life, emerges."[36] From the bacteria in our gut to our influence on the ecosystem, human bodies are entangled with nonhuman bodies, and our present is enmeshed with other times. "Monsters," the editors assert, "are bodies tumbled into bodies."[37] The Anthropocene narrative is that we are all then monsters, everything is monstrous, everything is a monster: "monster."

There is both peril and promise here. As the editors of *Arts of Living on a Damaged Planet* argue, "suffering from the ills of another species: this is the condition of the Anthropocene, for humans and nonhumans alike. . . . We are mixed up with other species; we cannot live without them."[38] Humans are not the center of things but nodes in a decentered network. This highlights our vulnerability as a species—indeed, rather than the futuristic cyborg of science fiction, in some respects a more apropos posthuman avatar for the twenty-first century might be the DC Comics superhero Swamp Thing, a humanoid/plant creature vulnerable to pollution. And there is danger here in another respect: reconstruing human beings as objects among objects as part of a "flat ontology"[39] in which all things are equal in existing can license rather than diminish exploitation—which is why Jane Bennett in *Vibrant Matter: A Political Economy of Things* (2010) suggests "a touch of anthropomorphism" as a strategy to "catalyze a sensibility that finds a world filled not with ontologically distinct categories of beings (subjects and objects) but with variously composed materialities that form confederations."[40]

At the end of "Seven Theses," Cohen foregrounds a kind of hope inherent in the monster for living more justly. "Monsters are our children," he writes. "They ask why we have created them."[41] Reflective consideration of what we consider monstrous can prompt reconsideration of sedimented ways of thinking that participate in forms of political violence and exclusion—no doubt important. But twenty-first-century cultural theory has gone further. The promise of Anthropocenic monstrosity inheres in that catalyzed sensibility that recognizes the human entanglement with the nonhuman. From this perspective, human survival requires shaking off humanist conceptions of the discrete Individual and instead acknowledging our shared monstrosity. We have always been posthuman "monsters," but current threats to the planet and human survival now require that we acknowledge this and take appropriate steps to stave off catastrophe.

Apocalypse

If we do not do this, we go the way of the dinosaurs—assuming we are not already too late—and the planet, better off without us, will not mourn our passing. The third master trope of the gothicized narrative of the Anthopocene I wish to address is the darkest: apocalypse, associated as well with the extinction of the human species. From global pandemics to climate change to nuclear annihilation, the Anthropocene is the age of apocalypse. To be fair, speculation about the end of the world is nothing new and plays a significant role in many world religions and traditions; however, awareness of the possibility of catastrophe now structures our thinking about ourselves, our relations to others, and the (im)possibility of a future.

Popular culture is awash with apocalyptic and postapocalyptic narratives ranging from the bombast of supervillains threatening human existence to the horror of hordes of ghouls to the quiet majesty of Emily St. John Mandel's postapocalyptic *Station Eleven* (2014). The world is constantly ending everywhere we look, including in contemporary cultural theory. Unlike spectrality and monstrosity, however, there is not, as far as I am aware, a single foundational text catalyzing an "extinctionist turn" of cultural criticism—Susan Sontag's "The Imagination of the Disaster" (first published in 1965) seems important,[42] as does Ray Brassier's 2007 *Nihil Unbound: Enlightenment and Extinction*[43] and, more recently, Claire Colebrook's 2015 collection *Deaths of the PostHuman: Essays on Extinction, Vol. 1*[44] and Patricia MacCormack's 2020 *The Ahuman Manifesto: Activism for the End of the Anthropocene*,[45] but none of these seems yet to have established itself as a kind of touchstone text directing subsequent criticism in specific ways. Instead, apocalypse and extinction appear for the most part to serve as the backdrop against which much contemporary cultural theory is articulated: we need cultural criticism because our way of life is killing us. Indeed, it may well be that all the ghosts and monsters have emerged in popular culture and cultural criticism precisely because we seem poised on the edge of catastrophe—we are haunted by the prospect of apocalypse, we are committing slow (but accelerating) suicide, we are the monsters. One master trope, then, to control them all: the Anthropocene as apocalyptic narrative breeding ghosts and monsters.

This is more or less the conclusion of philosopher Eugene Thacker, whose work is often associated with that of the speculative realists and with philosophical nihilists such as Brassier. In *In the Dust of This Planet* (2011), the first of Thacker's Horror of Philosophy trilogy, Thacker explores horror narrative as a kind of thought experiment that seeks—like speculative realism—to consider what things are like in their unknowable essence. Here Thacker distinguishes among the "world-for-us," which is the world "we interpret and give meaning to"; the "world-without-us," which is a depopulated planet that we can still imagine; and the "world-in-itself," the inaccessible real world.[46] Horror, asserts Thacker—and here he has in mind in particular, like Harman, weird fiction and the cosmic horror of Lovecraft—"is a non-philosophical attempt to think about the world-without-us philosophically."[47] Horror is "about the enigmatic thought of the unknown."[48] Horror narrative is the natural outgrowth of the Anthropocene thought of as the age of extinction, in which the human species is forced to confront its monstrosity in the sense articulated in *Arts of Living on a Damaged Planet*—that is, as bodies tumbled into other bodies, inflicting and receiving suffering as a consequence of entanglement in human–nonhuman networks and bad decisions.

The questions of how to respond and what to do about being on the brink of apocalypse are taken up by Matthew J. Wolf-Meyer in his *Theory for the World to Come: Speculative Fiction and Apocalyptic Anthropology* (2019)—an at-times personal and lyrical meditation proposing an approach but no easy answers (because there are none). According to Wolf-Meyer, speculative fiction and social theory both confront questions about catastrophe, aftermath, ramifications, and response. The true problem, however, is that, as Wolf-Meyer puts it, the "apocalypse is never singular; it is always multiple. In its multiplicity, the apocalypse is unimaginable. What is to be done when the future eludes our capacities for imaginative play and scientific modeling?"[49] How do we prepare for the unimaginable future? How do we grasp the ungraspable hyperobject? How do we know the unknowable real object? How do we negotiate the weirdness of the Anthropocene? "The end of the world," writes Morton, "is correlated with the Anthropocene, its global warming and subsequent dramatic climate change."[50] Myra Hird articulates a similar sentiment, correlating Anthropocene with the end of the world, "our vulnerability to planetary forces,"[51] which she sees connected to anxieties about the "consequences of human proliferation."[52] And she agrees with Wolf-Meyer that the future is ungraspable: "At the limits of the Anthropocene, the future cannot be visualized: It is an unknown aesthetic in excess of scientific prediction, human agency, and good will. It is indeterminate."[53] "Speculative fiction—and social theory—that considers desolation and its aftermath," responds Wolf-Meyer, "helps to point to ways forward, ways to live through the apocalypse, even if living through doesn't manage to keep things the same as they were."[54]

This, then, is an important chapter in the story of the Anthropocene thus far as articulated both in twenty-first-century critical and cultural theory and in popular culture: a gothic tale of a haunted planet, filled with monsters, framed against the backdrop of apocalypse. Late twentieth- and twenty-first-century cultural theory and popular culture have pivoted around these three master tropes: spectrality, monstrosity, and apocalypse. So much about them seems to "naturally" express our contemporary structure of feeling—the uncanny hauntedness of our present moment, the strategic deployment of monstrosity and the "monster" as a way to refuse destructive philosophical paradigms, the weirdness of a universe in which we are entangled with nonhuman actors we cannot fully know, the ever-present specter of catastrophe: Anthropocenic anxiety. ~~Anthropocene~~.

The question to end with, though, is: Must the story be told this way? The very naturalness of these tropes—ghosts, monsters, catastrophe—to tell the story of the Anthropocene should at least prompt us to pause because, as Roland Barthes developed in *Mythologies* (1957), disguising history as nature is how ideology functions.[55] So we at least need to ask: What is at stake in seeing the world as haunted? What is at stake in deploying the rhetoric of monstrosity to reformulate the notion of the human? And what is at stake with the omnipresent apocalyptic imagery? What avenues of investigation do they open and foreclose? Who benefits, and who does not? It may be that the gothic tale is the one we need right now. Indeed, this might even be the beginning point for something called an ethics of the gothic. But before we can go there, we need at least to speculate about how the story could be told otherwise—which will bring us back round again to where we are now: the gothic tale of the Anthropocene.

NOTES

1. Richard Grusin, ed., *The Nonhuman Turn* (Minneapolis: University of Minnesota Press, 2015).

2. María Del Pilar Blanco and Esther Peeren, "Introduction: Conceptualizing Spectralities," in *The Spectralities Reader: Ghosts and Hauntings in Contemporary Cultural Theory*, ed. María del Pilar Blanco and Esther Peeren, 6–10 (London: Bloomsbury, 2013).

3. Jeffrey Andrew Weinstock, "Introduction: The Spectral Turn," in *Spectral America: Phantoms and the National Imagination*, ed. Jeffrey Andrew Weinstock (Madison: University of Wisconsin Press, 2004), 4.

4. Anna Tsing, Heather Swanson, Elaine Gan, and Nils Bubandt, eds., *Arts of Living on a Damaged Planet* (Minneapolis: University of Minnesota Press, 2017), book jacket.

5. Tsing et al., G2.

6. Mark Fisher, *The Weird and the Eerie* (London: Repeater Books, 2016), 8.

7. Fisher, 10.

8. Fisher, 10.

9. Fisher, 10–11.

10. Fisher, 13.

11. Fisher, 20.

12. Fisher, 61.

13. Fisher, 61.

14. Fisher, 62.

15. Fisher, 64.

16. Ian Bogost, *Alien Phenomenology; or, What It's Like to Think Like a Thing* (Minneapolis: University of Minnesota Press, 2012), 4.

17. Graham Harman, *The Quadruple Object* (Winchester, U.K.: Zero Books, 2011), 39.

18. Steven Shaviro, "Speculative Realism—a Primer," *Terremoto* 2 (June 1, 2015), https://terremoto.mx/article/speculative-realism-a-primer/, emphasis added.

19. Graham Harman, *Weird Realism: Lovecraft and Philosophy* (Winchester, U.K.: Zero Books, 2012), 4–5.

20. Fisher, *The Weird and the Eerie*, 20.

21. Quentin Meillassoux, *After Finitude: An Essay on the Necessity of Contingency*, trans. Ray Brassier (New York: Continuum International, 2008), 7.

22. Timothy Morton, *Hyperobjects: Philosophy and Ecology after the End of the World* (Minneapolis: University of Minnesota Press, 2013), 1.

23. Morton, 1.

24. Morton, 3, Figure 1.

25. Morton, 70.

26. Morton, 70.

27. Morton, 17.

28. H. P. Lovecraft, *Supernatural Horror in Literature* (Mineola, N.Y.: Dover, 1973), 16.

29. Jeff VandeerMeer, "Hauntings in the Anthropocene: An Initial Exploration," *Environmental Critique,* July 2016, http://environmentalcritique.wordpress.com/2016/07/07/hauntings-in-the-anthropocene/.

30. VandeerMeer.

31. VandeerMeer.

32. Jeffrey Jerome Cohen, "Monster Culture (Seven Theses)," in *Monster Theory: Reading Culture,* ed. Jeffrey Jerome Cohen (Minneapolis: University of Minnesota Press, 1996), 4.

33. Jack Halberstam (writing as Judith), *Skin Shows: Gothic Horror and the Technology of Monsters* (Durham, N.C.: Duke University Press, 1995), 22.

34. See Donna Haraway, "A Cyborg Manifesto: Science, Technology, and Socialist-Feminism in the Late Twentieth Century," in *Simians, Cyborgs, and Women: The Reinvention of Nature,* 149–81 (New York: Routledge, 1994).

35. See Donna Haraway, "The Promises of Monsters: A Regenerative Politics for Inappropriate/d Others," in *Cultural Studies,* ed. Lawrence Grossberg, Cary Nelson, and Paula A. Treichler, 295–336 (New York: Routledge, 1992).

36. Tsing et al., *Arts of Living on a Damaged Planet,* M3.

37. Tsing et al., M10.

38. Tsing et al., M4.

39. On the concept of a "flat ontology," see Levi R. Bryant, *The Democracy of Objects* (Ann Arbor, Mich.: Open Humanities Press, 2011), 19ff.; see also Bogost, *Alien Phenomenology,* 17.

40. Jane Bennett, *Vibrant Matter: A Political Ecology of Things* (Durham, N.C.: Duke University Press, 2010), 99.

41. Cohen, "Monster Culture," 20.

42. Susan Sontag, "The Imagination of the Disaster," in *Liquid Metal: The Science Fiction Film Reader,* ed. Sean Redmond, 40–47 (London: Wallflower Press, 2004).

43. Ray Brassier, *Nihil Unbound: Enlightenment and Extinction* (London: Palgrave Macmillan, 2007).

44. Claire Colebrook, *Death of the Posthuman: Essays on Extinction,* vol. 1 (London: Open Humanities Press, 2011).

45. Patricia MacCormack, *The Ahuman Manifesto: Activism for the End of the Anthropocene* (London: Bloomsbury, 2020).

46. Eugene Thacker, *In the Dust of This Planet: Horror of Philosophy* (Winchester, U.K.: Zero Books, 2011), 1:4.
47. Thacker, 1:9.
48. Thacker, 1:8–9.
49. Matthew J. Wolf-Meyer, *Theory for the World to Come: Speculative Fiction and Apocalyptic Anthropology* (Minneapolis: University of Minnesota Press, 2019).
50. Morton, *Hyperobjects,* 7.
51. Myra J. Hird, "Proliferation, Extinction, and an Anthropocene Aesthetic," in *Posthumous Life: Theorizing beyond the Posthuman,* ed. Jami Weinstein and Claire Colebrook (New York: Columbia University Press, 2017), 255.
52. Hird, 251.
53. Hird, 264.
54. Wolf-Meyer, *Theory for the World to Come,* 15.
55. See Roland Barthes, *Mythologies,* trans. Annette Lavers (New York: Farrar, Straus, and Giroux, 1972).

« 2 »

De-extinction

A Gothic Masternarrative for the Anthropocene

MICHAEL FUCHS

In the superhuman scale of geological time, extinction is an inescapable component of any species' evolutionary cycle; extinction, the late evolutionary biologist Stephen Jay Gould explained, is "the normal fate of species."[1] Indeed, 99 percent of the 4 billion species estimated to have populated our planet in the last 3.5 billion years have disappeared. Since 1900, extinction rates have, however, soared to about a thousandfold the background rate.[2] Currently, more than 40 percent of insects, about one-third of all freshwater fishes, 25 percent of all mammals, 20 percent of all plant species, and 13 percent of all bird species are threatened with extinction.[3] More than thirty thousand species are threatened with extinction, according to the International Union for Conversation of Nature's Red List—and this number has been rising steadily. Extinction does not simply surround us but an extinction event of epic proportions is on the horizon.

If scientific reports are increasingly clear on the inevitability of an extinction event of catastrophic proportions, recent decades have also seen a culture "filled with depictions of zombies, plagues, and other spectacular representations of ecological catastrophe," all of which testify to the fact that "the specter of extinction haunts the popular imagination today."[4] This proliferation of death, in combination with its cultural companion of the undead, renders the current natural-cultural moment inherently gothic. Indeed, the Anthropocene, which is defined by the future recovery of human traces in the Earth's layers—by "future fossils . . . that will endure into the deep future"—has, as the present volume demonstrates, "gothic" written all over it.[5]

The sheer omnipresence of extinction has not only brought forth countless depictions of apocalyptic scenarios and barely inhabited postapocalyptic worlds but also fueled the popular and scientific imagination in another way. In the Introduction to his edited volume *After Extinction,* for instance, Richard Grusin invokes a future ghost by wondering, "what comes after extinction?"[6] For some scientists, the answer to this question seems relatively simple, maybe even too simple: de-extinction. Indeed, as Stewart Brand has noted, "that something as irreversible and final as extinction might be reversed is a stunning realization. The imagination soars. Just the thought of mammoths and passenger pigeons alive again invokes the awe and wonder that drives all conversation at its deepest level."[7] Brand pictures de-extinction as a reset button that will allow humankind to undo past mistakes.[8] This desire to resurrect species is nostalgia literalized—the longing for the future return of a past that never was. After all, passenger pigeons *(Ectopistes migratorius)* and woolly mammoths *(Mammuthus primigenius)* did not live in an age suffering from the weight of close to eight billion human beings. And while the passenger pigeon's extinction was a first sign of the "accumulation of extinctions" typical of capitalism, it was, arguably, not until the Great Acceleration that the workings of capitalism truly became tangible.[9]

This chapter draws on these various contexts to discuss actual de-extinction projects, discourses surrounding them, and representations of resurrection science in popular culture. I will suggest that de-extinction epitomizes the Anthropocene. In doing so, I will rely on Jeffrey Weinstock's contribution to this volume, in which he argues that spectrality, monstrosity, and extinction are three key narratives, and omnipresent tropes, of the Anthropocene, all three of which converge in de-extinction. In fact, de-extinction exacerbates the proliferation of Anthropocene specters by unlocking a future in which the undead will quite literally walk upon the Earth (perhaps only to vanish again). Akin to a kind of necromancy, de-extinction scientists try to make possible the return of the dead, as they seek to transport the past into the present while effectively transforming fantasy into reality and guaranteeing the constant reproduction of capital and the attendant exploitation and annihilation of the planet. Exemplifying Jeff VanderMeer's point that *"the uncanny has infiltrated the real"* in the Anthropocene, the fantastic, inherently gothic notion of bringing the dead back to life thus becomes a reality.[10] As the specters of species eradicated by anthropogenic activity are turned into necrofaunal revenants reminding of their past extinctions, such phantom species—paradoxically—also promise hope for a "better" future. Indeed, whereas the gothic generally functions as a projection screen for contemporaneous fears and anxieties, de-extinction promises to offset the constant state of "out-of-controlness" characteristic of the Anthropocene condition and promises humans to regain control over the fate of the planet.[11] De-extinction "look[s] to the past in the service of the future" in an attempt to reassert human exceptionalism,[12] yet inevitably also extrapolates past wrongs into the future and hence contributes to the proliferation of specters in the Anthropocene.

The Anthropocene Extinction

Recent research has suggested that

> predicted patterns of future ocean O_2 loss under climate
> change . . . are broadly similar to those . . . for the P/Tr
> [Permian–Triassic] boundary. Moreover, greenhouse gas
> emission scenarios projected for the coming centuries . . .
> predict a magnitude of upper ocean warming by 2300 CE that
> is ~35 to 50% of that required to account for most of the end-
> Permian extinction intensity.[13]

In other words, the geological and climatological similarities between the near future and previous mass extinctions cannot be denied—they are horrifying when considering the scope of the ecological catastrophe and the attendant species loss that is to be expected in the (relatively) near future. Indeed, "there are clear indications that losing species now in the 'critically endangered' category would propel the world to a state of mass extinction. . . . Additional losses of species in the 'endangered' and 'vulnerable' categories could accomplish the sixth mass extinction in just a few centuries."[14]

"Could accomplish" is a key phrase here, because leading paleontologists, such as Douglas Erwin, have repeatedly stressed that the proclamation of an *ongoing* sixth mass extinction constitutes a grave misunderstanding of the extent of the "Big Five" and exaggerates the implications of the environmental collapse we are facing right now.[15] Although "the recent loss of species is dramatic and serious," the current extinction numbers do "not yet qualify as a mass extinction in a palaeontological sense."[16] Nevertheless, acknowledging the potential dawn of the sixth mass extinction as a fact of life in the early twenty-first century not only emphasizes the destruction humankind has been wreaking upon the planet but also affirms that our ways of conceiving of the world have radically shifted. After all, extinction events are generally determined retrospectively. Paleontologists identify the vanishing of species based on traces these life-forms have left in the planet's crust, which indicate that these creatures used to inhabit the planet. The idea that what Earl Saxon calls the "Anthropocene extinction" will, at some future point in time, turn out to be a mass extinction exemplifies the changing realities characteristic of the Anthropocene.[17] As Claire Colebrook has explained:

> the positing of an anthropocene era . . . deploys the idea of human imaging—the way we have already read an inhuman past in the earth's layers—but does this by imagining a world in which humans will be extinct. The anthropocene thought experiment also alters the modality of geological reading, not just to refer to the past as it is for us, but also to *our* present as it will be without us.[18]

This viewpoint exposes the planetary insignificance of the individual human being. At the same time, it acknowledges that *Homo sapiens* "rival[s] the great forces of Nature" and (both consciously and unconsciously) leaves behind traces in the planet's layers.[19] A basic tenet of geology maintains (or, rather, *used to* maintain) that human time scales are inconsequential in view of geological deep time. But the Anthropocene condition suggests otherwise. As humankind has evolved from a biological into a geological agent, its planetary role has magnified and been implanted into deep time. The species' future-past role on the planet is imagined to be recovered or remembered by some post- or nonhuman life-form whose existence is projected into a future that will inevitably become reality.

While this post- or nonhuman life-form might appear to be little more than a neat rhetorical construct at first, it is required for conceptualizing the present moment remembered in the future-to-come, as *Homo sapiens* will have ceased to exist (at the very least in its current form). "Most of us can imagine humans living in a future full of space elevators, and even cities on the Moon," as "we usually picture our distant progeny in that future looking exactly the way we do now," Annalee Newitz notes in her book *Scatter, Adapt, and Remember* (2013). However, as Newitz stresses, our species is "going to evolve into creatures different from humans today—perhaps as different as we are from *Australopithecus*."[20]

Both the anticipation of human vanishing and the disappearance of a disproportionate number of species have rendered extinction "something to be sensed and imagined *here and now*."[21] Extinction hence combines a feeling of guilt concerning other species' past and ongoing vanishings and an anxiety about future extinctions, humans included. Traditional temporal categories collapse, as today's human beings (and arguably the planet) become aware of past, present, and future extinctions—indeed, not just "aware" but rather haunted by their present and future memories. The resultant condition is akin to what Paul K. Saint-Amour, in the context of nuclear anxiety, describes as an "inverted or *preposterous* phenomenon of traumatic symptoms . . . that exist not in the wake of a past event, but in the shadow of a future one," with the difference being that this inverted trauma adds to the trauma caused by the accumulation of species extinctions caused by anthropogenic activities in the last ten thousand plus years.[22] What perhaps becomes particularly troubling for individual human beings is the acknowledgment of future human extinction, as it "afflicts humanity with a case of anticipatory mourning, a mourning in advance of loss."[23] The inevitability of human extinction (and the long-term efforts needed to decrease the rate of other species' extinctions) causes paralysis. In fact, the contemporary fatalist discourse dominated by human-caused extinction (and self-extinction) in the past, present, and future potentially "undermin[es] all sense of agency" and "produc[es] melancholic forms of subjectivity deprived of capacity for action."[24]

Becoming Un-extinct

But extinction is not as "final and irreversible" as we generally believe it to be.[25] As a matter of fact, there are sometimes zombies lurking in the fossil records of past extinctions. In 1996, paleontologist J. David Archibald described the "zombie effect" as the process by which fossils, due to erosion and other natural causes, are redeposited in layers millions of years younger than the fossils themselves.[26] The no-longer-extinct hence walk through deep time and stratigraphic space.

Biblical undead likewise haunt paleontology. The Lazarus taxon was named after the New Testament tale of Lazarus returning from the dead and includes species that disappear from the fossil record or the historical now, leading paleontologists and biologists to believe that these species are extinct. However, the believed-to-be-extinct species suddenly reappears. The Lazarus effect is closely connected to mass extinction events, as "the population density of numerous species declines drastically and they disappear from the fossil record. For many species, the decline in abundance is terminal and they become truly extinct, but some species may survive in much reduced numbers."[27]

The coelacanth (*Latimeria chalumnae* and *L. menadoensis*) is probably the most famous Lazarus taxon. The fish was believed to have died out during the end-Cretaceous extinction sixty-six million years ago, only to be caught by fishers off the coast of South Africa in 1938. Since then, specimens of the West Indian species have been discovered in five more African countries and specimens of the Indonesian variety in the waters off Indonesia.[28] Similarly, scientists assumed that the pygmy right whale *(Caperea marginata)* disappeared from the face of our planet about two million years ago, until a carcass washed up in New Zealand in 2002.[29] And the Laotian rock rat *(Laonastes aenigmamus)* was thought to have vanished about eleven million years ago, until a scientist discovered "bodies of two unusual-looking rodents on sale as food" at a market in Lao People's Democratic Republic in 1996.[30]

Arguably, these believed-to-be-extinct species were, to draw on Avery Gordon's elaborations on ghosts, "seemingly not there to our supposedly well-trained eyes" but made themselves "apparent to us."[31] Indeed, in a paper on Lazarus taxa, Emmanuel Fara explains that the Lazarus effect exposes not only the incompleteness of the fossil record but, more importantly, paleontology's tendency to suppress these gaps in knowledge, as the field usually pretends that the current level of knowledge "is adequate to document major evolutionary patterns."[32] Lazarus taxa accordingly mark a return

of the repressed, as their "appearances signal epistemological uncertainty and the potential emergence of a different story and a
competing history," to quote from Jeffrey Weinstock's elaborations
on specters.[33] Taxa of "un-extinct" (or "undead") species allow paleontologists to acknowledge that the fossil record is incomplete,
thereby "call[ing] into question the veracity of the authorized version of events," to draw on Weinstock again.[34] At the same time,
seemingly never-ending reports in pop science publications inform
the public that species thought to have been extinct have been re-
discovered and that entirely unknown species have been discovered. Whenever one such species appears or reappears as a result
of humankind's increasing penetration of Earth, the media tend to
stress the number of species likely yet to be discovered and the variety of Lazarus taxa. Unfortunately, both of these numbers pale in
comparison with all the species lost for the same reason that new
ones are discovered—human encroachment upon the nonhuman
world. As a result, the becoming-un-extinct of species exposes the
omnipresence of extinction in our age.

Becoming De-extinct

On another level, the zombie and Lazarus effects reveal humankind's eagerness to categorize and name natural phenomena in an
attempt to create the illusion of understanding them. At the same
time, these attempts expose the inability to comprehend "nature."
Twenty-first-century technologies have made possible a similar,
yet at the same time very different, phenomenon: de-extinction. A
shadow companion of extinction, de-extinction—also referred to
as resurrection biology and species revivalism—denotes the restoration of extinct species.

The idea to resurrect an extinct species might sound like fantasy
or "soft" science fiction at first, but de-extinction is not a figment
of the imagination—not quite. The Pyrenean ibex (Capra pyrenaica pyrenaica), also known as bucardo, was one of four subspecies
of the Iberian wild goat. After the endling, Celia, was found dead,
the bucardo was officially declared extinct on January 6, 2000.[35]
The taxon vanished from the face of the Earth due to anthropogenic activities and their effects—overhunting in the nineteenth
and twentieth centuries and habitat loss, which led to overgrazing.
In the 1980s and early 1990s, ibex populations were decimated by

sarcoptic mange outbreaks, with some populations suffering mortality rates of more than 95 percent.[36] As early as 1992, Spanish scientists succeeded in creating bucardo embryos, but assisted reproductive technologies were not available for the species. Inspired by the successful cloning of the sheep Dolly in 1996, scientists collected DNA samples from Celia in 1999. Soon after Celia's death, they began to inject bucardo DNA into domestic goat eggs emptied of their own genetic material. Still in a lab, the scientists started the process of cell division and the creation of embryos. These embryos were implanted into domestic goats, with disturbing results, as the domestic goat's uterus cannot properly nourish a bucardo.[37] The photographs which Alberto Fernández-Arias showed at the TEDx conference in 2013 testify to the fact that the domestic goats gave birth to ghastly abominations, seemingly mummified creatures that rendered manifest the monstrous reproduction and Frankensteinean resurrection in which the scientists were engaged.[38]

The malformed offspring apparently inspired the genetic engineers to conquer the next frontier of science. In their ongoing attempts to revive the bucardo, French and Spanish scientists took the next step: hybridizing domestic goats with Spanish ibex over several generations before using the hybrids as breeding vessels. On July 30, 2003, one of the hybrids calved a Pyrenean ibex, rendering the bucardo de-extinct (while nevertheless remaining *functionally extinct,* as one specimen cannot secure the species' future). However, when Fernández-Arias "held the newborn bucardo in his arms, he could see that she was struggling to take in air, her tongue jutting grotesquely out of her mouth."[39] The little creature died after a few minutes due to a deformation of her lungs. A hideous progeny produced by crossbreeding and other forms of human tampering with life, the calf saw the light of the Earth without any chance of survival; she was, effectively, stillborn, and her subspecies practically went extinct for a second time as soon as it had become de-extinct.

We see this serialized extinction reflected in fiction too. For example, in the second book of Piers Anthony's Xanth series, *Source of Magic* (1979), the main character, a magician named Bink, encounters thirteen black cats. The narrator remarks, "Bink had never seen a pure cat before, in the flesh. We regarded the cat as an extinct species. He just stood there and stared at this abrupt de-extinction, unable to formulate a durable opinion." Bink knows that he has to overcome the cats in some way. The narrator wonders, "If he killed these animals, would he be re-extincting the species?"[40] If *Source of Magic* thus arguably exposed the linguistic conundrums that the de-extinction (and possible future re-extinction) of species entails nearly a quarter-century before the bucardo re-extincted minutes after it had become de-extinct, the Jurassic Park franchise presciently broaches some of the ethical and legal questions de-extinction raises. In *The Lost World* (1995), a character opines that "an animal that is extinct, and is brought back to life, is for all practical purposes not an animal at all. It can't have any rights. It's already extinct. So if it exists, it can only be something we have made. We made it, we patent it, we own it."[41] In *Jurassic World* (2015), a character who wants to deploy velociraptors in warfare echoes these ideas: "We do own them. Extinct animals have no rights." However, the raptor wrangler Owen corrects him: "They are not extinct anymore."[42] The sequel, *Fallen Kingdom* (2018), highlights the unclear legal situation (and its moral and ethical implications). A long-dormant volcano becomes active on Isla Nublar, the fictional island where both the original Jurassic Park and Jurassic World were built, and which has become a haven for the last dinosaurs. "Geologists now predict that an extinction-level event will kill off the last living dinosaurs on the planet," remarks a female BBC reporter. As the newswoman discusses the dinosaur situation, the news ticker at the bottom of the screen announces, "Earth warming at a pace unprecedented in 1000 years," thereby suggesting that the impending re-extinction of dinosaurs addresses quite real issues on our planet. The reporter goes on to describe the potential re-extinction of the dinosaurs as "the flashpoint animal rights issue of our time" and explains that the U.S. Senate has convened a special committee "to answer a grave moral question: Do dinosaurs deserve the same protections given to other endangered species or should they be left to die?"[43]

Of course, *Fallen Kingdom*'s depiction of the situation could be said to satirize the media hype surrounding the potential disappearance of animals biotechnologically recreated from DNA samples more than sixty-five million years old, thereby ridiculing conservation efforts and the animal rights movement. Nevertheless, the movie also raises important questions: What would we do if a de-extinct species would turn out to be unfit for survival in a world altered by anthropogenic activities and their consequences? *Consciously* eradicate it *again*? Or follow an approach Jurassic Park creator John Hammond suggests in *The Lost World* film—to accept that "these creatures require our absence to survive, not our help"? The problem here, of course, is that in a world characterized by the entanglements between nature and culture, we cannot just "step aside and trust in nature," as Hammond adds.[44] "We cannot suddenly stop being involved," because of our role in species' extinctions (and possible de-extinctions and re-extinctions) and because our involvement will not simply end from one day to the next, even if our entire species were to vanish overnight.[45] The main problem, however, is that no matter whether we decide to interfere, we cannot predict the long-term consequences of our measures and whether the actions taken would not further escalate the ever-increasing extinction rate.

Reversing Species Loss

In the paper in which José Folch and his team describe the bucardo de-extinction project, they conclude that

> cloning is . . . not [a] very effective way to preserve endangered species, because [of] the complexity [of] handling the experimental wild animal and the insufficient knowledge on both the cellular mechanisms involved in the technique and on the reproductive characteristics of the animals. . . . However, [for] species [such] as bucardo, *cloning is the only possibility to avoid its complete disappearance.* The present work encourages to appropriately store somatic tissues and cells of all endangered species or suitable animals, as they may be useful for future cloning-based conservation programs.[46]

Besides the loaded word choice of "avoiding the complete disappearance" of an already extinct species, this short passage reveals that the scientists imagine the establishment of a global gene bank with an eye toward cryopreserving tissue samples and genetic information to guarantee future life by reawakening dormant (i.e., extinct) life. "Genetic *information*" proves key here, for the bioinformatic discourse surrounding life, defined by the decoding, re-sampling, and encoding of life, considers extinction not the loss of a species, an individual specimen, or even "life as such" but rather the loss of data and information.[47] Having access to this information, on the other hand, allows scientists to decipher the code of life and, more importantly, to manipulate the code and change it according to their will, giving them control over life. Stephanie Turner has tellingly explained that "in genome time, evolutionary histories, including extinction narratives, are revised, forestalling or even reversing absolute endpoints in the endless reproducibility of the DNA code."[48] As a result, genetic engineering emerges as a vehicle for assuaging fears about biodiversity loss—indeed, a tool for *reversing* species loss.

The nonprofit organization Revive and Restore taps into the same idea. Its mission is "to enhance biodiversity through the genetic rescue of . . . extinct species." Through collaborations with "the world's leading molecular biologists, conservation biologists, and conservation organizations," Revive and Restore seeks "to develop pioneering, proof-of-concept genetic rescue projects using cutting-edge genomic technologies to solve problems posed by inbreeding, exotic diseases, climate change, and destructive invasive species" with the final goal being "to restore ecological biodiversity."[49] Such a project, of course, raises a number of moral, ethical, and economic questions—and none of them can be answered unambiguously: resurrecting a species human beings (or the effects of anthropogenic activities) recently eradicated might seem like a well-intentioned act, but can we guarantee that humans will not, for example, kill a male northern white rhino (*Ceratotherium simum cottoni*) if one were to appear again? Would anyone actually own these bioengineered creatures? Even Beth Shapiro, herself a genetic engineer involved in resurrection science, has stressed "the high cost of resurrecting extinct species and the myriad risks of reintroducing organisms into the wild whose environmental impacts are—because they are extinct—necessarily unknown."[50] More important, with projects focusing on the de-extinction of species like the passenger pigeon (extinct since 1914) and the woolly mammoth (extinct for about four thousand years), Revive and Restore's website uncannily (or consciously?) invokes the ghost of Dr. John Hammond:

> My colleagues and I determined, several years ago, that it was possible to clone the DNA of an extinct animal, and to grow

it. That seemed to us a wonderful idea, it was a kind of time travel—the only time travel in the world. Bring them back alive, so to speak. And since it was so exciting, and since it was possible to do it, we decided to go forward.[51]

Beyond apparently being too preoccupied with figuring out whether or not they *could* instead of thinking if they *should*, Revive and Restore scientists do clearly consider the question which animals they *should* resurrect. While the website offers detailed rationalizations focusing on the biological niches that the woolly mammoth and the passenger pigeon occupied, which try to explain why they should be among the species destined to walk upon the face of the Earth *again*, they, more importantly, make for very iconic representatives for de-extinction.

The mammoth, Matthew Chrulew has argued, "is the totem animal of *post*modernity," as it symbolizes "today's ecological *crisis*," which "push[es] the earth's natural limits."[52] "It is [the] perception of human culpability for the mammoth's extinction," he continues, "that provokes the desire to simulate or even resurrect them today."[53] Inverting narrative blueprints of gothic tales, reawakening these ghosts of the past hence suggests that humanity's past sins are atoned for (yet, in truly gothic fashion, they nevertheless haunt the future). The passenger pigeon, on the other hand, epitomized the natural abundance of North America when European colonists encroached upon the New World. Up until the American Civil War, hunters and early naturalists were awed by flocks counting millions of birds. While traveling along the Ohio River in 1813, John James Audubon, for example, reported that he saw a flight of pigeons so massive in size that "the light of noon-day was obscured as by an eclipse."[54] Tellingly, "a flock that the eye cannot see the end of" even appears in James Fenimore Cooper's novel *The Pioneers* (1823).[55]

The idea behind reintroducing the passenger pigeon to the forests in the Northeast of the United States echoes the middle part of the Hammond quotation referenced above—the resurrection of the passenger pigeon evokes a nostalgic return to a place of natural resources aplenty and a time characterized by simplicity and living in harmony with nature while erasing the devastating effects of colonialism's extractive and exploitative practices. Ursula Heise has diagnosed that this nostalgic harking back to an imagined past is "a curiously 'retro' way of moving into the future," which raises a number of questions. After all, "the conceptual paradoxes of de-extinction are such that what emerges from this nostalgia might be something quite different from a reconstruction of the past. Would a de-extincted passenger pigeon be a passenger pigeon or an innovative product of biotechnology, a 'Franken-pigeon'?"[56] Bruno Latour has rightfully stressed that Victor Frankenstein's "crime was not that he invented a creature through some combination of hubris and high technology, but rather that he *abandoned the creature to itself.*" Of course, Latour does not endorse a simplistic celebration of (bio)technology here; instead, he emphasizes the entanglements that define life on Earth and seeks to promote a "becoming ever-more attached to, and intimate with, a panoply of nonhuman natures."[57] Although Heise would probably agree with Latour on this issue, her conjuring of Frankenstein's ghost suggests that no matter how hard we might try, in the incredibly complex system that is the planet we inhabit, we cannot control the long-term consequences of our actions. After all, irrespective of whether it's climate change, ocean acidification, or biodiversity loss, none of this was planned. Similarly, no one can tell whether reintroducing a de-extincted species into the wild would not lead to the quick re-extinction of this species or maybe even the extinction of other species that have to compete with the de-extincted-turned-invasive species. And even if the reintroduction of a de-extincted species turned out to be successful, this success would not automatically mean that a different project trying to reintroduce another de-extinct species would be effective as well.

Necrocapitalism

In addition, de-extinction projects like Revive and Restore might be driven by noble ideas and might want to steer clear of Dr. Frankenstein's mistakes. However, one cannot suppress the feeling that the invisible hand of hypercapitalism will soon take control of such ventures. When Revive and Restore's website envisions that "exciting collaborative projects in genomic conservation are rapidly emerging," including "the production of commercially viable synthetic alternatives to wildlife-derived products," the capitalist, business-oriented language jumps at you.[58] Indeed, Revive and Restore's mission makes explicit that capital has been shifting into "a new space of production—molecular biology."[59] Giant corporations may soon literalize "the exploitation of past extinctions" Justin McBrien considers characteristic of capitalism.[60] De-extinction will then not only become a money-making machine but lead to ever-new extinctions that will be undone, as extinct species are constantly and repeatedly brought back to life, only to be eradicated again.

The fate of the Indominus Rex in *Jurassic World* exemplifies this serialized cycle of predetermined extinction. As Jurassic World's operations manager Claire Dearing stresses early in the film, to guarantee continued growth, Jurassic World's "asset development" must respond to market demands—"consumers want them [i.e., the dinosaurs] bigger, louder, with more teeth"—and hence their bioengineers "designed" the Indominus Rex.[61] Even if the Indominus had not been killed in the film's conclusion, it would soon have been replaced by an updated version—and the Indominus hence made extinct. *Fallen Kingdom* makes this capitalist logic explicit through the introduction of the Indoraptor, which is a "direct descendant" of the Indominus and which embodies "potential for growth [that] is more than you can fathom."[62] This "potential for growth" is founded upon the future substitution of the Indoraptor by a new "product." The flurry of extinctions leading to de-extinctions leading to re-extinctions exponentiates the "accumulation of extinctions" that defines the Necrocene.

In the end, the very concept of de-extinction bespeaks humankind's hubris, as it "will . . . make us into gods by allowing us . . . to resurrect extinct life-forms . . . according to our needs."[63] As such, de-extinction embodies the Anthropocene: de-extinction is inextricably tied to the mass extinction event into which humankind maneuvers this planet; de-extinction produces monstrous abominations (as the bucardo experiments showcased); and de-extinction exposes that the ghosts of lost species—past, present, and future—haunt us today. In the Anthropocene, our (Western) scales are simply off—the global is entangled with the local; individual human acts are simultaneously implicated in global anthropogenic activities and rendered meaningless in view of the insignificance of individuals within the context of global phenomena such as climate change; the differences between geological deep time and human history have faded away; and past, present, and future extinctions—along with future de-extinctions and re-extinctions—haunt the present moment.

Man-made extinctions of the past ten thousand plus years have depleted and deprived planetary life. Paradoxically, the de-extinction of these creatures simultaneously perpetuates human technological imperialism *and* seeks to atone for it. De-extinction promises *Homo sapiens* a tool to reassert dominion over the planet and embellishes human exceptionalism by signposting that humankind can develop beyond, can out-evolve, evolutionary processes like extinction. However, this ideal of control cannot be but an illusion, as it suppresses the realities of life on a planet whose resources dwindle away and which barrels toward environmental catastrophe at an alarming rate. In the Anthropocene, anthropogenic activities can no longer *not* impact the more-than-human world. The (potentially paralyzing) question thus becomes, how *can* humans intervene in planetary systems at this point in an attempt not only to stop ecocide but also to remediate past and present ecologically destructive anthropogenic activities?

NOTES

1. Stephen Jay Gould, *Eight Little Piggies: Reflections on Natural History* (London: Vintage Books, 2007), 46.

2. Stuart L. Pimm et al., "The Biodiversity of Species and Their Rates of Extinction, Distribution, and Protection," *Science* 344, no. 6187 (2014): 1246752.

3. See Francisco Sánchez-Bayo and Kris A. G. Wyckhufys, "Worldwide Decline of the Entomofauna: A Review of Its Drivers," *Biological Conservation* 232 (2019): 8–27; William R. T. Darwall and Jörg Freyhof, "Lost Fishes, Who Is Counting? The Extent of the Threat to Freshwater Fish Biodiversity," in *Conservation of Freshwater Fishes,* ed. Gerard P. Closs, Martin Krkosek, and Julian D. Olden, 1–36 (New York: Cambridge University Press, 2016); David Tilman, Michael Clark, David R. Williams, Kaitlin Kimmel, Stephen Polasky, and Craig Packer, "Future Threats to Biodiversity and Pathways to Their Prevention," *Nature* 546 (2017): 73–81; Kathy J. Willis, ed., *State of the World's Plants* (London: Royal Botanic Gardens, 2017). Note that animal and—at a distant second—plant species are dramatically overrepresented in discussions of extinction numbers. Barely any studies have investigated fungi, not to mention the other four kingdoms. Nevertheless,

as early as 2010, studies suggested that at least 10 percent of European macrofungi are also affected by the Anthropocene extinction. See Anders Dahlberg, David R. Genney, and Jacob Heilmann-Clausen, "Developing a Comprehensive Strategy for Fungal Conversation in Europe: Current Status and Future Needs," *Fungal Ecology* 3, no. 2 (2010): 50–64.

4. Ashley Dawson, *Extinction: A Radical History* (New York: OR Books, 2016), 16.

5. David Farrier, *Footprints: In Search of Future Fossils* (London: 4th Estate, 2020), loc. 315.

6. Richard Grusin, ed., Introduction to *After Extinction* (Minneapolis: University of Minnesota Press, 2018), loc. 54.

7. Stewart Brand, "Opinion: The Case for Reviving Extinct Species," *National Geographic News,* March 12, 2013, https://www.national geographic.com/news/2013/3/130311-deextinction-reviving-extinct -species-opinion-animals-science/.

8. My use of "humankind" (and its derivatives) and "we" follows Dipesh Chakrabarty, who has argued that humans "can become geological agents only historically and collectively." Chakrabarty, "The Climate of History: Four Theses," *Critical Inquiry* 35, no. 2 (2009): 206. The sweeping generalization typical of the Anthropocene discourse "challenges traditions of thought that have relied, over the past half century, on the assumption of some foundational difference—whether it be gender, sexual orientation, class, or race." Ursula Heise, *Imagining Extinction: The Cultural Meanings of Endangered Species* (Chicago: University of Chicago Press, 2016), loc. 4450. Of course, rather than "challenging" these differences, one may also argue that the Anthropocene discourse, in fact, erases them. See, e.g., Jason W. Moore, "The Capitalocene, Part 1: On the Nature and Origins of Our Ecological Crisis," *Journal of Peasant Studies* 44, no. 3 (2017): 594–630; Kathryn Yusoff, *A Billion Black Anthropocenes or None* (Minneapolis: University of Minnesota Press, 2019); and Duncan in this volume.

9. Justin McBrien, "Accumulating Extinction: Planetary Catastrophism in the Necrocene," in *Anthropocene or Capitalocene: Nature, History, and the Crisis of Capitalism,* ed. Jason W. Moore, 116–37 (Oakland, Calif.: PM Press, 2016).

10. Jeff VanderMeer, "Hauntings in the Anthropocene: An Initial Exploration," *Environmental Critique,* July 2016, https://environmental critique.wordpress.com/2016/07/07/hauntings-in-the-anthropocene.

11. Nigel Clark, "Panic Ecology: Nature in the Age of Superconductivity," *Theory, Culture, and Society* 14, no. 1 (1997): 88.

12. Dolly Jørgensen, *Recovering Lost Species in the Modern Age: Histories of Longing and Belonging* (Cambridge, Mass.: MIT Press, 2019), loc. 443.

13. Justin L. Penn, Curtis Deutsch, Jonathan L. Payne, and Erik A. Sperling, "Temperature-Dependent Hypoxia Explains Biogeography and Severity of End-Permian Marine Mass Extinction," *Science* 362 (2018): 5.

14. Anthony D. Barnosky, Nicholas Matzke, Susumu Tomiya, Guinevere O. U. Wogan, Brian Swartz, Tiago B. Quental, Charles Marshall et al., "Has the Earth's Sixth Mass Extinction Already Arrived?," *Nature* 471 (2011): 56.

15. Douglas Erwin, quoted in Peter Brannen, "Earth Is Not in the Midst of a Sixth Mass Extinction," *The Atlantic,* June 13, 2017, https://www .theatlantic.com/science/archive/2017/06/the-ends-of-the-world/ 529545/.

16. Barnosky et al., 56.

17. Earl Saxon, "Noah's Parks: A Partial Antidote to the Anthropocene Extinction Event," *Biodiversity* 9, no. 3–4 (2008): 5–10.

18. Claire Colebrook, *Death of the Posthuman: Essays on Extinction* (Ann Arbor, Mich.: Open Humanities Press, 2014), 28.

19. Will Steffen, Paul J. Crutzen, and John R. McNeill, "The Anthropocene: Are Humans Now Overwhelming the Great Forces of Nature?," *Ambio* 36, no. 8 (2007): 614.

20. Annalee Newitz, *Scatter, Adapt, and Remember: How Humans Will Survive a Mass Extinction* (New York: Doubleday, 2013), 242.

21. Joanna Zylinska, "Photography after Extinction," in Grusin, *After Extinction,* loc. 1274.

22. Paul K. Saint-Amour, *Tense Future: Modernism, War, Encyclopedic Form* (Oxford: Oxford University Press, 2016), 24–25.

23. Saint-Amour, 25.

24. Jussi Parikka, "Planetary Memories: After Extinction, the Imagined Future," in Grusin, *After Extinction,* loc. 1064.

25. Christopher Belshaw, *Environmental Philosophy: Reason, Nature and Human Concern* (London: Routledge, 2014), 163.

26. J. David Archibald, *Dinosaur Extinction and the End of an Era: What the Fossil Record Says* (New York: Columbia University Press, 1996), 70–72.

27. Paul B. Wignall and Michael J. Benton, "Lazarus Taxa and Fossil Abundance at Times of Biotic Crisis," *Journal of the Geological Society* 156 (1999): 453.

28. See, e.g., Peter Forey, *History of the Coelacanth Fishes* (London: Chapman and Hall, 1998).

29. Ewan R. Fordyce and Felix G. Marx, "The Pygmy Right Wale *Caperea marginata*: The Last of the Cetotheres," *Proceedings of the Royal Society, Series B* 280 (2012): 20122645.

30. Paulina D. Jenkins, C. William Kilpatrick, Mark F. Robinson, and Robert J. Timmins, "Morphological and Molecular Investigations of

a New Family, Genus and Species of Rodent *(Mammalia: Rodentia: Hystricognatha)* from Lao PDR," *Systematics and Biodiversity* 2, no. 4 (2005): 420.

31. Avery Gordon, *Ghostly Matters: Haunting and the Sociological Imagination* (Minneapolis: University of Minnesota Press, 1997), 8.

32. Emmanuel Fara, "What Are Lazarus Taxa?," *Geological Journal* 36 (2001): 291.

33. Jeffrey A. Weinstock, "Introduction: The Spectral Turn," in *Spectral America: Phantoms and the National Imagination*, ed. Jeffrey A. Weinstock (Madison: University of Wisconsin Press, 2004), 7.

34. Weinstock, 5.

35. Robert M. Webster and Bruce Erickson, "The Last Word?," *Nature* 380 (1996): 386. Today, taxidermied Celia welcomes visitors at the reception center of the National Park of Ordesa and Monte Perdido in Aragon, Spain.

36. Paulino Fandos, *La cabra montés (Capra pyrenaica) en el Parque Natural de Cazorla, Segura y Las Villas* (Madrid: ICONA–CSIC, 1991), 36.

37. Alberto Fernández-Arias, J. L. Alabart, J. Folch, and J. F. Beckers, "Interspecies Pregnancy of Spanish Ibex *(Capra pyrenaica)* Fetus in Domestic Goat *(Capra hircus)* Recipients Induces Abnormally High Plasmatic Levels of Pregnancy-Associated Glycoprotein," *Theriogenology* 51, no. 8 (1999): 1419–30.

38. TEDx Talks, "The First De-extinction: Alberto Fernández-Arias," *You Tube*, April 1, 2013, https://www.youtube.com/watch?v=5eMqEQw9Fbs.

39. Carl Zimmer, "Bringing Them Back to Life: The Revival of an Extinct Species Is No Longer a Fantasy," in *Animal Ethics Reader*, ed. Susan J. Armstrong and Richard G. Botzler (New York: Routledge, 2017), 479.

40. Piers Anthony, *The Source of Magic* (New York: Del Rey, 2002), 273.

41. Michael Crichton, *The Lost World* (New York: Ballantine Books, 2012), 102–3.

42. Colin Trevorrow, dir., *Jurassic World* (Universal City, Calif.: Universal Pictures, 2015).

43. J. A. Bayona, dir., *Jurassic World: Fallen Kingdom* (Universal City, Calif.: Universal Pictures, 2018).

44. Steven Spielberg, dir., *The Lost World: Jurassic Park* (Universal City, Calif.: Universal Pictures, 1997).

45. Bruno Latour, "Love Your Monsters: Why We Must Care for Our Technologies as We Do Our Children," in *Love Your Monsters: Postenvironmentalism and the Anthropocene*, ed. Michael Shellenberger and Ted Hordhaus (Oakland, Calif.: Breakthrough Institute, 2011), 412.

46. José Folch, M. J. Cocero, P. Chesné, J. L. Alabarta, V. Domínguez, Y. Cognié, A. Roche et al., "First Birth of an Animal from an Extinct Species *(Capra pyrenaica pyrenaica)* by Cloning," *Theriogenology* 71 (2009): 1033, italics added.

47. See, e.g., Eugene Thacker, *The Global Genome: Biotechnology, Politics, and Culture* (Cambridge, Mass.: MIT Press, 2005).

48. Stephanie S. Turner, "Open-Ended Stories: Extinction Narratives in Genome Time," *Literature and Medicine* 26, no. 1 (2007): 59.

49. Revive and Restore, https://www.reviverestore.org/.

50. Beth Shapiro, *How to Clone a Mammoth: The Science of De-extinction* (Princeton, N.J.: Princeton University Press, 2015), x.

51. Michael Crichton, *Jurassic Park* (New York: Ballantine Books, 2012), 305.

52. Matthew Chrulew, "Hunting the Mammoth, Pleistocene to Postmodern," *Journal for Critical Animal Studies* 9, no. 1–2 (2011): 34.

53. Chrulew, 41.

54. John James Audubon, *Ornithological Biography; or, An Account of the Habits of the Birds of the United States of America* (Philadelphia: E. L. Carey and A. Hart, 1832), 321.

55. James Fenimore Cooper, *The Pioneers; or, The Sources of the Susquehanna: A Descriptive Tale* (London: Routledge, 1852), 213.

56. Heise, *Imagining Extinction*, loc. 4265.

57. Latour, "Love Your Monsters," loc. 271.

58. Revive and Restore.

59. Melinda Cooper, *Life as Surplus: Biotechnology and Capitalism in the Neoliberal Era* (Seattle: University of Washington Press, 2008), 23.

60. McBrien, "Accumulating Extinction," 117.

61. *Jurassic World.*

62. *Jurassic World: Fallen Kingdom.*

63. Ashley Dawson, "Biocapitalism and De-extinction," in Grusin, *After Extinction*, loc. 3633.

« 3 »

Lovecraft vs. VanderMeer

Posthuman Horror (and Hope?) in the Zone of Exception

RUNE GRAULUND

The Anthropocene is a waking nightmare. Stuck in an awkward temporal position between a past, a present, and a future that is at one and the same time terrifyingly identifiable and bafflingly unknowable, it is difficult to orient oneself in the fugue state of the past-present-future that is the Anthropocene. As global modernity sluggishly awakens from a centuries-long slumber of anthropocentric thinking, gradually realizing just how (self-)destructive such behavior has been, the majority even of those who have become fully woke nevertheless tend to continue a life of somnambulant paralysis. As walking but woken dead, we are therefore as a species not, like the classic zombie, "braindead." Yet we seem as mindlessly ravenous, even as we become increasingly cognizant of the fact that unbridled growth and consumption cannot continue. As Patricia MacCormack phrases it in *The Ahuman Manifesto*, "humans now find ourselves in the difficult situation of knowing what we are doing and why it is literally murdering the earth, but we do not know how to get out of this scenario."[1]

In this chapter, I will examine how the Anthropocene is simultaneously exceptional while in fact also a return to the normality of a nonanthropocentric universe. Intimately familiar but also ultimately unknowable and, above all, uncontainable, the Anthropocene presents a horrifying new normal that will remain in a constant state of exception as long as we cling to former anthropocentric beliefs in endless progress and the rightful dominance of the human species, yet potentially far less horrifying once such positions are abandoned. With this in mind, I will examine the challenge to the supposed normativity of anthropocentric thought

offered through the idea of the "zone of exception" as portrayed in
H. P. Lovecraft's short story "The Colour out of Space" (1927) and
Jeff VanderMeer's *Annihilation* (2014). Weird, limited, and temporary to begin with, zones of exception threaten to overflow and
in time disturb and subvert the landscapes of normality. As the
perimeter of a containment zone is compromised and spills over
into the outside world (and vice versa), humanist assumptions of
dominance, control, and normativity are disturbed. I will argue
therefore that the zones of exception evoked by Lovecraft and
VanderMeer can be read into the emergence of two very different
kinds of strategies and philosophies for dealing with the Anthropocene. For whereas Lovecraft's zone of exception is one that evokes
nostalgia, denial, and eventual paralysis, VanderMeer's revolves
around openness, acceptance, and hope that allows for alternate
realities to the status quo to emerge.

The Zone of Exception and the New Normal of the Anthropocene

Historically, *zones of exception* have been employed to control un-
desired peoples and disease. The ghetto, the camp, and the quarantine zone all spring from a demand to manage and sometimes
eradicate contaminants that the surrounding environment deems
to be undesirous. Indeed, from the sixteenth-century Venetian
Ghetto over the infamy of the twentieth-century Warsaw Ghetto
and on to the *banlieues* of present-day Paris or the *favelas* of Rio de
Janeiro, urban zones of containment have been in effect for centuries. While some of these urban zones of confinement have been
directly enforced by violence (the Warsaw Ghetto), allowing little
to no exchange between the zone of containment and the outside
world, most of them have mainly been indirectly limited by socioeconomic forces (the Chicago South Side, Kowloon Walled City in
Hong Kong, Glasgow's East End). Prisons, asylums, and camps,
on the other hand, tend to be far more rigorously controlled by
physical force. In all cases, whether they are motivated by financial,
medical, racial, or criminal concerns, ghettos, camps, asylums, and
prisons are all intended to contain and control the movement of
people who are deemed undesirable and perhaps also dangerous
by the larger community in which they find themselves. *Quarantine zones* are different in that they are far more broadly defined

in terms of their subject matter. Originating from the Italian *quaranta giorni,* from the forty days that foreigners were forced to wait before entering a city during the reign of the Black Death,[2] quarantine zones have evolved to refer to the containment of life-forms other than human, primarily animals but on occasion also plants as well as a range of hazardous material. Other than disease (e.g., the plague, hoof-and-mouth disease, Dutch elm disease), quarantine zones can also be invoked by, for instance, gas leaks, oil spills, or nuclear fallout. Most recently and spectacularly so, quarantine has of course been evoked in a wide manner of ways due to the outbreak of Covid-19 and the following pandemic that, at the time of writing, is still raging.

In film and fiction, the notion of containment through quarantine has been employed for many different purposes. From the vaguely defined plague of Albert Camus's *The Plague* (1947) on to Jose Saramago's magical realist onset of a mass epidemic of the sudden loss of sight in *Blindness* (1995), literature has repeatedly explored the brutal indifference and absurdity with which power operates in the zones of containment elicited by the state of exception. It makes a regular appearance in science fiction too, with science fiction film in particular routinely employing the quarantine zone as a safeguard against the potential danger of an extraterrestrial menace. In some cases, these visitations turn out to be benign (*Close Encounters of the Third Kind* [1977], *E.T.* [1982], *District 9* [2009], *Arrival* [2016]), whereas in others, they prove, as suspected, to be malevolent (*Alien* [1979], *The Thing* [1982], *Life* [2017]). In either case, they invariably turn out to be either unnecessary or insufficient. As a mechanism of division and control, the lessons learned are that such machinery is unjust and harmful or that it cannot be enforced strictly enough.

We see the latter taken to its logical extreme once we enter the gothic territory of the infection narrative and in particular that of zombie fiction, film, and games. Overwhelmed and overrun by the zombie horde, the central plot device of almost all zombie tales is the drive of the human survivors to ensure distance and division between the living and the dead, a need that is almost without a fault geographically envisaged by the protagonists' continuous (and continuously unsuccessful) quest for a territory cleansed of zombie influence. In fiction, as in real life, containment zones can, however, also be evoked to keep out and exclude normality, rather than the other way around. The containment zones of experimental weapons testing like Los Alamos National Laboratory or the highly secretive commercial labs of Apple, Google, and Huawei are in place not to secure the safety of the general public but to safeguard the development of innovations so fundamental that they will in time upend the status quo forever. Eventually released into the greater world beyond the containment zone, nuclear bombs and smartphones were never intended to be contained ad infinitum. Also, once they were in fact released into the greater world, they ended up having such a radical effect on "normality" as to fundamentally change it forever.

This proves a telling dilemma of the containment zone as a state of exception, namely, whether it signifies a breach of the normal that must be quarantined so as to be rectified or destroyed or whether the abnormalities of the state of exception are in fact heralding a paradigm change that will mean the beginning of a new normal. As pointed out by Alison Bashford in *Quarantine: Local and Global Histories* (2016), such ambiguity has historically always destabilized the supposed strict demarcations of such zones in that "quarantine was at once part of the world forged through connections of capital, trade and empire, and one of the responses perceived to hinder those connections."[3] Indeed, as the repeatedly breached quarantine zones of science fiction and zombie fictions remind us, containment zones are bound to fail simply because they are the exception to the rule. As a state outside the normal, any containment zone will over time suffer unintended breakdown of its barriers or turn out to become the norm as the rules of normality are rewritten around it. This is of course precisely also what fascinates but also bothers Holocaust philosophers like Giorgio Agamben. For decades viewed as extreme states of exception in which the rules and norms of civilization were temporarily set aside, the possibility that the atrocities committed in the camps were not in fact the exception but the rule of modern society is almost as horrifying to contemplate as the actual atrocities themselves.[4]

As a concept originating from the attempt at restoring normative (human) mastery, the containment zone may historically have acted as a place of enforced equilibrium of a supposed ideal normality, but it has philosophically and imaginatively often acted in the opposite capacity. In the readings of Lovecraft and Vander-

Meer that are to follow, I will argue that while the zones of exclusion and containment envisioned in the two texts are employed for very different purposes, they do at least initially come to the same conclusion, which is to say, in the grand scheme of things, the human matters not at all. Both texts can therefore be seen to channel a widespread conception of the Anthropocene as a state of exception defined by an "anthropogenic planet that is predicted to *defy all prediction*,"[5] while also making clear what humanity in its anthropocentric worldview has conveniently but naively ignored, namely, that any attempt at human control and prediction has always been a sham. Accordingly, "'Anthropocene' is the first fully antianthropocentric concept," Timothy Morton has suggested, for while it may seem to elevate the human as an all-powerful force, it in fact dethrones it "from its pampered, ostensibly privileged place set apart from all other beings." Trapped as we are in the "vicelike death grip of a gigantic entity—ourselves as the human species,"[6] humanity finds itself to be peculiarly omnipotent and impotent at the same time. As Claire Colebrook points out, the very era named after us is thus also the era that most poignantly reminds us that "there was a time, and there will be a time, without humans: this provides us with a challenge both to think beyond the world as it is *for us,* and yet remain mindful that the imagining of the inhuman world always proceeds from a positive human failure."[7] Significantly, we see the development of such "positive human failure" played out in both Lovecraft and VanderMeer, but with very different consequences.

Lovecraft's Cosmic Humanist Pessimism

Zones of containment and the state of exception are central to many of H. P. Lovecraft's narratives as well as fundamental to his overall philosophy and worldview. As Mark Fisher has pointed out, "Lovecraft's stories are obsessively fixated on the question of the outside: an outside that breaks through in encounters with anomalous entities from the deep past, in altered states of consciousness, in bizarre twists in the structure of time. The encounter with the outside often ends in breakdown and psychosis. Lovecraft's stories frequently involve a catastrophic integration of the outside into an interior that is retrospectively revealed to a delusive envelope, a

sham."[8] In "The Call of Cthulhu" (1928), for instance, the protagonist discovers a sculpture of a frightful and fantastical being, the
great Cthulhu, but eventually realizes that the monster is real and
that he will from this point on be hunted by Cthulhu worshippers,
but even more terrifyingly that "mankind was not absolutely alone
among the conscious things on earth."[9] Similar revelations take
place in "At the Mountains of Madness" (1936), in which a group
of scientists travel to Antarctica on a scientific journey only to discover an ancient city of "the Elder Things," a race of alien beings, as
well as a giant monster—the shoggoth—that end up chasing them
out of the city. While one surviving member of the expedition goes
insane, the other must forever after live with the terrible conviction that "it is absolutely necessary, for the peace and safety of
mankind, that some of earth's dark, dead corners and unplumbed
depths be let alone."[10] And in "The Shadow over Innsmouth" (1936),
the protagonist decides to investigate the provincial town of Innsmouth but gets more than he bargains for. Initially shocked to discover that the town is populated by the human/monstrous hybrid
descendants of "the deep ones," a race of monstrous species from
the bottom of the sea, the narrator eventually realizes that he himself is turning into a deep one and that he, too, will enter the sea
and become one of them.

Common to all these stories is the transformation of their
protagonist-narrators from relatively confident, and content,
(human) beings certain of their place and their importance in the
world, followed by a descent into a state of horror as they realize
just how insignificant human lives, and humanity at large, are in
the grander scheme of things. As David Peak remarks, Lovecraft's
fiction can therefore be said to be characterized by

> the horror of the void: humans coming face to face with dis-
> placement, alienation, and the meaninglessness of life. . . . The
> great revelations contained within Lovecraft's stories suggest
> that man's place among the stars lie in darkness. . . . In this
> sense, the true purpose of the void is to create a portal to the
> beyond—from within. Much like the remnants of an ancient so-
> ciety created by primordial beings buried deep below the earth's
> crust, the void cosmically infects the inner with the outer.
> Essentially, the internalization of horror ultimately leads to a
> cosmic understanding of one's own meaninglessness.[11]

In "coming face to face" with the "horror of the void," it is important to note that Lovecraft's protagonists never come to terms with it. At first detecting some anomaly—a state of exception in that which they have until now considered to be normal—this initially limited zone of horror inadvertently expands to the point at which "the void cosmically infects the inner with the outer," to the point at which there is nothing but horror left. In Lovecraft's world, it is not possible to "face" the void and come out the other end. The protagonist of a Lovecraft story will inevitably end up insane, dead, or, at very least, forlorn, lost, and terrified in the cosmic horror of realizing the insignificance of humankind. The rest of humankind may continue to live on in blissful ignorance of its own insignificance. But the protagonist-narrator has internalized the void, always conscious of its indifference to human affairs.

This sense of a loss of control, of letting in the void and seeing the earth's crust as well as our own bodies and psyches "infected" by "the outside" of the cosmos, has led to a recent renaissance of Lovecraft's writing in a surprising array of fields. Conservative, male, white, fiercely racist and misogynist, zoophobic and anthropocentric,[12] Lovecraft is hardly the obvious choice for posthumanist scholars advocating care for the animal, the vegetative, and the planetary, and yet his writing has resonated widely with a range of thinkers of the nonhuman and materialist turns.[13] As Carl H. Sederholm and Jeffrey Andrew Weinstock have argued in their Introduction to *Age of Lovecraft* (2016), one of several recent edited anthologies on Lovecraft,[14] the author has become so popular that he "now seems to be everywhere, cropping up in places both anticipated and surprising."[15] In her review of Sederholm and Weinstock's book for the *LA Review of Books,* Alison Sperling affirms this as she muses on her own bewildered and even embarrassing continued interest in a writer with whom she, as "someone invested in non-oppressive, queer, and feminist critiques of literature and culture," knows she does not share many, if indeed any, values. The answer to this renewed and often surprising interest in a writer who should by accounts of his misogyny and racism alone have been rendered obsolete, Sperling reasons, is that for all the author's faults, Lovecraft's "fiction serves as a link between the modernist period and the contemporary one through this de-emphasis of the human and the inherent inability to fully comprehend the mysteries of the universe. In the Anthropocene . . . it is perhaps clear why a writer with what S. T. Joshi has called Lovecraft's 'cosmic pessimism' would serve as a contemporary philosophical model."[16] In what follows, I will question the degree to which Lovecraft's cosmic pessimism works as a contemporary philosophical model of the Anthropocene. For while Lovecraft may seem prescient of the Anthropocene in his realization that an anthropocentric worldview is now not only moot but has in fact always been a sham, the fact that he so ardently longs for a world in which anthropocentrism and the distinction between the human and the nonhuman is upheld at any cost, even to the point of ignorance, points to a somewhat different conclusion than what we have seen emerging out of a range of theoretical formations coming out of the materialist and nonhuman turns in recent years.

Reading "The Colour out of Space" in the Anthropocene

"The Colour out of Space" (1927) begins, like many of Lovecraft's tales, with a protagonist-narrator recalling his first encounter with the anomaly that will in time change his outlook on the world forever. Sent to an area of New England in which "there are valleys with deep woods that no axe has ever cut," the narrator is in his role as a surveyor the spearhead of modernity, sent to do the groundwork for the construction of a reservoir, in time meaning that "the dark woods will be cut down and the blasted heath will slumber far below blue waters." Warned by the townspeople of Arkham that "the place was evil," the narrator at first thinks these notions "odd and theatrical." Yet once "I saw that dark westward angle of glens and slopes for myself, [I] ceased to wonder at anything beside its own elder mystery." In the zone of abnormality he is about to enter, everything is off, and out of, in some way or other. "The trees grew too thickly, and their trunks were too big for any healthy New England wood. There was too much silence in the dim alleys between them, and the floor was too soft with the dank moss and mattings of infinite years of decay."[17] This is as much a landscape of excess, then, as of exception, and it is clearly one to which the narrator takes objection.

As the narrator is soon to learn, this strange zone in which everything is too big, too silent, too soft, and too off-color has not always been so transgressively excessive. Prior to what the locals refer to as "the strange days," these "were not haunted woods." Yet then came "the meteorite," "the weird visitor from unknown stellar space," an entity described as being "nothing of this earth, but a piece of the great outside; and as such dowered with outside properties and obedient to outside laws."[18] Here we see Fisher's argument regarding Lovecraft's obsession with "the question of the outside" as well as Peak's "horror of the void" neatly aligning in what Lovecraft describes as "that cryptic vestige of the fathomless gulfs outside; that lone, weird message from other universes and other realms of matter, force, and entity."[19] After the meteorite breaks through the atmosphere and slams into the earth, the area around the impact site soon begins to change, seemingly first for the better, but soon to collapse into decay and disease. The "orchards were prospering as never before" and the "fruit was growing to phenomenal size and unwonted gloss," yet it turns out that for "all that gorgeous array of specious lusciousness not one single jot was fit to eat."[20] As summer turns to winter and then to spring, it becomes clear that the "outside properties" of the meteor have spread to the surrounding lands, creating a zone in which everything is "very peculiar," "in a queer way," "monstrous," and of "strange colours that could not be put into words."[21] This "chromatic perversion" continues throughout the story, an explosion of visual input "hectic and prismatic," until suddenly it stops and all turns gray. Plants, crops, flowers, poultry, even the "swine began growing grey and brittle," spreading a blight throughout the affected zone and eventually leading to the demise of "everything organic," including a number of unfortunate humans. As the story concludes, a "rainbow of cryptic poison" shoots skyward, and the visitor once again leaves the infected zone behind, yet the land remains tainted by a mark it cannot be rid of.[22]

In most ways, "The Colour out of Space" follows the standard Lovecraft formula. Yet in terms of the outside influence, the "weird visitor" from "the great outside," the short story is at one and the same time atypical as well as the inevitable conclusion to a Lovecraftian logic taken to its extreme. First of all, the visitation from the outside did not happen in the ancient prehuman past but within living memory. Second, the visitor is precisely that: a temporary cosmic caller that both literally and ontologically rips open the sheltering sky to let in the cosmic horror from beyond, but then again takes to the void from which it came. Having pierced the sky twice, on entry and exit, it has forever changed not just the actual terrain with which it has been in contact but also the worldviews

of those who have witnessed such change. Third, and most significantly, this is a being that is defined solely in terms of the effects it
has on the outside world rather than in any bodily or other essential form that can be pinned to a specific physical object or quality.

The latter is particularly important in our reading of the entry-
way of the "outside" of Lovecraft's characteristic horror of the void.
For, as Michel Houllebecq and Graham Harman (and many others)
have pointed out, Lovecraft has a tendency to denote something
"unutterable" and "unspeakable," only to then go on to describe it
in overwhelming detail. Writing with "the fury of a demented opera,"[23] Lovecraft's "language is overloaded by a gluttonous excess
of surface and aspects of the thing."[24] In "The Colour out of Space,"
while as imaginatively excessive as always in his vocabulary, Lovecraft's monstrous visitor from the void is however reduced, or perhaps exalted, to color and light. Unlike "The Call of Cthulhu," no
comparisons to real or mythic bodily mixtures of "cuttlefish head,
dragon body, scaly wings"[25] are made, nor to the hybrid humanoid-
amphibian masses "alive with a teeming horde of shapes"[26] that we
encounter in "The Shadow over Innsmouth." Rather than present a
grotesque and monstrous body utterly unlike the human, or a hybrid mix of human and monster both, the monstrous being in "The
Colour out of Space" is perhaps best summed up as a "strange beam
of ghastly miasma."[27] For, while it arrives on the back of the physical
object of a meteorite, the being itself can only be known through
the properties of other things and beings as they themselves take
on properties that are alien to them. Plants, animals, and humans
take on unnatural hues, grow prodigiously, act weirdly, and eventually turn to dust or primeval "ooze and slime."[28] In "The Colour
out of Space," contact with the outside manifests by not manifesting in anything, or anybody, in particular but in a zone in which all
life breaks down and shifts shape in a miasma of mixtures in which
the very notion of essence, human and otherwise, is no more. Facing such a zone of shapeless and therefore potentially illimitable
horror, the narrator can only hope to flee, or at best flood the place
in an attempt to forget and contain its existence through the creation of a reservoir, an endeavor that is bound to fail, as the menace
clearly refuses to go away.

Reading "The Colour out of Space" from the perspective of an
Anthropocene twenty-first century, it is hard not to be reminded,

however anachronistically, of contaminated zones of exclusion plagued by radiation and nuclear fallout. Lovecraft's description of a malign entity manifested solely through light and rays that over time infect an area to greater and greater detrimental effect is oddly prescient of the horrors described in, for instance, John Hersey's description of the first military use of the atomic bomb in *Hiroshima* (1946), or perhaps even more fittingly of Svetlana Alexievich's nonfiction account in *Chernobyl Prayer* (1997) of the 1986 accident at the Chernobyl power plant, as in the dramatized but historically highly accurate HBO mini-series *Chernobyl* (2019). Hersey's description of a landscape reduced to a "reddish-brown scar, where nearly everything had been buffeted down and burned";[29] Alexievich's reportage of how the pollution of the land will remain "for thousands of years to come";[30] or the HBO television series' graphic depiction of human bodies turning to translucent mush due to radiation sickness—all are prefigured by Lovecraft's short story. In fact, "The Colour out of Space" can certainly be seen as a prophetic forecast of many other kinds of insidious forms of pollution—chemical and biological—introduced in the twentieth century, doubly frightening precisely because they are not directly visible. The zones of containment of Rachel Carson's *Silent Spring* (1962) come to mind, as do later cautionary tales like Marla Cone's *Silent Snow* (2005), a reminder that almost half a century post-Carson, not only do we still live in a world in which "pollution knows no borders"[31] but the problem has in fact gotten (much) worse.

If we recall the nature of Lovecraft's cosmic humanist pessimism, though, it is also important to stress that "The Colour out of Space" is precisely *not* a horror brought on by anthropogenic change, nuclear, chemical, or biological, but by the decidedly nonhuman horror that is explicitly witnessed to come from "out of space." To read Lovecraft's tale as a fable of the Anthropocene may therefore seem not only anachronistic but also counterintuitive. In what way, then, can we meaningfully read Lovecraft's story in the light of the Anthropocene? Furthermore, why is it that so many contemporary thinkers have taken to Lovecraft as a model for contemporary Anthropocene philosophical thought? Before this question can be answered in full, we must turn to Jeff VanderMeer's *Annihilation,* as it offers a wildly different approach to the beastly, the monstrous, the human, and the posthuman.

Becoming (Area) X

Justin D. Edwards identifies a "paradigm shift" in contemporary gothic in that the "Gothic monster is not necessarily an icon of terror, threatening humanity by consuming blood or brains or creating more of the undead. In contemporary Gothic, these figures are often humanized and engender sympathy."[32] As opposed to more traditional forms of gothic, in which the protagonist either flees or sets out to vanquish the monster, thereby creating distance or annulment of monstrous difference either through distance or destruction, contemporary gothic tends to annul the terrifying abnormality of the monster through assimilation. Quoting Fred Botting's claim that in willingly seeking out the monster, "radical difference is diminished: they become familiar, recognized, expected, 'normal' rather than 'monstrous' monstrosities, domesticated to the point of becoming pets," Edwards concludes that in contemporary gothic, "monsters are invited into the home."[33]

In VanderMeer's *Annihilation,* the monstrous has made itself home in what was once a human landscape. The unnamed protagonist, known simply as "the biologist," is initially tasked with breaching the perimeter of the mysterious and monstrous zone of "Area X" to "continue the government's investigation."[34] As in "The Colour out of Space," in which the government-sponsored narrator likewise encounters abandoned "hillside farms, sometimes with all the buildings standing, sometimes with only one or two, and sometimes with only a lone chimney or fast-filling cellar,"[35] this, too, is a place where "rotting cabins" remind the biologist that "long ago, towns had existed here" but also a space in which all that is left are "eerie signs of human habitation."[36] Unlike in Lovecraft's tale, in which the visitation from out of space is clearly and spectacularly marked, it is not entirely clear when or how the strange phenomena that is Area X began. "When Area X first appeared, there was vagueness and confusion,"[37] the biologist remarks, and this is a state of affairs that has not cleared up much by the time she arrives, in that confusion and ambiguity seem to rule Area X in every respect. "According to the records we had been shown, the first expedition reported nothing unusual in Area X, just pristine, empty wilderness," the biologist continues, later describing it as an area "devoid of human life" and as a place of "preternatural silence."[38] Yet if the early expeditions experienced it as a region bereft of the human, later expeditions rediscover human presence, of a kind. Entering the emptied buildings of those who once lived there prior to the appearance of Area X, the biologist sees "peculiar eruptions of moss or lichen, rising four, five, feet tall, misshapen, the vegetative matter forming an approximation of limbs and heads and torsos." A little later, walking close to a canal, she sees a dolphin that "stared at me with an eye that did not, in that brief flash, resemble a dolphin eye to me. It was painfully human, almost familiar."[39] Other encounters lead the biologist to doubt how to classify the samples of tissue she collects in Area X: "Was it really human? Was it *pretending* to be human?"[40]

As the two following volumes of the Southern Reach Trilogy reveal, the biologist will over time herself turn into a human-animal-landscape hybrid, ending up as a leviathan composed of different human, vegetative, animal, and mineral matter. Accordingly, the biologist remarks, in the closing pages of *Annihilation*, that "the thought of continually doing harm to myself to remain human seems somehow pathetic."[41] Read in comparison to "The Colour out of Space," we thus see a remarkable range of similarities between the two tales, albeit with one fundamental difference. Both feature a first-person narrator, both are tasked with collecting information about an unruly area of unnaturally vibrant wilderness (indeed, another member of the biologist's expedition is, like Lovecraft's narrator, a surveyor), both include strange metamorphoses of the human into nonhuman assemblages, and finally, both stories ultimately revolve around the impossibility of using human classificatory systems to describe a world that refuses to bow to human mastery, let alone recognize the human in the first place. As in Lovecraft's story, the otherworldly presence ruling Area X can only ever be experienced indirectly, a "faint golden glow"[42] shimmering around those who have been in contact with it, as in the metamorphic effect that gradually breaks down any individual form and category so as to merge it with something else. The essence and intent of Area X, if indeed any such thing can be said to exist, seems to be transformation itself.

In terms of the question of turning home, as of their position on the monstrous, Lovecraft's and VanderMeer's stories could, however, not have been more different. For while Lovecraft's narrator always desires to go home, to return to the safe confines of a world in which the human ruled supreme, VanderMeer's protagonist goes by a very different route. At first compliant with her mission and continuously attempting mastery of the area through the constant collation of "data to process,"[43] the biologist becomes increasingly reluctant to honor these demands, culminating in the decision that, as the concluding sentence of the novel reads, "I am not returning home."[44] Not only does the biologist refuse to be domesticized by the scientific and governmental human authority that has so far ruled her life but she also refuses to recognize Area X as "monstrous" in the first place. "Everyone had died or been killed, returned changed or returned unchanged, but Area X had continued on as it always had,"[45] the biologist muses as she ponders the remains of the many human lives altered by Area X, and hence concludes that Area X simply *is*.

From a Lovecraftian perspective, such indifference to human life is precisely what constitutes the hollow and horrific core of his cosmic humanist pessimism—of an ancient evil that puts the human under erasure physically as well as semiotically. Yet, for evil to exist in the world, VanderMeer's biologist seems to suggest, we need to be able to identify "*intent* or *purpose*," neither of which she can locate in Area X. Similarly, while we may "tell stories of heroism or cowardice, of good decisions and bad decisions," no such agency can be said to govern Area X, nor can such actions be said to have any effect on it whatsoever. As a zone of exception outside human jurisdiction, Area X seems ruled by one thing, and that is "a kind of *inevitability*."[46] This the biologist at last accepts and gives in to, while also clearly realizing that the greatest fear of those outside Area X, the people in power, is that the expeditions fail to "*hit upon some explanation, some solution, before the world becomes* Area X."[47] Ultimately, the one thing the exception zone of Area X has to teach humanity may precisely be that an anthropocentric worldview is the exception and not the rule; hence any attempt at human authority and mastery of the area, and indeed of the world at large, is not only doomed to fail but in fact an aberration.

A Metaphysics of Mixture: From Lovecraft to VanderMeer (and Beyond)

In a comparative analysis of the distinctions between weird fiction and the new weird in general, and the "weird prose" of Lovecraft and VanderMeer in particular, Gry Ulstein suggests that whereas "the traditional weird leans heavily on nihilism [and] does not typically evoke affects like hope or affirmation," the new weird is far more likely to lean into "hope as an embrace of the unknown and the unknowable."[48] While certainly far less negative in tone than "The Colour out of Space," it is however questionable whether a text like *Annihilation* is necessarily more "hopeful" than Lovecraft's story—not that it should be. As E. Ann Kaplan remarks, environmental approaches to anthropogenic change tend to veer toward a "utopian/dystopian duality," but perhaps a path somewhere between horror and hope would constitute a more constructive approach: "We need both hope and courage in order to change our ways of being, as we seek solutions and adapt to the new world. But we also need to understand and admit the reality of the dire situation—to take that in fully and try to understand the history of how we got here as we seek to deal with it."[49] *Acceptance*, which is the title of the third and final volume of the Southern Reach series, is perhaps a more fitting term than *hope*, exemplified nowhere better than in the biologist's journey into what she at first perceives to be a zone of exception but eventually accepts as something else.

As a biologist "specialized in transitional environments,"[50] the narrator is described as having both a disciplinary and a natural affinity with the animal and the vegetative over the human. This is partly due to her knowledge of nonhuman life-forms but mostly due to her interests in transitional ecologies, a liminality of which Area X supplies plenty, in that "within the space of walking only six or seven miles, you went from forest to swamp to salt marsh to beach."[51] This interest in transition and transformation, we eventually learn, mirrors her own mercurial nature, as, of course, her decision to willingly go through with her own metamorphosis into a nonhuman or more-than-human state. Bidding the world of the human goodbye, the biologist warns us on the penultimate page of the novel, "Don't follow. I'm well beyond you now, and traveling very fast."[52] On a literal level, this is expressed to ward off potential pursuers sent to chase her down by the human world outside Area X. On another literary and figurative level, it is a nod toward us, her (human) readers, who must at the end of the novel necessarily be left behind. Bogged down by our human bodies, our human worldview, and our human language, we cannot possibly hope to keep up with that which was once the biologist but is soon to be something else. Far "beyond us" and "traveling very fast" toward a new state

of being, the testimony to the earlier stage of this journey—this
the text we are holding in our hands—must at some point end.
Yet if we, her human readership, cannot follow her any further, at
least we are left with an idea of how better to conceive, or rather
fail to conceive, the place and the state of being toward which the
biologist is heading.

"Like a horror movie, evolution is as much about disintegration as it is about things coming together,"[53] Timothy Morton
remarks, in part recognizing that such a realization would from
a Lovecraftian perspective lead to terror and revulsion. The "cataclysmic molting"[54] that VanderMeer's biologist at first observes
and eventually becomes part of in (and of) Area X does not lead to
horror though. As Benjamin R. Robertson argues in his reading of
Annihilation, "Area X does not presuppose a complete world before
violation because Area X is not an invasive force from a spatial outside or a temporal afterward. It is what already exists here around
us, affecting us while remaining imperceptible to and unaffected
by us."[55] What Area X ultimately teaches the biologist, and perhaps
also us as readers, is that we can never stand apart from the world.
Initially defined as a zone of exception, Area X proves to be the
very opposite, exemplifying French philosopher Emanuele Coccia's
notion of a "metaphysics of mixture" in which "being in the world
no longer means finding oneself in an infinite space that contains
everything else; it means being no longer able to experience being
in a place without finding this place in yourself, and thus becoming
the place of your place."[56]

Ultimately, Area X turns out not to be the zone of exception
but the rule, reinstating the order of things as they always were.
Whether it is that of Morton's "ecology without nature," Donna
Haraway's "sympoiesis" described as a "becoming with," or Eben
Kirksey's "unruly assemblages," where "emerging ecologies" spring
from environments that cannot be said to clearly belong to nature
or culture,[57] VanderMeer's novel is therefore in line with a general
trend in environmental humanities responding to the conceptual
and concrete problems of the Anthropocene with a recognition of
the necessity to shed former supposed boundaries between nature
and culture, human and nonhuman, individual and environment.
As Robertson concludes, "Area X's refusal to reveal itself fully to
the human does not indicate there is more to it. . . . It knows nothing of partialness or wholeness because it can neither be analyzed

nor contained. It is there all along, too big and too close to see."[58] To observe the world, we the human have to stand apart from it. Yet even as we attempt to do so, this proves a futile gesture, as it proves that "we," the human, never really were. Moving forward, there is no way around, no temporary state of exception, no retreat from the dark, no escaping the zone, the monstrous, the weird. We can only, like the biologist, go through.

NOTES

1. Patricia MacCormack, *The Ahuman Manifesto: Activism for the End of the Anthropocene* (London: Bloomsbury, 2020), 11.
2. Jane Stevens Crawshaw, "The Places and Spaces of Early Modern Maritime Quarantine," in *Quarantine: Local and Global Histories*, ed. Alison Bashford (London: Palgrave Macmillan, 2016), 16.
3. Alison Bashford, "Maritime Quarantine: Linking Old World and New World Histories," in Bashford, *Quarantine*, 11.
4. See Giorgio Agamben, *Homo Sacer: Sovereign Power and Bare Life*, trans. Daniel Heller-Roazen (New York: Zone Books, 1998), 166, or Agamben, *Remnants of Auschwitz: The Witness and the Archive*, trans. Daniel Heller-Roazen (New York: Zone Books, 2002), 20.
5. Jennifer Fay, *Inhospitable World: Cinema in the Time of the Anthropocene* (Oxford: Oxford University Press, 2018), 9.
6. Timothy Morton, *Dark Ecology: For a Logic of Future Coexistence* (New York: Columbia University Press, 2016), 24–25.
7. Claire Colebrook, *Death of the Posthuman: Essays on Extinction* (Ann Arbor, Mich.: Open Humanities Press, 2014), 1:32–33.
8. Mark Fisher, *The Weird and the Eerie* (London: Repeater, 2016), 16.
9. H. P. Lovecraft, "Call of Cthulhu," in *Omnibus 3: The Haunter of the Dark* (London: Grafton, 1985), 79.
10. H. P. Lovecraft, "At the Mountains of Madness," in *Omnibus 1: At the Mountains of Madness* (London: Grafton, 1985), 138.
11. David Peak, *The Spectacle of the Void* (New York: Schism, 2014), 59–60.
12. See, e.g., Gina Wisker, "'Spawn of the Pit': Lavinia, Marceline, Medusa, and All Things Foul: H. P. Lovecraft's Liminal Women," in *New Critical Essays on H. P. Lovecraft*, ed. David Simmons (New York: Palgrave MacMillan, 2013); Jed Mayer, "Race, Species, and Others: H. P. Lovecraft and the Animal," in *The Age of Lovecraft*, ed. Carl H. Sederholm and Jeffrey Andrew Weinstock (Minneapolis: University of Minnesota Press, 2016); or James Kneale, "'Indifference Would Be Such a Relief': Race and Weird Geography in Victor LaValle and Matt Ruff's Dialogues with H. P. Lovecraft," in *Spaces and Fictions of the Weird and the Fantastic: Ecologies, Geographies, Oddities*, ed. Julius Greve and Florian Zappe (Cham, Switzerland: Palgrave Macmillan, 2019).

13. Graham Harman, *Weird Realism: Lovecraft and Philosophy* (Winchester, U.K.: Zero Books, 2011); Eugene Thacker, *In the Dust of This Planet: Horror of Philosophy,* vol. 1 (Winchester, U.K.: Zero Books, 2015); or Eric Wilson, *The Republic of Cthulhu* (New York: Punctum Books, 2016).

14. See also David Simmons's edited volume *New Critical Essays on H. P. Lovecraft* (New York: Palgrave Macmillan, 2013).

15. Carl H. Sederholm and Jeffrey Andrew Weinstock, "Introduction: Lovecraft Rising," in *The Age of Lovecraft,* ed. Carl H. Sederholm and Jeffrey Andrew Weinstock (Minneapolis: University of Minnesota Press, 2016), 1.

16. Alison Sperling, "Acknowledgment Is Not Enough: Coming to Terms with Lovecraft's Horrors," March 4, 2017, https://lareviewofbooks. org/article/acknowledgment-not-enough-coming-terms-lovecrafts -horrors/.

17. Sperling; H. P. Lovecraft, "The Colour out of Space," in *Omnibus 3: The Haunter of the Dark* (London: Grafton, 1985), 236–37.

18. Lovecraft, 241 and 243.

19. Lovecraft, 244.

20. Lovecraft, 245.

21. Lovecraft, 246–47.

22. Lovecraft, 248, 252, 265, 267.

23. Michel Houllebecq, *H. P. Lovecraft: Against the World, Against Life,* trans. Dorna Khazeni (London: Weidenfeld and Nicolson, 2006), 49.

24. Graham Harman, *Weird Realism: Lovecraft and Philosophy* (Winchester, U.K.: Zero Books, 2011), 25.

25. Lovecraft, "Call," 90.

26. H. P. Lovecraft, "The Shadow over Innsmouth," in *Omnibus 3,* 444.

27. Lovecraft, "Colour," 262.

28. Lovecraft.

29. John Hersey, *Hiroshima* (London: Penguin, 2002), 67.

30. Svetlana Alexievich, *Chernobyl Prayer,* trans. Anna Gunin and Arch Tait (London: Penguin, 2016), 136.

31. Martha Cone, *Silent Snow: The Slow Poisoning of the Arctic* (New York: Grove Press, 2005), 7.

32. Justin D. Edwards, "Contemporary American Gothic," in *American Gothic,* ed. Jeffrey Andrew Weinstock (Cambridge: Cambridge University Press, 2017), 72.

33. Edwards.

34. Jeff VanderMeer, *Annihilation* (London: 4th Estate, 2014), 4.

35. Lovecraft, "Colour," 237.

36. VanderMeer, *Annihilation,* 5.

37. VanderMeer, 94.

38. VanderMeer, 55 and 95.

39. VanderMeer, 96–97.

40. VanderMeer, 73.

41. VanderMeer, 194.

42. VanderMeer, 61.

43. VanderMeer, 33.

44. VanderMeer, 33 and 195.

45. VanderMeer, 158.

46. VanderMeer.

47. VanderMeer, 159.

48. Gry Ulstein, "'Through the Eyes of Area X': (Dis)Locating Ecological Hope via New Weird Spatiality," in *Spaces and Fictions of the Weird and the Fantastic: Ecologies, Geographies, Oddities,* ed. Julius Greve and Florian Zappe (Cham, Switzerland: Palgrave Macmillan, 2019), 130–31.

49. E. Ann Kaplan, *Climate Trauma: Foreseeing the Future in Dystopian Film and Fiction* (New Brunswick, N.J.: Rutgers University Press, 2016), 147.

50. Kaplan, 11.

51. Kaplan, 12.

52. Kaplan, 194.

53. Timothy Morton, *Hyperobjects: Philosophy and Ecology after the End of the World* (Minneapolois: University of Minnesota Press, 2010), 44.

54. Morton, 193.

55. Benjamin J. Robertson, *None of This Is Normal: The Fiction of Jeff VanderMeer* (Minneapolis: University of Minnesota Press, 2018), 115.

56. Emanuele Coccia, *The Life of Plants: A Metaphysics of Mixture,* trans. Dylan J. Montanari (Cambridge: Polity Press, 2019), 71.

57. Donna Haraway, "Anthropocene, Capitalocene, Plantationocene, Chthulucene: Making Kin," *Environmental Humanities* 6 (2015): 159–65; Timothy Morton, *Ecology without Nature: Rethinking Environmental Aesthetics* (Cambridge, Mass.: Harvard University Press, 2007); Eben Kirksey, *Emergent Ecologies* (Durham, N.C.: Duke University Press, 2015), 218.

58. Robertson, *None of This Is Normal,* 122.

4

Monstrous Megalodons of the Anthropocene

Extinction and Adaptation in Prehistoric Shark Fiction, 1974–2018

JENNIFER SCHELL

> MISCONCEPTION: Humans can't negatively impact ecosystems, because species will just evolve what they need to survive.
>
> CORRECTION: Some species may possess traits that allow them to thrive under conditions of environmental change caused by humans and so may be selected for, but others may not and so may go extinct.
>
> —University of California Museum of Paleontology, "Misconceptions about Evolution"

In *The Great Derangement: Climate Change and the Unthinkable* (2016), Amitav Ghosh highlights several of the representational challenges that anthropogenic climate change poses to authors of what he calls "serious" or "realist" fiction. According to Ghosh, this type of writing tends to be invested in the more mundane aspects of the lives of individual characters, who interact at particular times in specific localities. As such, it is incapable of depicting the catastrophic impact of the "slow violence" affiliated with global climate change—rising temperatures, melting ice caps, thawing permafrost, ocean acidification, and mass extinction—with any degree of accuracy or urgency.[1]

Though he decries realist writing as problematic, Ghosh posits that other generic forms—fantasy, gothic, horror, and science fiction—possess a good deal of potential in terms of their ability to depict the scope and gravity of contemporary environmental issues. Significantly, Ghosh is not alone. Ursula Heise claims that some kinds of experimental science fiction are capable of representing the "complexities and heterogeneities of cultures joined in global crisis."[2] Meanwhile, Rebecca Evans argues that "the generic tools on which cli-fi draws are varied, encompassing genres that have historically been subject to critical denigration."[3] She adds that "these supposedly 'lesser' generic tendencies, in fact, can play a significant role in environmental conversations."[4] Building on this scholarship, a number of the essays in this volume explore the potential of the gothic to provide humans with more productive ways of representing the devastating environmental problems of the Anthropocene.[5]

Much of the ongoing critical work on the ecological importance of the gothic mode is both cogent and compelling, and my goal here is not to undermine it. Rather, I wish to sound a note of caution about the reactionary capacities of some forms of gothic writing, especially those that revolve around monstrous, prehistoric animals that live deep in the undersea realm. Here I am referring to the myriad popular novels about extant megalodon sharks published in the wake of Peter Benchley's *Jaws* (1974). Much like *Jaws*, these texts tend to endorse speciesist attitudes, promote sexist discourse, and sensationalize violent acts. In terms of plot, they pit heroic adventurers—most of whom are white American men—against gigantic prehistoric elasmobranches who stray from the confines of their deep-sea habitats and attack unsuspecting swimmers and boaters.[6] Not coincidentally, they characterize sharks as brutal predators, incapable of coexisting with other life-forms, and humans as superior beings, capable of exerting mastery over the natural world.

These are not their only reactionary elements, however. Although these texts acknowledge the dangers posed to oceanic ecosystems by anthropogenic threats like overfishing and climate change, they do not endorse habitat conservation or species preservation. Instead, they advance scientifically irresponsible misconceptions about the evolution of species, describing megalodons as highly resilient, endlessly adaptable fish whose remarkable abilities include

the capacity to adjust to dramatically different environmental
conditions in a single generation or less.[7] In so doing, these novels promote the idea that humans need not take action to protect
the organisms living in the world's oceans because they can take
care of themselves. As this evidence suggests, ecocritics would be
wise to temper their endorsement of gothic fiction, some forms of
which can be enlisted to promote decisively antienvironmentalist
projects and agendas.

Megalodon Rising: The Origins of the Prehistoric Shark Novel

For all intents and purposes, the origins of megalodon fiction can
be traced to a particularly influential passage in *Jaws*. After catch-
ing sight of the titular great white shark for the first time, marine
biologist Matt Hooper starts speculating about the existence of
even larger monsters lurking in the depths of the ocean:

> We have fossil teeth from *megalodon*. They're six inches long.
> That would put the fish at between eighty and a hundred
> feet. . . . What's to say *megalodon* is really extinct? Why should
> it be? Not lack of food. If there's enough down there to support
> whales, there's enough to support sharks that big. Just because
> we've never seen a hundred-foot great white doesn't mean they
> couldn't exist.[8]

Although Hooper never again mentions megalodons—largely because his companions dismiss his ideas as the ravings of an im-
practical intellectual with an overactive imagination—this passage
inspired numerous subsequent authors, who recognized the potential appeal of stories about prehistoric sharks and produced novels
about them. Some of the first of these texts include Robin Brown's
Megalodon (1981), George Edward Noe's *Carcharodon* (1987), Tom
Dade's *Quest for Megalodon* (1993), Steve Alten's *Meg: A Novel of
Deep Terror* (1997), and Charles Wilson's *Extinct* (1997). Later examples include Jonathan Rand's *Mississippi Megalodon* (2008) as well
as Alten's six subsequent shark novels and myriad books issued by
Severed Press, a small Australian publisher specializing primarily
in horror fiction.[9]

Generically speaking, megalodon novels are difficult to categorize, for they contain elements of action adventure, science fiction, animal horror, and nautical literature. Drawing on Emily Alder's scholarship on maritime writing, I would emphasize that they also possess gothic qualities. In her essay "Through Oceans Darkly: Sea Literature and the Nautical Gothic," Alder observes that literary critics have largely ignored the gothic aspects of seafaring texts despite the fact that

> ships can be isolating, claustrophobic structures; ocean depths conceal monsters, secrets, bodies; the sea and its weather provide storms, sunsets, and remote locales for sublime and terrifying experiences; deep water is a useful metaphor for the interiority of the self; the ocean's precarious surface interfaces between life and death, chaos and order, self and other.[10]

Though incomplete, this list of maritime gothic tropes—many of which appear in megalodon fiction—provides ample evidence for Alder's claim that sea writing offers important "opportunities for rethinking or extending the scope of the Gothic in literary culture."[11]

While megalodon novels often involve isolated men trapped aboard claustrophobic ships or stuffed into cramped submersibles, I am more interested in some of their other gothic elements, such as their representations of monstrous sharks and their treatment of marine science. Importantly, many literary and cultural critics highlight the subversive potential of monsters. For example, in her essay "The Promises of Monsters: A Regenerative Politics for Inappropriate/d Others," Donna Haraway situates herself in the "womb of a pregnant monster" in an attempt to "find another relationship to nature besides reification and possession."[12] And in "Monster Culture (Seven Theses)," Jeffrey Jerome Cohen posits that monsters "ask us to reevaluate our cultural assumptions about race, gender, sexuality, our perception of difference, our toleration toward its expression."[13] Megalodon novels make no attempt to appropriate sharks for progressive social or environmental purposes, however. They use them as a foil to showcase the extraordinary physical and intellectual abilities of those humans—white American men—capable of subduing or slaughtering the largest oceanic predators the planet has to offer. In so doing, these novels exploit megalodon monstrosity to reinforce long-standing

Western ideas about humanity's capacity to exert dominance over the natural world.

Scientifically speaking, paleontologists know very little about the actual megalodons that populated the seas of the Miocene and Pliocene epochs, because, like other elasmobranches, their skeletons consisted primarily of cartilage, not calcium. As a result, they did not leave behind many fossils, just a few scattered teeth, coprolites, and vertebrae.[14] Scientists who have studied these remains estimate that female megalodons ranged somewhere between forty-four and fifty-six feet long, and their smaller male counterparts ranged somewhere between thirty-four and forty-seven feet long. Insofar as their physical appearance is concerned, experts suggest that megalodons possessed gaping jaws, replaceable teeth, and "streamlined yet powerful bodies built to efficiently cut through the water," much like their present-day analogues, the great white sharks and the mako sharks.[15]

Perhaps not surprisingly, authors of megalodon novels often play fast and loose with established science, exaggerating the size and appearance of the sharks to make them more formidable and monstrous. Thus the female shark in *Megalodon: Apex Predator* measures seventy-five feet long, while the male shark in *Carcharodon* measures eighty feet long. In *Extinct,* Wilson describes five megalodons: two sizable pups that are twenty-five feet long, one massive adolescent that is fifty feet long, and two titanic adults that are two hundred feet long.[16]

Taking advantage of the fear factor established by *Jaws,* some authors—Noe and Wilson among them—depict megalodons as morphologically similar to great white sharks. Others describe them in far more unsettling terms. In *Deep Terror,* Alten explains that megalodons adapted to their deep-sea environment by changing their skin color to an eerie, bioluminescent white.[17] In *Quest for Megalodon,* Dade describes the sharks as possessing "leprous and rotted" skin, as well as "a mass of dangling feelers" not unlike "catfish barbells."[18] And in *Megalodon,* Brown maintains that the prehistoric sharks living in the Molokai Fracture "did not look like sharks at all," because they evolved gigantic heads and teeth and camouflaged themselves "snout to tail, with a layer of living and dead mollusks."[19] Note that in these novels, evolution is both the mechanism that enables the sharks to survive across time and the source of their monstrosity.

Though their appearance differs from book to book, megalodon character traits and behavior patterns do not. All the novels depict these elasmobranches as monstrous predators and insatiable eating machines, incessantly prowling the ocean in search of human and nonhuman prey. Like many authors, Noe amplifies the horror by adopting Peter Benchley's strategy of writing from the cold-blooded fish's point of view. At the beginning of *Carcharodon*, he explains that the megalodon "was so large that he could eat hundreds of pounds of flesh and still hunt again the same day. No shark had ever been as ravenous as this one. He was well equipped for killing; his razor-sharp, serrated teeth were as large as a grown man's hand."[20] Then, he proceeds to describe, in quick succession and brutal detail, the manner in which the shark locates, slaughters, and devours its food:

> The shark descended and searched the ocean for anything worth eating. He saw a manta ray and he ripped off one of its six-foot wings with one quick bite, turned and snapped the other wing off. The manta's lacerated muscles quivered and bled profusely from the stumps, where his magnificent wings had once received their power. As the manta's wingless body settled on the ocean floor, Carcharodon turned once more and scooped up the remaining five hundred pounds of the ray and swallowed it easily. The shark continued to hunt.[21]

As he concludes these paragraphs, Noe foreshadows the death and destruction that occurs later in the novel, noting how "he was never satisfied, he always hungered and he always stalked."[22]

If megalodon eating habits are monstrous, then so are their reproductive behaviors and pup-rearing strategies. *Megalodon* features two adult sharks that devour the carcass of their progeny after he is killed by humans, and *Quest for Megalodon* features a female fish that gives birth to two live offspring, the survivors of an intense in utero cannibalism competition. In *Megalodon: Apex Predator*, an angry mother shark destroys an aquatic Antarctic research station when she attempts to free two of her drugged, captive offspring from their tanks. And in *Megalodon: Feeding Frenzy*, a pregnant, cannibalistic female megalodon leaves her secret underwater cavern in search of food and returns to give birth to hundreds of live young.[23] In these novels, characterizing the sharks as violent cannibals who cannot control their ravenous appetites serves to heighten their monstrosity.

Another prominent gothic element in megalodon novels is a pronounced preoccupation with science. According to Fred Botting, the figure of the scientist—especially the mad scientist—looms large in gothic writing because "the boundaries crossed by science transform the understanding of humanity's place in the natural world," often in terrifying ways.[24] Megalodon novels are not cautionary tales about the limits of science, like *Frankenstein* (1823), *The Strange Case of Dr. Jekyll and Mr. Hyde* (1886), and *Jurassic Park* (1990). Rather, they are science-as-savior books that revolve around the exploits of highly intelligent, hypermasculine scientists, determined to rescue the world from the onslaught of gigantic prehistoric sharks. Frank Acreman, the hero of *Megalodon*, is a marine biologist, and so is Scott Thompson, the hero of *Quest for Megalodon*. Meanwhile, Professor Benson, the protagonist of *Carcharodon*, is an oceanographer, and Jonas Taylor, the protagonist of *Deep Terror*, is a paleontologist. All of these men are athletic and attractive; all are convinced of the extant status of megalodons; and all are determined to vanquish them, no matter what the public or private cost. As Benson puts it, "the beast must be destroyed because it has no place in our world."[25]

To augment the heroic stature of their protagonists—and to make their claims about prehistoric sharks more convincing—these novels gothicize the ocean as an unfathomable realm of mystery, capable of concealing all manner of strange creatures in its dark, watery depths. They also employ what ecocritic David Ingram calls a "rhetoric of 'scientific' plausibility," citing the relatively recent discovery of new deepwater species or those long thought to be extinct.[26] Sometimes they move rapidly back and forth between these two forms of discourse. In one of his lectures to his students, Scott Thompson remarks, "The world's oceans remain virtually inaccessible, unexplored by humankind. Water covers 75 percent of our planet. With depths of seven miles, we can only *guess* at the secrets awaiting discovery." After exciting the interest of his pupils, he reveals that the sea contains several extant species that scientists once regarded as extinct:

A prime example is the *coelacanth*, a strange metallic-blue fish over six feet long which was classified as having been extinct for seventy million years. A living specimen was taken by fishermen in the Indian Ocean in 1938. . . . Another, even more recent case is *megamouth,* a species of shark similar to a whale shark that has no teeth and feeds on plankton by seining water through its oversized mouth. A fourteen footer was caught several years ago in the deep Pacific near Hawaii. Two other specimens have been encountered since.

As he concludes, Thompson returns to the gothic mode and indulges in a wildly speculative monster fantasy, exclaiming, "Other creatures *must* exist, incomprehensible in size and adaptability, which we have not met since our ability to penetrate their aqueous world is somewhat limited."[27]

For Thompson and the other scientists in contemporary megalodon novels, proving the existence of the sharks is not enough. These men also feel compelled to explain how these fish survived across time and why they left their secret hideaways. Most of them elaborate theories similar to that outlined by Frank Acreman:

Millions of years had committed the Megalodons to the deep Fracture. Once the seas had teemed with predators and only the development of massive cartilage and muscle had kept the Megalodons ahead, and even then it had been a closely run race. The fast-swimming sea lizard, *Icthyosaur,* with its saw-blade snout, had savaged the Megalodon ancestors of the remote past. With their better swim bladders and delicate fin structure, the Megalodons had evaded this assault by living ever deeper.

This special niche of dominance had been obtained at a price. Very little food existed naturally and like that much smaller species of the deep, *Argyropelecus,* the hatchet fish, the Megalodons had been forced to enlarge their mouths and their teeth.[28]

This passage and those appearing elsewhere in megalodon fiction ignore the fact that few, if any, organisms can move back and forth between the ocean's epipelagic and hadalpelagic zones because of the extreme light, temperature, and pressure differences.[29] Instead, they employ plausible scientific rhetoric to advance an unrealistic vision of the evolutionary process in which a threatened species saves itself simply by relocating to an alternate habitat and rapidly adapting to it.

As I observed earlier, these scientists also reveal the sharks' reasons for coming into contact with humans, most of which have to do with intrusive anthropogenic activities. In *Megalodon,* a submarine searching for gold in the Molokai Fracture provokes the sharks into an attack; in *Extinct,* nuclear testing forces the megalodons from their deepwater home; in *Quest for Megalodon,* noise pollution irritates the sharks into rising from the depths; and in *Megalodon: Feeding Frenzy,* an oil rig in the Chukchi Sea releases the megalodons when it accidentally drills into an undersea cavern. Once they surface, the sharks run amok, creating even more problems in oceanic ecosystems already stressed by overfishing, pollution, and climate change.

If humans and their exploitative environmental activities release megalodons into the known world, then humans also put them back where they belong, either by killing them or forcing them to return to the deep-sea trenches from which they came. At the end of *Megalodon,* a Russian submarine torpedoes one shark, while the other two sharks retreat to safer waters. Characters in *Megalodon: Feeding Frenzy* and *Megalodon: Apex Predator* kill the prehistoric fishes using rocket launders and nuclear bombs, respectively. In *Carcharodon,* Professor Benson and his protégé Marc destroy the shark with an explosive harpoon intended for whale hunting, and in *Extinct,* scientist Alan Freeman blasts one of the smaller megalodons with dynamite and drives the remaining four sharks out to sea.[30] In the end, then, these novels reinforce the reactionary idea that humans—especially white American men with access to high-tech weaponry developed by the military–industrial complex—possess mastery over nature.

Megalodon Evolving: Steve Alten's *The Meg* and Its Sequels

No prehistoric shark novels are more popular with reading audiences—and none are more invested in exploiting megalodon monstrosity and promoting human exceptionalism—than those written by Steve Alten.[31] For these reasons, they are particularly important to scrutinize. As the series begins in *Deep Terror,* navy-diver-turned-paleontologist Jonas Taylor discovers two megalodons, a male and a pregnant female, when he descends into the Pacific Ocean's Mariana Trench in a small submersible. The male dies after accidentally ensnaring himself in an undersea cable, and Jonas's crew members try to tow him up to their ship. Attracted by the smell of blood in the water, the female follows the carcass of her mate to the surface, penetrating through the thermocline that had trapped both fish in the depths of the trench. Ravenous with hunger, she proceeds to wreak havoc throughout the Pacific, pausing only to give birth to three offspring, one of which she cannibalizes and one of which dies in an orca attack. Eventually, she is killed by Jonas, who captures the surviving pup and places it in a special exhibit in an aquatic theme park at the Tanaka Institute in Monterey, California.

Alten's subsequent novels represent increasingly outlandish variations on these events. In *The Trench,* the captive female megalodon—now named Angel—goes into estrus and escapes from her tank at the institute into the open ocean. Driven by her reproductive instincts, she travels back to the trench, where she encounters a male of her species, mates with him, kills him, and bears him two pups. *Primal Waters* recapitulates this plotline in reverse, as Angel again goes into estrus and leaves the depths, accompanied by her two male offspring. Just before she arrives back at the institute, where she is recaptured by Jonas, she copulates with and kills one of her progeny. In *Hell's Aquarium,* Alten's characters engage with a new set of concerns. At the beginning of the novel, scientists at the institute perform DNA tests on Angel and her five pups—Belle, Lizzy, Angelica, Mary Kate, and Ashley—and discover that they possess the ability to reproduce through parthenogenesis. Although Angel and her weaker progeny perish, Belle and Lizzy escape the institute and claim the Strait of San Juan de Fuca as a nursery for their future, fatherless offspring. And in *Nightstalkers,* Belle and Lizzy leave their pups in the Salish Sea to travel back to the institute, where they are killed by a captive liopleurodon, a gigantic, prehistoric aquatic reptile taken from the Panthalassa Sea. Toward the end of the book, Jonas's son David makes plans to capture the remaining sharks for the new owner of the institute, who wants to put them back on public display.

At first glance, Alten's novels seem to indulge the fantasy—especially comforting in the age of the Sixth Extinction—that some extinct species are actually extant. I would argue, though, that the soothing aspects of this fantasy are mediated by the fact that the books contain several troubling contradictions. First, they represent megalodons as brutal apex predators, boundary-crossing monsters who are incapable of coexisting with humans; thus they indicate that these fish belong in the past, not the present. To further underscore this point, they anthropomorphize the conflicts between humans and sharks as stereotypical battles of the sexes in which male scientists use incredible amounts of violence to subdue or destroy female sharks. Second, Alten employs seemingly plausible scientific rhetoric to describe these fish as capable of responding to extinction threats by swiftly evolving new survival abilities, such as parthenogenetic reproduction. In this view, species naturally possess the intelligence, consciousness, and agency they need to take care of themselves (unless they are confronted directly by humans seeking to eradicate them). Like most other megalodon novels, then, Alten's books promote dangerously misinformed views of human exceptionalism, evolutionary processes, and the ecological problems of the Anthropocene.

With respect to their monstrosity, Alten's prehistoric elasmobranches embody many of the characteristics that Jeffrey Jerome Cohen outlines in "Monster Culture (Seven Theses)." According to Cohen, monsters "refuse easy categorization" and cause "scientific inquiry and its ordered relationality to crumble."[32] As long-lost relics of another era, Alten's megalodons transgress the boundary between extant and extinct species, thereby flouting the natural process of the evolution of life on earth, which requires the extinction of some species to make way for the evolution of new ones. As soon as they surface in the twentieth century, they throw marine food chains and ecosystems into complete chaos, and they baffle scientists, who argue among themselves about whether to classify the sharks as endangered or invasive, as amoral or evil, as natural or supernatural.[33]

Importantly, Alten's monstrous megalodons also possess bizarre physical characteristics—their ghostly skin, tremendous size, and eerie bioluminescence—that serve to differentiate them from other known shark species. When Jonas first sees the male at the bottom of the Mariana Trench, he is shocked by its outward appearance: "the conical snout, the thick triangular head, the crescent-moon tail. He estimated the Megalodon to be a good forty-five feet long, 30,000 pounds. Pure white. Florescent, just like the giant clams, just like the tubeworms."[34] Here the shark's similarity to strange, deep-sea mollusks and annelids—as opposed to other elasmobranches—makes it particularly disturbing. Elsewhere, Alten emphasizes the horrifying aspects of the sharks by describing the megalodons according to a set of stock metaphors, most of which he elaborates in *Deep Terror*. Thus he refers to them both in supernatural terms as ghosts and devils and in mechanistic terms as rockets, torpedoes, missiles, and trains. In later volumes, he also relies on monarchical language, demon imagery, and animal similes, comparing sharks to pit bulls, wolves, and tigers.[35]

All of this figurative language clearly demonstrates—to borrow a phrase from Cohen—that monstrous megalodons "dwell at the gates of difference" as an absolutely horrifying nonhuman other.[36] I would emphasize, though, that their strange physical appearance is not their only repugnant aspect, for they routinely practice behaviors that transgress the norms accepted by most human societies, including incest, infanticide, and cannibalism. Shortly after seeing the megalodons for the first time, Jonas witnesses the female devouring the carcass of her mate, "her snout buried deep within the male's bleeding body, her swollen white belly quivering in spasms as she engulfed huge chunks of flesh and entrails."[37] She later gives birth to three pups and eats one of them.[38]

As Cohen emphasizes, "representing an anterior culture" or, I would add, a nonhuman animal species "as monstrous justifies its displacement or extermination."[39] By constantly othering the female megalodon in *Deep Terror*, Alten makes Jonas's extreme violence against her—he steers his submersible into her stomach and cuts out her heart from the inside—seem both necessary and heroic. For contrast, consider the difference between this representational strategy and that employed by Jonathan Balcombe in his book *What a Fish Knows: The Inner Lives of Our Underwater Cousins* (2016). Throughout, Balcombe describes recent scientific discoveries about piscine sentience in an effort to encourage readers to identify with fish and "cultivate a new relationship with them," one that involves less thoughtlessness and more mindfulness, less exploitation and more conservation.[40]

Not insignificantly, Alten's megalodon novels also serve to reinforce the masculinist monster myth that Val Plumwood discusses in "Being Prey." Describing the aftermath of the crocodile attack that nearly took her life, Plumwood explains, "As a story that evoked the monster myth, mine was especially subject to masculinist appropriation. The imposition of the master narrative appeared in a number of different forms: in the exaggeration of the crocodile's size, in the portrayal of the encounter as a heroic wrestling match, and especially in its sexualization."[41] In *Deep Terror*, Jonas's story, too, evokes this myth, especially insofar as it represents him enmeshed in a biblical struggle of epic proportions against the inner anatomy of a giant female shark. Ironically, his only weapon consists of an improvised knife made from a fossilized megalodon tooth:

> Jonas Taylor could not maintain a grip on the slippery cords. From the angle of the cardiac chamber, he realized the Meg was rising, probably to attack. He thought of Terry. Wrapping the crook of his left arm around the bundle of cords, he braced his bare feet against the soft tissues of the inner chamber walls above him and, inverted, pulled the beating muscle downward with all his might. His right hand tightened his grip on the tooth. With one powerful slash, he cut into the cords.[42]

True to form, this confrontation results in the demise of the shark, as man proves himself superior to monstrous nature. Here, as elsewhere in Alten's books, the gender of the shark—and the extreme violence involved in destroying it—lends an uncomfortably misogynist tone to the encounter.

Although these novels tend to demonstrate the impossibility of the coexistence of humans and megalodons, they express at least some concern about the fish and their potential extinction. In *Deep Terror*, a federal judge lists megalodons "as a protected species of the Monterey Bay Sanctuary," and in *Nightstalkers*, an environmentalist wonders whether preserving endangered orcas should take precedence over preserving endangered sharks.[43] Meanwhile, in *Hell's Aquarium*, RAW, an animal rights organization concerned for the health and well-being of the captive elasmobranches, insists that the Tanaka Institute release them into the wild. Of note, the books ultimately adopt a reactionary attitude toward these individuals and organizations, criticizing the measures they take to ensure the preservation of the prehistoric sharks as insensitive, selfish, and harmful. Thus Jonas's friend Mac proves that some whale scientists care more for cetaceans than they do humans, and Jonas's wife, Terry, exposes RAW as an "extremist group" whose "leaders espouse animal rights only as an excuse to draw public attention and monetary contributions."[44]

According to the novels, the sharks might not be able to rely on marine scientists or environmental activists for protection, but they can rescue themselves from adverse circumstances through evolutionary adaptation. Crucially, they employ a rhetoric of scientific plausibility that draws on recent discoveries about shark reproductive behavior to do so. In *Hell's Aquarium*, Jonas's researchers inform him that their captive female megalodon gave birth to three genetically identical offspring, conceived through a parthenogenetic process similar to that observed in hammerhead and blacktip reef sharks. After some pointed discourse on the efficiency of this mode of reproduction and the irrelevancy of male organisms, Jonas's scientists posit that "man has been decimating the ocean's shark populations . . . perhaps nature found a way to counteract some of the effects."[45] They conclude that "with their numbers dwindling close to extinction, it makes perfect sense that Megalodons would eventually evolve to sex free reproduction."[46]

What makes these sections of the novels plausible is the fact that they draw on recent scientific discoveries. Some animals—including several species of insect, amphibian, reptile, and fish—possess the ability to reproduce through parthenogenesis. Some of them can even shift back and forth between sexual and asexual modes of reproduction, depending on environmental circumstances.[47] The problem in the novels lies in the fact that Alten uses these scientific details to support the reactionary idea that humans need not worry about endangered species because they possess the means to save themselves from eradication. In so doing, Alten misrepresents the precarity of those species not already endowed with special capacities, those species that must rely on the slow mechanisms of evolution to adapt to their changing circumstances. Along the way, he also perpetuates masculinist monster myths that endorse outdated ideas about human exceptionalism.

In the end, then, Alten's megalodon novels—just like their numerous predecessors and successors—showcase the various ways in which certain gothic tropes can be appropriated for antienvironmentalist purposes. Ironically, in a few rare moments, these books gesture toward the potential of sea monsters to inspire more progressive ideas. Toward the end of *Nightstalkers*, Jonas and Zach, a

Scottish cryptid hunter, travel to Antarctica, where they discover a prehistoric sperm whale from the Miocene epoch. Determined to slaughter the animal, Jonas aims the submersible's laser weaponry at the cetacean, but Zach stops him with some stirring words:

> Seeing what ye were about tae do, I realized that we're supposed tae be better than this . . . not jist me and ye, but mankind . . . humanity. It's a lesson I had learned before but forgot until this very moment; that at the end of the day our survival as a species may jist come down tae whether or not we respect the rights of other species tae live. God, listen tae me, I sound like a bloody Disney character.[48]

Although Jonas allows the whale to live, he shows no evidence that his attitude toward and relationship with the natural world have changed, and neither does anyone else in the novel. At the conclusion of the book, Jonas's son David kills a rampaging female liopleurodon in spectacularly violent fashion and sets out to capture Belle's and Lizzy's pups from their nursery in the Salish Sea. As these events indicate, none of Zach's enlightened ideas about the peaceful coexistence of human and nonhuman animals were meant to be taken seriously.

NOTES

1. Amitav Ghosh, *The Great Derangement: Climate Change and the Unthinkable* (New York: Penguin, 2016), 11, 22–31; Rob Nixon, *Slow Violence and the Environmentalism of the Poor* (Cambridge, Mass.: Harvard University Press, 2011), 2.
2. Ursula Heise, *Sense of Place and Sense of Planet: The Environmental Imagination of the Global* (Oxford: Oxford University Press, 2008), 208.
3. Rebecca Evans, "Fantastic Futures? Cli-Fi, Climate Justice, and Queer Futurity," *Resilience: A Journal of the Environmental Humanities* 4, no. 2–3 (2017): 106–7.
4. Evans, 107.
5. Throughout, I use the term *human* with the recognition that some humans—those who live in the industrialized nations of the Global North—are far more responsible for anthropogenic climate change than others. Likewise, I use the term *Anthropocene* with the recognition that it obscures the capitalist and colonialist forces that have contributed to the current precarity of the planet.

6. Sharks, rays, and various other cartilaginous fish belong to the sub-class elasmobranchii.

7. University of California Museum of Paleontology, "Misconceptions about Evolution," 2012, https://evolution.berkeley.edu/evolibrary/misconceptions_faq.php.

8. Peter Benchley, *Jaws* (New York: Random House, 1974), 229–30.

9. Steve Alten's series includes *Meg: A Novel of Deep Terror* (New York: Bantam, 1997), *The Trench* (New York: Pinnacle, 1999), *Meg: Primal Waters* (New York: Forge, 2004), *Meg: Hell's Aquarium* (New York: Tor, 2019), *Meg: Origins* (Portland, Oreg.: Gere Donovan Press, 2011), *Meg: Nightstalkers* (New York: Tor, 2016), and *Meg: Generations* (New York: Forge, 2018). Some of Severed Press's megalodon offerings include Jake Bible's *Mega* (2014), Eric S. Brown's *Megalodon Apocalypse* (2015), Matthew Dennion's *Operation Megalodon* (2018), J. E. Gurley's *Megalodon: Feeding Frenzy* (2016), S. J. Larsson's *Megalodon: Apex Predator* (2016), Flash Rex's *Megalodon Lives* (2011), and Viktor Zarkov's *Megatooth: A Deep Sea Thriller* (2015).

10. Emily Alder, "Through Oceans Darkly: Sea Literature and the Nautical Gothic," *Gothic Studies* 19, no. 2 (2017): 1.

11. Alder.

12. Donna Haraway, "The Promises of Monsters: A Regenerative Politics for Inappropriate/d Others," in *Cultural Studies,* ed. Lawrence Grossberg, Cary Nelson, and Paula A. Treichler (New York: Routledge, 1992), 295–96.

13. Jeffrey Jerome Cohen, "Monster Culture (Seven Theses)," in *Monster Theory: Reading Culture,* ed. Jeffrey Jerome Cohen (Minneapolis: University of Minnesota Press, 1996), 20.

14. *Coprolite* is the scientific term for a specimen of fossilized feces.

15. Danielle Hall, "The Megalodon," Smithsonian, February 2019, https://ocean.si.edu/ocean-life/sharks-rays/megalodon.

16. Gurley, *Feeding Frenzy,* 81; George Edward Noe, *Carcharodon* (New York: Vantage, 1987), 118; Charles Wilson, *Extinct* (New York: St. Martin's, 1997), 309.

17. Alten, *Deep Terror,* 103.

18. Tom Dade, *Quest for Megalodon* (New York: Swan, 1993), 103.

19. Robin Brown, *Megalodon* (New York: Playboy Paperbacks, 1981), 65, 97.

20. Noe, *Carcharodon,* 2.

21. Noe, 5.

22. Noe, 6.

23. Brown, *Megalodon,* 221–22; Dade, *Quest for Megalodon,* 20–21, 222–23; Wilson, *Extinct,* 307–10; Larsson, *Apex Predator,* 78–87; Gurley, *Megalodon,* 170–90.

24. Fred Botting, *Gothic*, 2nd ed. (London: Routledge, 2014), 13.

25. Brown, *Megalodon*, 12; Dade, *Quest for Megalodon*, 18; Noe, *Carcharodon*, 88, 90; Alten, *Deep Terror*, 6.

26. David Ingram, *Green Screen: Environmentalism and Hollywood Cinema* (Exeter, U.K.: University of Exeter Press, 2000), 7.

27. Dade, *Quest for Megalodon*, 18–19.

28. Brown, *Megalodon*, 65.

29. *Epipelagic* refers to surface waters, and *hadalpelagic* refers to oceanic trench waters. See National Weather Service, "Layers of the Ocean," https://www.weather.gov/jetstream/layers_ocean.

30. Brown, *Megalodon*, 221–24; Gurley, *Megalodon*, 123–24; Larsson, *Megalodon*, 185–86; Noe, *Carcharodon*, 193; Wilson, *Extinct*, 230, 309.

31. According to Alten's website, *Deep Terror* "hit every major best-seller list, including #19 on the New York Times list (#7 audio)." Many of his subsequent novels also achieved best-seller status. The film version of *Deep Terror*, released in August 2018 as *The Meg*, earned more than $530 million at the box office. See https://www.stevealten.com/bio/; Mark Hughes, "'Aquaman' Tops 'The Dark Knight' with $1 Billion Box Office," *Forbes*, January 13, 2019, https://www.forbes.com/sites/markhughes/2019/01/13/aquaman-tops-the-dark-knight-with-1-billion-box-office.

32. Cohen, "Monster Culture," 6–7.

33. Alten, *Nightstalkers*, 58–59, 284–86.

34. Alten, *Deep Terror*, 103.

35. Alten, 104, 129, 147, 162, 166, 167, 198, 239; Alten, *The Trench*, 15; Alten, *Primal Waters*, 56, 85; Alten, *Nightstalkers*, 36, 217.

36. Cohen, "Monster Culture," 7.

37. Alten, *Deep Terror*, 112.

38. Alten, 221.

39. Cohen, "Monster Culture," 7–8.

40. Jonathan Balcombe, *What a Fish Knows: The Inner Lives of Our Underwater Cousins* (New York: Scientific American, 2016), 8, 22.

41. Val Plumwood, "Being Prey," in *The New Earth Reader*, ed. David Rothenberg and Marta Ulvaeus (Cambridge, Mass.: MIT Press, 1999), 86.

42. Alten, *Deep Terror*, 322.

43. Alten, 244; Alten, *Nightstalkers*, 59, 285.

44. Alten, *Hell's Aquarium*, 92–93, 361.

45. Alten, 181.

46. Alten, 183.

47. Melissa Hogenboom, "Spectacular Real Virgin Births," *BBC Earth*, December 22, 2014, http://www.bbc.com/earth/story/20141219-spectacular-real-virgin-births.

48. Alten, *Nightstalkers*, 363.

5

A Violence "Just below the Skin"

Atmospheric Terror and Racial Ecologies
from the African Anthropocene

ESTHIE HUGO

> Let us return to that atmosphere of violence, that
> violence which is just below the skin.
>
> —Frantz Fanon, *The Wretched of the Earth*

Traditional gothic tales, as many critics have shown, glean much of their terror from their claustrophobic spatial settings, in locations such as closed-off cellars, chambers, and attics, which "bespeak abandonment and unlife."[1] Chris Baldick writes that gothic tales attain their "Gothic effect" through a combination of "a fearful sense of inheritance in a time with a claustrophobic sense of enclosure in space . . . to produce an impression of sickening descent into disintegration."[2] Baldick's description of the sickening disintegration experienced through the enclosure of space reads starkly in light of recent global events. As I write, the world is in the throes of a protracted lockdown period resulting from a new virus named SARS-CoV-2 and the Covid-19 pandemic it engendered. The virus contaminates through droplets that can spread through the air via coughing and sneezing, attacking the respiratory system, causing inflammation, and making it difficult to breathe. To curb its spread, countries across the world have implemented various stay-at-home-measures, framing confinement and isolation as necessary precautions against contamination. So, how do we read gothic under these new conditions, when the meaning of terror once again becomes reconfigured—no longer located in the enclosure of space but in the very air we breathe? Such events force us to reconsider how the gothic form reconfigured might give expression to a world suffocated and suffocating, radically reframed, in other words, by the terrors of an atmosphere.

The pandemic has unfolded across various fault lines, particularly in terms of racial inequality. Evidence shows that the Covid-19 disease has more severely affected people of color across the world.[3] In the United States, the phrase "I Can't Breathe," which memorializes the dying words of Eric Gardner, Byron Williams, and George Floyd, has become both an anthem of dissent against the American state's deadly toll on Black lives and a slogan that captures the racial inequalities structuring the current racialized experience of the pandemic.[4] In Africa, the proliferation of Covid-19 has similarly exposed how global crisis is shouldered disproportionately by Black bodies, which have long borne the effects of airborne toxicity in particularly violent ways. Like the Black men who recently died at the hands of American police brutality, African civilians regularly describe air quality in urban Africa through fears of asphyxiation. In Johannesburg, the center of South Africa's gold mining sector, the air quality is so poor that it has been dubbed "airpocalypse."[5] In Niger, also known as the "Uranium Capital of Africa," locals employ a similarly gothic lexicon to describe the contamination of land, water, and air by radioactive dust. "Have you seen the soil in the country?" asks a local mining worker from Arlit, an industrial town in north central Niger. "It is dry and lifeless. . . . There is something evil in the dust."[6]

Focusing on the uneven experience of global environmental crisis, this chapter is interested in mapping new directions in the gothic through an analysis of West African forms of cultural production in which the site of gothic terror becomes reconfigured and located in atmospheric racism. I chart the evolving politics and aesthetics of racial toxicity by focusing on the mobilization of atmospheric terror in the writings of Nigerian author Ben Okri and in the artistic portraits of Beninese photographer Fabrice Monteiro. Comparing these works allows for the interrogation of how different African artistic mediums draw on gothic aesthetics to give shape to the racist history of toxic exposure and, in the process, enable us to model a new analytic framework for understanding global environmental crisis as a political and ecological project that distributes life and death unevenly.

The racialized experience of deathly atmospheric exposure is not a new issue. The World Health Organization (WHO) has long argued that air pollution is the world's most severe environmental health concern.[7] Recognizing that nine out of ten people worldwide breathe air containing levels of pollutants that exceed WHO guideline limits, the organization has implemented a series of air quality programs across Europe, the Western Pacific, and the Americas, which recommend "threshold limits for key air pollutants that pose health risks and provide a reference for setting air pollution targets at regional and national levels to improve air quality."[8] While the WHO acknowledges that the effects of pollution are intensified by poverty, no air quality program currently exists for sub-Saharan Africa, despite the fact that pollution-related deaths have increased in the region by nearly 60 percent over the last two decades.[9]

Pavithra Vasudevan argues for the espousal of the term *racial ecologies* to describe these uneven geographic zones, in which corporeal vulnerability is experienced through the "slow violence"[10] of poisoned air, water, and land, which recomposes Black bodies "through intimate relations with . . . non-human species and inorganic matter."[11] Vasudevan's critique draws on emergent Fanonian readings that attempt to account for the place of race and empire in popular understandings of the Anthropocene, which, as a planetary condition framed by the name of the Anthropos, has been criticized for ignoring the uneven history of development in favor of analyses that opt instead "for indictments of the entire species."[12]As Rebecca Duncan notes in chapter 9 of this collection:

> The broad category of human activity cannot bring into focus the principle that organizes patterns of violence and security over time and that is clearly bound up with geopolitical distributions of wealth and power, with legacies of empire and colonial settlement, and with race.

Similarly suspicious of the fault lines encoded in Anthropocenic thinking, a number of scholars have opted for a range of alternative terms to account for the formative role played by transatlantic slavery in the instantiation of capitalism as modern-world-system.[13]

Racial ecologies thus nudge us usefully toward what Christina Sharpe describes as "monstrous intimacies"—intimate violences inherited from slavery that continue to shape Black subjectivities into the present.[14] Espousing Sharpe's formulation of postslavery subjectivity in her study of aluminum smelting in twentieth-century North Carolina, Vasudevan argues that the logics of racial ecologies are manifested in the "everyday corporeal negotiations [that Black communities experience] with waste materials,"[15] leading to "a transgenerational inheritance that manifests in chronic illness and premature death."[16] Like the intimate violences of the colonial slave system, which resulted in "Black bodies serv[ing] as both lifesource and toxic sink,"[17] the materiality of toxic exposure in contemporary Black communities substantiates arguments made by Saidiya Hartmann about the continuities between field and factory in the postslavery era.[18] Borrowing Hartman's insights into how slavery "lives on" through racial capitalism, Vasudevan shows how afterlives of the forcible use of Black labor in sugarcane and cotton production become embedded in racial ecologies that intertwine race, waste, and extrahuman natures in new and disturbing ways, as the "ghostly agents" of corporeal toxicity supplement slavery's "ball and chain."[19]

Racial ecologies give expression, then, to the lived experience of consumptive capitalism's intimate bodily invasions, elucidating imperialism's social-ecological violence as *suffocation*. As a material manifestation of the socio-natures of ongoing forms of coloniality across urban Africa, suffocation gives expression to Fanon's critique of colonialism as Manichaean spatial demarcation. As Fanon argues,

> the zone where the natives live is not complementary to the zone inhabited by the settlers. The two zones are opposed, but not in the service of a higher unity. . . . They both follow the principle of reciprocal exclusivity.[20]

Fanon's description here of the settler town and the native town are reanimated through environmental crisis, where the global centers responsible for climate crisis are more secured against its violence, while African cities are left vulnerable—"smother[ed]," as Jonathan Silver puts it in "Suffocating Cities," under "new extreme conditions" that replicate the processes of underdevelopment and racial capitalism that shaped African urbanization.[21] In thinking about the coloniality of this global condition, Silver pushes us to consider how climate change cannot be understood "as a series of dramatic events"; rather, it forms part of a long history in which violence is "disproportionately centred on the black body."[22] In what follows, I trace the toxic history of atmospheric terror in West Africa as both corporeal violence *and* contestation and insurgency, concluding by exploring how Okri and Monteiro draw on gothic to give expression to what we might understand as a decolonial praxis for understanding the Anthropocene.

Waste, Race, and the Suffocating City

Atmospheric toxicity plays a central role in Ben Okri's short story "In the City of Red Dust."[23] This tale charts the travails of two friends and ghetto dwellers—Emokhai and Marjomi—in an unnamed Nigerian city during the day on which the country's military governor celebrates his fiftieth birthday. The story is set during the Harmattan period, when great winds carry vast amounts of mineral dust from the Sahara Desert toward the Gulf of Guinea from November to March every year. Though a common annual occurrence throughout West Africa, the Harmattan haze in Okri's story brings with it more than the usual seasonal discomfort "of dry skins and chapped lips."[24] Instead, the narrative is replete with images of decay and suffocation caused by an unusually "massive cloud of red dust"[25] that hangs over the city, coating in red sediment "all natural life," from "the cockroaches, the cats, the dogs [and] the leaves of the stunted orange tree" through to "the zinc rooftops"[26] of the houses among which Emokhai lives.

No reason is provided for the Harmattan season's abnormal levels of dust, but we can surmise that the dust cloud has formed as a result of the country's near-complete reliance on the extraction of oil to grow the postcolonial economy. As is well known, Nigeria's political economy has been shaped by the petroleum sector throughout its postcolonial history. "Nigeria," writes Michael Watts, "is an archetypical petrostate, the eleventh largest producer and the eighth largest exporter of crude oil in the world."[27] Many critics have read Okri's narrative, which employs a series of gothic images and devices adapted from African folklore, as mediating the neocolonial logics of petro-predation. For Elleke Boehmer, the gothic elements of the story, in particular Okri's use of the vampire figure, "act[] as a powerful reminder of the vampire-like (post)colonial economy that the friends inhabit, in which the state feeds upon the blood of its citizens."[28]

Resource extraction and labor relations are given form through Okri's turn to the Yoruba myth of the *obayifo*. This myth is based on Ashanti vampire lore, which dictates that the *obayifo* is a witch that preys on children and crops by draining their "life-energy."[29] Drawing on the Yoruba belief in this creature's "insatiable appetite" for both human and extrahuman natures, Okri reifies capitalist predation through the corporeal practice of bloodletting.[30] Broke, hungry, and unable "to make money honestly," Emokhai and his friend Marjomi survive by selling their blood to a local hospital in exchange for a pitiful two naira per pint—less, they complain, "than what a prostitute gets."[31] Marjomi, prized for his "expensive . . . high-grade blood," sells so regularly that he exists in a state of near zombification. The hospital's nurses complain that his body is "like a skeleton with dried skin," and when he walks, he does so "muttering to himself, stumbling forward."[32] As it literally exhausts his lifeblood, the exsanguination also results in Marjomi being overcome by a seemingly supernatural stupor. While his blood is being drawn, Marjomi feels "that he has fallen into a dream"; his eyes become "liverish" with "a tortured light" as "a strange demented energy tak[es] over his movements."[33]

Barely alive, and suggestively "possessed" by the extractive economy, Marjomi and Emokhai stagger through the streets as military planes circle the sky, releasing large reams of paper stamped with the portrait of the city's dictator, "a soldier who had reputedly saved the city during a siege in the war."[34] This scene directly links the depleted bodies of Marjomi and Emokhai to the petro-economy via the figure of its petro-chemical coordinator. While these papers are meant to remind the city's citizens of the governor's birthday celebration, they simply exacerbate the city's high level of existing pollution. Watching as this "cascade of confetti . . . pirouetted towards the ground," Emokhai laments that the "formless" rubbish dump near to where he lives merely "grows bigger each day."[35]

Like Boehmer, many critics have read Okri's turn to a gothic vocabulary as an extension of "peripheral irrealist"[36] forms of narrativization that mediate the contradictions of Nigeria's first petroleum cycle, in which the contrast between boom and bust, growth and contraction, development and inertia, windfall and precarity, became particularly spectacularized.[37] In Okri's tale, oil capital explicitly produces inequality. Roaming the streets in search of work and food, Emokhai and Marjomi notice how the city's uneven development produces wealth for some and poverty for others. The street where Emokhai lives is covered in rotting "garbage heaps," while the city's wealthy live on "clean avenues . . . sealed behind barbed wire fences [and] named after rich men, governors, and freedom fighters."[38] The figure of the military dictator is embellished with "gold necklaces from secret societies and multinational concerns," while Marjomi and Emokhai must literally sell their lifeblood to make ends meet. Moreover, while the friends exist in a state of depravity and atrophy, above them the skies roil with the threat of military action. The thousands of fighter planes, which make Emokhai feel "as if he were under invasion, as if a new war had been declared,"[39] emblematize how, under such extreme inequities, order can only be maintained under threat of military force.

The "shock" of oil in Nigeria has not only resulted in forms of governance that reproduce social and political violence but has also led to the emergence of "occult economies,"[40] in which "bewitched accumulation" is generated through the discourse of "market-monstrosity."[41] Pointing to the increased circulation in urban Africa of "tales of enrichment via cannibalism, vampirism and extraordinary interactions between the living and the dead," David McNally suggests that Okri turns to the "fantastic genre" to provide a vessel for "the systematic assaults on bodily and psychic integrity that define the economic infrastructure of modernity."[42] Like Jennifer Wentzel, who coined the influential concept of "petro-magic-realism" to describe how Nigerian fiction aestheticizes the "magic" of petro-modernity,[43] McNally argues that Okri's fiction disturbs "the naturalization of capitalism" through the fantastic mode, which offers "a kind of grotesque realism that mimics the absurdity of capitalist modernity."[44] Rather than view them as "expressions of traditional values in opposition to the forces of modern capitalism," McNally sees in Okri's fantastical aesthetics a counterhegemonic disruption. This grows out of an experience of "social life in the age of globalising capitalism,"[45] which, in Okri's novel, is framed via an unevenness that is inflected specifically by a Yoruba cosmology.

Written in the aftermath of Nigeria's 1980s oil crash, the text is shaped by a need both to make sense of the wreckage of a once hopeful future and to come to terms with the legacy of faltering development and the political instability cemented by the perversity of oil wealth. The metaphor of vampiric corporeal predation responds to this dual imperative, making legible the devastating effects of the postcolonial petrostate through its figuring of oil as "blood circulating through the national body."[46] Key here is that Okri draws an explicit comparison between medicalized blood-letting, which takes place at the tellingly named Queen Mary Hospital, and the predatory methods of accumulation that continue to structure the postcolonial state through what Immanuel Wallerstein terms the "world-system."[47] As such, Okri's vampirism also encodes the coloniality of socioecological violence and the inextricability of human and extrahuman resources in the context of the extraction economy. Just as the hospital appropriates the life energies of Emokhai and Marjomi, so, too, does the global oil economy draw both on the life energies of African labor power and the potential energies of the extrahuman through its extraction of oil from the literal "veins" of the earth. The seemingly "fantastic" operations of foreign oil investment—which obscures the transactions between human bodies, ecology, and capital—are powerfully captured, then, in Okri's espousal of the vampire figure of the *obayifo,* which feeds not only on human life but also on crops—which is sustained, in other words, by both human and extrahuman prey.

While Okri highlights the mechanics of oil predation through the metaphor of vampirism and the Black bodily vulnerability this produces, the narrative places equal emphasis on the effects of oil through its inclusion of the blood red color of the dust that covers and consumes all who inhabit the city, thereby making use of the gothic mode to figure both the systemic extraction of labor and the aftereffects of this process of capitalization. As critics have noted, some of the most devastating effects of oil extraction concern its waste products and pollutants. Since the onset of the petro-regime, Nigeria has been home to some of the worst cases of oil pollution in the world. Hundreds of oil spills have occurred over the last few decades, but oil spills are not the only hazards produced by the oil economy. The flaring of petro-associated gas remains commonplace in oil-producing Nigeria, despite governmental promises to ban the practice since 1984.[48] Gas flaring, in which the natural gas associated with petroleum extraction is burned off into the atmosphere, significantly impacts air quality. Pollutants released by gas flaring are carried far from the actual sites of extraction into the city, where rising levels of airborne toxins have been linked to cancer and lung damage, as well as reproductive and neurological problems.[49]

Like his delineation of petro-extraction, Okri's illustration of atmospheric toxicity underscores how its distribution reproduces neocolonial oppression. Looking out at a city "obscured in dust, plaster and smoke," Emokhai sees "the patterns of an empire stifled in history."[50] Emokhai literally breathes in the dust of empire as he passes "an area which used to be a market where slaves were sold a hundred years before," feeling "his nose and lungs getting clogged from the dust and air."[51] Walking through this toxic cloud, Emokhai's body becomes recomposed and remade in the ghostly image of the dust that chokes him; he emerges from the dust "whittled . . . a shade more invisible"[52] than before. In this ghostly specter, Okri proffers the suffocating confines of the slave hold, as the very air Emokhai breathes becomes as terrifying as the injurious tomb of "racial terror" that was the slave ship.[53] As the violence of empire becomes diffused and expanded to permeate the everyday, Emokhai, in an uncanny invocation of the dying words of Floyd, Gardner, and Williams, describes walking through a city so hazardous that he feels as though "he [can't] breathe."[54] Moreover, as a trope that gothically registers both the processes of historical consumptive extraction and their toxic afterlives, Marjomi's zombie-like stupor similarly takes on new meaning, drawing into sharp focus how bodies become gothically "undone"[55] through the uneven transformation of human lives and extrahuman geographies, here reified through Black exposure to airborne toxicity.

Thus, while Okri's turn to a fantastical lexicon stylistically mediates the Nigerian state's "enchantment" with the global oil market, the gothic aesthetics of the story, in particular its invocation of the suffocating and zombified body, can equally be read as giving fictional meaning to the material realities of racialized toxic exposure. By shifting our focus from the actual time and site of extraction to the "monstrous intimacies" effected by the corporeal interaction of race and waste, Okri's tale allows us to look more closely at the living residues to which planetary extractive industries gave rise. In the process, his narrative opens up ways of viewing the Anthropocene that move away from common historical points of departure that prioritize the Industrial Revolution, focusing not on the temporal delineation of a single historical event but rather on "the temporally diffuse violence of an atmosphere."[56] To borrow from Christina Sharpe, who in turn draws on Fanon, Okri's story shows "how it is not the specifics of any one event or set of events that are endlessly repeatable and repeated, but the totality of the environments in which [Black bodies] struggle."[57]

Summoning colonial and contemporary conditions of racial vulnerability through gothic bodily suffocation and debility, Okri calls up the horrifying afterlives of human-made matter, in the double sense. Such visions of Black corporeal debility point to the cumulative weight of what Fanon saw as the colonized subject's "permanent struggle against omnipresent death . . . and the absence of any hope for the future."[58] In Okri's tale, the omnipresence of toxicity gives potent expression to the unlivable life of racial ecologies, in which the terms of a racist world continue to be lived "as a suffocating and inescapable atmosphere—as necessary sustenance, even as it sickens and depletes."[59] In this sense, Okri's delineation of atmospheric toxicity gives new meaning to Fanon's urgent descriptions of the Wretched of the Earth, those racialized subjects who are forced to live in a "narrow world strewn with prohibitions,"[60] where conditions of being "hemmed in" and "smothered" give way to the act of living as a form of "combat breathing."[61] The continual repetition of breath required for life becomes a site of struggle, making breathing itself part of the fight to maintain life in a suffocating and suffocated world.

Animated Monsters of the African Anthropocene

Alongside Okri's narrative, more recent West African artistic forms have begun to emerge that similarly look to portray how Black bodies disproportionately bear the bodily burden of industrial waste through gothic modes of representation. The photographic portraits of Beninese photographer Fabrice Monteiro are particularly instructive here, as his work extends Okri's focus on racialized bodily asphyxiation through the creation of what he describes as "visions of a world strangled by waste."[62] Monteiro was born in Namur, Benin, but currently lives and works in Dakar, Senegal. The city of Dakar plays a formative role in his work, as many of his most famous portraits from his 2015 collection The Prophecy were shot in the infamous Mbeubeuss: Senegal's largest waste dump. This landfill was created six years after Senegal's independence from French rule, in 1968, and sits on a floodplain outside Dakar, close to the ocean. It sprawls across the floodplain, covering more than 175 hectares and taking in more than 475,000 tons of waste every year. This makes it one of the largest open waste dumps in the world.[63] Not only is Mbeubeuss home to some of the world's worst pollution but it is also a lifeline for thousands of the city's poor. Working in a constant stream of poisonous gas and smoke, an estimated thirty-five hundred workers salvage materials collected from the site, selling these in bulk to Chinese and Indian scrap metal companies in the hope of earning a daily wage.[64]

Like these workers, who generate life from the "castoffs" that make up the waste dump, Monteiro draws from the landfill a range of waste materials to construct huge, monstrous figures that emerge from the city's excessive refuse and devastated landscape. Monteiro's figures are at once gothically monstrous and strangely beautiful, uncanny in their use of abject garbage to create prized objects of great beauty. Alongside his use of waste objects, Monteiro's photographic series takes inspiration from the ancient story of the Greek goddess Gaia.[65] As he puts it himself, the narrative of his series reconstructs Gaia's "incapacity to maintain the natural cycles of the planet in front of new modes of life and consumption."[66] Infuriated by what she sees, Gaia "resolves to send her djinns to let them appear to the humans and deliver a message of warning and empowerment."[67]

Of the images that compose Monteiro's 2015 collection, one is particularly striking for its comparative framing of slave histories and present-day Black corporeal negotiations with the wastes of the global oil economy. Unlike Okri's narrative, which hinges on the airborne residues of land-based oil extraction, this portrait takes us offshore, to the oceanic site of extractive capitalism. Here Monteiro depicts his monstrous goddess emerging on the Atlantic shores of Dakar's Hann Bay, from which the ancestors of modern Senegalese citizens were forcibly transported via the transatlantic slave trade centuries before. Monteiro's figure resembles the pan-African deity that goes by the various names of Mami Wata, water-mamma, Liba-Mama, and mama dlo. This aquatic divinity typically takes the form of a "beautiful black woman with black braids and the tail of a colourful fish"[68] and can be found across the African diasporas, in the Americas, and in the Caribbean under many different guises.[69] She is believed to have "developed from a local water

Esthie Hugo

Figure 5.1. A black-clothed figure, in the image of the pan-African deity Mami Wata, emerges from the polluted oceans of Dakar's Hann Bay. Copyright ADAGP, Paris and DACS, London 2021.

goddess within a wider pantheon of gods connected with various societies."[70] As other critics have shown, "the origins of this figure lie in a combination of Amerindian mythology, European mermaid lore, and the water-spirit beliefs brought to the region by enslaved Africans."[71]

While many have read Mami Wata as emblematic of the "cultural mixing" that emerged from the colonial encounter,[72] Michael Niblett has argued that versions of the deity from the Atlantic World, which emphasize her "violent, death-dealing" qualities, should rather be "interpreted with reference to the brutal violence and structural inequalities imposed on the Caribbean by capitalist imperialism."[73] Like Niblett's analysis of this water spirit's Caribbean manifestation, Monteiro's West African Mami Wata encodes the ongoing ecosocial imperialism of extractivist systems in postcolonial Senegal via offshore oil exploration. His Mami Wata takes the familiar form of a mermaid, but Monteiro renders her in decidedly more gothic terms than those in which she normally appears. In place of her vibrant scales, Monteiro's goddess is clothed in black fabric and white feathers that appear slick with crude oil. The black fabric makes her appear as if she is in the throes of death, as it consumes her entire body, from her face, which is drawn in an expression of pain, to the rolls of shiny black plastic—one of oil's main by-products—that compose her mermaid's tail.

The reason for her emergence from the water is ambiguous, but the deathly mask of her face suggests she has been forced out of her oceanic home as a result of the oil pollutants that cloud the black water frothing at her feet. As such, Monteiro's gothic contortion of the Mami Wata figure registers how capitalist transformations of the biosphere distort what Jason W. Moore refers to as the "relations of life-making"[74] into corrosive, monstrous configurations, recalling how "existing socioecological unities are violently disaggregated" under capitalist incursion, giving rise to "strange new configurations of human and extra-human nature."[75] Monteiro's work registers the "strange" new configurations of capitalist appropriation, then, by encoding them into this gothic figure, who is incapable of supporting life as it is habitually lived.

Certainly Monteiro's depiction of this water spirit clothed in slick black cloth plays on the proliferation of images of marine creatures writhing in thick murky waters, gasping for breath in oceans increasingly contaminated by the millions of barrels of crude oil that are released into the sea each year.[76] As such, the black residue that cloaks Monteiro's figure gives life to the devastating aftereffects that attend the search for and claiming of raw materials. Unlike Nigeria's administration, the Senegalese government has only recently become interested in the profit potentials offered by foreign oil investment. Since 2014, a series of foreign multinationals have marked the country as the new oil frontier, when Senegal's deepwater wells opened up a new basin on the Atlantic Margin.[77] In collaboration with Australian oil giant Woodside Energy and U.K. company Cairn Energy, the Senegalese administration has invested in the creation of a new "world-class" oil rig called the Sangomar Field, which promises to deliver "billions of dollars of revenue to the government of Senegal and provide social and economic benefits for generations to come."[78]

Yet, in Monteiro's photographic imagination, oil investment is framed not through celebration but through gothic images of ruination and decay. The new arrival of offshore oil extraction is given expression via a large ship in the background that lies perilously on its side, the source—it seems clear—of the ocean waters' deathly color. However, the ship could equally be a fishing vessel, thus referencing the Senegalese fishing economy, which is the backbone of local life, accounting for up to 75 percent of the protein consumed by millions of the country's citizens.[79] In addition to domestic industrial and artisanal fishing fleets, many foreign countries—including Japan, China, and states from within the European Union—maintain access to Senegalese waters, and this has placed unsustainable pressures on limited fish stocks over the last three decades.[80] But the Senegalese ocean has not only seen plummeting fish reserves. Since Senegal's independence from French rule, its beaches have become some of the most contaminated on earth. Lacking systematic municipal waste collection and disposal, residents regularly deal with their waste by discarding it along the country's shorelines.[81] As the beaches and ocean waters become dumping grounds that threaten to reach the size of the Mbeubeuss landfill, local fishermen sense that the sea's character is changing. Alongside lamentations of rising sea temperatures and pollution, locals describe the damage done to their once-plentiful fishing stocks through the oft-repeated refrain "There are no more fish in Senegal."[82]

As Monteiro's image of the oil-consumed ocean divinity suggests, the looming extraction of offshore petroleum is only set to exacerbate further the fragility of this already unstable ecosystem, leading to what many see as Senegal's "dystopian future."[83] Like these critics, Monteiro's Mami Wata similarly warns of an imminent apocalypse wrought by oil. In her one hand, she carries the skeletal remains of a white dove splattered with black resin. This is a reference to the archetypal white dove released by Noah in the biblical tale of Noah's Ark, in which Noah, his family, and the world's animals survive God's wrath though the construction of an ark that protects them from a world-engulfing flood. Unlike the bird in this scenario, Monteiro's dove does not bring the safe harbor of good fortune and a hopeful future; rather, it symbolizes the ruinous trajectories of resource extraction. Such signs make visible how Senegal's ocean is being remade, once more, into a site of death for Black African bodies and communities, recalling from its polluted depths the submarine history of New World slavery and "hundreds of thousands, perhaps millions" of African captives thrown overboard during the Middle Passage.[84] Invoking these histories through a gothic dynamic of the returning of the repressed, Monteiro shows how the conditions of this racist history become lived in an ocean made *unheimlich*, in the terms elucidated by

Figure 5.2. A large and brightly colored female figure stands on top of Mbeubeuss, Senegal's largest landfill. Copyright ADAGP, Paris and DACS, London 2021.

Freud's seminal essay.[85] Such conditions have led the simultaneous unhoming of Black bodies and marine life in asphyxiating waters that recall Fanon's meditation on the violence of the colonial state, which amplifies its wounding effects across the Black body by reducing the colonial subject to a state of combat breathing.

Moreover, while the biblical Noah survives the terror of a collapsing planet in the original tale, Monteiro's figure can only move from one strangled world to another. In a further image, a larger-than-life female figure stands above Mbeubeuss's trash-filled mound. Elaborating Okri's aesthetics of asphyxiation, this figure's face is adorned with a black oil mask, presumably as protection against the cloud of black smoke in which she is encircled. Her skirt is fabricated from pieces of brightly colored refuse that flow into the rubbish that collects at her feet, making her body indistinguishable from the trash heap on which she stands commingled with "other things."[86] Neither human nor nonhuman, the figure is simultaneously both and neither, a reminder of the "transcorporealities"[87] produced between the human and the extrahuman under the conditions of racialized toxicity from which she emerges.

The extreme largeness of Monteiro's figures also forces the viewer to confront how the peripherialization of Africa has resulted in its creation as "waste-world"—as the site in which modernity's cast-offs are "carried away into obscurity"[88] and "forgotten," thereby transforming the continent into "a convenient sink for toxic waste."[89] Monteiro reframes these colonial categories of human surplus—of "waste and waste beings"[90]—to include contemporary interactions of Black bodies with the toxic products of capitalism. In this sense, Monteiro's gothic figures serve as urgent allegories for the unevenness of capitalist development, where foreign investors prepare to feast on the profits of new ventures, while locals must endure the horrors of a dying planet shaped by centuries of social and ecological violence that have inaugurated "an environment of fatality"[91] from which they cannot escape.

New Genres of the Human

Yet, both Okri narrative and Monteiro's photographs retain a sense of hopefulness. As Julietta Singh argues with reference to Monteiro's series, there is a "breath-taking endurance in each of these figures" that not only reminds viewers of the ecological catastrophes produced by globalization but also points toward "other ways of generative living, of human and more than human cohabitation."[92] Indeed, while Monteiro's turn to gothic evokes the terrorized and terrorizing environments of racial ecologies, it simultaneously pays homage to the strategies of survival that are opened by the violent socioecological realities of contemporary African life. Such visions, in which "beauty, debris, danger and hope [become] closely interwoven,"[93] point in turn to the emancipatory potential encoded in the coproduction of life-making that takes as its foundation the intertwining of human and extrahuman natures. Niblett similarly argues, with reference to combined and uneven development in the Caribbean during the twentieth century, that gothic figures such as the *massacouraman* signal "a different kind of existence—a different way of being human," via their bodily manifestations of the "reorganisation of existing ecological unities."[94] For Niblett, the transcorporealities of gothic bodies allow for both the registration of the transformations attendant on the expansion of imperialist capitalism *and* the embodiment "of an amalgam of multiple orders of existence" that do not ascribe to "the contained corporeality of the isolated individual of capitalist modernity."[95]

Viewed with Niblett, Monteiro's gothic becomes particularly

powerful, as it provides a visual vocabulary that enables him not only to give form to the "ghosts" of past environments that contour Black bodies under conditions of global crisis but also to approach the human in ways that avoid recourse to the modern "Western" subject—the same subject who gives to the Anthropocene its name. In this sense, Monteiro's gothic bodies resonate with Alexander Weheliye's description of "different genres of the human,"[96] which attend to the "always enfleshed alterities of being human."[97] These corporeal alterities, to which gothic has long been attuned, simultaneously recall Sylvia Wynter's delineation of a decolonial project that unsettles the production of "Man-as-Human" through attention to "the worldviews of those who have been cast as non-Human or less-than-Human."[98] Monteiro's work is alive to this imperative, as it maps the modalities of an uneven geography of global crisis in which racial violence is practiced and lived, while also paying tribute to the emancipatory Black corporealities that both emerge in its wake and exceed its terms.

While Monteiro's use of gothic may be more explicitly attuned to such a decolonial praxis, Okri's short story offers "distinctive understandings of suffering" that equally serve as "speculative blueprints" for "new forms of humanity."[99] Like Monteiro's work, Okri's narrative highlights the devastating effects of atmospheric toxicity on Black bodies and environments but places equal emphasis on the forms of endurance that emerge under the lived conditions of racial ecologies. Salient here is that Okri's tale concludes with a poignant reflection on the relations of care that structure the friendship between Marjomi and Emokhai. As the story draws to a close, Emokhai searches the polluted "red city" for Marjomi, eventually finding him asleep in his makeshift dwelling.[100] Marveling "at the gentle ferocity of his spirit," Emokhai watches over his slumbering friend, careful to maintain the peace he finds in sleep, noticing how his face is "completely devoid of its [previous] tortured expressions."[101] Here, then, the act of caring becomes framed in terms that emphasize the resilience that remains even in the absence of obvious agency. While Emokhai and Marjomi dwell in the "intimate monstrosities" produced by petro-capitalism, this lived condition also inspires a commitment to forms of caring rooted in "the shared materiality of suffering."[102] When Marjomi awakes, Okri concludes his story with a final scene in which the friends smoke dope stolen from "the governor's secret farms."[103]

The story ends, then, with this final act of defiance, in which the act of breathing—the narrative's key source of traumatic wounding and pain—is reconfigured into a practice of insurgence that takes the form of social bonding and pleasure.

Thus, by recentering the historical conditions of atmospheric toxicity, and by constructing alternative forms of humanness that respond to the realities of racial ecologies, both Okri and Monteiro reject the universalized version of Western man in favor of gothic visions that emphasize "a lived experience of modernity's violence."[104] Situating this experience as "historically and systemically produced within an uneven global geography,"[105] the gothic aesthetics in Okri's story and Monteiro's photographs construct new forms of humanity that work against concepts of the human that are embedded in colonial capitalist systems and, in so doing, breathe life into a decolonial praxis for understanding the Anthropocene that might usefully disorientate us from our inherited habits of interpreting and acting in the world.

NOTES

1. Jack Morgan, "Toward an Organic Theory of the Gothic: Conceptualizing Horror," *Journal of Popular Culture* 32, no. 1 (1998): 73.

2. Chris Baldick, Introduction to *The Oxford Book of Gothic Tales* (Oxford: Oxford University Press, 1992), xix.

3. For a delineation of the racial disparities of Covid-19, see Robert Booth and Caelainn Barr, "Black People Four Times More Likely to Die from Covid-19, ONS Finds," *The Guardian*, May 7, 2020, https://www.theguardian.com/world/2020/may/07/black-people-four-times-more-likely-to-die-from-covid-19-ons-finds.

4. Mike Baker, Jennifer Valentino-DeVries, Manny Fernandez, and Michael LaForgia, "Three Words. 70 Cases. The Tragic History of 'I Can't Breathe,'" *New York Times*, June 29, 2020, https://www.nytimes.com/interactive/2020/06/28/us/i-cant-breathe-police-arrest.html.

5. Sipho Kings, "Breath, Death and Data: The Air in Our Cities Is Killing Us," June 28, 2019, https://mg.co.za/article/2019-06-28-00-breath-death-and-data-the-air-in-our-cities-is-killing-us/.

6. Abhijit Mohanty, "Extracting a Radioactive Disaster in Niger," *Down to Earth*, March 5, 2019, https://www.downtoearth.org.in/blog/health-in-africa/extracting-a-radioactive-disaster-in-niger-63451.

7. World Health Organization, "Air Pollution," https://www.who.int/health-topics/air-pollution.

8. World Health Organization, "Air Quality Guidelines," https://www .who.int/airpollution/publications/aqg2005/en/.

9. Priyom Bose, "How Africa Is Tackling Pollution (Plastic/Emissions)," *AzoCleanTech,* September 25, 2019, https://www.azocleantech.com/ article.aspx?ArticleID=977.

10. Rob Nixon, *Slow Violence and the Environmentalism of the Poor* (Cambridge, Mass.: Harvard University Press, 2011).

11. Pavithra Vasudevan, "An Intimate Inventory of Race and Waste," *Antipode* 4 (2019): 1–21.

12. Stacey Balkan, "Anthropocene and Empire," *The Caravan: A Journal of Politics and Culture,* October 19, 2016, http://www.caravanmagazine .in/vantage/anthropocene-and-empire-amitav-ghosh.

13. Of these critics, Donna Haraway, Monique Allewaert, and Jason Moore have risen to prominence for their formulation of terms such as the "Plantationocene" and the "Capitalocene," proposing that the extractive processes of capitalist slavery might be taken as the key transition into the current planetary condition of ecological devastation. See this collection's Introduction for more.

14. Christina Sharpe, *Monstrous Intimacies: Making Post-slavery Subjects* (Durham, N.C.: Duke University Press, 2010).

15. Ruth Wilson Gilmore, "Fatal Couplings of Power and Difference: Notes on Racism and Geography," *Professional Geographer* 54, no. 1 (2002): 15–24.

16. Vasudevan, "An Intimate Inventory," 11.

17. Vasudevan, 11.

18. Saidiya Hartman, "The Belly of the World: A Note on Black Women's Labors," *Souls* 18, no. 1 (2016): 166–73.

19. Vasudevan, "An Intimate Inventory," 17.

20. Frantz Fanon, *Wretched of the Earth,* trans. Constance Farrington (London: Penguin, 2001), 30.

21. Jonathan Silver, "Suffocating Cities: Climate Change as Social-Ecological Violence," in *Urban Political Ecology in the Anthropo-obscene,* ed. Henrik Ernstson and Erik Swyngedouw (Arlington, Va.: Routledge, 2019), 143.

22. Silver, "Suffocating Cities," 139.

23. Ben Okri, "In the City of Red Dust," in *Stars of the New Curfew* (London: Vintage, 1999).

24. Adam Voiland, "Choking on Saharan Dust," NASA Earth Observatory, February 2, 2016, https://earthobservatory.nasa.gov/images/144970/ choking-on-saharan-dust.

25. Okri, "In the City," 74.

26. Okri, 61.

27. Michael Watts, "Oil Frontiers: The Niger Delta and the Gulf of Mexico,"

in *Oil Culture,* ed. Ross Barret and Daniel Worden (Minneapolis: University of Minnesota Press, 2014), 197.

28. Ellekhe Boehmer, "Foreword: Empire's Vampires," in *Transnational and Postcolonial Vampires: Dark Blood,* ed. Tabish Khair and Johan Höglund (New York: Palgrave Macmillan, 2013), ix.

29. Theresa Bane, *Encyclopedia of Vampire Mythology* (Raleigh, N.C.: McFarland, 2010), 111.

30. Bane, 111.

31. Okri, "In the City," 49, 46.

32. Okri, 42, 43, 46.

33. Okri, 45.

34. Okri, 48.

35. Okri, 48.

36. Benita Parry, "Aspects of Peripheral Modernisms," *Ariel* 40, no. 1 (2009): 27–55.

37. Peter M. Lewis, "Nigeria's Petroleum Booms: A Changing Political Economy," in *The Oxford Handbook of Nigerian Politics,* ed. Carl Levan and Patrick Ukata, 7:502–19 (Oxford: Oxford University Press, 2018).

38. Okri, "In the City," 39.

39. Okri, 47.

40. Jean Comaroff and John Comaroff, "Occult Economies and the Violence of Abstraction: Notes from the South African Postcolony," *American Ethnologist* 26, no. 2 (1999): 279–303.

41. David McNally, *Monsters of the Market: Zombies, Vampires and Global Capitalism* (Leiden: Brill, 2011).

42. McNally, 6.

43. Jennifer Wenzel, "Petro-magic-realism: Toward a Political Ecology of Nigerian Literature," *Postcolonial Studies* 9, no. 4 (2006): 449–64.

44. McNally, *Monsters,* 7.

45. McNally, 185.

46. Andrew Apter, *The Pan-African Nation: Oil and the Spectacle of Culture in Nigeria* (Chicago: University of Chicago Press, 2005), 201.

47. Immanuel Wallerstein, *The Modern World-System I* (New York: Academic Press, 1974).

48. Leonore Schick, Paul Myles, and Okonta Emeka Okelum, "Gas Flaring Continues Scorching Niger Delta," *Deutsche Welle,* November 14, 2018, https://www.dw.com/en/gas-flaring-continues-scorching-niger-delta/a-46088235.

49. Godson Rowland Ana, "Air Pollution in the Niger Delta Area: Scope, Challenges and Remedies," *IntechOpen,* September 26, 2011, https://www.intechopen.com/books/the-impact-of-air-pollution-on-health-economy-environment-and-agricultural-sources/air-pollution-in-the-niger-delta-area-scope-challenges-and-remedies.

50. Okri, "In the City," 61.

51. Okri, 42.

52. Okri, 57.

53. Hartman, "Belly of the World."

54. Okri, "In the City," 41.

55. Vasudevan, "An Intimate Inventory," 17.

56. Romy Opperman, "A Permanent Struggle against an Omnipresent Death: Revisiting Environmental Racism with Frantz Fanon," *Critical Philosophy of Race* 7, no. 1 (2019): 69.

57. Sharpe, *In the Wake,* 111.

58. Frantz Fanon, *A Dying Colonialism,* trans. Haakon Chevalier (New York: Grove Press, 1994), 128.

59. Opperman, "A Permanent Struggle," 74.

60. Fanon, *Wretched of the Earth,* 29.

61. Fanon, *A Dying Colonialism,* 65.

62. Fabrice Monteiro, "Bio," https://fabricemonteiro.viewbook.com/bio-1.

63. Nadia Beard, "Senegal Waste Pickers Fight Dump Closure amid Hazards and Health Risks," Reuters, November 23, 2016, https://uk.reuters .com/article/us-senegal-environment-landrights/senegal-waste -pickers-fight-dump-closure-amid-hazards-and-health-risks -idUKKBN13I1KV.

64. Simeon Ehui, "'You Only See Trash. We See a Treasure Trove': Why Waste Management in Senegal Is a Critical Step toward Sustainability," *World Bank Blogs,* March 9, 2020, https://blogs.worldbank.org/ nasikiliza/you-only-see-trash-we-see-treasure-trove-why-waste management-senegal-critical-step.

65. Gaia has, of course, become a central concept in environmental science and the humanities. See James Lovelock, *The Ages of Gaia: A Biography of Our Living Earth* (New York: W. W. Norton, 1995), and Bruno Latour, *Facing Gaia: Eight Lectures on the New Climatic Regime,* trans. Cathy Porter (Cambridge: Polity Press, 2017).

66. Zahra Jamshed, "'The Prophecy': Photographer Captures Terrifying Vision of Future," *CNN Edition,* November 17, 2015, https://edition .cnn.com/style/article/photographer-fabrice-monteiro-the-prophecy/ index.html.

67. Jamshed.

68. Esthie Hugo, "Looking Forward, Looking Back: Animating Magic, Modernity and the African City-Future in Nnedi Okorafor's *Lagoon,*" *Social Dynamics* 43, no. 1 (2017): 49.

69. Henry Drewal, "Introduction: Charting the Journey," in *Sacred Waters: Arts for Mami Wata and Other Divinities in Africa and the Diaspora,* ed. Henry Drewal (Bloomington: Indiana University Press, 2008), 2.

70. Alex van Stipriaan, "Creolization and the Lessons of a Watergoddess

in the Black Atlantic," in *Multiculturalism/Power and Ethnicities in Africa,* ed. Antonionio Custodio Goncalves (Porto: Centro de Estudos Africanos, 2002), 93.

71. Gordon Gill, "Doing the Minje Mama: A Study in the Evolution of an African/Afro-Creole Ritual in the British Slave Colony of Berbice," *Wadabagei* 12, no. 3 (2009): 7–29.

72. See Drewal, *Sacred Waters.*

73. Michael Niblett, "Peripheral Irrealisms: Water-Spirits, World-Ecology, and Neoliberalism," in *Marxism, Postcolonial Theory and the Future of Critique: Critical Engagements with Benita Parry,* ed. Sharea Deckard and Rashmi Varma (New York: Routledge, 2019), 81.

74. Jason W. Moore, *Capitalism in the Web of Life: Ecology and the Accumulation of Capital* (London: Verso, 2015), 13.

75. Michael Niblett, *World Literature and Ecology: The Aesthetics of Commodity Frontiers, 1890–1950* (Cham, Switzerland: Palgrave Macmillan, 2020), 61.

76. "11 Major Oil Spills of the Maritime World," *Marine Insight,* January 10, 2020, https://www.marineinsight.com/environment/11-major-oil-spills-of-the-maritime-world/.

77. "Operations: Senegal," https://www.cairnenergy.com/operations/senegal/.

78. "Operations: Senegal."

79. "'Fish Are Vanishing'—Senegal's Devastated Coastline," *BBC News,* November 1, 2018, https://www.bbc.co.uk/news/world-africa-46017359.

80. Meaghan Beatley and Sam Edwards, "Overfished: In Senegal, Empty Nets Lead to Hunger and Violence," *Medium,* May 30, 2018, https://gpinvestigations.pri.org/overfished-in-senegal-empty-nets-lead-to-hunger-and-violence-e3b5d0c9a686.

81. Sushmita Roy, "Senegal, One of the World's Biggest Ocean Polluters, Will Enforce Fines on Plastic Use," *Global Citizen,* August 1, 2019, https://www.globalcitizen.org/en/content/senegal-will-enforce-fines-on-plastic-use/.

82. Beatley and Edwards, "Overfished."

83. Matthew Green, "Plundering Africa: Vicious Fishmeal Factories Intensify the Pressure of Climate Change," Reuters, October 30, 2018, https://www.reuters.com/investigates/special-report/ocean-shock-sardinella/.

84. Meg Samuelson, "Thinking with Sharks: Racial Terror, Species Extinction and the Other Anthropocene Fault Lines," *Australian Humanities Review* 63 (2018): 31.

85. Sigmund Freud, "The "'Uncanny,'" 1919, *Standard Edition* 17 (1954): 219–52.

86. Julietta Singh, "Disposable Objects: Ethecology, Waste, and Maternal Afterlives," *Studies in Gender and Sexuality* 19, no. 1 (2018): 53.

87. Vasudevan, "An Intimate Inventory," 8.

88. Singh, "Disposable Objects," 49.

89. Vasudevan, "An Intimate Inventory," 4.

90. Gabeba Baderoon, "Surplus, Excess, Dirt: Slavery and the Production of Disposability in South Africa," *Social Dynamics* 44, no. 2 (2018): 257–72.

91. Vasudevan, "An Intimate Inventory," 2.

92. Singh, "Disposable Objects," 49.

93. Priscilla Frank, "Afrofuturist Photos Transform Senegal's Trash into Haute Couture," *Huffington Post,* October 7, 2015, https://www.huffingtonpost.co.uk/entry/fabrice-monteiro-senegal-trash_n_560f1262e4b0af3706e0fbf4.

94. Michael Niblett, "Demon Landscapes, Uneven Ecologies: Folk-Spirits in Guyanese Fiction," in *Cultures of Uneven and Combined Development: From International Relations to World Literature,* ed. James Christie and Nesrin Degirmencioglu (Leiden: Brill, 2019), 335.

95. Niblett, 337, 328.

96. Alexander Weheliye, *Habeas Viscus: Racializing Assemblages, Biopolitics, and Black Feminist Theories of the Human* (Durham, N.C.: Duke University Press, 2014), 2–3.

97. Julietta Singh, *Unthinking Mastery: Dehumanism and Decolonial Entanglements* (Durham, N.C.: Duke University Press, 2018), 4.

98. Walter D. Mignolo, "Sylvia Wynter: What Does It Mean to Be Human?," in *Sylvia Wynter: On Being Human as Praxis,* ed. Katherine McKittrick (Durham, N.C.: Duke University Press, 2014), 108.

99. Weheliye, *Habeas Viscus,* 14.

100. Okri, "In the City," 78.

101. Okri.

102. Vasudevan, "An Intimate Inventory," 17.

103. Okri, "In the City," 79.

104. See chapter 9.

105. See chapter 9.

Part II

PLANTATIONOCENE

According to Donna Haraway, the Plantationocene is a way of conceptualizing the planetary impacts of the exploitation of natural resources, monoculture expansion, and forcible labor. These practices began in the 1600s and have underpinned modernity, climate change, and ecological destruction. The impacts of these structures have unevenly affected various populations and regions, with the Global South being the area that has suffered from the worst exploitation of extractive practices, environmental damage, and coercive work. This particular *-cene* calls attention to the devastating history of colonization and imperialism and underscores asymmetrical hierarchies based on gender, racial difference, sexual orientation, class distinctions, and economic privilege. But the Plantationocene is not located only in the annals of colonial history: the plantation, which we often consider to be a long-abandoned system, continues to shape us today.[1] This is because it is part of the present landscape of a current world order that has shifted, altered, and impacted the conditions of what is broadly conceptualized as a model inspired by the plantation's unbound exploitation of land and people. It can thus be seen in the structures of oppression that continue to be defined by racial difference; it can be found in what is often defined as the "natural" system of manufacturing and labor based on industrial capitalism; it can be witnessed in the factory system of exploited labor and in the disciplining of animals and plants in the agricultural and factory farm models of reproduction.

The Plantationocene productively shifts conceptions of the Anthropocene away from the Eurocentric focus on the Industrial Revolution, the steam engine, and coal as the center of planetary ecological change. The plantation points to the crucial role of capitalism in the hierarchical relations between the Global North and Global South and how the power dynamics related to various forms of exploitation highlight the crucial role of plantations in shaping the present global crises. The Plantationocene is simultaneously connected to, and distinct from, the Capitalocene, for it arises out of the fourteenth- and fifteenth-century capitalism of European metropoles like Florence and Bruges but marks a shift in the transcontinental movement of people, plants, and animals. By the sixteenth century, the technologies of travel engendered a triangulation in the movements of commodities and the forced migration of people from the west coast of Africa. Nations in the North Atlantic exploited the natural resources and people in parts of Africa and Asia, developing plantations for sugar, cotton, coffee, tea, and other products on land that was often farmed by the free labor of chattel slavery, indentured servants, or a subaltern workforce. Moreover, the plantation calls attention to the interconnectedness of species and, as such, challenges the distinctions between human and nonhuman while also eroding the binary of human embodiment and nature/society.

Like all -cenes, there are limitations to the Plantationocene. Janae Davis et al. have argued that the definition of this concept currently circulating in environmental humanities risks cementing the notion that the plantation is a space of human control over nature, in the process sidelining critical examination of the plantation as a racist mode of development.[2] With these limits in mind, we also recognize that the term *Plantationocene* has benefits for underscoring the critical dynamics shaping the current socioeconomic crisis: the planetary movements of people and plants, reductions of biodiversity, transnational corporate interests involved in long-distance capital investments, and the processes of coercion and control that define the labor market. "Situated at the intersection of forcibly displaced labor, long-distance financial investment, and intensive cultivation of the soil, the plantation is a systematic practice of relocation that initiates major upheaval in the relations between humans, animals, plants, and other organisms."[3] The term is also useful in that it highlights the "historical relocations of the substances of living and dying around the Earth as a necessary prerequisite to their extraction."[4] Anna Tsing pushes this further by arguing that plantation logics are characterized by scalability and interchangeability. The notion of scalability, she writes, refers to the proficiency through which the plantation was able to expand using an established blueprint, which includes the decimation of local peoples and plants, installation of plantation infrastructure on cleared lands, and importation of foreign people and crops. Her notion of interchangeability refers to the ability to exchange one species for another, evident in the plantation practice of substituting cane stock for enslaved people.[5] In the context of massive factory farming, the clear-cutting of ancient forests, the ecological destruction of mining for fossil fuels, and so much more, it is productive to reflect on how gothic and the Plantationocene informs our understanding of the current ecological crisis and how it is rooted in logics of environmental modernization, homogeneity, and control, that were developed on historical plantations.

To date, the Plantationocene has begun to gain theoretical and critical currency. The term is particularly useful because it underscores gothic narratives of the United States and Global South, intersecting with a history of settler gothic and slavery in the Black Atlantic and plantation histories in the Americas and across the Global South. The planetary impacts of the Plantationocene and its cultural productions are located in the intersections of race and colonialism and their material conditions. Significant for us are the ways in which plantation ideologies and structures continue to be woven into our everyday lives, from Amazon warehouses to factory farms to plantation tourism to the practice of hiring workers on no-hours contracts. In this, the Plantationocene calls attention to the planetary effects of extractive practices and monocultural development, as well as coercive, neoliberal labor practices that underscore modernity and climate change from the 1600s to the present and provide a useful way of reflecting on human-agented ecological change.

The essays in this part engage with how the Plantationocene is the basis for monstrous human animal and nonhuman animal forms: agricultural and horticultural practices, factory farming, and colonial and neocolonial exploitations of the land. In Lisa M. Vetere's chapter "Horrors of the Horticultural: Charles Brockden Brown's *Wieland* and the Landscapes of the Anthropocene," the horror is located within the landscape of the garden and Plantationocene through ornamental plants as well as crops. Here the colonial garden is the site of a gothic imagination in which plants are not just aesthetic spectacles but also part of monocultural production that feeds horrific ecological presences that turn plants into monstrous forms: the more a gardener tries to rid the land of unwanted plants, the stronger and more resistant those plants become. Likewise, in Dawn Keetley's "*True Detective*'s Folk Gothic," the reading of the television series moves from the plantation landscapes of Louisiana's sugar and petro-economies, with their historical exploitations of bodies and natural resources, to a racialized past that connects bodies to plantation landscapes. The bodies found in fields are inextricably linked to the racialized history of an environmental racism unearthed in the presence of a monoculture that links sugar and slavery, as well as a gothic environment that is a significant form of folk gothic.

Bodies and plantations—particularly nonhuman animal bodies on factory farms—are the subjects of Justin D. Edwards's chapter "Beyond the Slaughterhouse: Anthropocene, Animals, and Gothic," which explores animal agriculture, mass death, food production, and climate change. Here Edwards examines animals and gothic, not from the perspective of animal revenge horror or animal torture in gothic texts, but in narratives of animal agriculture and the ways in which the structures that support meat consumption and factory farming are destroying ecosystems and generating methane gases that impact climate events. On the plantations of corporate animal agriculture and animal product producers, the greed that fuels consumption engenders the destruction of animal, nonanimal, and animal human life. This indifference to planetary life, Edwards maintains, meshes with the difference toward the life that is consumed within the factories that raise and slaughter nonhuman animals for meat.

NOTES

1. Michael Warren Murphy and Caitlin Schroering, "Refiguring the Plantationocene," *Journal of World-Systems Research* 26, no. 2 (2020): 400–415.
2. Janae Davis, Alex A. Moulton, Levi Van Sant, and Brian Williams, "Anthropocene, Capitalocene, . . . Plantationocene? A Manifesto for Ecological Justice in an Age of Global Crises," *Geography Compass* 13, no. 5 (2019): 124–38.
3. Pieter Vermeulen, *Literature and the Anthropocene* (London: Routledge, 2020), 13.
4. Donna Haraway, Noboru Ishikawa, Scott F. Gilbert, Kenneth Olwig,

Anna L. Tsing, and Nils Bubandt, "Anthropologists Are Talking—about the Anthropocene," *Ethnos* 81, no. 3 (2016): 557.

5. Anna Tsing, *The Mushroom at the End of the World: On the Possibility of Life in Capitalist Ruins* (Princeton, N.J.: Princeton University Press, 2015), 38–40. See also Alfred J. López, "The Plantation as Archive: Images of 'the South' in the Postcolonial World," *Comparative Literature* 63, no. 4 (2011): 402–22, and Janae Davis, Alex A. Moulton, Levi Van Sant, and Brian Williams, "Anthropocene, Capitalocene, . . . Plantationocene? A Manifesto for Ecological Justice in an Age of Global Crises," *Geography Compass* 13, no. 5 (2019): 124–38.

« 6 »

Horrors of the Horticultural

Charles Brockden Brown's Wieland *and the Landscapes of the Anthropocene*

LISA M. VETERE

> Art should never be allowed to set a foot in the province of nature, otherwise than clandestinely and by night. Whenever she is allowed to appear here, and men begin to compromise the difference— Night, gothicism, confusion and absolute chaos are come again.
>
> —William Shenstone, *Unconnected Thoughts on Gardening* (1764)

What are the landscapes of the Anthropocene? An investigation into the etymology of the word *landscape* itself reveals the entanglement of human and nonhuman. In nearly every sense of the word, *landscape* signals a process and not a thing—the process of framing and rendering the "natural," whether in pictures, scenes, points of view, perspectives, or sketches.[1] In eleven out of its fourteen definitions for *landscape,* the *Oxford English Dictionary* dates the word's first usages to the years between 1599 and 1725, not coincidentally an era of large land seizures on a global scale, whether enclosures in England or the colonization of the Americas. The claiming, clearing, and cultivation of these lands in the pursuit of profit have created enormous devastation—on an unimaginable scale for peoples, places, animals, plants, and the ecosystems that encompass and sustain them. Such destruction has firm roots in the eighteenth century, when the mechanization of the Industrial

Age, driven by Enlightenment notions of scientific mastery, allowed for mass production in both factories and plantations. We
in the twenty-first century still bear witness to the magnitude of
this legacy: the wreckage of Hurricane Katrina in 2005, Deepwater
Horizon's horrific 2011 oil spill, monstrous heaps of plastics menacing increasingly acidified oceans, species on the brink of extinction, CO_2 pollution at irreversible levels, and, here in 2020, swarms
of killer hornets and the lethal Covid-19 disease, all spreading horror and terror throughout the globe. The temporalities and scale of
such events unsettle; enormous quantities of space and time separate cause from effect. As Nathan Hensley and Philip Steer declare,
"our anthropogenic present has scrambled the narrative templates
and historical logics previously available for organizing experience."[2] Hensley and Steer suggest that literary logics could foster a
better understanding of the Anthropocene. With its haunted cas-
tles, tortured bodies, menacing monsters, and supernatural powers, the gothic mode provides just such a coherent form with which
to make sense of a senseless reality.

In this essay, I will examine what is known as the "first American
gothic novel," Charles Brockden Brown's *Wieland,* for the ways it
helps to make sense of the Anthropocene. Published in 1798—a
key historic moment in the unfolding of the Anthropocene—the
novel tells the story of the Wieland family in the years between the
French and Indian War and the American Revolution (1763–76) as
the Pennsylvania family haunted by disembodied voices and then
afflicted by the tragedy of the murder of a family by its patriarch.
Wieland recounts an invasive presence in the family's Pennsylvania plantation who contaminates its landscape and buildings with
his unruly behavior, behavior that may (or may not) have incited
the grotesque murder. I argue that the plantation's ornamental
landscape—and the horticultural logics that shape it—plays a major role in the horrors of the novel. The logic of ornamental gardens
banishes unwanted plants and people; it seeks control and order,
the violation of which evokes fear and dread—surely the territory
of gothic narrative and an explanation of the power of Anthropocene texts ranging from Nathaniel Hawthorne's "Rappaccini's
Daughter" (1844) to films such as *Little Shop of Horrors* (1986) and
Swamp Thing (1982). "Plant horror" capitalizes on the terrors of
human encounters with the vegetal being that characterizes so
many a multispecies assemblage.[3] Hence the surprise that critics

have not investigated the first American gothic, *Wieland,* for its horticultural horrors. When considering the role of land in the gothic tale, scholars recognize Brown's novel as agrarian or frontier gothic,[4] but the horticultural dimension of Brown's tale has thus far gone unexplored.

In my reading, *Wieland* registers the logic of what Anna Tsing terms the "Patchy Anthropocene," or the "uneven conditions of more-than-human livability in landscapes increasingly dominated by industrial forms."[5] "Patches" are "landscape structures, that is, morphological patterns in which humans and nonhumans are arranged,"[6] and their analysis begins with attention to the multispecies history of specific landscapes. With that concept, Tsing seeks to reconcile universality and particularity to pair "systems" thinking with an acknowledgment of the heterogeneity insisted upon by critics of the homogenizing effects of the term "Anthropocene." Tsing argues that "the plantation landscape" was the very "avatar" of Enlightenment Man (Tsing's capitalization is intentional—designed to implicate and particularize the "Anthropo" of the Anthropocene). His plantations, she claims, "spread everywhere; they are modern proliferation. As machines of replication they manufacture proliferation."[7] Man as Planter declared his plantation an agricultural "improvement," serving the purpose not only of enhanced productivity but also of signaling his claim to its legitimate ownership. Part of the claiming involved representing the land as Nature with a capital *N,* a tabula rasa without a trace of prior peoples and plants—hence the drive to empty the land before establishing the landscape structure. Only when emptied could Enlightened Man then transport both human and nonhuman from other places to stake his claim in this "New" World. He regarded both as mere matter—the bodies that performed the work organized for them by the owners—and so His abduction, enslavement, and torture of Africans left His conscience clear.[8] Reduced to the cultivation of single crops at the expense of all others, plantations thus become, as Tsing explains, "ecological simplifications in which living things are transformed into resources—future assets—by removing them from their life worlds. Plantations are machines of replication, ecologies devoted to the production of the same."[9]

Plantation landscapes function with their headquarters in the metropole—their land dedicated to production managed from afar and their products shipped back to the metropole for consumption. This division of the globe into separate production and consumption zones replicated and accelerated the scale and logic of industrial mass production. Like European (and eventually North American) factories, plantations separated their intense monocultural production from all other activity, both rigidly and geographically. Planters functioned as the plantation's "Mind," governing and maintaining discipline over the bodies in a global division of labor that cultivated interdependencies but also deeply entrenched and devastating inequalities enduring for generations. Tsing considers the plantation so impactful a machine that she, along with Donna Haraway, supplements (rather than replaces) the contested term of *Anthropocene* by identifying the geological epoch as the "Plantationocene."[10] The Plantationocene's "simplifying" of ecologies has had insidious unintended consequences, as so often happens with so many practices throughout the Anthropocene. Complex ecosystems cannot be simplified and instead produce cycles of resistance and increasing violence against that resistance. Resistance inevitably emerges because peoples, plants, soil, and animals do not remain inert; they do not stand still or stop growing. When "disentangled" from their "life world," to use Tsing's terms, beings act unpredictably; they become what she calls "feral proliferations" that proliferate precisely because of "the affordances of specific landscape forms," in this case, the plantation.[11] Because humans cannot function as mere matter, displaced and enslaved peoples resist, run away, and rebel. "Cleared" land does not remain so, despite the demarcation of surveyor lines. Plants may be removed, but they leave their roots behind. Birds and other "wild" animals may spread seeds from other plants and drop them into the fields, where they root and grow once again.

The transplants, both human and nonhuman, brought into the fields fail to behave as expected. Unruly plants interfere with monocultural production and are labeled pests or "weeds" that must be removed, thus tasking agricultural workers to weed as well as sow and reap. Weeding seeks, by definition, to reduce biodiverse ecosystems and thus, by necessity, continually disentangles multispecies ecologies. Yet its goals are also continually foiled, as such land disturbances transform the soil into an even more appealing place for even more weeds. According to Clinton Evans, eighteenth-century agricultural texts characterized weedy plants as demons, their language growing increasingly hostile as the century wore on: "enemies," "spurious Kindred," robbers and rapists even. Evans quotes eighteenth-century writer William Ellis, who "used terms such as 'abominable,' 'stinking,' 'venomous,' and 'rampant' to describe some of the more troublesome weeds."[12] This invective, not surprisingly, led to even harsher responses to the weed: a "war," says Evans, that expends "more human energy" than "any other single human task."[13] Weeds became plants to exterminate rather than to tolerate. This war of extermination was fought on the fields of the plantation and led the weeds to grow physiologically stronger and more lethal. This ever-escalating cycle creates the kind of horrific ecological feedback loop described by Timothy Morton in *Dark Ecology* (2018) and is characteristic of the horrors of the Anthropocene. To return to the Anthropocene as gothic, this loop itself is what turns plants into monsters. The more planters try to purge fields of unwanted plants, the stronger and more resistant those plants become. The more virulent the invasives become, the more toxic the treatment. Tsing calls plantations "breeding grounds for virulence."[14] With monsters created through such a loop, it becomes difficult to locate the blame.

But the Plantationocene created monstrous plants not only through its agricultural but also through its horticultural practices; colonial plantations, that is, grew ornamental plants as well as crops. Ornamental gardens and cultivated plantation fields may seem like absolute opposites: one exists purely as aesthetic spectacle—plants to look at—and the other as monocultural production zone, or plants to eat. In his study of "the country and the city," however, Raymond Williams discerns a foundational link between farms and pleasure gardens. Landscape gardening of the eighteenth century may have emerged as a benign aesthetic, a "high point of agrarian bourgeois art,"[15] but Williams insists on its economic impacts and its necessary entanglement with the materiality of agricultural production:

And we cannot then separate their decorative from their productive arts; this new self-conscious observer was very specifically the self-conscious owner. The clearing of parks as 'Arcadian' prospects depended on the completed system of exploitation of the agricultural and genuinely pastoral lands beyond the park boundaries. There, too, an order was being imposed: social and economic but also physical. The mathematical grids of the enclosure awards, with their straight hedges and straight roads, are contemporary with the natural curves and scatterings of the park scenery.[16]

Williams goes on to observe that the mandate to banish "the facts of production"[17] determines the very purpose of landscape design: to create a view of "Nature" without laborers or the traces of their work. To naturalize the landowner's rightful and moral claim to the property, landscape gardens presented (and constructed) both a "commanding prospect" and an "unspoiled nature."[18] Hence an emotional need to deny production motivated the art. Jill Casid's work on the plantations of the West Indies goes a step further and traces their presence in the gardens constructed by owners for their European country homes. In fact, Casid calls the picturesque gardens created by the arrangement of such aesthetic plants a "displaced referent"[19] of the colonial plantation. Paintings, narratives, poems, or landscapers' designs all inscribe this use of ornamental plants to mark land enclosures and, at the same time, to deny their dependence on productive labor. Transplanted majestic oaks lined the entrance to the master's manor, and imported shrubs and flowers marked the boundaries of his property. Such plants performed similarly to the hedges and lines enclosing the English (and Irish) countryside. Casid extends Williams's analysis by noting the "hybridity" crafted by such views, arguing that they further indexed the "natural" basis of such command: "the discourse of picturesque intermixture endeavored to 'make a landscape' that would appear as a spectacle of variety rather than monoculture, an oasis of harmony and repose rather than violence and deadline labor."[20] Additionally, and unmentioned by both Williams and Casid, both plantations and garden landscapes also share the mandate to "banish" plants serving as bodily nourishment as well as the evidence of production. The plantation system's vegetation, whether growing in an ornamental garden or throughout a sugarcane field, provides only "empty" calories for both cultivator and consumer.

Charles Brockden Brown specifically identifies the patriarch of *Wieland*'s eponymous family, Theodore Wieland, as an avid practitioner of horticulture. In her epistolary account of the family history, his sister Clara Wieland alludes to the nature of her brother Theodore's work with cultivars on Mettingen, the family estate on the banks of the Schuylkill River, just miles north of Philadelphia:

"The ground which receded from the river was scooped into valleys and dales. Its beauties were enhanced by the horticultural skill of my brother."[21] While Clara's use of passive voice effaces the agent of the "scooping" of dirt, she does tell us that her brother's work included "bedecking" the constructed slopes "with every species of vegetable ornament, from the giant arms of the oak to the cluttering tendrils of the honey-suckle." Furthermore, the novel classifies Theodore's work as "skill," driven by his mental capacity, rather than as menial labor, performed only by his body. As an ornamental gardener with book learning, the patriarch of Mettingen exploits the aesthetic pleasure and symbolic meaning of the plants rather than their power to nourish life—to feed his family. In Williams's terms, Theodore "banishes" the "facts of production" and instead imposes the design of Mind.

Theodore the horticulturalist crafts this landscape precisely as prescribed by English garden theorists like Thomas Whately and William Shenstone—writers of botanical tomes studied by plantation owner Thomas Jefferson and emulated by the owners of English country homes, such as Alexander Pope and Horace Walpole, the latter known as the author of the first gothic novel, *Castle of Otranto* (1764). Whately's *Observations on Modern Gardening* identifies four essential elements of landscaping, which endow the first four chapters of his book with their titles: "Of Ground," "Of Wood," "Of Water," and "Of Rocks." To achieve picturesque gardens, he advises that the ground be varied in elevation, its shapes creating the most beauty through curves, both concave and convex; unevenness; irregularities; hollows; swells; and other irregularities.[22] Whately recommends that its outline be "advanced sometimes boldly forward, sometimes retired into deep recesses; broke all the sides into parts, and marked even the plain itself with irregularities."[23] Theodore meticulously follows this expert's instructions in his design of Mettingen's landscaping; he includes rocky cliffs, dangerous precipices, rollicking water, and grounds both convex and concave. Clara, Theodore, and their families wander serpentine pathways through the shade of orchards and down "declivities" to their summerhouse and temple. The novel describes the location of the Wieland property: "The eastern verge of this precipice was sixty feet above the river which flowed at this foot. The view before it consisted of a transparent current, fluctuating and rippling in a rocky channel, and bounded by a rising scene of cornfields and orchards" (12). Like her father's estate, Clara's house borders a "river bank [that] is . . . so rugged and steep as not to be easily descended" (71). All this is designed only to evoke emotion, whether pleasure or admiration of its owner's governing prowess.

The novel reinforces horticulture's association of plants with mind rather than body by totally erasing any trace of actual food being eaten; quite the contrary, thought, not food, most often nourishes the characters. In fact, Brown often uses words associated with eating to describe thought. For example, Clara's description of her brother reveals that while agriculture is practiced at Mettingen, the estate nonetheless is devoid of food; Clara has no buttermilk to give Carwin when he first appears at her home, only water (58). Indeed, the novel defines Theodore by the way that he *chews* the cud of thought: "what distinguished him was a propensity to *ruminate* on these truths" (25). He "ruminates" (38) first hearing Carwin's voice. Clara also "ruminates" after first hearing the voices in her bedroom (68). The siblings, alas, come by their habits honestly, as their father "entertained no *relish* for books" until he discovered the "book written by one of the teachers of the Albigenses, or French Protestants" (8), which satisfied a "*craving* which had haunted him" (9). Clara further describes her father as having *imbibed* his opinions on missionary work on the frontier (10). When the Wielands actually do encounter meals, they are only mentioned because the characters do *not* eat them: Clara "could taste no food, nor apply to any task" while waiting for Pleyel to arrive at Mettingen for a dramatic reading of a German play (91). Clara's brother is similarly averse to nourishing his body. Catherine describes how Theodore "scarcely ate a morsel, and immediately after breakfast went out again" after Pleyel informed him of Clara's supposed intrigues with Carwin (122). It's as if the Mettingen plantation seems to cultivate "thought" as its single crop, feeding mind alone. As landscape paintings elide the facts of production, *Wieland* banishes any trace of food and sustenance, turning the necessary biological process into an abjected other that, as all gothic scholars know, will certainly return to haunt someone or something.

Yet while the novel represents Theodore Wieland as the model gentleman landowner of the eighteenth century, seeking to sow the seeds of his disembodied universalized intellect throughout the globe, it nonetheless roots its story in a very particular place. For Charles Brockden Brown's *Wieland*, that particular place is his villa, Mettingen, on the "suburban" outskirts of Philadelphia: a very particular urban landscape and heir to the specific environmental history of its construction. Philadelphia provided nourishing ground for a tale of horticultural horror. The settlement itself was practically founded on the notion of the affective power of gardens. When planning his Pennsylvania colony, William Penn expressed his intention to ornament Philadelphia with garden cultivation on all original city lots, and the city is still known as "a greene Country Towne." Early maps, such as *A Portraiture of the City of Philadelphia,* drawn by Penn's surveyor general, Thomas Holme, in 1683, imagined the future city as a grid of streets interspersed with green spaces ornamented with fictional trees. Thus, as Elizabeth Milroy declares in *The Grid and the River: Philadelphia's Green Places, 1682–1876,* "Philadelphia was a picture before it was a city."[24] Perhaps this sense of Philadelphia as fertile ground on which to build art also lured someone like Ben Franklin, a young artisan from Boston, who disciplined—or "managed"—himself there into an international legend.

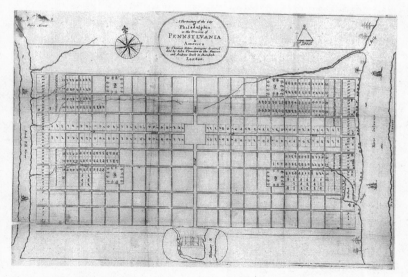

Figure 6.1. Thomas Holme, *A Portraiture of the City of Philadelphia in the Province of Pennsylvania in America,* 1683. This early map illustrates the "Enlightened" plan to deforest and establish the land composing the core of the future city of Philadelphia. This grid design depends on the lines of fictionalized and homogenous trees to mark the boundaries between urban living and natural spectacle. Courtesy of Barry Lawrence Ruderman Antique Maps Inc.

As Philadelphia grew and prospered, the wealthier families built "country homes" adorned by picturesque English gardens in the Schuylkill River Valley. Scull and Heap's maps encode the increasing popularity of this "country" life during the 1750s, depicting hundreds of houses within ten miles of the city limits. Such "villas" functioned as leisure, or "pleasure," grounds for those who worked primarily in the city. As Philadelphia's grid of streets named after trees became a prototype for cities growing throughout the colonies (e.g., *Nightmare on Elm Street*), so too did these villas provide a blueprint for suburban development throughout North America. An essential element of this blueprint was that those country homes be not of the country but easily accessible from the city—of the city, but not in it. These villas were, perhaps not incidentally, known as "plantations," an association to which *Wieland* calls attention when it exposes the family estate's reliance on slave labor: "The cheapness of land, and the service of African slaves, which were then in general use, gave him who was poor in Europe all the advantages of wealth" (11). Brown indirectly references Philadelphia's role in the slave trade, as merchants, sailors, and consumers in the seaport city purchased commodities like rum from the West Indies. For many of the owners of these Schuylkill plantations, like Wieland's father, the capital to dedicate themselves to the design of ornamental gardens attached to the villa derived from such commerce.

Pleasure gardens continued to shape Philadelphia's history for the second half of the eighteenth century. In the 1770s, Philadelphians gathered at public gardens along the banks of the Schuylkill to celebrate colonial victory in the American Revolution; locations such as Bush Hill and Gray's Gardens hosted patriotic fetes staged on "greens" conveniently cleared by the British army during its 1778 occupation. As Milroy observes, such deforestation gave spectators a clear prospect for these influential performances of nationalism. The private gardens of the Schuylkill villas also drew many tourists to consume these views, as the area grew into a popular tourist site and, at the same time, a "formative site within the early Republic's literary and artistic canon: some of the earliest landscape painting and prints produced in the new United States were views of the Schuylkill and Wisshickon."[25] Misrepresented as pristine forests, the prospects featured in this body of artistic work sent the message that estate owners were the natural "stewards of these picturesque landscapes."[26]

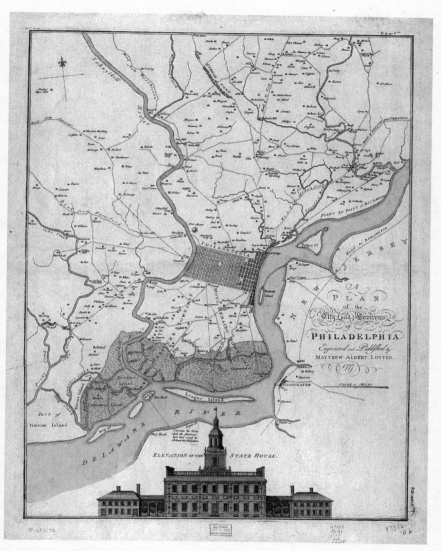

Figure 6.2. Nicholas Scull, George Heap, and William Faden, *A Plan of the City and Environs of Philadelphia,* 1777. This later edition of the 1752 map attests to the expansion of the Schuylkill villas into the surrounding "countryside" of the city. Holmes's city grid maintains its position at the center. Library of Congress, Geography and Map Division, http://www.loc.gov/item/74692193/.

One of the best-known owners of these landscapes, William Hamilton, fashioned his estate, the Woodlands, along the west bank of the Schuylkill—the same side of the river where Theodore Wieland Sr. built his Mettingen plantation. Grandson of the famous lawyer who successfully defended Peter Zenger's freedom of the press, William Hamilton frequently corresponded with founders such as Thomas Jefferson and George Washington as they modeled their own landscapes on Hamilton's Woodlands.[27] An amateur botanist himself, Hamilton worked with the prominent traders John Bartram and his son William, who collected and exchanged seeds (mostly of ornamentals) throughout the globe. His commerce was driven in part by the demand for ornamentals from the owners of the Schuylkill villas. Bartram's exchanges with European naturalists, such as Linnaeus and Hans Sloane, helped make Philadelphia a hub of the international horticultural movement. Hamilton brought many an ornamental to his Philadelphia grounds, a habit that also earned him the dubious honor of introducing several invasive botanicals that still trouble North American landscapes: the tree of heaven and the lombardy poplar.[28]

Charles Brockden Brown exploits the horror that such invasive species evoke by having his novel's villain, Carwin, also first emerge as an uninvited guest on the lawns of the fictional Schuylkill estate. Similar to a noxious weed, Carwin's invasion of the Wieland estate precipitates (if not causes) a chain of events leading to the murder of the Wieland family. Clara, in fact, first sees Carwin in places that weeds typically inhabit: the edges of riverbanks, "the road, and in the harvest field" (57). She further describes the weedy invasive as "rustic and aukward," with "a careless and lingering" pace. Carwin moves out of Clara's view and enters into "a copse at a small distance" (58). Carwin's presence on a lawn that customarily "was only traversed by men whose views were directed to the pleasures of the walk or the grandeur of the scenery" (58) surprises and bewilders her. The intruder's presence on her picturesque lawn unsettles her emotions so intensely that she spends hours afterward trying to capture his image in a portrait. She can't sleep: "half the night passed in wakefulness and in contemplation of this picture" (61), her mind turned into a rapidly proliferating field of entangled, weedy thoughts.

Weedy thought, feral proliferations—vining, growing without restraint or competitors—then infect the plantation of Wieland

Figure 6.3. James Peller Malcolm, *Woodlands, the Seat of W. Hamilton Esquire, from the Bridge at Gray's Ferry, Philadelphia*, c. 1792–94. Note the name of the estate: "Woodlands" refers not to the image's center but to the careful layout of its arboreal margin, acting as a microcosm of the design of Philadelphia itself (and later North American suburban plans more generally). Courtesy of the Dietrich American Foundation.

and all of its residents as Carwin's mischievous biloquism entwines them in circuitous thought and unresolved confusion. It is on this picturesque property—not only its lawn but its serpentine paths, its orchards, copses, rugged precipices, and hidden recesses—where Carwin performs much of his early ventriloquist's magic, the magic that begins to confound the minds and then ruin the lives of the Wielands. They hear mysterious voices in Theodore Wieland's meticulously landscaped backyard, up the hill on the way to the temple; and not much later, the voices are heard at Clara's—when she falls asleep in her summerhouse and nearly kills herself sleepwalking into a chasm (dreaming of such chasms even, showing how they have seeped into her unconscious)—and then when Pleyel thinks that he hears Clara and Carwin together in the "recess," another word that repeatedly appears. Carwin is able to throw his voice and deceive these suburban denizens because the very winding paths and crevices and recesses in the rocks characteristic of the English landscape garden disguise and distract their ability to link sight and sound and thus make sense of the sensory input that should produce reasoned thinking.

With the venomous rage against weeds of an eighteenth-century agricultural writer, Clara Wieland never ceases to blame Carwin for the madness of her brother, the murder of her family, and the destruction of her home and idyllic lifestyle, despite witnessing firsthand her brother's attempt to kill her. No doubt the murder of the Wielands is a brutal and horrific act. Yet the novel resists an easy explanation of the cause for such abhorrent violence. Thinking the novel through the Plantationocene, one might reconsider the virulence of its homicide. What causes a weed to become monstrous vegetation? In *Memoirs of Carwin the Biloquist* (1803–5), Brown's sequel to *Wieland,* he provides a glimpse into the transplanted Carwin's functioning in his original "life world," a family farm in the "western district" (281) of Pennsylvania. On his family farm, Carwin's father discouraged his son from book learning and even physically punished him for the ambitions that it fostered. Yet Carwin nonetheless manages to learn something very important, and very useful: to observe and contemplate the prospect of a landscape—the very skill that owners of Schuylkill estates used to demonstrate their particular kind of Enlightenment authority.

Carwin recounts an event in his fourteenth year that began when his father insisted that his son perform some pastoral labor—fetching cattle from their pastures. Fear of his father's wrath, in fact, pervades the scene and propels Carwin's behavior and thought. When arriving at the meadow to satisfy his father's demands, Carwin discovers that it's not as easy as he'd expected: a cow has escaped. In contemplating the broken fence that seems to have allowed it, Carwin succumbs to the deep pleasure of contemplation, wondering about its causality. Panic once again erupts and disrupts his wastrel ways, forcing Carwin to figure out a way to get back home quickly. The "beaten road" (283) is too long and circuitous, as it winds *around* rather than *through* a high rocky precipice overlooking a stream "agitated by an eddy" (283).

But the terrified son decides to risk taking the shorter but more perilous route. He stumbles through "abrupt points and gloomy hollows," "entangled in a maze" (284), until happening upon a concealed "narrow pass" that could bring him home more safely than the stream yet more quickly than the beaten road. This "hollow," however, is dark and steep. Carwin becomes fearful of its shade, imagining "goblins and spectres" (284), as he admits, and then starts to sing to fight off the fear. That's when he hears the first echo, though it's indistinct at first. He repeats his "ditty" to the lost cow, "in the shrill tones of a Mohock savage" (284), and wonders at hearing his voice repeated at least five times. "My terrors were quickly supplanted by delight," Carwin observes, and his amusement with his experiment delays him yet another hour. Hurrying home, Carwin arrives to find his father only mildly reproachful, and so he finds himself eager to return to the "recess," a "glen" "which overlooked a wide extent of this romantic country, [and] gave himself up to contemplation and the perusal of Milton's Comus" (287). He practices more, tries something else—a "notion of sound, similar to these, but produced by other means than reverberation" (287). His "experimenting" (287) initially fails, but then through sheer will and repetition, he manages to master his skill.

This origin story demonstrates several significant things about Carwin's power. First of all, he coproduced it with a very intricate and picturesque landscape. Here in Carwin's lifeworld, such geological structures function not as setting and background but as actants and figures. Without the material properties of its rocks, serpentine paths, recesses, streams, precipices, mazes, and uneven elevations, Carwin could not have learned the biloquism that brought the horrors to the Wieland's estate. The hollow literally sang to him; the stream and the precipice guided his way; the fence and the rocks dictated the rhythm and movement of his thoughts. Though acting in an ecology nearly identical to Mettingen's, though performing nearly exactly the same act, Carwin here is kept in check, his powers failing to result in lethal consequences. Although Clara tries to represent Carwin as a force of ungovernable nature invading the temple of art and intellect, Brown's backstory for Carwin reveals that his toxic effects on the plantation derive not just from an untrammeled nature but from art and nature interwoven over generations. His history shows that Carwin developed his art in a natural theater (itself probably a product of deforestation happening in the area of Carwin's small family farm for at least fifty years prior) and that his art at that time did not foster a murderous virulence. In the agricultural fields of his birth, Carwin was mischievous, but not homicidal. Among other factors, Carwin's father and brother acted as "natural competitors" in that ecosystem and constrained him. Only when removed from this "lifeworld" does Carwin become a catalyst of unimaginable horror. But the murder does happen at Mettingen, a plantation designed to cultivate a pure mind disentangled from its material roots, a place whose monoculture is vigilantly bounded by ornamental plants and the affective power of horticulture.

But what is at stake in the recounting of a single fictional incident of a virulent homicide? To return to the horrors of the Plantationocene and its geological temporalities, the node that is this novel operates in a much wider network, on a much grander scale. The kind of horticulture that Charles Brockden Brown represents in *Wieland* has grown exponentially since his gothic novel was first published in 1798. Throughout the nineteenth century, expert agricultural writers relentlessly promoted gardening of ornamental plants as a means to "improve" (in both moral and aesthetic terms) American private properties. In his "Editor's Preface" to his edition of William Darlington's 1865 *American Weeds and Useful Plants*, botanist George Thurber explains one of the purposes of his revisions: to urge nineteenth-century Americans to grow more ornamentals on their properties. He cites his decision to add descriptions of both weeds and ornamentals to his botanical catalog, even though "these latter may not strictly come within the class of 'useful,'" as being driven by emotion:

> The hope of inducing farmers to render the exterior of their homes more attractive by surrounding them with beautiful shrubbery, which, once planted, will be a permanent source of gratification not only to the possessors, but to travelers who pass them. The yards of our country dwellings generally present a forlorn appearance, which the attempt often made to cultivate a few coarse flowering plants, rather increases than removes.[29]

With the belief in the moral and intellectual value of landscape improvement growing in strength throughout the first half of the nineteenth century, upper-middle-class professionals of the antebellum era described this horticultural reform movement as one to induce "the right feeling" or affect within those who grew ornamentals. Thurber, for instance, talks of the "gratitude" that could be felt by farmers if they would only surround themselves with beautiful shrubbery. In her study of "The Moral Dimensions of Horticulture in Antebellum America," Tamara Plakins Thornton asserts that horticultural societies and journals started to emerge in the 1830s.[30] Such periodicals as the *Horticultural Register* and the *Magazine of Horticulture* published many an article meant to popularize and democratize horticulture in America, their chief method being affective—or to inspire.[31]

During the Anthropocene's "Great Acceleration," the democratization of gardening proliferated the virulent cycle of pest extermination. As the mandatory setting for the American dream, the monocultural lawn became the ornamental plant for the masses, its care and cultivation becoming the obsession of millions of humans, especially in the United States—designed all for affect and not at all for sustenance. The affect associated with lawns is intense and obsessive, institutionalized in many ways. For example, zoning laws in many municipalities throughout the United States criminalize the growing of plants for sustenance on front lawns. Twenty-first-century gardeners, farmers, and agribusinesses invest billions of dollars to exterminate ever more resilient species of invasive pests from these affective machines, status symbols, and miniature plantations. The health and environmental costs of the desire to control these monstrous plants are staggering. *Newsweek*'s Douglas Main reported on a 2016 study published in the journal *Environmental Sciences Europe,* revealing that Americans have applied 1.8 million tons of the herbicide, or weed killer, glyphosate since its introduction in 1974. "Worldwide, 9.4 million tons of the chemical have been sprayed onto fields. For comparison, that's equivalent to the weight of water in more than 2300 Olympic–size swimming pools. It's also enough to spray nearly half a pound of Roundup on every cultivated acre of land in the world."[32] The report adds that in March 2015, the World Health Organization's International Agency for Research on Cancer unanimously determined that glyphosate is "probably carcinogenic to humans." Research has also shown that herbicides have become part of many human (and likely nonhuman) bodies, as "glyphosate is an endocrine disruptor, meaning that it interferes with the proper functioning and production of hormones."[33] The same *Newsweek* article recounts the response of weedy plants to this assault: they develop resistance to the herbicides, to which companies like Monsanto and Dow have responded by producing, selling, and spraying even more toxic herbicides. The weeds become monstrous, in other words. How did this happen? Who made these monsters? Perhaps beginning to understand them as uncanny and gothic materializations of Morton's notion of the "strange loops" of the Anthropocene might be a start.

NOTES

1. *OED Online*, s.v. "landscape," https://www-oed-com.ezproxy.monmouth .edu/view/Entry/105515.
2. Nathan K. Hensley and Philip Steer, eds., *Ecological Form: System and Aesthetics in the Age of Empire* (New York: Fordham University Press, 2019), 4.
3. See Timothy S. Miller, "Lives of the Monster Plants: The Revenge of the Vegetable in the Age of Animal Studies," *Journal of the Fantastic in the Arts* 23, no. 3 (2012): 460–79; Dawn Keetley and Angela Tenga, *Plant Horror: Approaches to the Monstrous Vegetal in Fiction* (Berlin: Springer, 2016); Daisy Butcher, *Evil Rule: Killer Tales of the Botanical Gothic* (London: British Library, 2020); and Natania Meeker and Antónia Szabari, "Plant Horror: Love Your Own Pod," in *Radical Botany: Plants and Speculative Fiction,* 144–70 (New York: Fordham University Press, 2020).
4. On *Wieland* as frontier Gothic, see Jeffrey Andrew Weinstock, *Charles Brockden Brown* (Cardiff: University of Wales Press, 2011). On Brown's novel as agrarian gothic, see Tyler Roeger, "Agrarian Gothic: Carwin, Class Transgression, and Spatial Horrors in Charles Brockden Brown's *Wieland*," *Literature in the Early American Republic* 6 (2014): 85–111.
5. Anna Lowenhaupt Tsing, Andrew S. Mathews, and Nils Bubandt, "Patchy Anthropocene: Landscape Structure, Multispecies History, and the Retooling of Anthropology," *Current Anthropology* 60, no. 20 (2019): S186.
6. Tsing et al., S188.
7. Anna Tsing, "Earth Stalked by Man," *Cambridge Journal of Anthropology* 34, no. 1 (2016): 4.
8. For a fascinating reading on how enslaved peoples deployed their own understanding of personhood that contested their objectification by the plantation system, see Monique Allewaert, *Ariel's Ecology, Plantations, Personhood, and Colonialism in the American Tropics* (Minneapolis: University of Minnesota Press, 2013).
9. Tsing, "Earth Stalked by Man," 4.
10. Donna J. Haraway, *Staying with the Trouble: Making Kin in the Chthulucene* (Durham, N.C.: Duke University Press, 2016), 99.
11. Tsing et al., "Patchy Anthropocene," S186.
12. Clinton Evans, *The War on Weeds in the Prairie West: An Environmental History* (Calgary, Alb.: University of Calgary Press, 2002), 38.
13. Evans, xi.
14. Tsing, "Earth Stalked by Man," 13.

15. Raymond Williams, *The Country and the City* (Oxford: Oxford University Press, 1973), 124.

16. Williams, 124.

17. Williams, 125.

18. Williams, 125.

19. Jill Casid, *Sowing Empire: Landscape and Civilization* (Minneapolis: University of Minnesota Press, 2005), 77.

20. Casid, 14.

21. Charles Brockden Brown, *"Wieland" and "Memoirs of Carwin the Biloquist,"* ed. Jay Fliegelman (1798; repr., New York: Penguin, 1991), 53–54.

22. Thomas Whately, *Observations on Modern Gardening: Illustrated by Descriptions* (1770; repr., London: Forgotten Books, 2012), 2.

23. Whately, 4.

24. Elizabeth Milroy, *The Grid and the River: Philadelphia's Green Places, 1682–1876* (Philadelphia: Pennsylvania State University Press, 2016), 3.

25. Milroy, 4.

26. Milroy, 4.

27. James A. Jacobs, "William Hamilton and the Woodlands: A Construction of Refinement in Philadelphia," *Pennsylvania Magazine of History and Biography* 130, no. 2 (2006): 181–209.

28. On the history of these "unruly" trees, see Joanna Dean, "The Unruly Tree: Stories from the Archives," in *Urban Forests, Trees, and Greenspace: A Political Ecology Perspective,* ed. L. Anders Sandberg, Adrina Bardekjian, and Sadia Butt, 162–75 (London: Routledge, 2014); Christina D. Wood, "'A Most Dangerous Tree': The Lombardy Poplar in Landscape Gardening," *Arnoldia* 54, no. 1 (1994): 24–30; and Behula Shah, "The Checkered Career of *Ailanthus altissima*," *Arnoldia* 57, no. 3 (1997): 21–27.

29. George Thurber, Editor's Preface to William Darlington, *American Weeds and Useful Plants: Being a Second and Illustrated Edition of Agricultural Botany: An Enumeration and Description of Useful Plants and Weeds, Which Merit the Notice, or Require the Attention of American Agriculturists* (1865; repr., Sydney: Wentworth Press, 2019), vii.

30. Tamara Plakins Thornton, "The Moral Dimensions of Horticulture in Antebellum America," *New England Quarterly* 57, no. 1 (1984): 6.

31. Thornton, 8.

32. Douglas Main, "Glyphosate Now the Most-Used Agricultural Chemical Ever," *Newsweek,* February 2, 2016, https://www.newsweek.com/glyphosate-now-most-used-agricultural-chemical-ever-422419.

33. Main.

« 7 »

True Detective's Folk Gothic

DAWN KEETLEY

The critically acclaimed first season of HBO's *True Detective* (2014) has already garnered significant critical attention, including numerous essays that take up the series' representation of the ecological damage wrought by the petroleum industry. Riding around the flat terrain of southern Louisiana with oil refineries omnipresent in the background, the two protagonists, Detectives Marty Hart (Woody Harrelson) and Rust Cohle (Matthew McConaughey), rarely comment on the taken-for-granted landscape of their lives. In one striking exception, though, Rust comments, "This pipeline is carving up this coast like a jigsaw. Place is gonna be underwater in thirty years" (1:3). The intertwined petrochemical industry, climate, and devastated communities of the Louisiana bayous that Rust describes here have attracted most of the criticism on the series.[1] Delia Byrnes writes, for instance, that the series is preoccupied with the "intimate entanglement of bodies and oil," and Min Hyoung Song adds that "bodies and landscapes are intermingled" as "part of some combined ecology."[2] Through attention to the ways in which refineries shape lives and permeate bodies, the criticism on *True Detective* has tended toward a presentist focus (with gestures toward an apocalyptic near future), a focus that tends to flatten both space and time. As Christopher Lirette eloquently puts it, in the Louisiana of *True Detective*, "pipes and roots and crosses and truck stops and abandoned schools and caves and the good life and the sad withering of imagination and bigger, national and global things are so enmeshed they flatten out."[3] These flattened landscapes of the series resonate with a phrase spoken twice (including by Rust and drawn from Nietzsche): "Time is a flat circle" (1:5).

True Detective certainly seems "flat," its story line spread out across the even landscape of the present moment. It thus seems the perfect text to read alongside certain posthuman/speculative realist/ecological theories that insist on the enmeshment of human lives with the agential nonhuman—the elements, the weather, the land, and refineries. *True Detective* offers up, in both its visual and narrative logics, the "flat ontologies" of posthuman theory, things entangled with people. Rob Coley epitomizes this dominant reading of the series when he names what he calls Rust Cohle's "geo-material sensibility": Rust engages in an "ecological detection," as he is able to attune himself to "the weird aesthetic entanglement of human culture and planetary matter."[4] As illuminating as such readings are, they also inevitably obscure; they exert pressure to emphasize the present and, in their propensity toward "flatness," tend not to see the unevenness of the effects of such things as the transnational petrochemical industry and hurricanes. As Jennifer Wenzel has claimed, "Anthropocene species talk" can be a "troubling new universalism that disregards the highly uneven roles that different groups of humans have played in the transformation of the planet, and the uneven distribution of risk and resilience in confronting this human-made world."[5] The "flat" readings of *True Detective* also fail adequately to recognize both race and the history, as well as the more recent history that lies between the present and what Coley calls the "temporality of the Anthropocene: a deep time, a planetary time."[6]

A more human, more recent history—the history of the sugar plantation and of race and slavery—is crucial to the plot and the landscape of *True Detective,* however. The dead white body that begins the series, the body of the murdered Dora Lange, is found in a sugarcane field. And that's important. It has also scarcely been addressed, with the exception of Sharae Deckard's provocative claims about the show's deployment of "the resource Gothic of the sugar plantation" and its linking of the "petroleum uncanny" to the "sugar uncanny."[7] Dora's body has instead been read primarily through its enmeshment with the petroleum industries of Louisiana. Dora Lange, Song writes, "embodies what humans become, even in life, if the extractive zone depicted in the show grows and proliferates."[8] But Dora Lange's body is inextricable from the cane fields of Louisiana and its racialized history. We must look, as Wenzel insists, to the intractability of "environmental racism and the toxic burdens borne unevenly by racialized minorities."[9] We must look to the monoculture—sugar—that created Louisiana's wealth, along with its slave system and its poverty.

To unearth the residues of sugar and slavery in season 1 of *True Detective* is also to recognize its gothic nature, specifically what I call its "folk gothic." Two critics have mentioned the gothic in relation to the HBO series, but only dismissively.[10] Attention to gothic objects, place, and time can, though, adumbrate a depth hidden within more "flat" readings. While the refineries are integral to the flat landscapes of the series, captured in the many wide-angle and extreme long shots, the gothic intrudes in tight close-ups, shots that emphasize foreground over background, detail over distance, the proximate over the remote.[11] Whereas the shots that capture the refineries, moreover, express a self-evident causality—literally linking the petrochemical industry to the eroding land, the encroaching water, the desperate poverty, and the ruined buildings and land—the shots that capture the gothic are isolating, atomizing; on the surface, they appear to inhibit connections rather than clarifying them. The elements of the gothic are also displaced from the self-evident contemporaneity of the petrochemical landscape, hinting at a lost pastoral, a more untouched nature—what one critic has called a "wilderness" that only appears to be separate from the pipelines and refineries scarring the landscape.[12] But the gothic objects and "wilderness" of *True Detective*, along with the "folk" who own, create, and inhabit them, are profoundly implicated in the Anthropocentric logic of the series, opening up a history of sugar crops and plantations that is more entangled with present ecological destruction than is apparent in the series' overwhelming visual focus on the petrochemical landscape.

Gothic Objects

The strange gothic objects of *True Detective* include Dora Lange's body itself, reified and out of place lying under an isolated oak tree in a sugarcane field. These objects include her spiral tattoo, the antlers and crown set on her head, and the strange objects woven of branches that both stand and hang nearby. The objects consist of a girl's drawing of the "green-eared spaghetti monster" who chased her through the woods; references to the "Yellow King" and "Carcosa"; a painting on the wall in an abandoned church; other strange

Figure 7.1. The object found in Marie Fontenot's playhouse. *True Detective* (1:2).

objects made of twisted branches; a photograph of masked figures on horseback; and a videotape of more masked figures performing a strange, horrifying, and ultimately unseen (by the viewer) ritual. These objects will get repeated, always visually and narratively unmoored from explanatory context. These are the "clues" that Rust and Marty strive to link together in their work of pursuing the killer.

In the second episode, the camera dwells on the shape made from branches found in the playhouse at the home of Marie Fontenot's uncle and aunt's house, where Marie used to play before she went missing five years before Dora Lange's body was found. The shot tells us the object is "Evidence," but of what nobody knows. All Rust can do at this moment is draw (rather than interpret) the strange things he sees—more details that are awaiting the "whole," the "system" that will (eventually, he hopes) explain them. In refusing any relation with what is around them—in refusing assimilation into the perceptual schemas of those who struggle to see them—these objects all persist in their strangeness: what Graham Harman has called a "weird realism," although, as he says, "realism is always in some sense weird," as it is about "the strangeness in reality that is not projected onto reality by us."[13] The very title of this second episode, "Seeing Things," draws attention to the series' weird "things," which defy explanation, and it suggests that these "things" may well contain a truth that could be hidden by the imposition of familiar systems. As Marty says to Rust, "you attach an assumption to a piece of evidence, you start to bend the narrative to support it" (1:1).

In their simultaneous visibility and withdrawn obscurity, the gothic objects of *True Detective* draw our attention away from the flat expanses and global entanglements of the petrochemical landscape to the strange, isolated detail. And there is nothing insignificant about the detail. As Rust, notorious for taking copious notes, says to detectives Maynard Gilbough and Thomas Papania (who are investigating a 2012 murder that uncannily resembles Dora Lange's), "you never know what the *thing*'s gonna be, do you? A little *detail* somewhere down the line ... breaks the case" (1:1; emphasis mine). Details carry weight. Details can illuminate a whole that is otherwise occluded. Details are synecdochic of systems we don't understand (yet), of ways of knowing that are visually represented in *True Detective* in their being cut off from their surroundings in close up, not splayed out and always already illuminated in wide-angle shots.

As detectives, Marty and Rust not surprisingly position "things" as evidence. But mystifying objects are also part of the gothic tradition. As Fred Botting has described it, the gothic includes "the partial visibility of objects, in semi-darkness, through veils, or behind screens ... denying a clearly visible and safe picture of the world."[14] *True Detective*'s gothic objects, however, are not concealed by darkness or veils or screens; they are always fully illuminated, fully visible in the camera's close-ups. They are obscure *in and of themselves,* the series insists. While Rust and Marty certainly hope that they will become explicable, the gothic objects of *True Detective* persist in defying the main characters' prevailing systems of knowledge.

Folk Gothic

The objects of *True Detective,* and the details to which they draw our attention, constitute a specifically *folk* gothic in that they are, it turns out, created by the "folk," a category grounded in what James Thurgill has called "perceived division in social classes, specifically between the burgeoning 'mainstream' of the middle classes and working rural communities: the 'folk.'"[15] Thurgill roots this class-based understanding in Alan Dundes's seminal study of folklore, in which he describes the "folk" as "predicated upon a two-tier system whereby folklore and folk communities were seen as the subjugated element of a classist society." The "folk" represent what Dundes calls the "uncivilized element of a civilized society," distinct from the entirely "primitive" but nonetheless "believed to have retained survivals of savagery."[16] The gothic objects of *True Detective* are *folk* gothic objects, then, in that they are created by largely invisible "swamp folk" who are "dug in off the grid" and who are definitely associated with the savage and the primitive (1:4); they are the impoverished, the marginalized, and the left behind in Louisiana's global petrochemical economy, and they can thus orient us to the uneven effects of the Anthropocene.

Indeed, the folk gothic objects of *True Detective* are associated almost exclusively with poor whites who cling to existence in the pockets of land and ruined buildings left behind by the processes of global industry.[17] But the notion of the "folk" as a (single) subjugated class—predicated on a "two-tier system" that separates the "middle class" and the "rural," as well as the ways in which environmental destruction is lived—is complicated in *True Detective* by race. If the poor whites of the Louisiana "wilderness" are hard to see, African Americans are as good as invisible. Song aptly states that African Americans, "with their few speaking parts and spectral presences, are depicted as mere objects."[18] Certainly Marty and Rust never recognize that race has anything to do with the crimes they are investigating; they never mention race as important. Rust ignores it entirely, and Marty recognizes it only to manipulate the presumed racism of his white colleagues (keeping his place as "one of them") and his boss (so he will allow them to continue their investigation).

It matters, though, that the cult to which the series' "monsters"—Dewall and Reggie Ledoux and Errol Childress—belong is explicitly white. While the Ledoux cousins and Childress are certainly "rural" and "uncivilized"—left behind by global capitalism and its urban, upwardly mobile middle class—they both enjoy and cling to a white heritage and privilege. It is no coincidence that Errol Childress is discovered to be living in a former plantation.[19] The cult includes not only poor, marginalized whites but also some of the most powerful white men in the state: former sheriff of Vermilion Parish Sam Tuttle; his son, Christian ministry magnate Billy Lee Tuttle; and his nephew and governor of the state Edwin Tuttle (none of whom are ever brought to justice). The "folk" in *True*

Detective, then, are a cross-class group firmly rooted in racial privilege. Importantly, one of the two glimpses we get of this "cult" is in a photograph of Dora Lange as a young girl with five horsemen wearing pointed hoods that clearly evoke the Ku Klux Klan (1:2).

That the "folk" of *True Detective*'s folk gothic constitute an explicitly racialized community is evident in the reason Billy Lee Tuttle set up the rural Christian schools, the Wellspring Program, which served to supply the cult with its (always white) sacrificial victims. The official explanation given to Rust and Marty is that Tuttle wanted to provide "an alternative to the kind of secular, globalized education that our public schools were promoting" (1:6). The "cult" is, then, bound up with both religion and the local and rural as opposed to the secular and the global, a very familiar dichotomy in folk gothic and horror. We also learn, though—more fleetingly, as race always flickers only fleetingly into view in this series—that the schools were also expressly designed to circumvent federally mandated "busing" designed to ensure the racial integration of the public school system. As one man on Pelican Island tells Rust and Marty, the local children either went to the Christian Light of the Way School "or they were bused to Abbeville. State said a kid got to be bused two hours to school," he comments in disgust. When Rust looks, a bit later, at the Light of the Way yearbook, the children are exclusively, and not surprisingly, white (1:3).[20] This reference remains undeveloped, but it is crucial to understanding the way in which the "cult" reinforces cross-class white power, erects an unbreachable racial divide, even as it sacrifices poor *white* children to do so. The often-invisible centrality of racial division to the narratives of folk gothic and horror emerges into view.

Anthropocene Gothic Place and Time

A critical gothic object in *True Detective* is the tree by which Dora Lange's body is found. The prominence of the tree highlights the particular *place* of the crime, and yet it is almost completely irrelevant to the detectives, as the series draws a stark line between the detective and the gothic imagination. When Marty and Rust arrive at the crime scene, Rust heads immediately for the body, and the camera dwells, with him, on the distinctive aspects of the crime, narrowly defined as Dora Lange's naked body, the tattoo on her back, the crown and the antlers, her tied hands, the marks on her body, and her teeth. Rust gets up close, sketching her body in his notebook and talking to Marty about the ligature marks and blood pooling. Rust later describes to Marty how the killer used Dora's body as a "paraphilic love map," attaching to her body "practices forbidden by society." Rust says, "This kind of thing does not happen in a vacuum." But the context in which he is interested is the *entirely psychological* relationship between the killer and his victim. Rust pulls his attention from the body, which Marty explicitly calls a "piece of evidence," only to look at the strange wooden structures placed on the ground and hung from the tree, and then he joins other police officers walking through the sugarcane to find more "evidence" as the camera cuts away (1:1). For Rust, and the police in general, all that matters is what strictly belongs to the victim and the killer—the properties of the murder, a very narrow and clearly bounded *crimescape* in which everything else about the place, including its particular history, fades into nonexistence.

The camera, however, does not only adopt Rust's point of view; it intermittently pulls out from the "clues" to show the oak tree by which Dora's body is placed, the dirt tracks for which it marks a crossroads, and the sugarcane that surrounds it on all sides. In these shots, the gothic objects that are the focus of Rust's strictly criminological attention pull another context into sight, a gothic context that insists on the centrality of a place that is marked by its past. "Place deeply involves time," as Timothy Morton puts it.[21] Indeed, the murder of Dora Lange—one of many sacrificial victims, it turns out—is integrally bound up with the history of the place in which she is found. As in all gothic narrative, what Tim Ingold calls the "temporality of the landscape" is critical—the landscape as a record of those who have lived there and "have left there something of themselves."[22]

While Dora Lange's body is visually detached from the otherwise almost ubiquitous refineries, it is nonetheless connected to the anthropogenic landscape of rising waters, pipelines, and petrochemical plants. The cane fields in which her body lies significantly appear in the opening iconographic image of the credit sequence—a photograph by Richard Misrach, *Sugar Cane and Refinery, Mississippi River Corridor, Louisiana, 1998*.[23] With the exception of Deckard, who eloquently notes that "oil and sugar frontiers are superimposed in the credits,"[24] critics have focused almost exclusively on the refinery in their readings both of this image and of

Figure 7.2. Dora Lange's body posed by the oak tree. *True Detective* (1:1).

the series itself. The cane fields are in the foreground of the shot, however, thus insisting on the entwinement within the Anthropocene of both the petrochemical industry (Louisiana's main industry in the present) *and* a sugar monoculture (Louisiana's main economy in the past and still thriving in the present). This image gestures to the centrality, in short, of sugar *as well as* oil in *True Detective*'s representations of ecological damage. The series makes manifest what Michael Niblett has argued: that "oil and sugar have been deeply imbricated in histories of colonial conquest, imperial domination, and the gross exploitation of human and extra-human nature."[25]

Certainly the Anthropocene "originated" before the petrochemical industry—before, in fact, the date many offer as the opening of the Anthropocene, the "Great Acceleration" beginning around 1945.[26] It originated even earlier than the Industrial Revolution of the late eighteenth century.[27] At a theoretical level, Morton has argued that the "Anthropocene is an event within agrilogistic space," while, more empirically, William F. Ruddiman has proffered extensive evidence of his "early anthropogenic hypothesis," arguing that the Anthropocene began with widespread land clearing for agriculture as far back as seven thousand years ago.[28] The origins of the Anthropocene may indeed lie in agriculture, but humans' profound impact on the Earth escalated when agriculture was spurred by the intertwined forces of technology, capitalism, global migration, and the slave trade. Indeed, some argue that the Anthropocene originated with the Columbian Exchange, the moment when "Old" and "New" Worlds became linked as Europeans sought "to extract wealth from the Americas."[29] Explaining her preference for *Capitalocene* over *Anthropocene*, Donna Haraway argues that the former term "suggests a longer history" than the latter, elaborating that "I think we are looking at slave agriculture, not coal, frankly, as a key transition."[30] Jason W. Moore has explicitly articulated the role of sugar in New World imperialist capitalism, arguing that the combined "New World sugar frontiers and African slaving frontiers" "freely appropriated (and exhausted)" land and humans and that the commodification of sugar "consumed forests, soils, and workers (usually slaves) at a ferocious pace" beginning in the fifteenth century.[31] *True Detective*, read through a gothic lens, illuminates the centrality of slavery and the sugar monoculture within discourses of the Anthropocene.

That Dora Lange's body is found in what Morton calls an "agrilogistic space"—by an oak tree in sugarcane fields—has been generally overlooked. Indeed, one critic, Casey Ryan Kelly, only notices it to erase its significance. He writes that Dora Lange's body was found in a "serene cane field" and then analogizes her body to "the other industrial waste products that pervade the rest of the contaminated community," thus actively expunging the violence and ecological damage wrought by agriculture, replacing sugar with oil.[32] The tree becomes more visible within the gothic register of the series, however. In the U.S. literary tradition, gothic trees are frequently entangled with the history of colonialism and slavery: the South Carolina tree where Crèvecoeur found a beaten slave suspended from a tree in a cage, for example, as well as the linden tree in Hannah Crafts's *The Bondwoman's Narrative*, from which the slave Rose and her dog were hanged and left to die.[33] *True Detective* extends this gothic tradition as its prominent tree invokes the violent appropriation of both people *and* nature.

One of the most striking aspects of the particular southern live oak tree by which Dora Lange's dead body is abandoned is that it stands solitary. This is unusual for trees and immediately signals the intervention of humans, who either planted it there alone or cut down the other trees around it. The oak tree is an immediate and graphic reminder of violent human manipulation of the natural world. The tree stands, moreover, at the crossroads of dirt tracks that cut through sugarcane fields, immediately broadening the scope to an entire agricultural system predicated on expropriating natural resources. The tree and the cane fields position nature as enmeshed, as Wenzel puts it, "within a *resource logic*, in which nature is understood as natural resource, disposed for human use and subject to human control."[34] While the petrochemical landscape invokes the vulnerability of *all* humans, the oak tree in the sugarcane fields insists on a history—specifically a slave economy—in which racialized bodies were designated as inherently precarious, disposable, and less than human. We might call this a shift in focus from the "Anthropocene" to what Haraway has called the "Plantationocene"—that is, the "devastating transformation of diverse kinds of human-tended farms, pastures, and forests into extractive and enclosed plantations, relying on slave labor and other forms of exploited, alienated, and usually spatially transported labor."[35] Both the tree and the cane fields, in short, invoke southern slavery, without which Louisiana's thriving sugarcane industry—"white gold," as one book calls it—would not have been possible.[36]

While the southern live oak is native to the region, and thus a "natural" part of the landscape, its location is at the same time "unnatural" within the diegesis of the series. The series diegetically locates Dora Lange's body in Erath, in Vermilion Parish, but the scene was filmed in a remote part of Oak Alley Plantation in St. James Parish, farther to the east, surrounded by the former great sugar plantations (almost all of them now tourist destinations). Built in the 1830s, Oak Alley is so named because of the avenue of twenty-eight large live oak trees that led from a nearby levee to the house. It was "built almost entirely by slave labor," which allowed its white inhabitants, the Roman family, to live in "princely style."[37] Jacques Roman was an "ante-bellum sugar baron" who owned 108 enslaved people at his death.[38] The oak tree by which Dora Lange's body is found, marker of the grandeur of Oak Alley, built entirely on slave labor, brings race and slavery from the periphery to the center of *True Detective*.

It is significant that Dora's body was found in a remote part of Oak Alley Plantation and thus away from the house—the seat of power. Dora's abandoned body in the first episode is mirrored by a scene we hear about in the last episode. Errol Childress's half sister and lover, Betty, describes how their grandfather (Sam Tuttle) caught her "alone in the cane fields" and raped her (1:8). Betty's brief story marks how distance (the remoteness of both the fields and those who worked in them) made plantation slavery, as well as murder and rape, possible. The geographical remoteness that amplified the ontological distancing of Black slaves from the human was itself inextricable from the appropriation of natural resources. As Wenzel puts it, "the species divide is the *ideological* fiction that colonialism uses to justify the *material* expropriation of the natural wealth of the colonized world, including enslaved human labor."[39] Like the ghosts of slaves who worked and died in the cane fields of Louisiana, Dora Lange's dead body and Betty's raped body are similarly far from the center of the plantation and from the powerful elite of the cult who sacrificed them. The antlers affixed to Dora's head evoke the species divide manipulated by those who lived in the plantations, who wielded the distinction against those who worked in their fields, and who appropriated both human bodies and the land.

Dora's crown, however, signals her difference (and Betty's) from enslaved bodies; she is white and thus, by southern planter logic, able to attain the sacredness demanded of the sacrificial victim. She is even associated with Christ through her "crown" of "rose thorns" (1:1), the wounds on her abdomen (akin to the wound on Christ's side), and her proximity to the tree: as the Acts of the Apostles claims, Jesus was "hanged on a tree."[40] Again, then, the oppression of poor whites by the elite is signaled only to also make it clear that even *poor* white bodies are higher on the scale of privilege and power than Black ones. Dora Lange and the other always white female victims of the cult were *sacrificed,* which must be distinguished, as Rey Chow points out, drawing on Giorgio Agamben, from the mere "extermination" of "bare life" in, for example, the Holocaust and, of course, southern racial slavery and its violent aftermath in Reconstruction, Jim Crow, and enduring systemic racism. This violence, the expendability of "bare life," is not covered with "sacrificial veils," Chow remarks.[41] Song has pointed out that the nonwhite characters of *True Detective* "blend into the background of the show, and as such are markers of the landscape."[42] While Dora Lange was manifestly sacrificed, Black people, both enslaved and free, are more akin to the warm soil Betty says she feels on her back as her grandfather rapes her.

Numerous critics have pointed out the perceived inadequacy of *True Detective*'s ending, in which Marty and Rust track down

Errol Childress to "Carcosa" and kill him. Song reads the finale as merely "uncovering a conventional serial killer," who, Lili Loofbou-row adds, "has nothing to teach us."[43] I would argue, though, that Errol Childress is profoundly significant, although his significance eludes Rust and Marty. Childress intentionally puts Dora Lange's body by the oak tree, in the cane fields; his murder of Dora Lange is a ritual sacrifice, and he is part of a larger cult predicated on racial segregation and oppression; his sacrificial murder is steeped in the centuries-old history of slavery, and specifically sugarcane farming, with its exploitation of people and things, of people *as* things. *True Detective* thus loops the older history of agriculture, growing and manufacturing "white gold" on the backs of enslaved people, into the petrochemical present. Both are equally depen-dent on global flows of humans and goods, both create similarly uneven effects on disparate groups of people, and both are equally implicated in humans emerging "as a 'great force of nature' in the historical record of Earth."[44] With its close attention to how "hu-mans" are divided by race, class, and access to capital, however, *True Detective* orients us to what we may better call the Plantation-ocene than the Anthropocene.[45]

Mowing Devils

Each pair of detectives sees and talks to Errol Childress before Rust and Marty confront him in "Carcosa" in the final episode. Marty and Rust see him mowing the grass at an abandoned school on Pelican Island in 1995, and Rust asks him about the school (1:3); Papania and Gilbough see him mowing a cemetery lawn in the pen-ultimate episode, and they stop to ask him directions (1:7). In both instances, the detectives see without seeing; they encounter their "monster" without realizing it. In both instances, curiously, Chil-dress is mowing in a circular fashion.[46]

Childress's circular mowing evokes, I argue, agricultural prac-tices that exceed the particular practices of growing sugarcane in nineteenth-century Louisiana; it evokes the harvesting of grain.[47] Morton begins *Dark Ecology* with a scene from Thomas Hardy's *Tess of the d'Urbervilles* (1891) in which people follow the reaping ma-chine as it moves in ever-narrowing circles around the field, inexo-rably trapping wild animals in its tightening loops.[48] For Morton, this passage, with its blurring of human and machine, represents the "twelve-thousand-year structure" of "agrilogistics" that is the "slowest and perhaps most effective weapon of mass destruction yet devised."[49] Childress's circular mowing seems a vestigial, unconscious mimicry of the reaping that Hardy depicts, and it is another image that roots Childress and his cult in agriculture and its originary damaging exploitations.

This Anthropocentric image of Childress is also folk gothic in that Childress mimics not only harvesting generally but more specifically a "mowing devil" of Hertfordshire folklore found on the title page of a 1678 pamphlet called *The Mowing-Devil; or, Strange News out of Hartford-shire.* The pamphlet describes how, in August 1678, a wealthy farmer in Hertfordshire saw that his three-and-a-half acres of oats were ready to be cut down, so he approached a poor neighbor who worked in the summer harvesting the crops of others. The poor neighbor, "as it behoov'd Him," attempted to sell his labor for a price a little above the going rate. This incensed the farmer, who then offered the man "much more under the usual Rate than the poor Man askt above it."[50] Angry words ensued, and when the poor man tried to mollify his wealthy neighbor by agreeing to mow his crop at much less than the usual rate, the farmer declared, *"That the Devil himself should Mow his Oats before he should have any thing to do with them."*[51] And, of course, that's exactly what the Devil did. In one night, the fields aflame, the Devil cut all the farmer's oats in a perfect circle. The farmer was too terrified ever to touch the field after that and it remained burned and barren. *The Mowing-Devil* thus demonstrates how a capitalist "agrilogistics" destroys both nature itself and a potentially equitable, cooperative relationship, as a field irreparably burns; and, like the devil, Childress sets the cane fields on fire in the very opening scene of *True Detective*.[52] The plight of the poor rural white man, who sees the means of employment and income slipping away in an agricultural system that will increasingly privilege only a wealthy few, will become a staple of folk horror into the twenty-first century. Errol Childress is one of those left-behind men, literally inhabiting the margins of Louisiana's sugarcane industry.[53] But then there is, in *True Detective*, the profoundly determining intervention of race. Significantly, while a rich and poor white man squabble over wages in *The Mowing-Devil*, a "black" man ends up doing the mowing and everyone, and everything, is damned. Such are the wages of slavery.

Errol Childress's reiterated circular mowing also definitively

Figure 7.3. Errol Childress mowing in *True Detective* (1:7) and the "mowing devil" from *The Mowing-Devil* (1678).

marks *True Detective* as folk *gothic* rather than folk horror. One of the most important characteristics of the latter is the sacrificial ritual, but the victim, importantly, is almost always an outsider, typically an avatar of the modern and the urban who has stumbled into the rural, archaic enclave. Borders are crucial to folk horror; they are what separates the two groups (urban and rural) who find themselves in conflict.[54] Certainly Marty and Rust, as well as Papania and Gilbough, serve as the "outsiders" typical of folk horror. They are ultimately *not* the sacrificial victims, however. The cult sacrifices its own in ways that draw on arcane, long-standing, and local traditions. *True Detective* is driven less by the transgressing of borders crucial to folk horror's narrative arc than by a vertiginous, inward circularity, exemplifying Chris Baldick's definition of the gothic as combining "a fearful sense of *inheritance in time* with a claustrophobic sense of *enclosure in space,* these two dimensions reinforcing each other to produce an impression of sickening descent into disintegration."[55] The cult in *True Detective* is in thrall to both the past and to the local, striving to renew lost power and privilege through what is in the end a form of self-cannibalization.

Although Rust and Marty eventually find and kill Errol Childress, they can't really be said to have solved the case, not least because they treat it as a murder case and not as a powerful ritual with a long history. They glimpse this truth, or at least Rust does, but only glancingly, only enough to see in the Dora Lange case a partial solution. Marty and Rust are never sure who is a part of this cult and, most important, what (and *why*) this cult actually is. Composed of wealthy and powerful as well as poor and disenfranchised white men, the cult is driven by a nostalgia for an agrarian past defined in Louisiana's immediate history by plantation slavery and racial segregation and hierarchy. While individual pathology and a twisted sexual gratification are part of the ritual (the part Rust can see), they are not all of it. Without explicitly mentioning slavery, Nic Pizolatto has written of his principal "monster," Errol Childress, that he is "a revenant of great historical evil," connected to a place "where Voudon and Santeria are practiced along the bayous and a primitivism still maintains in many places."[56] The "evil" in *True Detective* is indeed old, although it does not abide in "Voudon and Santeria." The "primitivism" of the cult's practices and rituals are tied instead, like the agricultural history they evoke, to a history that is colonialist, capitalist, and white—to an ongoing history that appropriates and destroys both people and nature.

NOTES

1. Christopher Lirette, "Something True about Louisiana: HBO's *True Detective* and the Petrochemical Aesthetic," *Southern Spaces,* August 13, 2014; Delia Byrnes, "'I Get a Bad Taste in My Mouth out Here': Oil's Intimate Ecologies in HBO's *True Detective,*" *Global South* 9, no. 1

(2015): 86–106; Rob Coley, "'A World Where Nothing Is Solved': Investigating the Anthropocene in *True Detective*," *Journal of Popular Television* 5, no. 2 (2017): 135–57; Casey Ryan Kelly, "The Toxic Screen: Visions of Petrochemical America in HBO's *True Detective* (2014)," *Communication, Culture, and Critique* 10 (2017): 39–57; Helen Williams, "Petrochemical Families: Landscape and Lineage in *True Detective*," in *True Detective: Critical Essays on the HBO Series*, ed. Scott F. Stoddart and Michael Samuel, 29–50 (Lanham, Md.: Lexington Books, 2018); and Min Hyoung Song, "*True Detective* and Climatic Horror," *Post45*, April 4, 2019, http://post45.research.yale.edu/2019/04/true-detective-and-climatic-horror/.

2. Byrnes, "I Get a Bad Taste," 88; Song, "*True Detective*."

3. Lirette, "Something True."

4. Coley, "A World," 152–53. For a discussion of "flat ontologies," see Peter Gratton, *Speculative Realism: Problems and Prospects* (New York: Bloomsbury, 2014), 93, 117, 127–28, 171.

5. Jennifer Wenzel, "Turning Over a New Leaf: Fanonian Humanism and Environmental Justice," in *The Routledge Companion to the Environmental Humanities*, ed. Ursula K. Heise, Jon Christensen, and Michelle Nieman (New York: Routledge, 2017), 165.

6. Coley, "A World," 140.

7. Sharae Deckard, "Ecogothic," in *Twenty-First-Century Gothic: An Edinburgh Companion*, ed. Maisha Wester and Xavier Aldana Reyes (Edinburgh: Edinburgh University Press, 2019), 181. Deckard makes compelling claims about the series but does not develop her reading as her focus is on contemporary postcolonial fiction. Byrnes, too, mentions Louisiana's history of plantation slavery twice, only to point out the "uneasy intimacy of Louisiana's plantation histories and its petrochemical futures," adding that it warrants further elaboration. Byrnes, "I Get a Bad Taste," 102; see also 94.

8. Song, "*True Detective*."

9. Wenzel, "Turning Over," 172.

10. Rodney Taveira merely lists tropes of southern gothic deployed within *True Detective*—"the grotesque and irrational, the supernatural and fantastical, the outré and excessive"—and leaves it at that. Taveira, "*True Detective* and the States of American Wound Culture," *Journal of Popular Culture* 50, no. 3 (2017): 586. Byrnes argues that such tropes limit the scope of the central murder and its causes, orienting the series toward the local when it is, she says, global. The series' southern gothic tropes, she writes, "have long been used to shore up geographic boundaries and associate region with ontological difference." Byrnes, "I Get a Bad Taste," 89.

11. The prominence of the gothic in season 1 is made particularly apparent in its contrast to season 3, which also follows the trails of sacri-

ficed children and is also set in the U.S. South (Arkansas), but which is not only itself signally bereft of the gothic but raises the narrative of season 1 only to strip away the gothic. Hart and Cohle were simply uncovering a "pedophile ring," we are told in season 3 (3:7).

12. Williams, "Petrochemical Families," 34, Williams's essay very effectively shows how Errol Childress is aligned with the "more primeval forces of nature" (29) and how neither is at all separate from the spaces of modernity.

13. Harman, *Speculative Realism,* 92.

14. Fred Botting, *Gothic* (New York: Routledge, 1996), 6.

15. James Thurgill, "The Fear of the Folk: On *Topophobia* and the Horror of Rural Landscapes," *Revenant: Critical and Creative Studies of the Supernatural* 5 (2020): 33–56.

16. Andrew Dundes, *Interpreting Folklore* (Bloomington: Indiana University Press, 1980), 2. Williams claims that Errol Childress represents "a primordial force that impinges on modern suburban life." Williams, "Petrochemical Families," 30.

17. It's worth mentioning *True Detective*'s evocation of another folk gothic narrative, Tobe Hooper's *Texas Chain Saw Massacre* (1974). The opening scene of *True Detective,* in which an unknown man is artfully arranging a body, replicates exactly the opening of *Texas Chain Saw*; both TV series and film feature strange "folk art" objects; and both also feature the inextricability of the past (in which some characters are pathologically mired) and the petrochemical present (the gas station in Hooper's film).

18. Song, *"True Detective."*

19. Childress's lair, "Carcosa," moreover, was filmed at Fort Macomb, near New Orleans, where Confederate soldiers camped for a while during the Civil War. Ella Morton, "The Real Location of True Detective's Carcosa," *Atlas Obscura* (blog), March 11, 2014, http://www.slate.com/blogs/atlas_obscura/2014/03/11/here_s_the_real_location_of_true_detective_s_carcosa.html.

20. The only critics who reference this crucial comment are Lirette, who mentions that one of the "traumatic events" of the series is "the aftermath of desegregation," and Deckard, who refers to the "incomplete process of desegregation" as one of the "compound catastrophes that structure contemporary life in Louisiana." Lirette, "Something True"; Deckard, "Ecogothic," 182.

21. Timothy Morton, *Dark Ecology: For a Logic of Future Coexistence* (New York: Columbia University Press, 2016), 11.

22. Tim Ingold, "The Temporality of the Landscape," *World Archaeology* 25, no. 2 (1993): 152.

23. Richard Misrach and Kate Orff, *Petrochemical America* (New York: Aperture Foundation, 2012), 50–51.

24. Deckard, "Ecogothic," 181.
25. Michael Niblett, "Oil on Sugar: Commodity Frontiers and Peripheral Aesthetics," in *Global Ecologies and the Environmental Humanities: Postcolonial Approaches,* ed. Elizabeth DeLoughrey, Jill Didur, and Anthony Carrigan (New York: Routledge, 2015), 268.
26. See Morton, *Dark Ecology,* 76, and Erle C. Ellis, *Anthropocene: A Very Short Introduction* (New York: Oxford University Press, 2018), 51, 73.
27. Ellis, *Anthropocene,* 2, 49.
28. Morton, *Dark Ecology,* 76; William F. Ruddiman, *Plows, Plagues, and Petroleum: How Humans Took Control of Climate* (Princeton, N.J.: Princeton University Press, 2005); see also Ellis, *Anthropocene,* 90–93, and Richard Blaustein, "William Ruddiman and the Ruddiman Hypothesis," *Minding Nature* 8, no. 1 (2015), https://www.humansandnature.org/william-ruddiman-and-the-ruddiman-hypothesis.
29. Ellis, *Anthropocene,* 95. The series actually explicitly, albeit fleetingly, evokes the migrations introduced in the Columbian Exchange. At one point, Rust and Marty realize the murderous cult uses the trappings of "Couris de Mardi Gras," a rural winter festival that, as Marty says, "went heavy on the saturnalia, a place where Santeria and Voudon all mash together" (1:7). Santeria and Voudon are both African religious practices, presumably brought to North America via the slave trade. Moreover, the strange wooden objects, which appear on numerous occasions, including near Dora Lange's body, are also connected to Santeria. The African American minister at the predominantly Black church in Erath tells Rust that they are what his aunt called "devil traps." When they have this exchange, the minister, Rust, and Marty are all standing in the church, crosses featuring prominently on the walls. The minister added that his aunt "loved" Jesus but "had a bit dat Santeria in her, you know?" (1:1). What most call people call "bird traps" in a Christian context are also "devil traps" in Santeria, then; the wooden objects mix both, characteristic of the hybrid religious practices that often inform folk beliefs (see also 1:7).
30. Donna Haraway, Noboru Ishikawa, Scott F. Gilbert, Kenneth Olwig, Anna L. Tsing, and Nils Bubandt, "Anthropologists Are Talking—about the Anthropocene," *Ethnos* 81, no. 3 (2016): 555.
31. Jason W. Moore, "The Rise of Cheap Nature," in *Anthropocene or Capitalocene? Nature, History, and the Crisis of Capitalism,* ed. Jason W. Moore (Oakland, Calif.: PM Press, 2016), 110, and Moore, "Wall Street Is a Way of Organizing Nature: An Interview with Jason Moore," *Upping the Anti: A Journal of Theory and Action* 12 (August 16, 2017), https://uppingtheanti.org/journal/article/12-wall-street-is-a-way-of-organizing-nature. See also Moore's study of the "sugar frontier": "Sugar and the Expansion of the Early Modern World-Economy: Com-

modity Frontiers, Ecological Transformation, and Industrialization," *Review* 23, no. 3 (2000): 409–33.

32. Kelly, "Toxic Screen," 47.

33. J. Hector St. John de Crèvecoeur, *Letters from an American Farmer* (1782; repr., New York: Penguin, 1986), 178; Hannah Crafts, *The Bondwoman's Narrative,* ed. Henry Louis Gates Jr. (New York: Grand Central, 2002), 20–26.

34. Wenzel, "Turning Over," 169.

35. Donna Haraway, "Anthropocene, Capitalocene, Plantationocene, Chthulucene: Making Kin," *Environmental Humanities* 6 (2015): 162; see also Haraway et al., "Anthropologists," 556–57, which is the transcript of a 2014 conversation in which the term "Plantationocene" was coined.

36. Glenn R. Conrad and Ray F. Lucas, *White Gold: A Brief History of the Louisiana Sugar Industry, 1795–1995* (Lafayette: Center for Louisiana Studies, University of Southwestern Louisiana, 1995).

37. Lillian C. Bourgeois, *Cabanocey: The History, Customs, and Folklore of St. James Parish* (New Orleans: Pelican, 1957), 31–32.

38. Bourgeois, 32.

39. Wenzel, "Turning Over," 168.

40. Acts of the Apostles 10:39.

41. Rey Chow, "Sacrifice, Mimesis, and the Theorizing of Victimhood (A Speculative Essay)," *Representations* 94, no. 1 (2006): 134.

42. Song, *"True Detective."*

43. Song; Lili Loofbourow, "Marty the Monster," in "'True Detective' Finale," *Los Angeles Review of Books,* March 11, 2014, https://lareviewofbooks.org/article/true-detective-finale/#!.

44. Ellis, *Anthropocene,* 2.

45. Both Haraway and others argue that the "Plantationocene" continues beyond the literal (southern, antebellum) plantation—into, for instance, factory farming and "monocrop agribusiness." Haraway, "Anthropocene," 162n5; see also Haraway et al., "Anthropologists," 556–57.

46. That mowing grass in a circle is unusual is highlighted in that Rust cuts Marty's grass at one point, and he cuts it, as is typical, in straight lines (1:3).

47. Williams mentions that Childress is mowing in circles but sees it only as a visual marker of the repetitions that punctuate the narrative. Williams, "Petrochemical Families," 39.

48. Morton, *Dark Ecology,* 3–4. This continued practice of reaping in a tightening circle has caused enormous damage to certain species, not least, for instance, corncrakes on Orkney. See R. E. Green, "The Decline of the Corncrake *Crex crex* in Britain Continues," *Bird Study* 42, no. 1 (1995): 73.

49. Morton, *Dark Ecology*, 5.

50. *The Mowing-Devil; or, Strange News out of Hartford-shire*, August 22, 1678, 2.

51. *Mowing-Devil*, 3, emphasis in original.

52. As Deckard points out, protesting slaves often set plantation fields on fire, forging another connection between Dora Lange's body and slavery. Deckard, "Ecogothic," 177.

53. As of 1995, even as sugarcane acreage continued to grow in Louisiana after losses to the oil industry in the 1970s and 1980s, "the number of farms continue to decline," as larger farming enterprises are owned by fewer people. Conrad and Lucas, *White Gold*, 72–73.

54. See Dawn Keetley, "Defining Folk Horror," *Revenant: Critical and Creative Studies of the Supernatural* 5 (2020): 1–32; Adam Scovell, *Folk Horror: Hours Dreadful and Things Strange* (Leighton Buzzard, U.K.: Auteur, 2017), 17–18.

55. Chris Baldick, ed., Introduction to *The Oxford Book of Gothic Tales* (New York: Oxford University Press, 1993), xix, emphasis added.

56. Kate Aurthur, "The 'True Detective' Creator Debunks Your Craziest Theories," *Buzzfeed*, March 6, 2014.

8

Beyond the Slaughterhouse

Anthropocene, Animals, and Gothic

JUSTIN D. EDWARDS

Speaking from the near ruins of a damaged planet, where tipping points are consistently identified and ignored, the gothic is more apt than ever. The ruins of gothic—the crumbling Otranto, Tinturn Abbey, the southern plantation—signal that which is lost: the shattered remains of a preeminent past. The landed gentry, the plantation owners, absentee landlords, the religious elites, are all economic realities that contain the specter of a powerful history that haunts the present and the future. Those economic waves that flow from eighteenth-century colonization into nineteenth-century industrialization into twentieth-century nuclear military industries into the twenty-first-century empire of globalization and neoliberalism all arise within the detrimental imperious power of the Anthropocene and crash against a gothic narrative that frames ecology in terms of darkness, death, and destruction.

In an environment where ecological understanding is continually repressed in favor of a devastating economic system that produces and consumes itself—the snake eating its own tail—the return of that which has been repressed pushes to the surface under the accumulating force of its own steam, ready to explode in a mushroom cloud of global destruction that can only be mapped out in burning fallouts and nuclear freezes. Has winter come yet? In the face of disaster capitalism, the answer is a resounding *yes*. Disasters offer hyperprosperity for the economic and political elite. Management by crisis becomes capitalism by shock: when New Orleans is flooded, public schools are replaced by charter schools; when a natural disaster hits Haiti, big-business government aid comes with the imposition of free market arrangements and debt obligations for those who are in dire need of assistance. Expressions such as "hurricane colonialism," sometimes associated with the aftermath of Hurricane Maria in Puerto Rico, underscore how the ideological agendas of the political-economic elite extend imperialist agendas that can be traced back to, among other things, the cotton plantations of Mississippi, the sugar plantations of Jamaica, and the tea plantations of Sri Lanka.[1] The collapse of a region due to climate change is, like the collapse of the stock market, an opportunity for the elite: they buy it all up, increasing their wealth and power. It is not surprising that climate change denials are disseminated from the top.

An anthropocentric point of view glimpses the ruins on the horizon—imagines the number of days left, calculates the years of melting ice and burning fires—but such a perspective can no longer be sustained. Wildlife thrives within the fallout zone of Chernobyl; the absence of the human animal is far from the eradication of life.[2] Gothic narratives point to that which is outside the anthropocentric, offering horrified expressions that decenter the human animal and devolve the self into an uncanny weirdness. Gothic has always decentered the Anthropos in its animal–human–animal hybrids, its monstrous forms and its undead creatures. All of this can be mapped from eighteenth-century colonization to twenty-first-century neoliberal managerial forces that we find in the plantation-like "mods" of the Amazon.com warehouses (unironically named "fulfillment centers"), where the "pickers" are run by electronic devices that continuously count down tasks against the clock.[3]

The plantation has been digitized. The Amazonian Plantationocene moves from the Global South to the North Atlantic, from the colonization of the Americas to the burning of the rainforests. The plantation has engendered the monstrously accelerated agro-industrial-economic structures that are set in a grotesque landscape of what might be, for the human animal at least, a derelict planet that can no longer sustain us, if only because we cannot contain ourselves. The exploitation of labor, the consumption of land, the production of destructive gases, and the massive consumption of water are engendered by a monoculture/product wherein life (human and nonhuman life) is meat: bodies are used up and consumed.[4] This is perhaps most apparent in the intensive livestock farming that is based on the modern process of cutting out, disconnecting, and reducing life to production and death in monstrous proportions. Disconnection eliminates biodiversity and negates multispecies complexes. But disconnection is also necessary to sustain an economic system that is ecologically unsustainable.

One way of thinking about gothic and Anthropocene is with reference to binaristic narratives that pit the human animal against the environment: haunted wildernesses, threatening jungles, dark forests, black lagoons, the gothic sublime. In the early European novel, the land is neither elevating nor enriching; it is vertiginous and plunging, threatening the individual with lost control. It is a destabilizing source of instability that must be domesticated in the greenhouse, the flower bed, the lawn, the botanical gardens. Likewise, in the territories beyond Mount Snowden, the Lammermuir Hills, and the Alps, the unmapped lands of other continents posed other threats: here there be monsters. The dark place "out there" is the ecological space—a source of terror—to be mapped and tamed into a homely sense of place. These by-products of (gothic) imperial conquest narratives appropriate the exotic and control the threat that is "out there" by bringing it "in here"—the untamed to the tamed, the colonies to the metropole—so the unhomely is pressed into the homely. This supports the human animal's belief that we can improve on environments that pose threats to us.

It is vital to think differently about gothic and Anthropocene. By bypassing binary thinking and moving outside the Anthropos, it might be possible to circumvent the teleological conception of the anthropogenic destruction of ecological systems (and the domination as well as extinction of other nonhuman animals), which are taken as inevitable results of the "development" of *Homo sapiens* as a species. The human animal has a destructive potency—a dominant force more powerful than ecology—that is wielded over a planet. We have the power to trigger a mass extinction event *and* the agency to prolong "tipping points" through planetary management and geoengineering. We are both the problem and the solution: a way of thinking that falls back on the self-referentiality of the human, its human-centeredness. There is, then, a need to de-center the human in discourses on the Anthropocene, even though the Anthropos of the epoch inherits so much from a philosophical tradition that places the human animal at the center of life and history. We too often revert to tropes, narratives, and concepts of humanity that position the human animal at the top of a hierarchical food chain where humankind has the sovereign right of dominion.[5]

Gothic, I suggest, offers up a diet of flesh and blood: vampires and zombies have insatiable appetites, reminding us that our bodies are meat. In this, gothic asks questions about human hierarchies, as it points to the fleshy body of the human as a source of protein and iron. Gothic thus poses questions about how and what we might eat: Is it possible to eat less destructively? Can we eat less violently? What are the ethics of consumption? How can gothic enable us to embrace an ethical ecocentric position? By reflecting on gothic, Anthropocene, and animals, I argue that we, the human animal, can place ourselves both inside and outside an anthropocentric position from which we can glimpse the interconnectedness of species and move toward a sense of multispecies that challenges hierarchies. The power dynamics in this way of thinking engenders an objectification of the nonhuman animal and negates the significance of seeing the Anthropocene in terms of its intertwining forces, conceived as human and nonhuman species, where the future of one determines the future of the other.

Throughout this book, the authors have pointed to the limits of the word *Anthropocene,* but one of its possibilities is its potential to identify the human as a species among many other species and, in so doing, shift human supremacy toward human–animal relationality. In other words, the term can be reappropriated as a way to reorient our thinking toward relationality and away from presumptions of human mastery and separation that are a big part of anthropocentric thinking. It can be, I suggest, a driver for overcoming the stranglehold of objectification, a path toward an interconnected subjecthood between human and nonhuman animals.

An important stage in the rise of the Anthropocene is animal agriculture and its accompanying slaughter. In fact, Paul Crutzen and Eugene Stoermer argue that there are three significant sites of human and animal interaction—the growth in global cattle populations, species extinction, and the expansion of industrial farming—and these are significant markers of the Anthropocene.[6] Approaching this from a different perspective, Foucault identifies animal and plant agriculture as a powerful political technology that impacts populations and species across a threshold of biological modernity, a form of biopolitical power that regulates birth and death, disease and health, and dovetails with the "anatomopolitics" by which capital disciplines the productive capacity of bodies.[7] Speciesism and biopolitical thinking both pinpoint animal domestication as a pivotal point in the human animal's ability to modify ecosystems, control bodies, and regulate power in communities that have contributed directly to the Great Acceleration.

Animal agriculture in the Anthropocene has led to narratives of catastrophe and apocalypse. Methane gases released into the atmosphere produce radically destructive climate events; mass drought and human suffering are brought about by water consumption and changing access to fresh water; the demolition of ecosystems such as rainforests and boreal forests distort micro- and macroclimates; and unsustainable feed for husbandry triggers extensive desertification and famine among human populations.[8] These catastrophic visions are fueled by multiple socioeconomic conditions, ranging from the increasingly large-scale animal agriculture corporations to massive factory farms to powerful animal product conglomerates and imperious meat lobbyists. The desire for profit sustains a disregard for life. This indifference to planetary life meshes with the indifference to lives that are consumed within the factories that raise and slaughter nonhuman animals for meat.[9]

Depending on where we live, animals used for livestock may or may not be visible, but they do fill up the planet. Their presence is seen in the biomass that exceeds the human animal, and one-third of the planet's surface is given over to feeding them. So even if we do not eat them or their products, we are still influenced by the capitalist biopower of the meat industry and its relation to the corporate enterprise and consumer culture that is woven into the fabric of the global bio-economy. Within this process, then, it is not only the nonhuman animals who are consumed. The planet is eaten away, and the workers who are exploited by the corporations are expendable. The same thinking that objectifies nonhuman animals intertwines with the objectification of human animals and a contempt for ecological concerns. What I am suggesting here is an extension to the central argument in Carol J. Adams's influential book *The Sexual Politics of Meat,* in which she argues that meat consumption and violence against animals are structurally related to other forms of violence, specifically violence against women. Adams demonstrates how many cultures equate meat eating with masculinity, and she points to the significant links between the prevalence of a carnivorous diet and patriarchal attitudes, particularly the idea that the end justifies the means, and the objectification of others.[10]

This objectification is integrated into the labor market of animal agriculture. The expenditure of bodies in this industry is not limited to cows, chickens, or pigs: human labor is also consumed, and with it the bodies of laborers. According to the U.S. Department of Labor, as well as Statistics Canada, there are more than one million full-time and part-time workers on Canadian and American factory farms, where billions of animals are raised and slaughtered for human consumption every year. Factory farm workers, often people of color and migrant workers from Latin America (many undocumented), are exploited so that their bodies become mangled, distorted, and disfigured, and sometimes expire. In most cases, they do not earn a living wage; they suffer from exposure to harmful gases, repetitive stress disorders, cardiovascular problems, and premature death. Driven by rigid contracts set forth by corporate employers, factory farms consume their workers to maximize profits. And the violence toward nonhuman animals extends to violence against human animals.[11]

This is the domino effect of objectification. We have reached a stage in the Anthropocene when the objectification of animals in corporate agriculture is indifferent to ecological decline, catastrophe, and devastation. This disregard for ecological life collapses into the structural disregard for nonhuman animal life, subjecting animals to torturous violence that is part of an objectification whereby the workers who are employed to raise and slaughter the nonhuman species are subjected to abuse by the corporations that exploit them. The binary separating the human from other species falls away. And what we are left with is a cannibalistic capitalism that extends Marx's vampire metaphor: the constant sucking of the workers' blood by a corporate body that appears to be vampire-like in its desire and ability to suck the life out of those on the abattoir floor. Yet instead of overcoming the stranglehold of objectification by moving toward an interconnected subjecthood, we continue to drive over the cliff edge of ecological collapse.

The treatment of animals—human and nonhuman—is vital for understanding the impact of the Anthropocene, and gothic narratives are rich sources of material for such an exploration.[12] For instance, the treatment of animals is intimately linked to violence against human animals in Edgar Allan Poe's "The Black Cat" (1843), in which the drunken narrator, who has always loved pets, has a deep bond with a beautiful black cat, Pluto. One night, though, in a gin-soaked rage, he turns on Pluto and gouges out the cat's eye with a penknife; this is a prelude to a murderous rage that leads to him killing his wife with an axe. Similarly, more than a hundred years later, Iain Banks's *The Wasp Factory* (1984) focuses on Frank Cauldhame's life on a small island in rural Scotland, where he takes pleasure in collecting the bodies and heads of the small animals he kills and the dogs he burns. As the narrative unfolds, it is revealed that he murders three of his relatives: two cousins and his younger brother. The violence directed at nonhuman animals is replicated in the violent acts toward human animals.

The literary critic Xavier Aldana Reyes correctly identifies the slaughterhouse as a significant gothic site for exploring violence against human and nonhuman animals and reads the abattoir as a place where the horrific treatment of nonhuman animals bleeds into the exploitation and abuse of people.[13] Reyes identifies abattoirs in gothic texts like Matthew Stokoe's *Cows* (1991) and Joseph D'Lacey's *Meat* (2008) as dehumanizing machines that are oblivious to the suffering of livestock or workers and driven by corporate giants. Here slaughterhouses foreground a potential collapse in speciesism, and given that human factory workers are regularly and severely physically compromised in animal-processing plants, people are frequently victimized and disenfranchised by monopolistic business practices in the animal-processing industry.[14] This means that community members are physically endangered by the presence of meatpacking factories at a local level, but human communities worldwide are also threatened by the overall effect of concentrated animal feeding operations on climate change.

This relationship between the local slaughterhouse and the global impact of the animal-processing industry is significant. In some cases, small-scale impacts have been seen in areas around large-scale animal-processing facilities, but the global concerns about land degradation and deforestation, air and water pollution, and the loss of biodiversity have been convincingly documented.[15] From a planetary perspective, animal agriculture contributes significantly to anthropogenic climate change. And if this continues at the current levels, the potential ramifications of meat production could have profound impacts on large populations of people due to the generation of methane, high levels of water consumption, and the high amounts of manure produced on industrialized farms. In addition, the thousands of animals in industrialized farms require large amounts of food, typically in the form of cereal grains. It is estimated that more than one-third of the world's cereal output is dedicated to farm animal feed, despite the fact that "it would be much more efficient for humans to consume cereals directly since much of the energy value is lost during conversion from plant to animal matter."[16]

Recognizing the impact of the local slaughterhouse can, I suggest, extend outward to the planetary effects of anthropogenic violence on human and nonhuman animals. And recent gothic texts, such as the French–Belgian coproduction *Raw* (2016), include representations of the mesh of violence that is incorporated into institutions not directly related to slaughterhouses or the animal-processing industry. Here the techniques of power around the consumption of meat work to induce docility by not questioning carnivorism. This extends to the suggestion that the living body must consume nonhuman animals to enliven the living body by fueling our energies. The normalized body eats meat; the rest are relegated to the margins, labeled abnormal. This, then, legitimizes a human speciesism that excludes nonhuman animals from the protection that is, at least in theory, afforded to the human community. On the other hand, though, following Foucault, the biopolitical form of governing in modernity includes a detached and technical stance toward lives, turning individuals into life as a mass and resource, so that speciesism is unsettled and humans enter the same biopolitical nexus as other animals. I am not suggesting a rejection of agency in the face of biopolitical power that includes the pure and simple capacity to legislate or legitimize sovereignty in the mesh of human and nonhuman animals. Rather, biopolitics is, above all, a strategic arrangement that coordinates power relations to extract a surplus power from living beings.[17]

A synopsis of *Raw* might go something like this: Strict vegetarian, Justine, enters a decadent, merciless, and dangerously seductive world during her first week at veterinary school. Desperate to fit in, she strays from her principles and eats raw meat for the first time. She soon experiences unexpected and terrifying reactions as another side of herself begins to emerge. Is this a true self? A core self? Surely not. For the film questions essentialist notions about *the* human and, more generally, the tenets of speciesism. More accurately, the emergence of the other Justine marks a corruption of the body whereby the corporeal is invaded—infected—by a foreign body of flesh that contaminates the living. The infection sees her collapse back into a primordial nature as her largely plant-based diet gives way to a craving for raw meat and she becomes the sign of a horrifying carnality, cannibalism, that overwhelms the distinction between nonhuman and human animals.[18]

It is this form of consumption—eating human flesh—that has provoked the strongest audience reactions to the film. When it premiered at the Toronto Film Festival, for instance, paramedics were called to the cinema after some viewers fainted during the scenes of cannibalism.[19] After another festival screening, the director, Julia Ducournau, was verbally attacked by a viewer during an interview; the man stormed out of the theater, yelling "the film makes no sense!" Ducournau takes these responses in stride. Referring to the representations of cannibalism, she asserts that "movies don't have to be easy. The important thing is the impact they have on you afterwards. And what traces they leave in you."[20] And when she is asked about the meaning of cannibalism in the film, she refuses to answer and insists that she wants to leave the meaning open to viewers. Contrast this to the director's dismissive response to suggestions that the film might support vegetarianism and veganism: "How? Where? Why?" she says to someone during an interview. "Have you seen the movie, really?" Here, her openness to meanings of cannibalism falls away, shutting down a vegetarian or vegan reading of the film. Perhaps this is because she does not want to see the film as entering into the discourses of the vegan killjoy. Or perhaps it is because she does not want her film to be labeled as a preachy text that promotes a pious veganism or naive utopianism.

The film begins with a cafeteria scene in which Justine and her parents have lunch. Suddenly Justine spits out the food in her mouth: there is meat in her meal. Her mother is outraged. She yells at staff, asking them what they would do if Justine had a lethal allergy to meat. Animal consumption is a form of contamination. It is a threat to life—human and nonhuman animals—and the emotive response illustrates a symbolic confrontation with the horrors of carnivorism. From this perspective, Justine's corporeality and her vegetarian diet threaten the carnivist and speciesist social order that underscores human–animal relations. Indeed, throughout the film, the viewer is reminded of the bodily connections between animals and humans. We see images of horses given tranquilizers alongside student parties where ketamine is consumed; cows are penned up beside the students forced into rows as they take exams or conduct lab experiments; new students are forced onto their hands and knees and led through the dark bowels of the university; horses run on treadmills as students take exercise in the yard. Human and nonhuman animals are linked: they are drugged, herded, examined, prodded, and abused.

The early cafeteria scene is mirrored in the vet school dining hall. Here Justine expresses her ideas about animal rights to explain her vegetarianism and her desire to become a vet. She links the suffering of animals and humans, asserting that an animal is self-aware and thus deserves the same rights as human animals. "I bet a raped monkey suffers like a woman," Justine says. This sparks a retort from a young woman at the table: "So a raped monkey, raped woman, same thing?" Justine answers a tentative yes, adding, "Why are we at vet school?" Why, indeed. The question is not answered, and the debate (and its ethical underpinning) is met with silence. Justine's equivalence between animals and humans is not shared by the other vets in training: an institution that is meant to promote the nurturing, care, and support of nonhuman animals is complicit in the ideology of speciesism that supports carnivist practices. Yet the film visually challenges this ideology: directly following the cafeteria discussion, there is a shot of students taking an exam that visually evokes animals in a cage.[21]

What is instituted here is a biopolitical form of governing that is characteristic of modernity, implying a detached and technical stance toward human lives. In this, biopolitical power in the vet school turns individual life into a collective noun whereby human life is treated as a resource and, as such, the human's self-proclaimed position as the crowning glory of planetary existence is unsettled and the students find themselves part of the same biopolitical nexus as other animals. The "caged" students in the exams are—as in the initiation rituals—identified by numbers, and an important link is made to the numbering of the animals in the labs. The dogs to be dissected or the cows to be prodded are tagged and reduced to numerical equivalence, just as the students in the labs find themselves identified with their student numbers and, by extension, their grades, impact factors, and h-index numbers. This dynamic of anonymization furthers a biopolitical treatment of life—human as well as nonhuman—as resource, thus reflecting a decentralized form of governing measures and the mobilization

of life itself through the technologies that support the animal agriculture industry. Justine's vegetarian ideology is gradually erased
as she becomes carnivore, and as a vet, she is trained to support
the institutions of a carnivore economy.

Being initiated into the institution is increasingly tied to a violence that is endemic in the alliance rites of being accepted into a
group. The initiation of the first-year vet students includes, among
other things, being bathed in pig's blood, being bullied in the corridors, and being pushed into performing sexual acts. Her fellow
students assure Justine that this is a harmless institutional tradition and that she will initiate the "rookies" in the following year.
Inflicting suffering on others, as well as witnessing that suffering,
is all in good fun. This particular notion of pleasure is, more and
more, part of institutional structures in which brutality is labeled
as amusement and violence is endemic in a group as an exuberant
kick. The practice of hazing includes a seemingly easy delight in the
violence toward and suffering of others; this has led to customs in
which the fantasies and the practice of violence are seen simply as
modes of entertainment. If we can find fun when witnessing the
suffering of human animals, then it is perhaps easier to accept the
suffering of nonhuman animals.

The most significant of these initiation rituals arises when Justine is forced to eat a rabbit kidney. This is the Ur-moment of
carnivism: it is the precise second when Justine's well-meaning
worldview begins to collapse and she adopts the principles es-
poused by the other students and teachers. Nonhuman animals
are merely resources to be objectified and reduced to meat that
can be consumed and used up by people. The message is clear: vets
are trained to support this ontology, regardless of the well-being
of animals or any reflection on animal rights. The Ur-moment is
heightened by the language—signaled in the film's title—and fur-
thered by the images of the uncooked meat that Justine cannot
resist. In fact, her consumption of a rabbit kidney calls attention to
the power of language within meat eating. Here there is no absent
referent, whereby the violence of slaughtering nonhuman animals
is veiled through metaphor: "cow" becomes "beef," "pig" becomes
"pork," "deer" becomes "venison," "fish eggs" become "roe." Instead, the raw language draws attention to a violence of predation
that is a central and defining characteristic of human domination
within the Anthropocene.

The institutional production of self is, in this instance, the metamorphosis of becoming-carnivore. It is about rejecting what is the perceived self-denial of vegetarianism and embracing some imaginary primal instinct to consume flesh. This practice of changing being—of becoming—is not just an ontological practice but also the erasure of an ethical position where the nonhuman animal is an accepted, though limited, resource to be exploited, abused, consumed. When asked by her doctor why she ate the raw rabbit kidney that made her so sick, Justine tells her that she said no. "Did they force you?" the doctor asks. "No," Justine has to admit. For she wishes to fit in and, as she says, be average. "Find a quiet corner and wait out the year," the doctor advises her. Here the film poses questions about holding certain principles as an individual in the face of institutional forces that challenge those views. And, by extension, the text picks apart the question of how we might transform ourselves and society to extend partial sympathies and, instead, embraces institutionalized power structures and carnivorous relations to others. The animal other does not figure in this particular equation.

It is from this perspective that the background of industrialized animal agriculture in *Raw* moves into a necropolitics that imposes the right to enslave beings, impose social or civil death, or simply kill others.[22] Within this system, the animals are a form of walking death, and the film displays the forms of subjugation of life to the power of death as the nonhuman animal lingers in a state of being positioned between life and death. There is, in other words, a continuum here in which necropower and politics work upon certain populations of beings to further life in some instances and deny life in others. In the latter, the nonhuman animal enables us to fully reflect on the implications of "the living death" within the context of the Anthropocene. Life is the path to the slaughterhouse; life is a process and precursor to death. This view of the factory farm conflates life as the resource for death. In this, necropower is tied to the central processes of the plantation system—simplification and enforcement—both of which are integral to the structure of industrial farming. By reducing the life of the nonhuman animal to the death of meat, the biomedical processes change biological and genetic life and move biodiverse regions into ecosystems that are cut off from multispecies interlocking, and the farmed animal is forced on multilayered but unidirectional levels into interacting with a single species: the human animal. The life of the nonhuman animal is transformed, but so are the land, the environment, and the life of the human animal that regulates the industrial farming system.

But *Raw* also pushes in other directions, for in the film, becoming-carnivore is an ongoing process that morphs into other practices. Justine moves from eating raw meat to consuming human flesh. Becoming-carnivore bleeds into becoming-cannibal. This erasure of difference signals how her relationship to others continues to change as the affirmation of speciesism begins to fall away. Eating meat moves into being eaten. Meat is meat, regardless of the source.

Raw is a long way from being a preachy film. It is filled with nuance and interpretive possibilities, posing significant questions without offering simplistic answers. Does the representation of cannibalism link the eating of nonhuman animal and human animal flesh? Is the film suggesting that we should stick to our principles in spite of institutional and peer pressures? Or are vegetarians denying important aspects of their primal appetites and thereby giving rise to something darker? Regardless of the answers to these questions, it would be too crude to read the film as narrating a coming-of-age story in which the protagonist finds growth and power only after she has consumed meat. This is not a story of denial. Nor is it a text that promotes eating meat. It does not include answers about how to be an ethical person in an anthropocentric world. But it does call attention to the biopower that relegates nonhuman animals to the margins, as well as an ongoing process in the Anthropocene, or, better, the Plantationocene: *Raw* enables us to reflect upon different ways of being in the world as a species. It calls attention to our relations to other species, particularly the differences and power between human animals and how these hierarchies are mapped onto other species.

Beyond vegetarianism, veterinary science is an integral cog in the biopolitical machine that drives the industrial farm. Dominating the maintenance of life for nonhuman animals through reproduction, a healthy life-span, and the precise moment of death is the basis for the complete biotechnological control and enforcement of the economic strata of meat production and consumption. The animal factory must produce optimally: meat, eggs, and milk must be supplied in bulk through clearly calculable criteria to maximize profits. Veterinarians are, like other industrial farm employees, workers who must rigorously assess the insemination process at the heart of reproduction through a complex calculus that involves the purchasing of animal sperm and eggs, spatial constraints, legal regulations, and health risks to human and nonhuman animals. Veterinary knowledge and zootechnological practice form the basis of these calculations. In this context, the animal commodity is a product that also gives the products (meat, milk, and eggs); or, to put this another way, the animal is the slave, the production tool, and the produce. The Plantationocene comes into sharp focus when we survey intensively farmed animals, for these plantations reduce life to a determining factor: assets for profit now and investments in the corporate future.[23] Any nuanced conception of life is overwritten by the bottom line, a one-dimensional ontology that negates the multispecies of biodiversity and promotes monocultures. The animal body is transformed into an organic machine.

Raw helps us reflect on the possibility of a future that is unique, different from current human animal and animal relations. It interrogates the boundaries between species and the ethics of killing, eating, and consuming meat (human meat or animal meat). It calls attention to the ethics of murder—meat as murder—and suggests that we need to understand a metaphysics of subjectivity that does not exclude the animal but deconstructs the human–animal boundary: the exclusion of the animal is part of the problem. As part of this process, the representation of cannibalism—becoming-cannibal—points to the subject of becoming by emphasizing consumption, for carnivorous culture and cannibalism haunt the text and suggest that the material basis of our culture is a problematic site that must be addressed if we are to have a transformed vision of companion species. This is all the more important now that we see how industrial farming damages ecological systems in many ways and that at the heart of its impact is a plantation structure based on the mass production of life for the purpose of death. This simplified practice strips away all complex multispecies entanglements, ambiguity, and complexity, engendering monocultural life that is easily managed and controlled to breed massive profits. In this, corporate animal agriculture is part of a monocultural sphere of plantations that turn our planet away from the complexities of biodiversity and regenerative ecosystems. Texts like *Raw* reveal the biopower of hierarchical arrangements that pave the way for a destructively transparent path that is easily accessible and unidirectional. But the corporate path that reduces all life—plant and animal—to profit will inevitably light the flame that will burn down the Plantationocene, leaving it in the ruins of gothic.

NOTES

1. Laura Weiss, Marisol Lebrón, and Michelle Chase, "Eye of the Storm: Colonialism, Capitalism, and the Climate in the Caribbean," *NACLA Report on the Americas* 50, no. 2 (2018): 109, as well as Sandy Smith-Nonini, "The Debt/Energy Nexus behind Puerto Rico's Long Blackout: From Fossil Colonialism to New Energy Poverty," *Latin American Perspectives* 47, no. 3 (2020): 64.

2. Mary Mycio, *Wormwood Forest: A Natural History of Chernobyl* (Washington, D.C.: Joseph Henry Press, 2005), 127–53.

3. Nichole Gracely, "Surviving in the Amazon," *New Labor Forum* 21, no. 3 (2012): 80–83.

4. Vanesa Ribas, *On the Line: Slaughterhouse Lives and the Making of the New South* (Oakland: University of California Press, 2016), 1–28.

5. HARN Editorial Collective, ed., *Animals in the Anthropocene: Critical Perspectives on Non-human Futures* (Sydney: Sydney University Press, 2015).

6. Paul J. Crutzen and Eugene F. Stoermer, "The Anthropocene," *Global Change Newsletter* 41 (2000): 17–18.

7. Chloë Taylor, "Foucault and Critical Animal Studies: Geologies of Agricultural Power," *Philosophy Compass* 8, no. 6 (2013): 540.

8. Henry N. Le Houérou, "Climate Change, Drought and Desertification," *Journal of Arid Environments* 34 (1996): 133–85.

9. Michael Kreyling, "Uncanny Plantations: The Repeating Gothic," in *The Palgrave Handbook of the Southern Gothic,* ed. Susan Castillo Street and Charles L. Crow, 231–44 (Basingstoke, U.K.: Palgrave, 2016). See also a discussion of plantation gothic in Sharae Deckard, "Ecogothic," in *Twenty-First Century Gothic,* ed. Maisha Wester and Xavier Aldana Reyes, 177–86 (Edinburgh: Edinburgh University Press, 2019).

10. Carol J. Adams, *The Sexual Politics of Meat* (1990; repr., London: Bloomsbury, 2015), 25–34. Adams's argument has been critiqued by, among others, Carrie Hamilton, who shows that Adams's version of vegan feminism relies on the silencing and exclusion of sex workers as subjects. See Hamilton, "Sex, Work, Meat: The Feminist Politics of Veganism," *Feminist Review* 114, no. 1 (2016): 112–29.

11. Several important studies have documented the abuse of workers in this industry. A. G. Holdier writes that in meat-processing plants, "physical effects are not the only harms to workers that must be considered; exposure to, and participation in, the violence of this

workplace also leads to profound psychological damage . . . and ille-gal drug use is not unheard of as a supplement to try and meet an employer's demands" (45). Holdier, "Speciesistic Veganism: An An-thropocentric Argument," *Critical Perspectives on Veganism,* ed. Jodey Castricano and Rasmus R. Simonsen, 41–66 (Basingstoke, U.K.: Pal-grave, 2016).

12. There are of course other aspects of animal gothic: the most common is the animal revenge narrative. Here a representative of the animal kingdom turns on humanity and threatens to usurp the power of the human animal. Examples include *The Birds* (1963), *Planet of the Apes* (1968), and *Jaws* (1975). Another strand of animal gothic nar-rative is the animal–human hybrid in such texts as H. G. Wells's *The Island of Dr. Moreau* (1896) and William Hope Hodgson's *The House on the Borderlands* (1908). See Bernice M. Murphy, "'They Have Risen Once: They May Rise Again': Animals in Horror Literature," in *The Palgrave Handbook to Horror Literature,* ed. Kevin Corstorphine and Laura R. Kremmel, 257–73 (Basingstoke, U.K.: Palgrave, 2018), as well as Katarina Gregersdotter, Johan Höglund, and Nicklas Hållén, *Ani-mal Horror Cinema: Genre, History and Criticism* (Basingstoke, U.K.: Palgrave Macmillan, 2015).

13. Xavier Aldana Reyes, *Body Gothic: Corporeal Transgression in Contem-porary Literature and Horror Film* (Cardiff: University of Wales Press, 2014), 99–101.

14. See Reyes, 99–100.

15. Bradley J. Cardinale, J. Emmett Duffy, Andrew Gonzalez, David U. Hooper, Charles Perrings, Patrick Venail, Anita Narwani et al., "Bio-diversity Loss and Its Impact on Humanity," *Nature* 486 (2012): 59–67.

16. Tara Garnett, "Livestock-Related Greenhouse Gas Emissions: Impacts and Options for Policy Makers," *Environmental Science and Policy* 12 (2009): 491.

17. Shukin and O'Brien explore the biopolitics of slaughter and the pow-ers of affect in cinema, focusing specifically on Sergei Eisenstein's early film *Strike* (1925). The images and idiom of striking are linked to the blow that fells an animal, thus calling attention to "the human's sovereign power to take animal life and cinema's aesthetic power to make feel." Nicole Shukin and Sarah O'Brien, "Being Struck: On the Force of Slaughter and Cinematic Affect," in *Animal Life and the Mov-ing Image,* ed. Michael Lawrence and Laura McMahon (London: BFI, 2015), 188.

18. C. Lou Hamilton, *Veganism, Sex and Politics: Tales of Danger and Plea-sure* (London: Hammeron Press, 2019), 72–77.

19. Adam Gabbatt, "Cannibal Horror Film Too Raw for Viewers as Paramed-ics Are Called," September 14, 2016, https://www.theguardian.com/film/2016/sep/14/cannibal-horror-film-raw-toronto-film-festival.

20. Kaleem Aftab, "Director Julia Ducournau on Her Cannibal Film *Raw*: 'I Asked My Actor, What Do You Think in Principle about Shoving Your Hand up a Cow's Arse?,'" *The Independent*, April 5, 2017, https://www.independent.co.uk/arts-entertainment/films/features/julia-ducournau-raw-a7666871.html, as well as "Julia Ducournau: Cannibalism, Feminism and Growing Up," https://www.52-insights.com/julia-ducournau-cannibalism-feminism-growing-art-movie-interview-french-cult/.

21. Dawn Keetley's blog *Raw (Meat): Are We Our Bodies* offers insightful readings of this imagery: http://www.horrorhomeroom.com/tag/raw/.

22. Achille Mbembe, "Necropolitics," trans. Libby Meintjes, *Public Culture* 15, no. 1 (2003): 39.

23. Anna L. Tsing, "A Threat to Holocene Resurgence Is a Threat to Livability," in *The Anthropology of Sustainability: Beyond Development and Progress*, ed. Marc Brightman and Jerome Lewis (London: Palgrave, 2017), 51–52.

Part III

CAPITALOCENE

The Capitalocene designates an era of destructive environmental practices in which the main culprits are capital and capitalism. As a term, *Capitalocene* thus redirects the accusatory finger of the Anthropos on to "capital" so as to lay bare a more specific chain of causality that the term *Anthropocene* elides. According to Jason W. Moore, while "Anthropocene is a worthy point of departure,"[1] it is important to make clear that "the Anthropocene argument poses questions that it cannot answer."[2] Not only does the Anthropocene potentially redirect earlier historical responsibility for planetary environmental destruction from the Global North on to all of humanity; it also fails to address the ills caused by a system that would over time migrate from its origins in Europe and on to the rest of the world, including the Global South. Finally, "it perpetuates the ontological dichotomy between humans and nature in which human agency is treated as a force acting *upon* rather than *in* or as a *part* of nature," just as it potentially exacerbates the anthropocentric conviction "that humans can shape the planet and re-create it in their image."[3]

Though the concept has earned considerable traction in environmental humanities and social sciences, some argue that capitalism is not the only force of environmental destruction. Timothy Morton thus suggests that "capital and capitalism are symptoms of the problem, not its direct causes. If the cause were capitalism, then Soviet and Chinese carbon emissions would have added nothing to global warming."[4] Yet, although it is certainly possible to trace the human impact on ecology further back in time, to eras before the rise of capitalism, as to anticapitalist modes of political and financial systems contemporaneous with capitalism, it is inarguable that capitalism has proven to be the most destructively efficient, wide-ranging, and persistent "way of organizing nature"[5] and one that has by now far outstripped, for instance, communism.

Indeed, as a much-repeated quote of (supposedly) Fredric Jameson goes, capitalism has been so ruthlessly efficient at taking on opposing financial systems and ideologic formations that we may have reached a point at which "it is easier to imagine an end to the world than an end to capitalism."[6] Or alternatively, while it may become increasingly obvious that "the global capitalist system is approaching an apocalyptic zero-point,"[7] very little action is being taken to revert or even slow down this trajectory toward a potential cataclysmic collapse.

In suggesting that we replace *Anthropocene* with *Capitalocene*, proponents of the latter term are often despairing, but sometimes also hopeful. Despair may seem only natural in a world in which capitalism is so ubiquitous and so ubiquitously destructive. Yet, to some, the destructive nature of capitalism is also hopeful precisely because the apocalyptic nature of a system reliant on an ever-continuous drive for profit and progress that knows no limit cannot but dismantle itself. As the writers of "Uncivilization: The Dark Mountain Manifesto" phrase it, "we do not believe that everything will be fine. We are not even sure, based on current definitions of progress and improvement, that we want it to be."[8] While such statements are certainly "dark" in that "not being fine" may lead to the deaths of millions and perhaps billions of humans if the process of "uncivilization" called for in the manifesto is indeed made manifest, advocates of such a philosophy should find encouragement in the fact that the world as we now know it is not worth living in: "The end of the world as we know it is not the end of the world full stop. Together, we will find hope beyond hope."[9]

The essays included in this part reflect the sentiments outlined in the preceding paragraphs in that they challenge an "Anthropocene discourse [which] veers away from environmentalism's dark idiom of destruction, depradation, rape, loss, devastation, deterioration and so forth of the natural world into the tame vocabulary that humans are changing, shaping, transforming or altering the biosphere."[10] Rebecca Duncan's chapter "Gothic in the Capitalocene: World-Ecological Crisis, Decolonial Horror, and the South African Postcolony," for instance, insists that we look at the colonial legacy of the Capitalocene. As she tackles the erasure of the Global North and Global South divide of the universalizing tendencies of the "Anthropocene" from a South African perspective, Duncan challenges us to reckon with uncomfortable aspects of imperialism and capitalism to which an approach based solely on the impact of the Anthropos may be blind. Reading Mohale Mashigo's *Intruders* (2018), Duncan argues that the short story collection is not most fruitfully read as the actions of a collective humanity. Rather, Duncan suggests, seeing as it is the violent and racialized regimes of capital that have configured the South African locality, a Capitalocene rather than Anthropocene approach will unearth both systemic and historically specific exploitation by capital that a more broadly universalist anthropocentric approach may miss.

Similarly, Timothy Clark's chapter "Overpopulation: The Human as Inhuman" questions the blanket assumptions following in the wake of (often un)critical discussions of overpopulation from Thomas Malthus up to and including the present day. As Clark points out in a discussion of what he terms "overpopulation gothic," if we reduce our current predicament simply to a rise in human numbers, then we become blind to a range of other, more important aspects. For instance, although there may be far fewer people in the Global North, people of the Global North tend to consume and pollute many times more than the inhabitants of the Global South, and a focus on numbers alone constitutes a shifting of blame onto people who have in fact done very little of the actual consumption and pollution that a drop in world population is supposed to mitigate.

Barry Murnane's chapter "Digging Up Dirt: Reading the Anthropocene through German Romanticism" examines capitalist mining practices in early nineteenth-century Northern Europe, but ultimately also traces the redistribution of such localized extraction of minerals in a global context. In an age long before oil and the combustion engine would lead to the revolution in transportation of goods and people that we today tend to think of when we envisage global capitalism, Murnane makes clear that the beginnings of the Capitalocene stretch back not only hundreds of years but also deep underground. Finally, in the chapter "Got a Light? The Dark Currents of Energy in *Twin Peaks: The Return*," Timothy Morton and Rune Graulund explore the destructive force of energy unleashed by the very shift to oil and the discovery of nuclear power in the twentieth century that would allow capitalism to become as dominant as it is today, not only through what Andreas Malm has termed "fossil capital"[11] but also through a nuclear arms race won over communism via sheer financial dominance.

These chapters underscore the destructive environmental practices of capitalism. But they also deal with topics that precede capitalist modes of production. In his reading of the practice of mining, Murnane's chapter, for instance, engages not only with human behavior preceding capitalism by millennia but also with stone and minerals preceding the human itself by millions of years, hence returning us to the questions and concerns of geology and deep (prehistoric and certainly also precapitalist) time from which the term *Anthropocene* was originally coined. Similarly, Morton and Graulund's essay on energy, while focusing on twentieth-century practices of fossil capital as well as the success of a capitalist system in creating the first atomic bomb, point to tendencies of human behaviors of cruelty and aggression that are primal, bestial, and prehistoric.

NOTES

1. Jason W. Moore, "Introduction: Anthropocene or Capitalocene? Nature, History, and the Crisis of Capitalism," in *Anthropocene or Capitalocene? Nature, History, and the Crisis of Capitalism,* ed. Jason W. Moore (Oakland, Calif.: PM Press, 2016), 2.
2. Moore, 5.
3. Anne Fremaux, *After the Anthropocene: Green Republicanism in a Postcapitalist World* (Basingstoke, U.K.: Palgrave Macmillan, 2019), 44.
4. Timothy Morton, *Dark Ecology: For a Logic of Future Coexistence* (New York: Columbia University Press, 2016), 23.
5. Moore, "Introduction," 6.
6. As Matthew Beaumont has pointed out, the exact origins and contexts of the by now seemingly ubiquitous quote are difficult to pin down, even by Jameson himself: "It has recently become something of a cliché, at least on the Left, to cite the claim, first made by Fredric Jameson in *Seeds of Time* (1994), that in the current conjuncture it is easier to imagine the end of the world than the end of capitalism. 'Someone once said,' Jameson writes in 'Future City' (2003), where he recapitulates and revises the point, and where it becomes apparent that he is probably misremembering some comments made by H. Bruce Franklin about J. G. Ballard." Beaumont, "Imagining the End Times: Ideology, the Contemporary Disaster Movie, *Contagion,*" in *Žižek and Media Studies,* ed. M. Flisfeder and L. Willis (New York: Palgrave Macmillan, 2014), 88.
7. Slavoj Žižek, *Living in the End Times* (London: Verso, 2010), x.
8. Paul Kingsworth and Douglas Hine, "Uncivilisation: The Dark Moun-

tain Manifesto," in *Walking on Lava: Selected Works for Uncivilised Times* (White River Junction, Vt.: Chelsea Green, 2017), 16.

9. Kingsworth and Hine, 23.

10. Eileen Crist, "On the Poverty of Our Nomenclature," *Environmental Humanities* 3, no. 1 (2013): 133.

11. See Andreas Malm, *Fossil Capital: The Rise of Steam Power and the Roots of Global Warming* (London: Verso, 2016).

Gothic in the Capitalocene

World-Ecological Crisis, Decolonial Horror,
and the South African Postcolony

REBECCA DUNCAN

Gothic Geology

In "The Parlemo," a short story published in her collection *Intruders* (2018), Mohale Mashigo maps the relation between past and present in her native South Africa. Drawing on a recognizably gothic symbology of buried remains, the author imaginatively excavates Johannesburg's built environment and focuses on a district in the grip of dynamic gentrification. A configuration of "grey paint, new bricks, repurposed school desks [and] copper fittings,"[1] this area is emerging as the domain of the hipster youth, belonging—in South Africa—to the so-called born-free generation that has come of age after the 1994 fall of the apartheid state. These urban renewals are, in fact, a specific effect of the conditions under which this political transition played out. To the extent that they register the rise of commercial development in the previously low-income inner city, they invoke the turn to macroeconomic neoliberalism that characterizes the dawn of democracy in the country. As elsewhere across the postcolonial world, the neoliberal agenda—which prioritizes privatization over redistribution, financialization over industry, individual responsibility over state support—has not worked in South Africa to redress long-entrenched economic inequalities cultivated along racial lines under formal white minority rule. Mashigo refers the reader to this reactivation of systemic violence via what appears initially to be an act of imaginative archaeology: "Beneath the buildings, stuck in the concrete, was the blood and sweat of those who had built the city. Beneath their sweat lay the limbs . . . of those who were digging the core of the earth on the promise of a better life."[2]

Johannesburg began its existence as a goldfield during South Africa's fin de siècle mineral revolution, thus named because it kick-started industrialization in the country. The rapid ascendance of diamonds and subsequently gold also provided the crucible in which a blueprint was developed by colonial administrators and mining capitalists for the racist organization that would shape the country over the following century. Briefly outlined, the mines satisfied their demand for cheap labor by implementing categories of race to identify a laboring class that could be remunerated at as low a wage as possible. A migrant system undergirded this strategy: African people were forcibly confined to reserve territories in the late nineteenth century, and taxes were levied by the colonial state on these enclosures to deliberately compel men into the mineral economy. This complex of geographical segregation, coercion, and racialized remuneration would then be refined and expanded after 1948 under the National Party government's policy of apartheid, which can thus be viewed, as John S. Saul and Patrick Bond note, as itself a system of racial capitalism organized around the coercive production of cheap labor.[3] It is, importantly, over the structures and effects of this system—a South Africa in which access to land, skilled work, education, and infrastructure was officially distributed in racist terms—that the postapartheid regime has rolled out the deindustrializations, privatizations, and welfare retractions characteristic of the neoliberal state, with the result that those bearing the brunt of apartheid's violence are faced with a postcolonial present in which that violence is not alleviated but reiterated in new and compound states of precarity.

When Mashigo writes of blood and bones in the foundations of a rapidly gentrifying Johannesburg, it is to these circumstances that her narrative points. Loren Kruger warns against a fetishization of the city's current dynamism because this risks a "foreshortened view of the . . . past":[4] a convenient amnesia that, "since the days of gold," has been summoned periodically to facilitate Johannesburg's strategic "reinvention"[5] for the ends of capital. This last is specifically significant in relation to Mashigo's tale. The violence embedded in her material cityscape is connected explicitly to a mysterious condition of memory loss, which in turn enables a hipster generation to embrace neoliberal gentrification. "Human-kind was prone to forgetting big things," the narrative voice re-lates: "this neglect changes the way history is shaped, so the soil, bricks and cement turn themselves into a vault."[6] If there are bod-ies in Johannesburg's built environment, the text implies, this is because the history of gold and race—of capital in South Africa—has not been adequately remembered in the democratic age.

Especially important to the argument that follows here is the sense in which Mashigo's amnesiac scenario signals an ontological shift, one that has taken place "all around the world"[7] and is thus global in scope. The human remains lodged in South African soil and concrete are in this way connected to a modulation that bears not only on a particular social organization but on the conditions under which (human) life has previously unfolded on a planetary scale. In this sense, the tale's quasi-gothic vision of Johannesburg is legible as a geological—and not only an archaeological—image, and it is here that we might turn to the Anthropocene: the age in which human activity precisely enters the geological record. However, if Mashigo's excavations can be read in this way, then her rendition of the record does not register the actions of a collective humanity. Rather, etched into it are the violent and racialized regimes of capi-tal that have configured the South African locality since the coun-try's rise to imperial priority after the discovery of gold.

This is not strictly an Anthropocene record, in other words, but one that bears traces of what Jason W. Moore has called the Capi-talocene: the age in which capital is the dominant force shaping the earth's systems.[8] It is significant that it is with recourse to a gothic lexicon—of buried bodies, of violent pasts secreted under bright veneers—that Mashigo constructs this vision from contemporary South Africa. Gothic is summoned here as the vocabulary in which to articulate a particular perspective on the current planetary condition, a viewpoint that looks out from a history of racialized power and systemic violence, and from which *Anthropocene* appears an inadequate term. Later in this essay, I will elaborate more fully on this mobilization of gothic forms, analyzing Henrietta Rose-Innes's *Green Lion* (2016) and another of Mashigo's tales, titled "Ghost Strain N." To situate these fictions, and the connections they draw between capital, colonialism, and extrahuman nature in South Africa, I turn now, however, to Moore's world-ecological conception of the Capitalocene and to the imperial principle that has structured this planetary formation from its inauguration into the crisis-ridden present.

Crisis, World-Ecology, and the Coloniality of Power

The postmillennial period is a time of accelerating transformations in the earth's systems. And yet, the causes and effects of these emergencies are not evenly distributed on a planetary scale. It is the global poor, concentrated largely across the postcolonial states of the Global South, who disproportionately suffer both the "slow" and "spectacular" violences of unfolding crises, as Rob Nixon, for example, has influentially noted.[9] Vishwas Satgar points out that the twenty nations most vulnerable to the effects of global heating—the so-called V20—are located across "Africa, Asia, the Caribbean, Latin America and the Pacific" and are already experiencing catastrophic shifts in temperature, sea level, weather patterns, and—concomitantly—mortality.[10] At the same time, responsibility for these changes—the weight of "climate debt"— lies overwhelmingly with "the rich industrialised countries of the global North [many of which] have been polluting since the advent of the Industrial Revolution . . . in the context of imperial international relations."[11] To account for these variegations and their roots, a sharper and more systemically attuned historical vocabulary is required than the one offered by Anthropocene thinking. The broad category of human activity cannot bring into focus the principle that organizes patterns of violence and security over time and that is clearly bound up with geopolitical distributions of wealth and power, with legacies of empire and colonial settlement, and with race. "There is a calculus that allows us to map where the bodies most affected by past climate change are buried," write Moore and Raj Patel, "and where future casualties are likely to be."[12]

To delineate this "calculus," Moore shifts the historical point of departure away from the Industrial Revolution prioritized by Anthropocene thought and turns instead to the long sixteenth century, drawing in part from Immanuel Wallerstein's assessment of the modern world-economy as the capitalist world-system. Capital, for Wallerstein, is defined by a principle of "endless accumulation,"[13] which concurrently requires endless economic expansion. Over capital's history, this has played out through cyclical boom and bust rhythms, in which the limits to expansion are reached within a certain formation, prompting stagnation, unrest, and eventually crisis. This then demands a reorganization of the (global) mode of production so that the conditions of crisis can be reinvented as new conditions for growth.[14] It is because of this in-built expansionist drive that, ultimately, capital cannot exist as anything but a world-economy, and this takes shape, Wallerstein shows, as an uneven planetary formation of economically strong core states and peripheral regions, all structurally interconnected by a geographical division of labor, which is in turn organized by an exploitative relation of power.[15] Historically, he writes, capital has solved its innate contradictions in crucial part "by expanding the pool of . . . workers elsewhere in the world, who . . . work at a lower level of wages"[16]—or, indeed, for no wage at all.

This exploitative strategy is starkly evidenced across the period of European colonialism that formally ended in the mid-twentieth century. But it is important that the modern world-system is *birthed* with the European colonial endeavor. It emerges after 1450 in the Atlantic world, as thinkers affiliated with the "decolonial option"[17] have emphasized. Aníbal Quijano identifies a "coloniality of power"[18] that has shaped geopolitical formations over the last five centuries, arguing that this emerges from the codevelopment of racial categories with the inaugural transoceanic division of labor.[19] On this account, racist discourse is produced in early imperial centers as a means of justifying the distribution of unpaid work among colonized peoples, which in turn facilitated the rapid economic development and global empowerment of Western Europe.[20] Moore reiterates this thought, and expands on it.[21] For him, however, the unpaid sphere encompasses not only colonized peoples but also the potential energy—the "capacity to do work"—of extrahuman nature.[22]

"Appropriation" is the term Moore gives to the process for harnessing this cheap work/energy.[23] He shows that this unfolds in tandem with an "epistemic rift" emergent in Enlightenment thinking[24] and which—via Cartesian dualism and Bacon's formative philosophy of science—defined relations between human and extrahuman in binary terms. "Capital's governing conceit is that it may do with Nature as it pleases," Moore writes. "Nature is external [to Society] and may be coded, quantified and rationalised to serve economic growth."[25] As Quijano also notes,[26] this account of

Nature is epistemically entangled with the production of geohistorical racial identities: along with the extrahuman components
of the biosphere, Moore reiterates, "Nature . . . encompassed virtually all peoples of color,"[27] who—as in the case of the South African gold mine and the policy of apartheid—are deemed less fully
Human than colonizing Europeans under the auspices of Eurocentric knowledge. The world-economy is thus, Moore argues, a
world-ecology, and the story of this planetary configuration is one
in which capital, empire, and Enlightenment epistemology have
worked together over the last five centuries to cyclically remake
historical Natures in their own image and to plunder these for certain humans' gain. On this account, apartheid and its precursors
should be seen as "ecological regimes":[28] institutionalized ways of
organizing the biosphere via permutations of the epistemic rift,
oriented toward the production of Nature as Cheap Labor.[29]

But "Cheap Nature"[30] is epistemically inexhaustive in its scope.
It is a material fiction that is only made violently concrete through
the historical operation of geopolitical power. In reality, Natures
are produced within a wider context, which Moore names the
oikeios or "web of life."[31] This designates—with a lowercase *n*—
"nature as a whole":[32] the condition within which life-making
processes unfold and which is characterized not by binary separations but by a real relationality.[33] Viewed with *oikeios,* human
and extrahuman, Society and Nature—and capitalism itself—are
coproduced through rhizomatic connections that "interweave[e]
symbolic and biophysical natures at every scale"[34] and in a way
that bears on those crisis periods that cyclically recur across the
history of capital. "While the manifold projects of empire, capital
and science are busy making Nature with a capital N . . . the web of
life is busy shuffling about the biological and geological conditions
of capitalism's process."[35] The effect of these "shufflings" is to ham-
per the operation of Nature-making, to the point where a given
construction is no longer available "on the cheap."[36] While this resistance to cheapening strategies has recurred across the history
of capitalism, prompting the phases of systemic reorganization
Wallerstein describes, for Moore, the proliferation of crises that
characterizes our neoliberal present suggests the terminal failure
of capital's pivotal Nature-making strategy, which seems unable
durably to reinstate the conditions for expansion by identifying

new frontiers for appropriation.[37] We are thus living in the twilight of the Capitalocene, and from this perspective the unprecedentedly totalizing commodifications of the neoliberal agenda signal the violent and frantic last gasp of a dying system.

And yet, the failing efficacy of capital's Cheap Nature strategy has not dismantled the coloniality of power. Across the history of the modern world and into the present, successive regimes of capital, working in conjunction with new permutations of the Enlightenment's epistemic rift, have reinvented the world's (post)colonies as the sites of new Natures, from the plantation to the mine, the cash crop, and the sweatshop—and others. Viewed in this way, the postcolonial present is characterized by "sedimentations" of histories, to borrow Ann Laura Stoler's vocabulary:[38] it is the site at which the structures and effects of formal capitalist colonialisms have been strategically reactivated—or strategically overlooked—for the benefit of a power that remains innately colonial in Quijano's sense. As it works cumulatively in this way through successive repurposings of violent pasts, coloniality emerges for Stoler as force of *ruin*—or "ruination"[39]—in the verbal sense.[40] From this vantage of active "imperial debris,"[41] the emergencies of the present are both frequently immediately experienced as radical states of lived precarity and—clearly bound up with compounded legacies of empire, exploitation, and settlement—emphatically not the effect of collective human activity.

World-Ecological Revolution and Gothic at the Periphery

There is a sense in which gothic, as a literary mode given over to scenes of threat, horror, and exaggerated violence, might be considered broadly appropriate to the circumstances of heightened vulnerability in which lives are currently lived across the postcolonial Global South. But it is also possible to chart a more direct and tangible relationship between the mobilization of gothic forms in contemporary fiction from the peripheries of the world-system and the end phase of the Capitalocene as Moore has described it. Here we might return momentarily to Mashigo's Johannesburg, which, in figuring historical regimes of racial violence as literally sedimented, notably offers a vision of ongoing ruination that corresponds closely with Stoler's own. To the extent that this image is interpretable, too, as a Capitalocene record, presenting the over-laying of colonial by neoliberal formations in a way that imbues both with geological force, it also provides a vision of the terminal present, which—as Moore has noted—is a signal moment of capi-talist crisis shaped precisely by the accumulating effects of succes-sive Cheap Nature strategies. In his analysis of "gothic periodicity," Stephen Shapiro has argued that, since its inception, gothic has tended to proliferate at just such cyclically recurring periods of world-economic transition.[42] On this account, gothic's figures of violence and excess encode and make concrete the disorientating local experience of world-systemic shifts, which—planetary in scope—are not fully graspable from the ground of any single lo-cality. Michael Niblett makes a related argument around fantasti-cal fictional forms and moments of crisis but routes this through Moore.[43] If literature registers world-economic shifts, then—because the world-economy is a world-ecology—it will also bear the imprint of rising and falling Cheap Nature strategies, "since," Niblett notes, "these organize in fundamental ways the material conditions, social modalities and areas of experience upon which literary form works."[44]

   It is important that these assessments invest gothic with a protocritical potential: in registering the violent experience of in-corporation into a rising regime of capital, in other words, gothic forms enable an exposure of that system's caustic effects. Noting this, the Warwick Research Collective (WReC), of which Shapiro is part,[45] suggests that contemporary gothic fictions produced in peripheral zones self-consciously capitalize on these interrogative possibilities. In this millennial corpus, gothic not only *registers* the violent disorientation of world-ecological shifts from the perspec-tive of those geopolitical spaces they most deeply affect but is also a species of what the WReC follows Michael Löwy in calling "criti-cal irrealism":[46] a mode of fiction-making in which fantastic forms are *mobilized* precisely to critique regimes of capital and their strat-egies of Cheap Nature. This is the case in the narratives I will go on to address across the rest of this chapter. Gothic is not written, here, in a world shaped by human activity. Rather, it is a local re-sponse to and interrogation of a world made (and remade) in the image of empire, power, and capital, at a moment when the es-tablished technics of Nature-making are collapsing—unevenly—under the cumulative weight of their own effects.

Capitalocene Uncanny

In Henrietta Rose-Innes's *Green Lion,* set in a near-future Cape Town, these biospheric transformations appear chiefly as massive species loss: indeed, it seems that wild animal life has, at the moment of the narrative's taking place, been almost entirely extinguished. And yet, the text is also full of animal figures—if not animal *life* as such—and these are frequently presented in the gothic language of the uncanny. Protagonist Con, who works in a facility for the re-breeding of extinct lions, makes his way early in the novel through a house that is strangely crowded with hunting trophies. These are rendered uncanny by a relentless sense that they are not *not* alive: "The smell . . . death and chemicals. The passage was . . . dim, lined with the shadowy forms of animals on plinths; mounted heads . . . birds frozen in flight."[47] Leaving the house, Con feels he has been in a "place of danger": "perhaps even now [the creatures] were stirring from their pedestals, cracking their glass domes and inching towards the stairs."[48] Uncanniness emerges, to paraphrase the Freudian perspective,[49] from the disturbing coincidence of the familiar and the strange, which, as it implies the internality of what appears to be outside the self, unsettles the presumed coherence of the subject.

Amitav Ghosh has influentially argued that currently unfolding climate change produces experiences of the "environmental uncanny": "the freakish weather events of today, despite their radically nonhuman nature, are . . . animated by cumulative human actions."[50] In this sense, they prompt "an awareness that humans were never alone": that humanity exists within "the presence and proximity of nonhuman interlocutors."[51] Rose-Innes's uncanny animal figures appear to provoke a similar realization through the staging of a gothic scene. Their creeping liveliness emblematizes a Nature that, though it seems to exist in object form, possesses a vitality akin to Humanity's own.

And yet, situated in the wider context of the novel, the preserved animals also resist interpretation in Ghosh's terms. Where the environmental uncanny describes the unruly consequences of collective human action, the uncanniness of Rose-Innes's figures turns on the process of their production. As *Green Lion*'s animal effigies invoke an apparently external Nature, they simultaneously emphasize that this has been constructed through taxidermic reification. If an uncanny effect is derived from their embalmed bodies, then this has less to do with the recognition of shared vibrancy between humans and the rest of nature than it does with a sense that what has been transformed into object may yet be alive with some unpredictable agency. Rose-Innes maps this dynamic in wider terms over the course of the narrative, tracing processes of Nature-making across South African history. At the same time, the text suggests that these productions are not inert; instead they are shown to live—actively and catastrophically—within an encompassing web of life. In these ways, the narrative develops around the structure of what might be called a *Capitalocene uncanny*, imagining the systemic production of external Natures, and their threatening reanimations. Ultimately, it mobilizes an uncanny gothic to interrogate "green" thought that is undergirded by Anthropocene logic, to point toward the covert violence of this conceptual scaffolding and to its unevenly allocated material effects.

To begin with, however, and in a maneuver symbolically reiterated by the taxidermic process, the novel dramatizes the production of Nature under the neoliberal state in postapartheid South Africa. At a point in the recent past, a fence is built around Table Mountain, with the intention of keeping the dwindling animal population in and humans out. The government oversees this project, but jointly with corporate enterprise, so that the fence reflects the privatization of the environmental commons that characterizes the neoliberal agenda in South Africa and elsewhere. To the extent that it literally demarcates territories of Society and Nature, it also offers a vision of this current capitalist formation as, in Moore's words, "a way of organizing nature," and one that turns on the epistemic rift. This is historicized in the text in much the way that Mashigo historicizes the neoliberal present: as shaped by the cumulative effect of previous regimes. To build the fence, an informal settlement of shacks is cleared, explicitly recalling earlier forced removals under the apartheid state, and its perimeter describes an estate once owned by the notorious colonial-era mining magnate Cecil John Rhodes. As it links together these three formations of capital—neoliberal, apartheid, and colonial—*Green Lion*'s fence between Society and Nature presents them in world-ecological terms: as dispensations that have hinged on permutations of the socioecological binary. At the same time, this narrative trajectory figures the local history of capital's Cheap Nature strat-

egy in a way that underscores its relationship to the ongoing coloniality of power: across the histories the mountain enclosure
invokes, the exploitability or disposability of human life—the
vulnerability of life to appropriation—is determined according to
historical categories of race.

At the same time as the production of these Natures is em-
blematized by the embalmed bodies of the animals, *Green Lion*'s
uncanny taxidermy also signals a symmetry between capital's
Nature-making logic and the narrative's delineation of "green" responses to accelerating species loss. Shortly after he has negoti-
ated the trophy-lined passage, Con meets the "green lion" of the
novel's title:

> It gazed on him . . . with its mismatched eyes, one . . . stitched
> on like a monstrous teddy bear's. But more damage had been
> done. . . . The fur was streaked with bilious green. . . . The crea-
> ture's jaws were forced open around . . . a bald old tennis ball.
> Con . . . did not want to inhale this madness.[52]

These grotesque modifications are related to a cultish group of animal enthusiasts who call themselves "Green Lion" and who, with
the disappearance of animal life, have come to view animals as
invested with a kind of mystical power. It becomes clear as the
narrative goes on, however, that much as this community seeks
to resacralize the animal in a world that is destroying it, they also
retain the logic of the epistemic rift. In their view, extrahuman nature is explicitly presented as "something outside . . . human lives,"
and this gives way to an appropriative agenda: "There's . . . *energy*
we get from wild animals," one member explains.[53]

A more conventional version of the same dualist rhetoric is replicated by Con's manager—Amina—who describes herself as "a
conservationist" and also—in the same breath—"a human being": "I want to find ways to do what we can with what we have
left."[54] Both these perspectives on biospheric change—esoteric
and mainstream—admit conspicuously of a conceptual schism
between Humanity and Nature, this last becoming an external domain on which humanity impacts in either sensitive or deleterious
ways. This logic, Moore argues, undergirds Anthropocene thinking, which—interpreting climate emergency as the effect of collective human actions *on* nature—admits of a "*consequentialist bias*"[55]

and remains "captive to the very thought structures that created the present crisis."[56] In fact, the narrative itself gestures to this point, signaling the possibility, raised by T. J. Demos, that Anthropocene rhetoric might *facilitate* capital's Cheap Nature strategy.[57] To generate money for the rebreeding project, Amina (the "conservationist") considers running a canned hunting program—"people would pay a lot . . . to be the person to kill the last . . . lion"[58]—but it turns out this is already under way behind the fence, overseen by South Africa's corporate–state alliance. Any sense that commercial hunting will help to arrest the unfolding extinction is, from here, clearly debunked. The enclosure is now empty, as Con notes: "It was dead. . . . This mountain was finished . . . used up, shot out." Analogous to the taxidermic animals, he concludes, "It is a relic in a museum case."[59]

The gothic figure of the green lion thus incarnates not only the vision of Nature underpinning "green" endeavors in the narrative but more specifically the extent to which this Nature segues into that conception mobilized by the regimes of racial capital the novel has traced across South African history and which—more widely implemented—has produced the emergencies of the text's present. It is not insignificant, in this sense, that the lion appears in a setting that metaphorically invokes a heating earth: Con discovers it at the center of "a room [that] heaved with unhappy life. The vapours on this planet were hot and moist and thronging."[60] There is a sense, in fact, in which the taxidermy's uncanniness—its strange familiarity—is deployed in part to symbolize this coincidence of environmental thought and the very processes against which it is oriented: the green lion, on this perspective, makes visible an uneasy relation between "green" rhetoric and the logic of systematized violence.[61]

But there is also another uncanny dimension to the text's preserved animal bodies, which has to do with that incipient sense that these are about to creak into life and break out of their glass cases. The scenario is not far from the truth: a lion does escape the confines of its artificial enclosure, but this is the living animal with which Con works at the breeding facility. She disappears and, in doing so, becomes less a real creature than a peripheral presence that haunts the narrative's final stages and—importantly—signifies an alternative to taxidermic Nature: "For Con, the lioness is everywhere . . . her form slipping around every corner . . . her

growl behind the traffic rumble. . . . At other times, it's as if he himself is looking through her eyes."[62] All-encompassing, and inter-
weaving human and extrahuman, Society and Nature, this spectral
lion—more an existential state than a figure—invokes a relational
sense of nature as a whole, its fugitive haunting quality signaling
the failure of the language of the epistemic rift, which (like cage
bars or glass cases) cannot capture its real complexity.

If this seems to return us to Ghosh's environmental uncanny—
to an imbrication of collective humanity and extrahuman nature
exposed by contemporary climate events—then Rose-Innes's
narrative counters that possibility. As the monstrous lion-body
in its planetary hothouse affirms, the novel imagines biospheric
change in terms that symbolically suggest a view close to Moore's
own. It envisions the emergencies of the heating present not
as spiraling outward from a human collective but as the *oikeios*-
effects of the Cheap Nature strategy. This is a perspective that
locates capital and colonialism themselves within the web of
life: Natures unfold within and transform nature as a whole, and
these violent modulations—to return—are currently distributed
throughout the world-system via the coloniality of power. *Green
Lion* has already invoked the entanglement of racial oppression
and capitalist ecology in its treatment of the fenced-in mountain.
Toward its end, this is revisited in the motif of the haunting lion,
which—especially when it is refracted through an anxious gothic
lens—realizes the monstrous potential of those incipiently living
taxidermic effigies. In part, the lioness's transition from actual lion
to emblem of nature takes place as she becomes inseparable from
Con's adolescent encounter with another, unseen and—the text
suggests—supernatural predator in the mountain reserve: "cold
swept over his skin. . . . There was a sensation that a large creature
was moving alongside him . . . but the shadow lay frictionless on
his face. And cold, colder than a terrestrial shadow should be."[63]

Shortly afterward, a child mysteriously disappears from the
enclosure, and the scene is replayed in the novel's present when
a young girl is killed, ostensibly by the escaped lion, on the Cape
Flats. This is Cape Town's suburban periphery, invented by the
apartheid state, where the effects of postdemocracy neoliberali-
zation continue to be experienced as poverty and—in the face of
this—high rates of violent crime. If, on one hand, the youthful
victims of the spectral lion imply a generational distribution of

vulnerability to the transforming *oikeios*—a sense that the planetary future is curtailed for the youth—then the site at which the second attack takes place also suggests that gradations of threat continue to be governed by a history of systemic racialized violence and by the successive renewal of coloniality into the present.

Decolonial Horror

Ultimately in Rose-Innes's narrative, gothic threats stalk those South African localities where the effects of successive Cheap Nature strategies accumulate with particularly destructive density. This approach is taken up and developed more fully by Mashigo, who throughout *Intruders* deploys figures of horror to encode experiences of ongoing ruination in South Africa's millennial present. The world that emerges across this collection is one shaped by sedimented regimes of racial capitalism, and, as "The Parlemo" demonstrates, these are presented not only as social organizations. Rather they produce ontological shifts that transform the way life unfolds within the biosphere. It is these transformations in turn that form the basis for the text's speculative imaginary. In this sense, stories in *Intruders* implicitly situate themselves in something like a Capitalocene reality: they figure histories of racialized violence as an accretive geological force. A tale titled "Ghost Strain N" is noteworthy in this respect specifically as a narrative that interrogates the cumulative effects of Cheap Nature in South Africa through a located gothic vocabulary. Here South Africa's youth are transforming into what the text calls "Ghosts," zombie figures who survive by "breaking into homes, tearing hearts out of peoples' chests and eating them."[64]

The scenario mapped out in "Ghost Strain N" is connected to epidemics of substance abuse among impoverished South African communities ("N" stands for *nyaope*, a heroin cocktail), but it also reflects a wider generational anxiety that emerges in the wake of the country's neoliberal turn. As the effects of privatization, financialization, and restricted state support overlay the unevenness cultivated under apartheid, young South Africans raised in the new democracy nonetheless "face the same, if not greater, levels of unemployment, poverty, inequality and hopelessness than their parents."[65] The text imagines existence under these conditions as a state of undeath incarnated in the bodies of the Ghosts. Fre-

quently presented as unnaturally static—"suspended in time"[66]—
these encode an arrested futurity, which relates to a generation
stripped of opportunity but also to a sense of the present as a
moment of terminal crisis. The plague of Ghosts, which spreads
rapidly, dramatizes this failure as it inaugurates planetary breakdown: "In just a few months, things had fallen apart over the whole
world."[67] At the same time as the Ghosts register the dying spasms
of the Capitalocene from the local vantage of contemporary South
Africa, the tale locates the roots of this end time in the systemic
violence that has configured the country's colonized pasts. The
Ghosts embody histories of ruination, a function clearly apparent
in another "strain" of the zombie virus ("W") afflicting the wine-
making regions of South Africa, where—in a peculiarly grotesque
permutation of apartheid's Cheap Labor regime—vineyard workers have historically been paid in alcohol: "Strain W made Ghosts
rip out the oesophagus from people because they had wine poured
down their throats instead of being compensated by . . . those who
profited from their labour."[68]

In this way, Mashigo's narrative underscores the relation between unfolding planetary crisis and the coloniality of power. This
is shown both to drive current states of emergency and to govern the distribution of vulnerability to their effects among formerly colonized peoples and places. Any meaningful challenge to
the transforming biosphere must, the text implies, engage with
these historical realities. In the Capitalocene, in other words, resistance must be *decolonial*: it must seek to remake the world as
this has been produced, via diverse permutations of Eurocentric
modernity's epistemic rift. If the coloniality of power works to
epistemically peripheralize and render materially exploitable or
disproportionately vulnerable those it locates beyond what Walter
Mignolo calls "the colonial difference,"[69] then decolonial thinking
centralizes this condition, beginning from "the biographical sensing of the . . . body in the Third World." To think decolonially is thus,
on Mignolo's account, to think both "geo- and body-politically."[70]
It is a response to modernity that emerges from a lived experience
of modernity's violence and situates that experience as historically and systemically produced within an uneven global geography. Viewed through the critical irrealist lens the WReC provides,
Mashigo's vocabulary of horror can be understood as giving shape
to just such a geo- and body-political perspective on Capitalocene

realities. As it mobilizes images of living death to imagine dispro-portionate exposure to current crises, and as it locates this condi-tion as the effect of colonial capitalist pasts, the narrative draws on gothic to critically figure and situate a lived experience of violence.

Though horrifying, Mashigo's Ghosts can thus be read as envi-sioning the site at which a decolonial sensibility emerges. They pro-vide a vantage that, because it makes visible the systems through which bodies and environments are rendered vulnerable, is also a point from which to reimagine the strategies that have made the world—and to do so such that it is not violently experienced. This, importantly, is the function Mashigo ascribes to speculative fiction in the millennial South African context. "There needs to exist a place in our imaginations," she writes in the preface to *In-truders*, "that is the opposite of our present reality where a small minority owns most of the land and lives better than the rest."[71] The final passages of "Ghost Strain N" gesture toward this space. The tale closes in the aftermath of the plague, which—apocalyptic in proportion—has precisely destroyed the inequalities to which Mashigo refers. The reader is left with protagonist Koketso car-rying Steven—his best friend, now a zombie—about the country in a coffin to protect him from incineration. This is warranted, it turns out: Steven begins to recover sentience, and Koketso, who has been attacked by the undead, nonetheless remains alive and is undergoing a strange biophysical transformation: "the places where Steven had bitten him . . . glowed a little in the dark, and Koketso liked it."[72] The text's icon of horror is here refigured, al-beit tentatively, into something different—and more hopeful. And Capitalocene gothic from millennial South Africa (and perhaps from across the Global South more widely) might be understood as oriented generally toward similar transformations. As they map the systemic roots and uneven experiences of current crises—causes and distributions that are uniquely visible from the vantage of postcoloniality—gothic forms in these narratives also point implicitly, uneasily, toward the possibility of a future that is not configured by those processes that shape the past, and the present.

NOTES

1. Mohale Mashigo, *Intruders* (Johannesburg: Picador Africa, 2018), 50.
2. Mashigo, 49.
3. John S. Saul and Patrick Bond, *South Africa: The History as Present:*

From Mrs Ples to Mandela and Marikana (Woodbridge, U.K.: James Currey, 2014), 36.

4. Loren Kruger, *Imagining the Edgy City: Writing, Performing and Building Johannesburg* (Oxford: Oxford University Press, 2013), 1.

5. Kruger, 2.

6. Mashigo, *Intruders,* 55.

7. Mashigo, 55.

8. Jason W. Moore, *Capitalism in the Web of Life: Ecology and the Accumulation of Capital* (London: Verso, 2015), 77.

9. Rob Nixon, *Slow Violence and the Environmentalism of the Poor* (Cambridge, Mass.: Harvard University Press, 2011), 2–4.

10. Vishwas Satgar, "The Climate Crisis and Systemic Alternatives," in *The Climate Crisis: South African and Global Democratic Eco-Socialist Alternatives,* ed. Vishwas Satgar (Johannesburg: Wits University Press, 2018), 4–5.

11. Satgar, 5.

12. Jason W. Moore and Raj Patel, *A History of the World in Seven Cheap Things* (Oakland: University of California Press, 2017), 35.

13. Immanuel Wallerstein, *World-Systems Analysis: An Introduction* (Durham, N.C.: Duke University Press, 2004), 23.

14. Wallerstein, 30–31.

15. Wallerstein, 24–25.

16. Wallerstein, 31.

17. Walter Mignolo, "Geopolitics of Sensing and Knowing: On (De)coloniality, Border Thinking, and Epistemic Disobedience," *Confero* 1, no. 1 (2013): 130.

18. Aníbal Quijano, "Coloniality of Power, Eurocentrism and Latin America," *Nepantla: Views from the South* 1, no. 3 (2000): 533.

19. Quijano, 534–37.

20. Quijano, 537.

21. Jason W. Moore, "The Rise of Cheap Nature," in *Anthropocene or Capitalocene? Nature, History and the Crisis of Capitalism,* ed. Jason W. Moore (Oakland, Calif.: PM Press, 2016), 91.

22. Moore, *Capitalism in the Web of Life,* 14.

23. Moore, 70.

24. Moore, 76.

25. Moore, 2.

26. Aníbal Quijano, "Coloniality and Modernity/Rationality," *Cultural Studies* 21, no. 2–3 (2007): 172–73.

27. Moore, "Cheap Nature," 91.

28. Moore, *Capitalism in the Web of Life,* 158.

29. Rebecca Duncan, "From Cheap Labour to Surplus Humanity: World-Ecology and the Post-apartheid Speculative in Neill Blomkamp's *District 9,*" *Science Fiction Film and Television* 11, no. 1 (2018): 49–53.

30. Moore, *Capitalism in the Web of Life*, 15.
31. Moore, 8–10.
32. Moore, 3.
33. Moore's perspective "unif[ies] humanity and nature not only epistemically, but ontologically" (25). He argues that across mainstream, twentieth-century environmental criticism, conversations around human-nature relationality have taken place largely at the level of "philosophy and meta-theory" (24). World-ecology, however, addresses the issue "on the terrain of modern world-history" (25). The *oikeios*, in other words, is not only a concept for thinking beyond the dualism of Society and Nature; it is part of a "historical method" for understanding how—in real and material ways—"human and extra-human natures [have] co-produce[d] historical change" (25).
34. Moore, 9.
35. Moore, 2–3.
36. Moore, 1.
37. Moore, 1.
38. Ann Laura Stoler, "'The Rot Remains': From Ruins to Ruination," in *Imperial Debris: On Ruins and Ruination,* ed. Ann Laura Stoler (Durham, N.C.: Duke University Press, 2013), 2.
39. Stoler, 2.
40. Stoler, 11.
41. Stoler, 2.
42. Stephen Shapiro, "Transvaal, Transylvania: *Dracula*'s World-System and Gothic Periodicity," *Gothic Studies* 10, no. 1 (2008): 31.
43. Michael Niblett, "World-Economy, World-Ecology, World-Literature," *Green Letters* 16, no. 1 (2012): 21.
44. Niblett, 20. See also Kerstin Oloff, "Greening the Zombie: Caribbean Gothic, World-Ecology and Socio-ecological Degradation," *Green Letters* 16, no. 1 (2012): 31–45; Sharae Deckard, "Uncanny States: Global Ecogothic and the World-Ecology in Rana Dasgupta's *Tokyo Cancelled*," in *EcoGothic*, ed. Andrew Smith and Bill Hughes, 177–93 (Manchester, U.K.: Manchester University Press, 2013); and Rebecca Duncan, "Writing Ecological Revolution from Millennial South Africa: History, Nature and the Post-apartheid Present," *ARIEL: A Review of International English Literature* 54, no. 4 (2020): 65–97.
45. Sharae Deckard, Nicholas Lawrence, Neil Lazarus, Graeme Macdonald, Upamanyu Pablo Mukherjee, Benita Parry, and Stephen Shapiro, as the Warwick Research Collective (WReC), *Combined and Uneven Development: Towards a New Theory of World Literature* (Liverpool: Liverpool University Press, 2015).
46. Deckard et al., 96–97.
47. Henrietta Rose-Innes, *Green Lion* (Cape Town: Umuzi, 2016), 39.
48. Rose-Innes, 41.

49. Sigmund Freud, "The 'Uncanny,'" 1919, in *The Uncanny*, trans. David Mclintock (London: Penguin, 2003), 124.

50. Amitav Ghosh, *The Great Derangement: Climate Change and the Unthinkable* (Chicago: University of Chicago Press, 2016), 32.

51. Ghosh, 30.

52. Rose-Innes, *Green Lion*, 40.

53. Rose-Innes, 168–69.

54. Rose-Innes, 95.

55. Moore, "Cheap Nature," 82, emphasis in original.

56. Moore, 84. This critique of Anthropocene thinking is one element in Moore's wider assessment of "Green Thought" (5), by which he intends environmental scholarship and activism, chiefly from the latter half of the twentieth century. It is worth pointing out that Moore is not suggesting that ecocriticism directly promulgates an anthropo-ecological binary. Even a cursory reading of major work in this and cognate fields—scholarship from Donna Haraway, Stacy Alaimo, Bruno Latour, or Timothy Morton—reveals a "broad agreement that humans are part of nature" (5). What existing criticism has resisted, however, is the possibility that "human *organizations*—families, empires, corporations, markets—are natural forces" (5, emphasis added). Writes Moore, "For critical scholars . . . the consensus is clear: capitalism acts upon a nature that operates independently. . . . It makes a 'footprint' on the earth, which must be reduced" (5). It is in this sense, on Moore's account, that Green Thought (Anthropocene thinking included) reverts to the dualism of Humanity and Nature. The intervention of world-ecology is to provide a different historical picture, in which "the stories of human organization are co-produced by . . . human and extra-human nature" (7).

57. T. J. Demos, *Against the Anthropocene: Visual Culture and Environment Today* (Berlin: Sternberg Press, 2017), 19.

58. Rose-Innes, *Green Lion*, 119.

59. Rose-Innes, 238.

60. Rose-Innes, 40.

61. As it suggests this coincidence of racialized capitalist violence and environmentalist praxis, the narrative should also be understood as critiquing the wider entanglement of "green" agendas with colonial politics. Graham Huggan and Helen Tiffin point out that environmentalism has frequently "had catastrophic results for people violently co-opted into western systems." Huggan and Tiffan, *Postcolonial Ecocriticism: Literature, Animals, Environment* (London: Routledge, 2010), 186. *Green Lion*'s engagement with conservation is specifically noteworthy in this sense, since conservation practice is broadly motivated by a "pressure to preserve non-human animal and plant species" (186) and, as Huggan and Tiffin note in line with Moore, it thus reiterates

the Society–Nature dualism that also "provide[s] justification for . . . colonisation" (187). Farieda Khan affirms this point in her historical analysis of conservationist environmentalism in colonial and apartheid South Africa. Not only were African people excluded from conservation organizations that emerged under colonial administration in the late nineteenth century but the conservationist understanding "of the ideal protected natural area as . . . uninhabited" was also mobilized within the framework of segregation politics across the twentieth century and used to dispossess communities of their land. Khan, "The Roots of Environmental Racism and the Rise of Environmental Justice in the 1990s," in *Environmental Justice in South Africa,* ed. David A. MacDonald, 15–48 (Athens: Ohio University Press, 2002), 18. These histories are subliminally invoked in Rose-Innes's narrative and linked with the socioecological binary, when it emerges that the preservative enclosure of the mountain entails the destruction of an informal settlement and the displacement of its occupants.

62. Rose-Innes, *Green Lion,* 261.

63. Rose-Innes, 202.

64. Mashigo, *Intruders,* 37.

65. Robert Mattes, "The 'Born Frees': The Prospects for Generational Change in Post-apartheid South Africa," *Australian Journal of Political Science* 47, no. 1 (2012): 140.

66. Mashigo, *Intruders,* 31.

67. Mashigo, 39.

68. Mashigo, 40.

69. Walter Mignolo, "The Geopolitics of Knowledge and the Colonial Difference," *South Atlantic Quarterly* 101, no. 1 (2002): 60–62.

70. Mignolo, "Geopolitics of Sensing," 132.

71. Mashigo, *Intruders,* xi.

72. Mashigo, 46.

10

Overpopulation

The Human as Inhuman

TIMOTHY CLARK

The Earth now carries an extraordinary and overwhelming number of human beings—toward eight billion and rising. Humans account for about 36 percent of the biomass of all mammals, with their domesticated livestock making up another 60 percent, leaving a mere 4 percent of biomass accounted for by mammals in the wild.[1] Despite global fertility rates declining, human numbers are already set to rise toward ten billion by midcentury, before perhaps slowing.[2]

"Population, to be meaningful, must be modelled,"[3] and the fraught topic of overpopulation has always tended toward modes of gothic representation. To think in terms of very large numbers necessarily conjures gothic tropes: the human as inhuman, a dynamic perceived in statistical projections as a kind of remorseless growth, an impersonal algorithm, the faceless mass, and so on. Thus, like other global environmental problems, concepts of overpopulation tend toward images of zombification, as in the crude video *Zombie Overpopulation* (2015),[4] released by the charity Population Matters, filmed in a mock-documentary style and featuring zombies blundering around destroying their environment. As this chapter will argue, gothic tropes are particularly suited to representing a crucial feature of overpopulation pressure, of the human become other by dint of sheer numbers. At the same time, to celebrate the gothic as a cognitive resource for representing the Anthropocene may also be problematic. First, however, before turning to questions of representation, we need to outline the broad context of debate about overpopulation and the environment.

That overpopulation is a crucial environmental issue seems at first utterly obvious—more people means increased human impact, more displacement and destruction of nonhuman life, more pollution from human activity. At the same time, as soon as accounts of overpopulation are analyzed with a view to countermeasures, they emerge as morally and politically intractable, liable to brutal simplifications, hidden moral dilemmas, undesirable implications, and implicit kinds of discrimination, and, finally, ugly debates about immigration—especially given that population growth is now overwhelmingly concentrated in the poorer Global South. The relative absence of overpopulation from green literary criticism may have less to do with disputing the reality of the issue than with the deeply unpalatable nature of the questions it raises.[5]

For many Malthusians and neo-Malthusians in the nineteenth and twentieth centuries, engagement with issues of population restraint were driven by the desire to eradicate global poverty.[6] But it is also hard to forget the repellent forms of biopolitics with which claims of "overpopulation" have been linked, such as the mass-sterilization programs of India's Emergency Period (1975–77).[7] Whenever a birth control policy is instituted solely for economic or demographic reasons, as opposed to issues of women's rights, it has too easily become a form of coercive pressure on more vulnerable women.

In the 1960s and 1970s the so-called population bomb was a central focus of alarm about the future, anticipating features of the current debate about a so-called Anthropocene. Yet this debate now appears simplistic in retrospect. One may ask, what is the prime agent of the Anthropocene?[8] It is not humanity per se but the interaction or contamination of human behavior (primarily but not solely that of a wealthier and exploitative minority), technology, and multiple natural processes acting together in often unpredictable ways on the working of Earth's natural systems. The agent of change is a hybrid and self-conflicted material/intentional entity, inhabiting the increasingly chaotic realm of its own interference effects, as these now precipitate both social deprivation and the extinction of other forms of life. Accordingly, even the most die-hard "population bomb" activist must concede that global human overpopulation is not in itself *the* agent of an Anthropocene. However, it is, as it were, a decisive *catalyst,* one that renders dangerously potent all the other factors in planetary change. (*Catalyst*: "A substance that increases the rate of a chemical reaction without itself undergoing any permanent chemical change" [*Oxford Online Dictionary*]).[9] For instance, to the commonplace objection that population is not "the real problem," but that overconsumption is, must come the retort that if such iniquitous consumption were limited to only a few million people, instead of being a matter of several billions, then there would still be injustice but no threat to the Earth System itself and to the viability of much life on Earth, and no "Anthropocene" debate.

Fatalism is another factor in the relative silence on the population question: why debate something about which one can do next to nothing? A vast population is already "gothic" in the sense of embodying the oppressive overshadowing of the present by the past, a pervasive if usually merely assumed or even unperceived context of day-to-day life. Fertility rates are such slow factors of change, and human numbers already so vast, that even a current rate not much above the replacement level must still mean the pressures of vast, increasing numbers of people.

Given the industrialization of agriculture (the "Green Revolution"), the issue with population has become less the demographic constraint of limited resources than environmental side effects in terms of greenhouse gases, loss of biodiversity, and such. This green focus also highlights a blind spot in much official demography, even beyond the issue of acknowledging the vast difference in resource impacts and responsibility between privileged and impoverished human groups. The dominant framework for debates about population scenarios, "carrying capacities" for instance, as exemplified in collections like *Is the Planet Full?* (2014)[10] is a strikingly immoral one, for it simply assumes an unquestioned and exclusive human entitlement to all the resources of the planet, making no reference to the claims of nonhuman life. The only nonhuman creatures mentioned in Goldin's Introduction to *Is the Planet Full?* are bacteria as related to human diseases and to animals as "meats."[11] The same immorality structures this whole collection of expert essays in demography. Without this frightening discounting of all nonhuman life, however, the concept of "overpopulation" at once becomes far more elusive. *Whose* lives are counted in the "population" at issue? What is the intrinsic value of nonhuman lives, and how would that feed into demographic accounting and definitions of the *over* in *overpopulation*?[12]

Questions of Representation

Like climate change, global human overpopulation is never per-ceptible *as such*, for population elsewhere in the world, or on the Earth overall, is not to be sensed from any one place. Its apparent partial manifestations can be deceptive—the impact of human overpopulation on the planet is already pronounced, yet large ar-eas of the earth remain almost deserted, while a crowded city in Ethiopia may well have less environmental impact than a small town in Australia. Both overpopulation and climate change are what Karin Kuhlemann describes as an "unsexy" risk factor for catastrophe:

> The creeping nature of unsexy risks obscures the extent and momentum of accumulated and latent damage to collective goods, while shifting baselines tend to go unnoticed, mislead-ingly resetting our perception of what is normal. Even where we recognise that something is a problem, we may still not recog-nise the underlying, catastrophic trendline, or just how much damage is already baked into states of affairs that we come to regard as normal.[13]

Being seemingly impersonal, statistical, and dispersed over large space and time scales, overpopulation does not have a human face. Individual people may well be rational, but viewed en masse, humanity is not behaving as a rational entity, even in the limited sense of observing calculations of future self-interest.

Climate change and overpopulation represent seemingly com-parable challenges of literary representation. As is now much discussed, including in the Introduction to this volume, climate change resists conventional narration because its causes are mul-tiple, sometimes opaque, and widely dispersed in time and space, all of which resists any clearly grasped story line in terms of a se-ries of actions unfolding in a definite sequence to a determinable end. Nevertheless, climate change is now provoking new kinds of inventiveness and formal experimentation in literature. Yet, what is striking about representations of overpopulation here is that, overwhelmingly, the literary tendency for decades has been in the very opposite direction, toward plots of cartoonish simplicity and crude and even ludicrous dystopian scenarios.

Samantha Morgan summarizes the nature of a large number of overpopulation dystopias thus:

> Time and again, the image of teeming and violent metropolis, its inhabitants crammed into tiny apartments, subsisting on vat-grown meat or processed algae, became standard in the futures imagined in the second half of the twentieth century. Isaac Asimov's *The Caves of Steel* (1954), Harry Harrison's *Make Room! Make Room!* (1966), and John Brunner's *Stand on Zanzibar* (1968), as well as short stories by Kurt Vonnegut and J. G. Ballard take place in cities where civil unrest increases as the availability of space, food, and water decreases.[14]

Much fiction on overpopulation still seems covered by these clichés, a kind of limited overpopulation gothic—as with Paolo Bacigalupi's more recent, trite "Pop Squad" (2008), which depicts illegal babies being tracked and shot in the head, in the context of a society in which the privileged no longer age.[15] All of these scenarios are basically evasive, for they jump over the issue of overpopulation as a challenge in the present in order to represent its extreme extrapolation in the future.

Henri Bergson famously described the nature of humor and jokes as arising often from when "a person gives the impression of being a thing."[16] The algorithmic dynamics of demography give a corresponding sinister, bad-joke quality to many literary dystopias about overpopulation, such as "Billenium" by J. G. Ballard.[17] In this short story, a city is depicted as having so many people that road traffic is now a thing of the past, as roads are now just streams of people on foot. There are so many that "people jams" at the junctions can last more than a day, and it can take hours to cross the street just to buy lunch. Ballard's main plot follows a simple dynamic: each person is strictly rationed to a tiny in-house space, but the central protagonist and his friend discover that their house has a whole, previously hidden room. Once the new room is taken, it is soon then subdivided to give space to two women friends, then further subdivided for parents, so that soon the initial situation of extreme confinement has merely repeated itself like an underlying law of life. In this, the "bad joke" structure lies in the reduction of human behavior and character to the simplicity of an algorithmic process, a kind of zombification. The attempt to represent demographic pressure in so direct and heightened a way pushes realism into the realm of the surreal, the fantastic, or the merely absurd.

Anthony Burgess's novel *The Wanting Seed* (1962)[18] presents one of the more incongruous versions of an overpopulation dystopia out of a seeming desire to shock. Overpopulation in the future is seen as leading to new forms of social discrimination. The main protagonist, Tristram, is disadvantaged for a possible promotion at work because he comes from a family of four children.[19] It is a world in which lack of space and restrictions on family size lead to a glorification of homosexuality, on the bizarre, homophobic assumption that same-sex couples do not want children, while Tristram adopts the mincing, "effeminate" manner of gay male stereotypes of the day. As social order disintegrates, cannibalism arises and is depicted as a ghastly version of the Roman Catholic Mass. Whereas Harry Harrison's novel *Make Room! Make Room!* (1966)[20] makes some plausible sense as a *noir* image of a future, vastly overcrowded New York of social degradation and basic shortages, its much-revised film version, *Soylent Green* of 1973,[21] caters to a more extreme taste as its central detective protagonist unearths the grim truth that soylent, a government-sponsored food, is actually made from reprocessed human flesh. Since the peak of concern in the 1960s and 1970s with overpopulation, the issue has hardly gone away but has become a standard, if under-analyzed, background feature of innumerable fictional dystopias since, in literature, cinema, comics, and computer games.

In the overpopulation dystopias by Burgess, Harrison, Bacigalupi, Ballard, and numerous others, the scenarios are often so grotesquely extreme as to risk disarming in advance any chance of being taken seriously in relation to overpopulation in a contemporary context, even when this is how they present themselves.[22] However, instead of simply dismissing all these texts as "bad" writing or sensationalism, it may be useful to consider why it is that depicting overpopulation seems to slide so easily into caricature. It is as if the more directly a text tries to home in on depicting increasing human numbers, the more simplistic it risks becoming. Thus it is that the more interesting fictions about overpopulation treat it *indirectly*, as one environmental factor among others. Brunner's *Stand on Zanzibar* (1968),[23] for instance, even though it features in Morgan's list of cliché overpopulation dystopias, also "resists unicausal explanations of environmental disaster, focusing on multiple social and governmental culprits."[24] Lionel Shriver's *Game Control* (1994)[25] (discussed later) engages overpopulation primarily in offering a subtle and humorous study of the language, psychology, and culture of demographers. The relatively simplistic nature of the other texts could be said to reinforce the fact that overpopulation is not, in itself, *the* agent of an Anthropocene but a catalyst whose force depends on its implication in other economic and social realities, such as overconsumption in some areas or the pressures of poverty in others.

The often crass nature of so many overpopulation dystopias suggests two thoughts. The first is that the plethora of absurd scenarios underlines the fact that to depict overpopulation as *the* decisive environmental problem is a serious misreading, and this is what becomes highlighted in these cartoonish extrapolations of planetary overcrowding. A second, more disturbing conclusion follows: that while human overpopulation is indeed a powerful catalyst of environmental violence, it is also, insidiously, of a nature to resist *credible* representation singly, as a force by itself. For how can you know or represent the nature of a catalyst considered on its own? This is the elusive nature of overpopulation as an object of environmental debate—such that a voice of hasty objection will always arise in the discomfort of discussing it, with the pertinent but only partly true retort "but the real problem is . . ."

Overpopulation and an Anthropocene Gothic?

Tobias Menely and Jessie Oak Taylor, discussing concepts of the Anthropocene as an event "that exceeds narrativization," write that

> the Anthropocene provides an opportunity for literary studies to test and transform its methods by examining how the symbolic domain might, or might not, index a historicity that exceeds the human social relation and encompasses planetary flows of energy and matter.[26]

The gothic uncanniness of overpopulation lies in the inhuman/human element of the demographic, a dynamic that seems to "exceed the human social relation," even while being inextricable from it. Questions of population include mathematical effects that escape the human symbolic domain but are nevertheless entirely immanent to human society—the emergent effects, both psychic and material, of sheer large numbers, vulnerability to disease epidemics for instance, or the fact that the more people there are concentrated in a region, the more the probable need for its administration and overview, the greater its organizational complexity, and the higher the probability of restrictions on individuals. It is one side effect of the Covid-19 pandemic that the general public has acquired a new familiarity with the sometimes daunting force and projections of population statistics and alarming multiplier effects.

Why "gothic" in particular? At issue here is an interpretation of the "gothic" different from its once-standard interpretation as a manifestation of a cultural or personal unconscious, of the repressed or the culturally disavowed. Jerrold E. Hogle's Introduction to *The Cambridge Companion to Gothic Fiction* (2002) is representative in its reading of gothic as making readers "confront what is psychologically buried in individuals or groups, including their fears of the mental unconscious itself."[27] For example, in Mary Shelley's *Frankenstein,* the monster made from pieces of dead bodies can be read both as its maker's fantasy of reembracing his dead mother and as a making manifest of tensions and choices "simmering at the subliminal levels of his culture (in his *political unconscious*)," such as "the rise of a 'monstrous' urban working class."[28] Gothic in this sense informed what became a standard reading of the numerous fictional dystopias on overpopulation from the second half of the twentieth century, texts such as Robert Bloch's *This Crowded Earth* (1958),[29] Burgess's *The Wanting Seed,* Harrison's *Make Room! Make Room!,* Kurt Vonnegut's "Welcome to the Monkey House" (1968),[30] Ballard's "Billenium," Max Ehrlich's *The Edict* (1971),[31] Ursula Le Guin's *The Lathe of Heaven* (1971),[32] and many others. These are plots in which a concern with the proliferation of people is explained by critics as really the manifestation of some more familiar and immediate political anxiety. For instance, in a survey of postwar gothic, Steven Bruhm writes of "the racist representation of vampires as Mexican immigrants in John Carpenter's 1998 film *Vampires*" and of "the fear of eastern Europeans in Stoker's *Dracula,* which additionally indicates the fear of the unknown 'foreign' parts of ourselves, be they sexual or 'spiritual.'"[33]

Andreu Domingo deploys a similar cultural diagnostic in his survey of accounts of population-focused dystopias, or "demodystopias."[34] These texts, with their crowds, social breakdown, and so on, can be explained, he argues, as their authors' fear of a contemporary unrest, of the masses as a "potential source of subversion, as a result of disquiet arising from inequalities and scarcities."[35] The tumultuous and populous cities fortify themselves; their precincts, packed or deserted, have become unsafe. The streets, whether labyrinthine or in the gridlike pattern of the Big Apple, have the same function as the forests of heroic medieval legends, the jungles of adventure novels, or the immensity of outer space in science fiction, transmuted into this sinister, dangerous, and uncontrollable place.

This is a consistent but surely also narrow reading. For Domingo and others, there seems no question that overpopulation, however simplistically fictionalized, might ever itself be taken as a real issue, instead of as a kind of fantasy topic that only reflects anxieties or prejudices about cultural power in its immediate context. While justified in significant ways, to read all these texts solely in terms of another race/class/gender diagnostic also remains inadequate: it is to internalize, in terms that admit of tidy moral accounting, issues that also remain not just a matter of individual or group psychology at all but the impersonal dynamics of large numbers, of an unassimilable exteriority.

Beyond the elements of cultural anxiety and abjection in these texts, the frequent grotesquery of "overpopulation gothic" can be traced to another cause. The distortions, contortions, absurdities, and deformations of much overpopulation fiction enact the strain of representing the broad time and spatial scales of world demography in a narrative form on the immediate human scale. With overpopulation, or climate change, what seems just normal, or discounted, on the day-to-day scale—the slight expansion of a settlement, a new power station, a third child, an academic flying to a conference—becomes part of a dynamic that could appear monstrous at the scale of decades or centuries, and which thus becomes engaged through a reverse literary strategy of depicting the day-to-day scale as a form of the monstrous or fantastic, as in the continually self-dividing rooms of Ballard's "Billenium."

An instance of this literary strategy is an early scene in Burgess's *The Wanting Seed*. There, a Dr. Acheson cheerfully consoles the main protagonist, Tristram, and his wife, Beatrice-Joanna, on the death of their infant son from meningitis. In this scene a mode of thinking that might seem rational or defensible when the topic is demographic statistics ("'We do care about human life,' said Dr Acheson, stern. 'We care about stability. We care about not letting the earth get overrun.'") becomes shocking and inappropriate when transposed into an individual attitude in an individual case ("'You've had your recommended ration. No more motherhood for you. Try to stop feeling like a mother.' He patted her again").[36] Likewise, a fact normally expressed en masse as a statistic about mortality rates is personified, as it were, in one doctor's statement about the death of one child, and the demographic focus on resource use is being extrapolated and caricatured in the image of the child's body as a source of recycled phosphorus pentoxide: "Think of this in national terms, in global terms. One mouth less to feed. One more half-kilo of phosphorus pentoxide to nourish the earth, in a sense, you know, Mr Foxe, you'll be getting your son back again."[37]

In effect, the grotesque in such texts can be read as a scalar disjunction made sensuous. It enacts a kind of scalar interference between representational frames. Other than being normalized as the internal/psychic made sensuous and external, such gothic tropes or plots would express external contexts whose force is precisely their resistance to being accountable or internalizable as matters of attitude or cultural politics alone, the effects of an impersonal scalar dynamic, the emergent effects merely of very large numbers.

Burgess's monstrous/comic scene encapsulates the basic rhetorical strategy of many of these texts and a resulting sense of the incongruous in many of them. In the most thoughtful of fictions on overpopulation, Lionel Shriver's *Game Control* (1994), set in a fast "developing" Kenya, the demographic expert and dangerously charismatic antihero Calvin Piper, with his pet monkey called "Malthus," is a villain in the gothic tradition of the deranged scientist, plotting a culling of the human species. The novel's main protagonist, Eleanor, is engaged in benevolent, noncoercive programs of social aid, including dispensing contraceptives, and she repeatedly irritates Piper with her sense of individual compassion and social conscience. She is his critic at first but later becomes a convert to his extreme, latently racist, and appalling views. Piper's statements gain their sense of horror by dramatizing at the immediate personal scale issues whose import and significance (or otherwise) could be apparent only on a time scale of generations. Shriver's grotesque comedy pivots around Piper's seeming plan to save humanity by developing a drug that will selectively cull one-third of the world population:[38]

> "In public we refer to our enterprise as the NAADP: New Angles on Active Demographic Prophylaxis. But that's not what it really stands for."
> "Which is?"
> Calvin grinned. "The National Association for the Advancement of Dead People."[39]

Demographic expertise seems to demand a drug that will affect only certain parts of the population (i.e., the issue of target groups that renders population talk often so unethical):

> "We have discussed designing an alternative pathogen for industrialized nations, with their below-replacement fertility rates. The North is threatened by an ageing population. Shrinking labour pools will force it to accept immigration, transforming the cultural complexion of these countries. The old are economically unproductive and burdensome to social systems. We recommend an agent that hits geriatric targets and leaves the juvenile cohort largely intact."
> Eleanor squirmed. She liked her grandmother.[40]

Likewise, in an exchange on HIV:

> "You find high infection rates *optimistic*?"
> "Threadgill is browned off with me. HIV—he thinks I invented it."
> "That's preposterous!"
> "Not really. And I was honoured."[41]

Piper queries what, taking a very long-term view, it is to be "kind" or "generous" in relation to day-to-day life. He objects to Eleanor's programs of humanitarian aid:

"You would be far more generous to launch into [the town of]
Mathare with a machine gun."

   "I don't think that kind of joke is very funny."

"It isn't a joke."[42]

Eleanor gradually comes under his influence, describing the culling
of elephants as "an act of love" ("Without culling, all the elephants
would have starved. However paradoxically, cropping was an act
of love").[43]

What is incongruous or absurd or bad-joke-like in the earlier
overpopulation dystopias is here artfully transmuted by Shriver
into a kind of deliberate and knowing shock tactic. While gothic
has always edged toward self-parody, these bizarre quotations from
Game Control are not merely mocking or satirical of bigotry: they
can also be read, with caveats, as engaging one of the most insidious features of the "Anthropocene," the discrepancy between the
appearance of human to human life at the daily familiar scale and
the (most often invisible or merely inferred) emergence of sheer
human numbers as a disruptively catalytic force in the workings of
the Earth System. An Anthropocene gothic, so to speak, express-
ing a disjunction between issues of ethics considered at conflicting
scales, becomes here a kind of horrific humor. Its force is to be more
of a provocation to debate than to offer any palatable solution, with
the question of whether issues of right and wrong are invariable, regardless of the spatial and temporal scales at which they are considered. Is shooting an elephant always a wrong to the species, or could
it somehow mutate, over a time scale of generations, into a "good"
or even "generous" action, "an act of love" even? What happens to
terms like *good, generous,* and *love* in the process? The provocative
wit of Shriver's villain lies in such dislocations of scale and the disturbing way they torque given ethical terms.

Shriver's "mad scientist" figure eventually gives himself over to
the police, his deadly virus proving in fact harmless and his whole
plot effectively a publicity stunt ("It so happens that intellectual
courage is the only kind I've got").[44] The provocative humor of Piper's grotesquery (e.g., shooting people seen as a kind of generosity)
highlights another aspect of the insidiousness of overpopulation
as an issue for literary representation. Does the fact that gothic
tropes come so easily and even so inevitably to hand when describing global environmental threats also help make these things ob-

jects of psychological evasion, dismissal, or disbelief? For, however seriously discussed "the gothic" may be in the academy, with the general public, gothic remains overwhelmingly an aesthetic category associated with sensationalism and entertainment. Studies of why people enjoy horror, fear, and anxiety in literature or film almost always relate this enjoyment to an accompanying feeling of pleasure received from the implicit or assumed knowledge that, whatever the horrors being represented, its consumers are themselves quite safe (just as it turns out always to have been the case behind Piper's plans for mass murder).[45] To represent the Anthropocene in gothic terms may risk aiding forms of environmental denial, insofar as it deploys material, images, and narratives whose underlying signal of "you are safe" may well be misleading. If overpopulation as a long-term environmental problem resists sensuous representation except in gothic form, this may be disconcertingly close to the statement that such overpopulation cannot be represented except in a form that resists its being taken as seriously as it should be.

The insidious elusiveness of the issue is apparent in other common fictional plots concerning overpopulation. In many texts, the scalar challenge of representing global overpopulation is effectively sidestepped, and the focus is on a single heroine or group depicted as a victim of population measures that have become a form of tyranny. This focus enables the text to realize itself as personal drama or adventure story on the normal individual human scale. We see repeatedly scenarios of a mother hiding her illegal additional child from the persecutions of the "population police," while in Margaret Peterson Haddix's young adult Shadow Children series,[46] the vicissitudes of an illegal and hidden third child are used to express standard issues of maturation and identity. Alternatively, we read of dystopias in which population politics instantiate a form of brutally intensified and institutionalized misogyny, as in Margaret Atwood's *The Handmaid's Tale* (1985).[47] Such texts, with their powerful focus on individual lives, engage crucial social questions, but they are not about overpopulation as a current, pressing global issue. The issue of the effect of human numbers over broad time scales is largely evaded by dramatizing issues of obvious individual or social wrong in the future.

Keith Clavin has highlighted the contradictory dynamics of such dystopian scenarios in two recent films, *Snowpiercer* (2013), directed by Bong Joon-ho, and *Mad Max: Fury Road* (2015), directed by George Miller.[48] In *Snowpiercer,* a seemingly genuine battle against an enemy is revealed as a constructed scenario to keep human numbers down, as in a similarly bizarre episode of Burgess's *The Wanting Seed* half a century earlier. In *Mad Max: Fury Road,* a viciously patriarchal tyranny in a severely resource-depleted world is overthrown by a rising matriarch, but the film ends on her moment of victory without any adequate sense of how this triumph and liberation will address the dearth of resources. Both films, Clavin argues, implicitly correlate measures for a sustainable population with a murderous tyranny, for the villains are always engaged in forms of population management, so that the audience will identify with the humanist and individualist values of those who resist it. Yet this is to evade the question of whether the triumph of issues of social equity can genuinely address those pressures of overpopulation out of which the tyranny arose. In using clichés of overpopulation as a whipping boy for the rather too automatic affirmation of humanist values, Clavin argues, such plots are surreptitiously endorsing modes of thinking that were implicated in the causes of overpopulation in the first place. In sum, it would seem that overpopulation can hardly be represented as an issue for the individual person except in the form of protests against hypothetical measures to engage it. The interest of overpopulation, from a rhetorical or formal point of view, becomes, why does it not seem representable as a serious and worthy environmental issue except in terms that come close to its evasive dismissal or denial? This challenge of its representation, on top of all the other moral issues it raises, renders overpopulation especially insidious as an environmental issue.

NOTES

1. "Humans and Big Ag Livestock Now Account for 96 Percent of Mammal Biomass," *Ecowatch,* May 23, 2018, https://www.ecowatch.com/biomass-humans-animals-2571413930.html.

2. "Today, the world's population continues to grow, albeit more slowly than in the recent past. Ten years ago, the global population was growing by 1.24 per cent per year. Today, it is growing by 1.10 per cent per year, yielding an additional 83 million people annually. The world's population is projected to increase by slightly more than one billion people over the next 13 years, reaching 8.6 billion in 2030, and

to increase further to 9.8 billion in 2050 and 11.2 billion by 2100." See "World Population Prospects: The 2017 Revision Key Findings and Advance Tables," United Nations, 2017, 2, https://population.un.org/wpp/Publications/Files/WPP2017_KeyFindings.pdf.

3. "The Stature of Man: Population Bomb on Spaceship Earth," in *Scale in Literature and Culture,* ed. Michael Tavel Clarke and David Wittenberg (Cham, Switzerland: Palgrave Macmillan, 2017), 157.

4. "Zombie Overpopulation," 2015, https://www.youtube.com/watch?v=tfl3zJA6HbY.

5. Roy Beck and Leon Kolankiewicz have analyzed how, in the period 1970–98, American environmental groups, such as the Sierra Club, by forming close alliances with and taking up the programs of civil rights groups, gradually came to downplay and eschew questions of overpopulation that had earlier been very prominent in their campaigning work on wilderness protection: "While the agendas of the human rights and environmental groups should not be seen as fundamentally at odds with each other, they nonetheless are not the same. . . . The human rights agenda is by necessity oriented toward the immediate needs of individuals. The environmental agenda has often also dealt with immediate threats but just as often works for goals that are far into the future. . . . Human rights work is about people getting their full share of rights; its ideal is freedom. Environmental work is often about asking or forcing people to restrain their rights and freedoms in order to protect the natural world from human actions, so that people who are not yet born might someday be able to enjoy and prosper in a healthy, undiminished environment. The fact that human rights work and environmental work involve tensions between goals and philosophy does not mean that either of them must be seen as wrong or right." "The Environmental Movement's Retreat from Advocating U.S. Population Stabilization (1970–1998): A First Draft of History," *Journal of Policy History* 12, no. 1 (2000): 144–45. The paper concludes that the issue of overpopulation was gradually dropped for political reasons, that is, preserving the public status of the environmental community: "By the 1990s, it may be that environmental groups had conceded priority to the human rights groups and at least tacitly had agreed to press for environmental protections only when they did not conflict with the human rights agenda. [Michael] Hanauer wrote that during the 1990s the moral high ground was often yielded to those who gave precedence to human rights over environmental protection" (145).

6. See Alison Bashford's *Global Population: History, Geopolitics, and Life on Earth* (New York: Columbia University Press, 2013), 41.

7. See Prajakta R. Gupte, "India: 'The Emergency' and the Politics of Mass Sterilization," *Asian Studies* 22, no. 3 (2017): 40–44.

8. I use this rather modish term guardedly, and in the sense defended in my *The Value of Ecocriticism* (Cambridge: Cambridge University Press, 2019), 19–22.

9. *Oxford English Dictionary*, s.v. "catalyst," https://en.oxforddictionaries .com/definition/catalyst.

10. Ian Goldin, ed., *Is the Planet Full?* (Oxford: Oxford University Press, 2014). In Anthony B. Atkinson's analysis of what overpopulation is, based on a version of utilitarian economics, we read "the cost of an additional person is equal to what they consume minus what they produce," an equation that only makes sense in a framework of a kind of human solipsism. Such brutal anthropocentrism is also the unexamined basis for such seemingly reasonable statements in demography as "the world could be 'overpopulated' with five billion people with unsustainably high consumption levels whereas over ten billion poor people with low consumption levels would not exhaust the planet's carrying capacity. This is not to say that poverty is good" (Goldin, 2). Toby Ord weighs the issues of whether increasing population should be considered a benefit, given that each additional human life has its intrinsic, positive value. Such anthropocentricism also underlies the notion of "sustainable development" stemming from the Brundtland Commission Report of 1987 (i.e., the aim of meeting current needs for the world's human population without compromising the ability of future generations to meet those same needs).

11. Goldin, 18.

12. The constitutive anthropocentrism of debates about population appears in a different guise in the rising concern with what is being called "underpopulation." With falling birthrates, now at less than replacement in the most "developed" countries, there is talk of the damaging effects of "underpopulation"—yet this *underpopulation* is an alarmingly slanted term. The sense of deficiency at work in the *under-* is predicated on the numbers needed by the projected demands of a capitalist economy. Whereas the term *overpopulation* usually describes a condition relating to ecological limits and notions of "carrying capacity," *underpopulation* has a primarily economic and political reference only, being a form of pressure on the perpetuation of current (overpopulated) modes of social organization that already doom innumerable kinds of nonhuman life to extinction. In sum, both terms in their very different ways condense within themselves multiple and conflicting assumptions and moral evasions.

13. Karin Kuhlemann, "Complexity, Creeping Normalcy and Conceit: Sexy and Unsexy Catastrophic Risks," *foresight*, March 2018.

14. Samantha Morgan, "Malthusian Ideas: Sheri S. Tepper's New Ecological Misery," *ISLE* 22, no. 2 (2015): 225.

15. Paolo Bacigalupi, *Pump Six* (San Francisco: Night Shade Books, 2018), 137–62.
16. Quoted in Simon Critchley, *On Humour* (London: Routledge, 2002), 55.
17. J. G. Ballard, *The Complete Short Stories* (London: Flamingo, 2001), 267–78.
18. Anthony Burgess, *The Wanting Seed* (1962; repr., New York: W. W. Norton, 1976).
19. Burgess, 31.
20. Harry Harrison, *Make Room! Make Room!* (1966; repr., London: Penguin, 2008).
21. Richard Fleischer, dir., *Soylent Green* (United States: Metro-Goldwyn-Mayer, 1973).
22. In fact, these twentieth-century overpopulation clichés continue urban gothic tropes established in nineteenth-century literature about overcrowding in vast cities, really a simpler and rather different issue from global overpopulation. For Victorian images of urban population, see Emily Steinlight, *Populating the Novel: Literary Form and the Politics of Surplus Life* (Ithaca, N.Y.: Cornell University Press, 2018).
23. John Brunner, *Stand on Zanzibar* (New York: Doubleday, 1968).
24. Neal Bukeavich, "'Are We Adopting the Right Measures to Cope?': Ecocrisis in John Brunner's 'Stand on Zanzibar,'" *Science Fiction Studies* 29 (2002): 56.
25. Lionel Shriver, *Game Control* (1994; repr., London: Borough Press, 2015).
26. Tobias Menely and Jessie Oak Taylor, eds., *Anthropocene Reading* (Philadelphia: Pennsylvania State University Press, 2017), 5.
27. Jerrold Hogle, ed., Introduction to *The Cambridge Companion to Gothic Fiction* (Cambridge: Cambridge University Press, 2002), 3.
28. Hogle, 4.
29. Robert Bloch, *This Crowded Earth* (1958; repr., New York: Belmont Books, 1968).
30. Title story of *Welcome to the Monkey House* (New York: Delacorte Press, 1968).
31. Max Ehrlich, *The Edict* (New York: Doubleday, 1971).
32. Ursula K. Le Guin, *The Lathe of Heaven* (New York: Avon Books, 1971).
33. Steven Bruhm, "The Contemporary Gothic: Why We Need It," in Hogle, *Cambridge Companion to Gothic Fiction*, 271.
34. Andreu Domingo, "Demodystopias: Prospects of Demographic Hell," *Population and Development Review* 34 (2008): 725–45.
35. Domingo also rightly objects that the disruption depicted in these dystopias is politically evasive, for these are contexts in which "scarcity is not a problem of production and distribution, but a simple consequence of too many people" (731).

36. Burgess, *Seed*, 5.

37. Burgess, 4.

38. This is a common supervillain plot, repeated for example in Dan Brown's thriller *Inferno* (New York: Doubleday, 2013) about a mad-scientist plot to release a drug that would sterilize a third of humanity. As often, overpopulation is not really being engaged as an issue but merely exploited as a handy motive for sensationalized crime.

39. Shriver, *Game Control*, 257.

40. Shriver, 250.

41. Shriver, 57.

42. Shriver, 55.

43. Shriver, 141.

44. Shriver, 372.

45. See Mathias Clasen, "Why Horror Is So Popular: And May Even Be Good for Us," *ScienceNordic*, January 7, 2018, http://sciencenordic. com/why-horror-so-popular. "Clasen and his team believe that people who seek out and enjoy horror may do so because it helps them feel a sense of control or mastery over their fears." Chelsea Whyte, "The Benefits of Being Scared," *New Scientist*, February 9, 2019, 8.

46. Shadow Children (boxed set): *Among the Hidden*; *Among the Impostors*; *Among the Betrayed*; *Among the Barons* (New York: Simon and Schuster, 2004).

47. Margaret Atwood, *The Handmaid's Tale* (Toronto: McClelland and Stewart, 1985).

48. Keith Clavin, "Living Again: Population and Paradox in Recent Cinema," *Oxford Literary Review* 38, no.1 (2016): 47–66.

« 11 »

Digging Up Dirt

Reading the Anthropocene through German Romanticism

BARRY MURNANE

Written in 1818 and first published in the *Serapionsbrüder (The Serapion Brethren)* collection (1819–21), E. T. A. Hoffmann's "Die Bergwerke zu Falun" ("The Mines of Falun") anchors critical thinking about the Anthropocene to the ground we live on and with.[1] Set against a background of Romantic *Naturphilosophie,* medicine, and mining science, Hoffmann's tale tells the story of a young sailor with the East India Company called Elis Fröbom who returns to his native Sweden, travels to work at a copper mine in Falun, and dies when the mines collapse in upon him while he pursues a fantastic, eroticized figure called the "mineral queen." The story ends with an uncanny reminder of the biological and geological intimacy central to experiences of the Anthropocene when decades later, a new generation of miners discovers his apparently petrified body. In Hoffmann's world, our intimacy with the earth we transform is profoundly unsettling and self-endangering, revealing how the ground beneath our feet becomes aberrant, the uncanny site of strange but familiar agencies, both human and otherwise.

As a result of a series of suggestive binary pairs of Elis's bride Ulla–the mineral queen, sexuality–aestheticized sensuality, and materialism–supernaturalism, most critics of Hoffmann's story have argued that the mines are an allegorical spatialized representation of Elis's mental life and unconscious desires.[2] I do not propose we ignore these psychological readings, but I argue that to focus solely on Elis's conflicting and narcissistic sexual desires ignores the technologies of global trade and metal extraction that frame his experiences in Falun. "Die Bergwerke" begins with a reference to Elis's colonial journeys with the East India Company and detailed descriptions of a violent extraction process, and countless references to economic interests punctuate the text with a frame of social reference beyond Elis alone.

In this chapter, I pursue a reading of "Die Bergwerke" as a multivalent document of the Anthropocene. Firmly anchored in discourses of geology, natural science, psychology, and environmental pollution,[3] Hoffmann's story enables twenty-first-century readers to historicize the Anthropocene in which we live. Moreover, "Die Bergwerke" also historicizes the Romantic ecological discourse of its own time by referencing the older colonial and technoscientific contexts from which it emerged, showing that the mines matter just as much as the mind does. Indeed, I argue that Hoffmann's story renders visible the blind spots of collective human economic and geological actions involved in extraction capitalism. Finally, I suggest that the place of the gothic in the Anthropocene might lie in its ability to represent the distortions and illusions of the dominant economic, political, and scientific discourses in modernity, deploying its central tropes and motifs like fantastic and monstrous figures, chronotopical disruptions, and experiences of *frisson* to represent the messiness of humanity's relationship with the nonhuman world.

The Mines Matter—"Die Bergwerke" between Psychology and Anthropocene

"Die Bergwerke" portrays a world infused with strange forces that simultaneously manifest themselves externally (the mineral world) and internally (Elis's visionary states). When in the mines, Elis experiences repeated unsettling mysterious visions, such as an old miner who appears to him while he is working "in dicke[m] Schwefeldampf gehüllt" ("wrapped in such sulphurous fumes") (*Bergwerke*, 227/*Mines*, 163, translation amended). Given this demonic apparition, it is no surprise that Elis is shaken with fear: "Elis sah mit Entsetzen, wie er behende gleich einer Eichkatz' die schmalen Sprossen der Leiter heraufhüpfte und in dem schwarzen Geklüft verschwand" ("Elis saw with horror how he scrambled up the narrow rungs of the ladder as nimbly as a squirrel and vanished in the black cleft"). Indeed, these mines "[bedünken] ihm ... ganz unheimlich" ("seemed quite uncanny to him") (*Bergwerke*,

229/*Mines*, 164). This uncanny experience reminds Elis that he is following in the footsteps of generations of miners; we might say that in the underground apparition of the old miner, Elis sees a spectral trace of previous anthropogenic geoactivity. Similarly, the discovery of Elis's own imperfectly preserved body by a mining community that has long since forgotten him—and continued to mine the earth that killed him—at the end of Hoffmann's story provides a similar uncanny human trace in the stones beneath their feet. These encounters of human and nonhuman forces in an inorganic nature constitute a fear-inducing, gothic experience of the Anthropocene.

These forces begin long before Elis arrives in Falun. The story starts with him having just returned to Göthaborg from sailing from the colonies to learn of his mother's death. Thrown into melancholic introspection, Elis is approached by a mysterious old man, who it later emerges could only be the ghost of Torbern, a miner who was buried in an explosion in Falun more than a hundred years previously and about whom uncanny legends have developed (*Bergwerke*, 229/*Mines*, 164–65). Torbern capitalizes on Elis's sense of alienation and his imaginative tendencies to tell him about the seemingly marvelous mines at Falun, putting Elis into a visionary state following which he decides to try his luck there instead (*Bergwerke*, 215/*Mines*, 154). Shortly afterward, Elis has a prevision not just of his later experiences in the mine but also of a mysterious mineral queen, a sensual but nonsexualized figure that fills him with awe: "in dem Augenblick leuchtete es auf aus der Tiefe wie ein jäher Blitz, und das ernste Antlitz einer mächtigen Frau wurde sichtbar. . . . Der alte hatte ihn umfaßt und rief: . . . das ist die Königin" ("Before Elis had time to be afraid, there was a sudden flash of lightning from the depths, and the solemn visage of a majestic woman became visible. . . . 'Take care, Elis Fröbom. That is the queen'") (*Bergwerke*, 217/*Mines*, 156–57). Inexplicably, Elis follows the miner out of the city and travels across the country to Falun. Riddled with skepticism once there, he spontaneously ("unwillkührlich"; *Bergwerke*, 224) pledges to stay and become a miner after meeting Pehrson Dahlsjö and his daughter Ulla. Dahlsjö owns an important local mine, and Elis is instantly infatuated with Ulla, later being allowed to marry her. Torn between the promise of material wealth and bourgeois family life aboveground and visions of the marvelous riches of the mineral queen in the mines below, Elis enters the mines on his wedding day and is crushed to death before his preserved corpse is found decades later.

Because of these binaries of fantasy–reality, underground–surface, sensuality–sexualization, supernaturalism–materialism, Theodore Ziolkowski has argued that Hoffmann's mine, as in German Romanticism more generally, is "a mine of the soul, not a technological site,"[4] and indeed this seems to be broadly accurate as a reading of "Die Bergwerke." Starting with the traumatic experience of his mother's death and finishing with his solipsistic, escapist vision of the mineral queen in opposition to the domestic reality of life with his fiancée, Ulla,[5] the mines' function as an allegorical representation of the unconscious layers of Elis's subjectivity is clear. Elis's behavior in Falun is readily visible as a process of repressing traumas, of sublimation, and of creating the neurotic substitute satisfaction of the mineral queen. Indeed, his prospective father-in-law, Dahlsjö, offers precisely such a "diagnosis" of his underground adventures: "Dem tiefsinnigen Neriker hat die Liebe den Kopf verrückt, das ist alles" ("Love has turned the head of the melancholy Neriker—that is all") (*Bergwerke*, 236/*Mines*, 170).

I do not propose that we ignore such psychological readings of the story, but the conclusion of Hoffmann's story should be a warning against reducing Elis's fate to one of narcissistic introspection alone. After all, Dahlsjö's "analysis" doesn't help Elis in the slightest—he still goes off to his demise in the mines. In the self-reflexive irony of Hoffmann's text, critics need to be wary of doubling such bourgeois, materialistic diagnoses in their modern interpretations by ignoring the technologies of global trade and the realities of metal extraction that frame Elis's experiences in Falun. In fact, Hoffmann's mine is remarkable by virtue of its very concrete depictions of the signs of destruction inflicted on the landscape through human extraction activity.[6] Shortly after Elis's arrival in Falun, we read:

Bekanntlich ist die große Tagesöffnung der Erzgrube zu Falun an zwölfhundert Fuß lang, sechshundert Fuß breit und einhundert und achtzig Fuß tief. Die schwarzbraunen Seitenwände gehen anfangs größten Teils senkrecht nieder; dann verflächen sie sich aber gegen die mittlere Tiefe durch ungeheurn Schutt und Trümmerhalden. In diesen und an den Seitenwänden blickt

hin und wieder die Zimmerung alter Schächte hervor, . . . Kein
Baum, kein Grashalm sproßt in dem kahlen zerbröckelten
Steingeklüft und in wunderlichen Gebilden, manchmal riesen-
haften versteinerten Tieren, manchmal menschlichen Kolossen
ähnlich, ragen die zackigen Felsenmassen ringsumher empor.
Im Abgrunde liegen in wilder Zerstörung durcheinander Steine,
Schlacken—ausgebranntes Erz, und ein ewiger betäubender
Schwefeldunst steigt aus der Tiefe, als würde unten der Höllen-
sud gekocht, dessen Dämpfe alle grüne Lust der Natur vergiften.
(*Bergwerke*, 220)

As is well known, the great entrance to the mine of Falun is
about twelve hundred feet long, six hundred feet wide, and one
hundred and eighty feet deep. The blackish brown sidewalls
at first extend more or less vertically; about halfway down,
however, they are less steep because of the tremendous piles of
rubble. Here and there in the banks and walls can be seen the
timbers of old shafts. . . . Not a tree, not a blade of grass was living in the barren, crumbled, rocky abyss. The jagged rock masses
loomed up in wonderful forms, sometimes like monstrous petrified animals, sometimes like human giants. In the abyss there
were stones—slag, or burned out ores—lying around in a wild
jumble, and sulphurous gases rose steadily from the depths as if
a hellish brew were boiling, the vapors of which were poisoning
all of nature's green delights. (*Mines*, 158, translation amended)

There is a disturbing realism and griminess to these images: the
Falun that Elis encounters is a shocking place showing a wide-
reaching transformation of the environment, producing dirt,
slack, and noxious fumes. Elis may subsequently endeavor to over-
look the damage done by mining, becoming enamored with a feminine vision of mineral riches, but the literary critic cannot afford
to follow him down this particular mineshaft.

Most readings of "Die Bergwerke," in particular psychological
interpretations, build on a metaphysical and spiritual approach to
nature represented by Torbern and Elis that contrasts with this
ecological violence. Both men profess an alternative relationship
to the earth that is not oriented toward extraction and commerce
but is described as a disinterested and nebulous "wahre Liebe
zum wunderbaren Gestein und Metall" ("true love for marvelous

rocks and metals") (*Bergwerke*, 230/*Mines*, 165). This holistic vision compares favorably with Elis's employer and future father-in-law, Person Dahlsjö. For him nature is an external threat that needs to be conquered; otherwise, "die mächtigen Elemente, in denen der Bergmann kühn waltet, [werden] ihn vernichten" ("the mighty elements among which the miner reigns, will annihilate him") (*Bergwerke*, 225/*Mines*, 161). Dahlsjö imagines a conceptual opposition between humanity and nature, which ecocritics such as Val Plumwood have identified as lying at the heart of the environmental violence of modernity's progress myth.[7] Dahlsjö stands in for an industrial mind-set that refers to the natural world as the material "other" of the agential human "self," thus creating a construct of "nature" that is subordinate to a hubristic humankind and hence available for widespread use and abuse (*Bergwerke*, 225/*Mines*, 161). Torbern's and Elis's "true love" for the inorganic, by contrast, seems disinterested in such material concerns.

This opposition is open to deconstruction. On the day he dies, Elis is not running away from Ulla to the mineral queen; he is actually trying to unite what on the preceding pages is termed his "zwei Hälften" ("split in half"), the bourgeois quotidian and the "besseres, sein eigentliches Ich" ("his better, his true being") (*Bergwerke*, 235/*Mines*, 169). Before leaving, he tells Ulla that the gems he is looking for will be his "Hochzeits-Gabe" ("wedding present") to her (*Bergwerke*, 237/*Mines*, 170). In Elis's ideal scenario, he would marry Ulla, have the mineral queen's gemstones, and run the mine without any negative consequences, meaning that the materialistic and environmentally disastrous tendencies of the mining community segue into the vision of disinterested riches and wealth here. Just as Böhme and others have argued that the mineral queen is a symbolic sublimation of Elis's displaced sexual desires,[8] I am suggesting a parallel symbolic displacement of the materialist economic desires of his mining activities in the dream of the mineral queen and her gemstones. Elis's mystical striving for the mineral world enables him to develop a programmatic blindness to the environmental price of extraction activities that filled him full of horror and abject disgust upon his arrival in Falun.

Far from being disinterested, Elis's pursuit of gemstones is extraction capitalism of the worst kind—just another human–nature entanglement that reshapes and damages the earth while imagining a vision that purposefully conceals the networks of anthropocentric science, technology, and capital underlying it. Noting that "geology is a mode of accumulation, on one hand, and of disposses-sion, on the other" involving "instrumentation and instrumental-ization" of nonhuman inorganic matter and those humans deemed to be inhuman in the pursuit of profit,[9] Kathryn Yusoff has devel-oped a powerful critique of the dirty work of precisely such a "geo-logics" of extraction as that advocated by Dahlsjö, Torbern, and, ultimately, Elis. She argues:

> It is not just that geology is a signifier for extraction but that a transmutation of matter occurs within that signification that renders matter as property, that makes a delineation between agency and inertness, which stabilizes the *cut* of property and enacts the removal of matter from its constitutive relations as both subject and mineral embedded in sociological and ecologi-cal fields.[10]

Extraction capitalism's generation of "a new geochemical earth" is a way of "world making that was for the few" rather than the many[11] and delivers genocide, transplantation of people as slaves, the creation of "alien" ecologies of monocultures, and transforma-tion of the ground beneath all our feet—but predominantly *black* feet—into a damaged, uninhabitable mass of poisonous caverns and slag heaps. There is no disinterested geological imagination.

The descent into the marvelous spaces of the mine in "Die Berg-werke" is not simply a descent into Elis's unconscious; it is also an arrival into the economy and slow violence of the Anthropocene in which he is living. From the "dicker Dampf" ("thick mist") ris-ing over the lakes to "dem ungeheuern Höllenschlunde" ("the huge jaws of hell") and "Anblick der fürchterlichen Zerstörung" ("the sight of the awful destruction") that freezes the blood in Elis's veins (*Bergwerke*, 219–20/*Mines*, 157, translation amended), from the "ewig betäubender Schwefeldunst" ("eternally stupefying sul-phurous gases") to the "ungeheurn Schutt und Trümmerhalden" ("monstrous accumulations of stones and refuse") (*Bergwerke*, 220/*Mines*, 157–58), mining produces horrifying effects. "Die Bergwerke" reminds us that our reshaping of the planet is first and foremost caused by what we extract, showing us that the pollution "that now fills our atmosphere was released by the combustion of stuff" drawn from the material with which we live daily.[12] The tale of Elis's demise is very much earth-bound, highlighting human entanglement in the world around us.

(S)Cenes of Digging: Matter and Mind

If the economics of mining and marrying for money seem less divisible than critics have previously suggested, they also underestimate the profound knowledge of Romantic travel writing, scientific, geological, philosophical, and proto-psychological intertexts lurking beneath the surface of "Die Bergwerke." From India to Falun, from gemstones to slag heaps, from the fascinating to the horrifying experience of human entanglement in and with nature, the world of Hoffmann's text merges the different "(s)cenes" of the anthropogenic (re-)shaping of our world that has become known as the Anthropocene. Critical discourse on the Anthropocene has multiple -cenes and, by association, many scenes and timelines. These stretch from cities to farmland, from the Global North to the Global South, from the oceans to the skies, from prehistoric events of mass extinction to the present climate crisis via colonial expansion in the Early Modern period and the Industrial Revolution some 250 years ago. Similarly, as discussed in the Introduction to this book, disagreement as to the causation of these anthropogenic effects has produced different -cenic descriptors of these phenomena, prioritizing variously colonialization (Plantationocene[13]) or industrial capital (Capitalocene[14]) and even trying to undo and overcome the homogenizing, undifferentiated anthropocentrism implicit in the term *Anthropocene* in favor of alternative and more liberating models of coexistence (Chthulucene[15]). "Die Bergwerke" offers a remarkable coalescence of these various -cenes. On one hand, Elis's previous occupation as a sailor engaged in the global trade of the East India Company frames the extraction processes firmly within the discourse of colonialist expansion of the Plantationocene, while on the other hand, the mining for copper and the anthropogenic effects this has on the landscape are framed within the industrial contexts of the Capitalocene. Likewise, Hoffmann's story was published in 1819 and thus at the onset of the Industrial Revolution in Germany, but it is set around 1700, during the period in which the modern scientific idiom was established through which the *Anthropos* ruptured *Himself* from a performatively generated *Nature*,[16] thus opening the earth up to exploitation in the manner embodied by Dahlsjö in Hoffmann's story.

"Die Bergwerke" was written in a period of radical reform of mining sciences and practices in Germany that enabled the rapid industrial takeoff of the mid-nineteenth century, and these reforms produced a large body of literature in various disciplines and media.[17] This discourse would have been immediately obvious to Hoffmann's contemporary readership familiar with the Falun story from popular scientist Gotthilf Heinrich Schubert's *Ansichten von der Nachtseite der Naturwissenschaft* (1808) and other more literary sources, such as a competition in the literary journal *Jason* in 1809.[18] Indeed, Schubert is name-checked by Ottmar in the discussions among the titular Serapion-Brethren that follow the tale (*Bergwerke*, 239–40). Hoffmann also draws on two further source texts from the burgeoning field of geosciences, Johann Friedrich Ludwig Hausmann's *Reise durch Skandinavien* (Journey through Scandinavia), which is referenced in a footnote in the story itself (*Bergwerke*, 220/*Mines*, 158), and Ernst Moritz Arndt's *Reise durch Schweden im Jahr 1804* (Journey through Sweden in the year 1804). These accounts differ significantly. Hausmann—professor for mineralogy and mining technology at the University of Göttingen—is interested in documenting the technologically and scientifically notable discoveries he makes on his journey through Sweden and Norway. Arndt—a professor for history at the University of Greifswald and later in Bonn—focuses more on social and cultural developments, offering an optimistic appraisal of Sweden's burgeoning industrial culture.

In keeping with his specialist scientific focus, Hausmann's *Reise durch Skandinavien* records the names, history, and technical details such as depth, pressure, tools and machines, levels of ore production, and gross profit, with minute detail.[19] He is clearly fascinated by the level of industrial extraction in Sweden compared with the more old-fashioned mines in his native Harz and Weserbergland mountains. He nevertheless notes the "schauerlichen Eindruck" (horrifying impression) that the vast slag heaps—the "schreckliche Bild einer durch Unordnung und Verschwendung herbeigeführten Zerrüttung" (the dreadful picture of a ruination produced by disorder and wastefulness)—leave on visitors.[20] Such brief moments of shock do not stop him from moving swiftly on to describe the pumping and extraction systems that make such environmental destruction almost inevitable, however. Indeed, the lengthy historical accounts of the founding fathers and owners of these mines that punctuate his account swiftly turn the reader's attention toward the captains of industry and away from a consideration of the environmental impact of their industriousness.[21] With brief exceptions, Hausmann's account of the mining and extraction industry generates an almost entirely uncritical progress narrative by banishing all signs of anthropogenic pollution to the margins.

Arndt follows a different approach. A historian, Arndt also studied natural sciences and geography, and his description vacillates between optimism about Sweden's industrial future and unsubtle criticism of the environmental effects of Falun's mining history. He describes the town's appearance as "düster" (dreary), noting "Rauch" that "für die Gesundheit unmöglich gleichgültig seyn [kann]" and "Fremde, die hierher kommen, [werden] leicht mit Nasenbluten, Kopfschmerzen, Husten und Augenschmerzen geplagt" (smoke . . . which simply must have an effect on the health. . . . Foreign visitors are often easily plagued with nosebleeds, headaches, coughing, and sore eyes).[22] The anthropogenic effects of the extraction industry and its by-products are palpable:

> Der Kupferrauch hat alle Häuser braun gefärbt. Er hat aber
> dabei noch die Wirkung, daß er das Holz fast unverweslich
> und eisenhart macht. Dieser feine Rauch färbt Silber, Messing
> und anderes Metall oft dunkel, macht das Eisen rostig und die
> Fenster trüb. Er ist zum Teil so scharf, daß man ihn auf einige
> Meilen von der Stadt oft noch weiter merkt.[23]

> The smoke from the copper has colored all of the houses brown.
> It also has the effect of making the wood as hard as iron and
> almost indestructible. This fine smoke often turns silver, brass,
> and other metals into a darker color, makes iron rusty, and
> darkens the windows. The smoke is so putrid that it can often
> be registered many miles from the city itself.

Such disturbing images of the environmental impact are clearly the source of Hoffmann's fictionalized Falun, which is constantly shrouded in sulfuric smog.

In "Die Bergwerke," Hoffmann uses Hausmann as a reliable source for the depictions of the mine, its workings, and the terminology with which to describe it. Where the text dwells precisely on those environmental effects that call Hausmann's "progress" narrative into question, the story pivots closer to Arndt's more critical viewpoint. When Elis learns that Torbern has long since died in a mining accident, only now to ghost around the text as a spectral reminder of man's hubristic attempts to penetrate and control nature, the idea that extraction supports progress is firmly debunked. It is precisely the programmatic blindness toward the anthropogenic side effects of mining that is opened up to view first in Torbern's death and then ultimately in Elis's own demise. Both their deaths are quite literally *Man*'s arrival in the Anthropocene: crushed by the debris of human hubris that had earlier disgusted him, Elis (like Torbern before him) becomes a trace element in the lithic records of the mining industry's environmental destruction. "Die Bergwerke" reveals a profoundly unsettling and self-damaging intimacy with the earth that we have transformed.

Like other German Romantic texts about mines, Hoffmann's focus is on minerals and metals rather than fossil fuels, a sign perhaps of Germany's comparatively late turn toward coal extraction compared with other European nations.[24] As we have seen, however, the fact that "Die Bergwerke" engages with contemporary literature on mineralogy and metallurgy underlines the fact that the mines and their matter really do *matter* in Hoffmann's story. While this is certainly true for the realistic depiction of environmental damage, the supernatural focus on Torbern's ghost and the "mineral queen" also draws on contemporary scientific debates— namely, Gotthilf Heinrich Schubert's *Ansichten von der Nachtseite der Naturwissenschaft*.

Written in the wake of Friedrich Schelling's *Naturphilosophie*, *Ansichten* was a version of a lecture series Schubert had held previously in Dresden in 1807.[25] Schubert was a professor of natural science at Erlangen and Munich for many years and one of the most widely known natural scientists of the early 1800s in Germany. Far from an original thinker, Schubert saw himself as a scientist who made complex theories more widely accessible, and the spectacular topics with which he engages in the *Ansichten* underline this. The lectures document phenomena that appear to be diametrically opposed to the rational account of the natural world, arguing instead for the existence of an all-pervading worldly entanglement of energy and matter, the organic and inorganic, mind and body, spirit and substance. He outlines this in the fourteenth and final lecture, arguing for "eine innige Beziehung und Wechselwirkung" (an intimate relationship and interdependency) and "eine[n] genauen Zusammenhang" (a definite relationship) of "alle Glieder des Systems" (all components of the universe), irrespective of their organic or inorganic, material or immaterial, status.[26] Matter for Schubert is not an inanimate assemblage; it is animated and agential by virtue of "eine Ursache" (one cause) behind all constituents of the "System." Or put differently, *matter* (noun) is because it *matters* (verb). According to Schubert, this erstwhile holistic state is now, in the age of rational science, barely recognizable and no longer self-explanatory.

Following on from this principle, Schubert's geological interests are focused on the presence of fossils in stones, which he views as evidence of the ability of organic material to become "sublimated" into the inorganic realm, and hence for materials to be capable of transmuting into other categories of materiality. Schubert "proves" these speculations by inserting a highly stylized story about a miner in Falun who disappeared and was later found preserved under the earth: "Auf gleiche Weise zerfiel auch jener merkwürdige Leichnam, von welchem Hülpher, Cronstedt und die schwedischen gelehrten Tagebücher erzählen, in eine Art von Asche, nachdem man ihn, dem Anscheine nach in festen Stein verwandelt, unter einem Glasschrank vergeblich vor dem Zutritt der Luft gesichert hatte." (That strange, apparently petrified corpse of which Hülpher, Cronstedt, and the learned Swedish journals speak also crumbled in the same manner into a type of ash after it had been brought to the surface in a glass container in the dashed hope that this might protect it from contact with the elements.)[27] It is this story that Hoffmann references in the discussion in the frame narrative of the *Serapionsbrüder*.

The actual origin of Schubert's preserved Swedish miner was a report published in the journal *Nye Tidender om lärde Sager* in July 1720,[28] and thus the period in which the modern, Enlightenment scientific episteme began to establish itself most clearly in Germany. As with Jeffery Jerome Cohen's story about the Avebury man crushed by a megalith before it was discovered six hundred years later by Alexander Keiler,[29] the Falun miner's body is a source of amazement among journalists and scientists in its now seemingly fossilized form. It is worthwhile noting that the discovery of fossils in the late eighteenth century is typically seen as the dawning of a sense of "deep" time,[30] and Schubert's story about a human crumbling to dust excellently captures this feeling of the irrelevance of the human in the expansiveness of lithic time. Unlike the imperfectly fossilized remains of the miner, stone "conjures spans that transient humans cannot witness and yet are called upon, anxiously, to narrate."[31] In his historical gaze backward toward the intellectual origins of modern scientific inquiry, and in the trope of the crumbling human body in opposition with deep geological time, Schubert's *Ansichten* indicates his rejection of this mode of scientific inquiry in pursuit of a less environmentally destructive Romantic *Naturphilosophie*.

Schubert's metaphysical realism also offers us a model of entanglement of mind and matter that enables us to deconstruct the clear opposition of "psychological" and "realist" readings of Elis's descent into the mines. As his preoccupation with phenomena such as somnambulism, mesmerism, and thought transference show, Schubert advocates a fluid transition between mind and matter, between psyche and substance. These ideas have their successor in contemporary ecological theory. Schubert's appeal to an all-pervading, all-encompassing dynamic complexity of organic *and* inorganic, of mind *and* matter, has much in common with the "new materialism" of thinkers like Karen Barad and Jane Bennett, which stresses the complexity of all relations among people, people and things, and things in their own right without relying on distinctions or priorities of certain forms of agency. Following Bruno Latour's deconstruction of agency as a demarcation between human and nonhuman nature,[32] Bennett's *Vibrant Matter* argues for "a vital materiality," according to which all matter exists as life force in an interlinked, entangled (but by no means homogenously manifesting) material universe.[33] For Ian Hoddard, entanglement allows broader ecological and historical critique of humans' development of extraction technologies; Hoddard argues, "Human existence and social life depend on material things that are entangled with them."[34] Criticizing the "common belief that there is an inherent boundary between the 'physical' and the 'metaphysical,'"[35] Barad likewise posits "the universe" as "agential intra-activity in its becoming,"[36] using the important prefix *intra-* to signal "the mutual constitution of entangled agencies."[37] Set against the background of Schubert's *Naturphilosophie*, the idea that there can be a distinction between the interior and the exterior is misplaced. An ecological reading of "Die Bergwerke" cannot afford to distinguish, nor should it presume, a primacy of one over the other.

That, however, is where Schubert and Hoffmann part ways. While Schubert retains a quasi-religious belief in a benevolent form of entanglement with an animated nature, Hoffmann's text undermines any such convictions. Although his relationship with *Naturphilosophie* is broadly sympathetic—visible especially in stories like "Der goldne Topf" ("The Golden Pot")—Hoffmann's response to these theories is not uncritical. Unlike other early German Romantics, Hoffmann's engagement with *Naturphilosophie* was not particularly intensive, and although he read Schelling's *Von der Weltseele* (On the world soul), his main source of knowledge was Schubert's more accessible writing. As Monika Schmitz-Emans and Gerhard Kaiser have shown, however, Hoffmann tends to treat Schubert's concepts as an "ästhetisches Spielmaterial" (material for aesthetic games).[38] Thus, in his underground vision of a union with the mineral queen, we see a form of entanglement with the inorganic that is exciting and positive:

> Sie erfaßte ihn, zog ihn hinab, drückte ihn an ihre Brust, da durchzuckte ein glühender Strahl sein Inneres, und sein Bewußtsein war nur das Gefühl, als schwämme er in den Wogen eines blauen, durchsichtig funkelnden Nebels. (*Bergwerke*, 232)

> She seized him, pulled him down, pressed him to her breast, and there flashed through his soul a glowing ray—and his consciousness became little more than a feeling of drifting in a blue, transparent, sparkling mist. (*Mines*, 167, translation amended)

What Hoffmann's fiction shares with Schubert here is the central idea that the rationally experienced quotidian world is merely one manifestation of the duplicitous "ambiguity" of all (natural) phenomena, behind which may lie the marvelous agency of nature. Unlike Schubert, there is no certitude of this, however. Hoffmann suspends "Die Bergwerke" in fantastic uncertainty, ambiguous as to whether Elis's union with the inorganic world is the vision of a mentally ill man or genuinely the presence of the supernatural in nature. In a narrative repeatedly focalized through Elis, indicated by phrases such as "it seemed to him," "as if," or the ubiquitous "sensed," the blending of subjective and objective reality frames most events as being potentially only imagined. In his fictionalization of Schubert, Hoffmann questions the metaphysical certitude of the scientist's worldview. It is in this critical reappropriation, I will now argue, that Schubert's version of the Falun story becomes "gothicized."

Digging Up Dirt: The Gothic Anthropocene's Uncanny Agencies

Contrary to Elis's desires, he ultimately exerts little mastery over the stones and minerals he seeks, and there is no security about his having become successfully initiated in the language of nature in the manner both he and Torbern envisage. Indeed, this is a failure that is already prefigured in Elis's first vision of the mineral queen following his encounter with Torbern in Göthaborg. This imagined encounter seems to be positive, consisting of a complete dissolution of his selfhood as he merges into the glistening inorganic nature around him:

> Elis gewahrte neben sich den alten Bergmann, aber sowie er ihn mehr und mehr anschaute, wurde er zur Riesengestalt, aus glühendem Erz gegossen. Elis wollte sich entsetzen, aber in dem Augenblick leuchtete es auf aus der Tiefe wie ein jäher Blitz, und das ernste Antlitz einer mächtigen Frau wurde sichtbar. . . . Sowie nun aber der Jüngling wieder hinabschaute in das starre Antlitz der mächtigen Frau, fühlte er, daß sein Ich zerfloß in dem glänzenden Gestein. Er kreischte auf in namenloser Angst und erwachte aus dem wunderbaren Traum, dessen Wonne und Entsetzen tief in seinem Innern widerklang. (*Bergwerke*, 217–18)

> Elis saw the old miner beside him; but as he stared at him, the miner changed into a gigantic shape, as if cast of glowing metal. Before Elis had time to be afraid, there was a sudden flash of lightening from the depths, and the solemn visage a majestic woman became visible. . . . But as soon as the youth looked down again into the majestic woman's rigid face, he felt his

being dissolved into the shining stone. He screamed in nameless fear and awoke from this marvellous dream, the rapture and terror of which resounded deep within his being. (*Mines*, 156, translation adapted)

This dissolution of the human subject into nature is a traumatic experience, not a joyous sense of release. "Die Bergwerke" maintains the entangled model of subjectivity and materiality found in the Romantic *Naturphilosophie* of Schubert, but rather than celebrating a benevolent, holistic vision of life in the Anthropocene, this entanglement of human and nonhuman, self and mineral world, is experienced as threatening and horrific.

This skeptical response to Schubert is most visible in the story's conclusion. Elis not only dies as a result of his unfulfilled striving for a mystical union in nature; he ultimately fails to find this union with the mineral world at all, turning to dust rather than becoming stone. The coda to the story notes that his body only "*appeared to be petrified*" ("der versteinert *schien*") (*Mines*, 171/*Bergwerke*, 239, emphasis added). Monika Schmitz-Emans has observed, "Anders als Schubert dämonisiert Hoffmann die Natur, um das Ich in seiner Hilflosigkeit zu zeigen" (Unlike Schubert, Hoffmann demonizes nature in order to show the subject in its helplessness).[39] The helplessness of the human subject in Schmitz-Emans's view is suggestive of a hostile external nature, but Hoffmann is more subtle than this. To demonize nature in the way Schmitz-Emans suggests merely reproduces the negative Othering of nature as a dangerous force to be feared, and therefore mastered, that defines characters like Dahlsjö and even Elis himself on the plot level. Elis's failed union with the mineral world, like Torbern's before him, was itself little more than a smokescreen for his striving after quite materialistic subterranean riches. I suggest instead that "Die Bergwerke" links the "demonization" of nature deliberately to human agency, and this is where we might identify a turn toward the gothic in Hoffmann's narrative.

As the Introduction to the present volume makes clear, hostile nature can indeed be one articulation of the gothic in the Anthropocene: "as an entity that has always been under threat, always questioned, by the Gothic, the human takes up an endangered position in the Anthropocene."[40] What becomes of this threat, however, if this is a nature that is always already anthropogenically modified, in which human and nonhuman entanglement is all-pervasive? In gothic fictions, the desire to go digging around to unearth things—family histories, sexual desires, or untold riches—is one that is better ignored. In the Anthropocene, this is even more true: the age that was coproduced by humans digging in the dirt has caused irreparable ecological destruction that is now coming back to haunt us with a vengeance.[41] As Jeff VanderMeer writes, "in the Anthropocene . . . hauntings and similar manifestations become emissaries or transition points between the human sense of time and the geological sense of time."[42] One instance of this in "Die Bergwerke" is Torbern's spectral presence. When traveling to Falun, Elis sees Torbern's shape: "wie er aus einer Schlucht, aus dickem Gestripp, aus dunklem Gestein plötzlich hervortrat . . . dann aber schnell wieder verschwand" ("he quite often saw the old man suddenly step from a ravine, or a thick copse or from behind some dark boulder . . . and then suddenly disappear again") (*Bergwerke*, 219/*Mines*, 157). Just as the chemical, toxic legacy of extraction capitalism diffuses globally—indexed in "Die Bergwerke" by Elis's work in the East India Company—we might say that Torbern's itinerant ghost is the uncanny trace of humankind's agency in the anthropogenic destruction of the environment—the result of a man-made explosion in the mines. This trace is uncanny because it is caused by an agency that had been banished from sight in an act of programmatic blindness that enabled modernity's progress narrative, only now it both reappears in the mining community's stories and—more worryingly—is offered up in the stones themselves. Torbern's spectral traces in cliffs, abysses, stones, and finally in the mine itself are an uncanny chronotopical disruption between human time and geological time of man's own making.

This is an uncanniness that characterizes the biological and geological intimacy that we experience in the Anthropocene,[43] and as such, we can use Torbern as a starting point for understanding the gothic *of* and *in* the Anthropocene. Torbern's story and the desire it awakens in Elis are suggestive of a risky biological and geological intimacy that we could call gothic rather than Romantic or *naturphilosophisch*: this is an ecology of fear and uncertainty rather than holistic conviction, and ultimately, the earth as a mineral body takes on threatening qualities.

Elis's entanglement with the earth's inorganic body is a similar source of terror. When his apparently fossilized remains are discovered decades after his disappearance, Elis's contemporaries, with the exception of the now ancient Ulla, are all long since dead. Life in the mines has continued unabated, and Elis's story—unlike Torbern—has been forgotten. Nobody tells any stories about his demise in the mines; the potential warning against the hubris of extraction goes unnoticed. When Elis's preserved corpse is found in the mines and is brought to the surface, this lack of knowledge is challenged. At first, Elis's corpse seems like a perfect example of a *naturphilosophische* union with nature: his untouched youthfulness contrasts diametrically with his former fiancée Ulla's now decrepit state. Precisely who the spectral remnant is and who is alive is thoroughly confused: "Und damit kauerte sie neben dem Leichnam nieder und faßte die erstarrten Hände und drückte sie an ihre im Alter erkaltete Brust, in der noch, wie heiliges Naphthafeuer unter der Eisdecke, ein Herz voll heißer Liebe schlug" ("She squatted down beside the body and seized the stiffened hands and pressed them to her withered breast beneath the icy sheath of which, like a holy naphta flame, a heart filled with ardent love was burning") (*Bergwerke*, 239/*Mines*, 172). Just as suddenly as it was found, and just as briefly as this uncanny embrace lasts, Elis's body crumbles to dust while Ulla herself dies: "Man bemerkte, daß der Körper des Unglücklichen, der fälschlicherweise für versteinert gehalten, in Staub zu zerfallen begann" ("They noticed that the corpse of the unfortunate man, which they had thought was petrified, was beginning to turn to dust. The appearance of petrifaction had been deceptive") (*Bergwerke*, 239/*Mines*, 172). It is the transience of human life in the face of the deep time of stones and minerals that is powerfully captured here.

For the spectators of this strange reunion, discovering the human remains of extraction capitalism in this way must be doubly shocking: these are the traces of man's past hubris literally deposited on and in the stones, which they now target in their own hubristic extraction activities. Elis's corpse, like Hoffmann's story, highlights the negative and destructive experiences of nature as transformed by man. Like Torbern, Elis is a haunting, uncanny presence, a ghost that rises out of the global landscape to remind these latter-day benefactors of extraction capitalism of the violence they inflict on the landscape around them and which in turn engineers their own endangered modern lives. The place of the gothic in the Anthropocene, "Die Bergwerke zu Falun" suggests, lies not simply in the horrific experience of nature's magnitude but also in gothic's ability to deploy its central tropes and motifs like fantastic and monstrous figures, chronotopical disruptions, and experiences of *frisson* as a means to represent the distortions and illusions of dominant economic, political, and scientific discourse in modernity, such as the practices of extraction that make modernity possible at all.

Dawn of the Anthropocene

This chapter has analyzed "Die Bergwerke zu Falun" as a document from the dawn of the Anthropocene, when technology provided greater access to minerals, metals, and hydrocarbon sources of energy, thus expanding the influence of mining and allowing a literal reshaping of the world in a profoundly more intense form than ever before. I use the phrase "dawn" of the Anthropocene broadly, however. On one hand, this refers to the fact that Hoffmann's story is written in a period of radical reform of mining sciences and practices in Germany that enabled the rapid industrial takeoff of the mid-nineteenth century. On the other hand, this refers to the actual origins of the Falun story in the period in which the modern, Enlightenment scientific episteme began to establish itself most clearly in Europe. Hoffmann's immediate source, Gotthilf Heinrich Schubert, like many Romantic scientists, positioned itself critically to this tradition, making "Die Bergwerke zu Falun" an artifact not simply of the period in which the Anthropocene emerged in a palpable manner but also of nascent ecological insights that rendered its origins and dangers visible. Hoffmann's story goes further than this, however. Although Elis's death and uncanny return from the underground challenge the anthropocentrism of modernity's narratives of progress, unlike the *Naturphilosophie* from which the novella emerges, "Die Bergwerke" offers no resolution and no reassuring counternarrative of empathetic initiation in the "book of nature." That does not mean, however, that it advocates the materialist, capitalist, and scientific status quo, of course. As Heather Sullivan writes, "Hoffmann keeps our eye on the dirt of materiality" by fictionalizing—and ultimately collapsing—Elis's attempts first to repress, then to sublimate in a mystical vision the awful destruction of nature in Falun.[44] These nascent ecological insights can, and perhaps should, be the task and nature of the gothic in the Anthropocene.

NOTES

1. E. T. A. Hoffmann, "Die Bergwerke zu Falun," in *Sämtliche Werke in 6 Bänden*, vol. 4, *Die Serapionsbrüder*, ed. Wulf Segebrecht, 208–41 (Frankfurt am Main: Deutscher Klassiker, 2001). English translations are from "The Mines of Falun," in *Tales of E. T. A. Hoffmann*, ed. and trans. Leonard J. Kent and Elizabeth C. Knight (Chicago: University of Chicago Press, 1972), 149–72, unless otherwise indicated. All further references are to these editions and will appear in the main body of the text with the abbreviation *Bergwerke/Mines* with the relevant page number.

2. See Hartmut Böhme, "Geheime Macht im Schoß der Erde. Das Symbolfeld des Bergbaus zwischen Sozialgeschichte und Psychohistorie," in *Natur und Subjekt*, ed. Hartmut Böhme, 67–144 (Frankfurt am Main: Suhrkamp, 1988), and Theodore Ziolkowski, *German Romanticism and Its Institutions* (Princeton, N.J.: Princeton University Press, 1990).

3. See Stefan Höppner, "Romantische Hohlwelten. Das Bergwerk bei Novalis, Schubert und Hoffmann," in *Hohlwelten. Les Terres Creuses. Hollow Earth*, ed. Hartmut Fischer and Gerd Schubert, 99–104, 124–25 (Berlin: Lehmanns Media, 2009); Kate Rigby, *Topographies of the Sacred: The Poetics of Place in European Romanticism* (Charlottesville: University of Virginia Press, 2004), 140–56; Heather I. Sullivan, "Dirty Nature: Ecocriticism and Tales of Extraction—Mining and Solar Power—in Goethe, Hoffmann, Verne, and Eschbach," *Colloquia Germanica* 44, no. 2 (2011): 117–21.

4. Ziolcowski, *German Romanticism*, 28.

5. See Friedrich Kittler, "Der Dichter, die Mutter, das Kind. Zur romantischen Erfindung von Sexualität," in *Romantik in Deutschland: Ein interdisziplinäres Symposion*, ed. Richard Brinkmann (Stuttgart: Metzler, 1978), 103; Detlef Kremer, *E. T. A. Hoffmann. Erzählungen und Romane* (Berlin: Erich Schmidt, 1999), 111 and 176–78.

6. Sullivan, "Dirty Nature," 118–19.

7. Val Plumwood, *Feminism and the Mastery of Nature* (London: Routledge, 1993), 3.

8. Böhme, "Geheime Macht," 130–31.

9. Kathryn Yusoff, *A Billion Black Anthropocenes or None* (Minneapolis: University of Minnesota Press, 2018), 16–17.

10. Yusoff, 19–20.

11. Yusoff, 26.

12. John Philip Usher, *Exterranean: Extraction in the Humanist Anthropocene* (New York: Fordham University Press, 2019), 1.

13. See Donna Haraway, Noboru Ishikawa, Scott F. Gilbert, Kenneth Olwig, Anna L. Tsing, and Nils Bubandt, "Anthropologists Are Talking— about the Anthropocene," *Ethnos* 81, no. 3 (2016): 556–57; John L. Brooke and Christopher Otter, "Concluding Remarks: The Organic Anthropocene," *Eighteenth-Century Studies* 49, no. 2 (2016): 281–302; Yusoff, *A Billion Black Anthropocenes.*

14. See Jason W. Moore, *Anthropocene or Capitalocene? Nature, History, and the Crisis of Capitalism* (Oakland, Calif.: PM Press, 2016); Andreas Malm, *Fossil Capital: The Rise of Steam Capital and Global Warming* (London: Verso, 2016).

15. Donna Haraway, *Staying with the Trouble: Making Kin in the Chthulucene* (Durham, N.C.: Duke University Press, 2016).

16. See Bruno Latour, *Politics of Nature: How to Bring the Sciences into Democracy,* trans. Catherine Porter (Cambridge, Mass.: Harvard University Press, 2004), 10; and Haraway, *Making Kin,* 40–41.

17. See Jason Groves, "Petrifiction: Reimagining the Mine in German Romanticism," in *Readings in the Anthropocene,* ed. Sabine Wilke and Japhet Johnstone, 247–52 (New York: Bloomsbury, 2017); Kate Rigby, "'Mines Aren't Really Like That': German Romantic Undergrounds Revisited," in *German Ecocriticism in the Anthropocene,* ed. Caroline Schaumann and Heather I. Sullivan (New York: Palgrave, 2017), 116–17.

18. See Georg Friedmann, "Die Bearbeitungen der Geschichte von dem Bergmann von Falun" (PhD diss., Berlin, 1887); Rolf Selbmann, "Unverhofft kommt oft. Eine Leiche und die Folgen für die Literaturgeschichte," *Euphorion* 94 (2000): 173–204.

19. Johann Friedrich Ludwig Hausmann, *Reise durch Skandinavien in den Jahren 1806 und 1807* (Göttingen: Johann Fr. Röwer, 1818), 5:96–102; all translations are my own.

20. Hausmann, 96.

21. Hausmann, 102–13.

22. Ernst Moritz Arndt, *Reise durch Schweden im Jahr 1806* (Berlin: G. A. Lange, 1806), 2:239; all translations are my own.

23. Arndt, 231.

24. See Groves, "Petrifiction," 249–50.

25. See Höppner, "Romantische Hohlwelten," 115–24.

26. Gotthilf Heinrich Schubert, *Ansichten von der Nachtseite der Naturwissenschaften* (1808; repr., Dresden: Arnold, 1840), 373–74; all translations are my own.

27. Schubert, 229.

28. John Neubauer, "The Mines of Falun: Temporal Fortunes of a Romantic Myth of Time," *Studies in Romanticism* 19, no. 4 (1980): 477.

29. Jeffrey Jerome Cohen, *Stone: An Ecology of the Inhuman* (Minneapolis: University of Minnesota Press, 2015), 75–76.

30. Noah Heringman, "Deep Time at the Dawn of the Anthropocene," *Representations* 129 (2015): 56–85.

31. Cohen, *Stone*, 85.

32. Latour, *Politics*, 237.

33. Jane Bennett, *Vibrant Matter: A Political Ecology of Things* (Durham, N.C.: Duke University Press, 2010), vii.

34. Ian Hoddard, "The Entanglements of Humans and Things: A Long-Term View," *New Literary History* 45 (2014): 19.

35. Karen Barad, "Posthumanist Performativity: Toward an Understanding of How Matter Comes to Matter," *Signs: Journal of Women in Culture and Society* 28, no. 3 (2003): 812.

36. Barad, 818.

37. Karen Barad, *Meeting the Universe Halfway: Quantum Physics and the Entanglement of Matter and Meaning* (Durham, N.C.: Duke University Press, 2007), 33.

38. Gerhard Kaiser, *E. T. A. Hoffmann* (Stuttgart: J. B. Metzler, 1988), 121; see also Monika Schmitz-Emans, "Naturspekulation als 'Vorwand' poetischer Gestaltung. Über das Verhältnis E.T.A. Hoffmanns zu den Lehren G.H. Schuberts," *Mitteilungen der Hoffmann-Gesellschaft* 34 (1988): 67–83.

39. Schmitz-Emans, "Naturspekulation," 81.

40. As the Introduction to the current volume states.

41. Heringman, "Deep Time," 57.

42. Jeff VanderMeer, "Hauntings in the Anthropocene: An Initial Exploration," *Environmental Critique*, July 7, 2016, https://environmental critique.wordpress.com/2016/07/07/hauntings-in-the-anthropocene/.

43. Compare Heather Sullivan, "The Dark Pastoral: A Trope for the Anthropocene," in Schaumann and Sullivan, *German Ecocriticism in the Anthropocene*, 26–28.

44. Sullivan, *Dirty Nature*, 128.

Got a Light?

The Dark Currents of Energy in Twin Peaks: The Return

TIMOTHY MORTON AND RUNE GRAULUND

> There is a sadness in this world, for we are ignorant of many things.
>
> —The Log Lady

1950s (Lynchian nostalgic heartland)

1990s (*Twin Peaks* original seasons 1 and 2, wide breakthrough of neoliberalism)

2017 (*Twin Peaks: The Return,* inauguration of Trump, support of coal, aftermath of Palin and Drill Baby Drill!)

The original season of David Lynch and David Frost's television series *Twin Peaks* (1990) is on a surface level "petro-nostalgic America"[1] at its most cozy and least troubled. The viewer may be perturbed by the murder of young Laura Palmer, yet the structure and tropes of the classic detective whodunit at least initially reassure us that while a wrong may have been committed, all will in time be well. As people drive their cars without a worry, drink damn fine coffee, and consume infinite amounts of cherry pie and donuts, the towering concerns of peak oil and financial crisis haunting contemporary America are nowhere in sight. Still, as is the case with any Lynch production, the coziness of small-town America turns out to be anything but. Soon revealed to be a supercharged gothic nightmare bursting with demons and doppelgängers, dwarves and giants, filicide and illicit desire, haunted houses and forests, it is the energy of the town itself and the structure that supports it that turn out to be wrong and not some glitch in the system.

This chapter will present a reading of season 3 of *Twin Peaks* through the perspective of (dark) energy in the light of the Anthropocene. Kicking off with a closer look at the viscous dark matter that Reza Negarestani has termed the "inorganic demon"[2] of oil, the chapter examines the petro-nostalgia running through Lynch's filmography from *Eraserhead* (1977) up to and including *Twin Peaks: The Return*. In this, we are particularly interested in the manner in which season 3 seems to break with the sometimes seemingly uncritical approach to petro-modernity otherwise present in much of Lynch's oeuvre, as of how this central source of literal dark energy ties up with many other forms of unclean energy fueling human society, from wood over coal and nuclear, on to the figuratively dark and malignant energies of patriarchy and misogyny that so dominate the Lynchian (demon) world. Most obviously and immediately so, we see these connections established in the shifting geography of the series. Largely ignoring the original setting of a small alpine town somewhere in the American Northwest, season 3 roams broadly over the North American continent, from the coastal metropolises to small-town life in the Midwest, on to the deserts and casino towns of the Southwest. For while the journeys to and in these places are portrayed through a series of trips by petrol-fueled car and jet travel, it is in the eerie extraplanar and time-travel trips that the series' often confounding but also richly suggestive (il)logic of energy truly unfolds. Yet as we will be arguing, the two should not be viewed separately, for where the original series focused on the intimate details of small-town life and interpersonal relations, season 3 casts a wider net. In episode 8, "Got a Light?," in what may be the series' (and perhaps television history's) most remarkable passage, we witness the Trinity Test, the explosion of "the Gadget," the first atomic device, in White Sands, New Mexico, on July 16, 1945, as the camera dives into and goes through the blast in a take lasting well over five minutes. It is the ultimate fantasy: looking where one simply cannot look, where even a remote camera cannot penetrate—inside the atom-shredding force of a sustained fission reaction.

With this, the unleashing of humanity's most devastating weapon of mass destruction, a burst of light that is all-encompassing and all-destructive, soon to snuff out the lives of hundreds of thousands of Japanese civilians, the horrific but in terms of lives lost comparatively speaking insignificant filicide of the original season pales in comparison. In what follows, we will therefore ask what our belated awakening from the dream world of 1950s petrochemical and atomic America may signify in a world in which we are finally coming to terms with the fact that damn good coffee never comes for free.

The Anthropo-scenic Route

If the original season of *Twin Peaks* was at a surface level detective television, at heart it was always gothic. In its mix of suburban gothic with forests dark and Grimm, incestuous desires and drug-fueled love affairs, pornography and domestic violence, madmen and freaks (dwarves, giants, cripples, and one-armed men), haunted houses, cabins and lodges, the original season of *Twin Peaks* was consistently dark, even if also often delightfully and mischievously so. Laura Palmer, the young and seemingly innocent murdered girl who soon turns out to be depravity personified, is but the first of many doubles that haunt the show (Good/Bad Cooper, Good/Bad Laura, Good/Bad Leland). Indeed, as the series unfolds, it is the rule rather than the exception that the population of the apparently sedate town of Twin Peaks harbors sinister secrets. Hinting toward a world in which neither we, the viewers, nor the cast of the show can ever hope to be quite at ease, the original season thus retains a sense of existential dread that even in its most lighthearted and silly moments it never quite manages to dispel.

As *Twin Peaks* went into its second season, whatever remained of the original scaffolding of the classic detective television show dissolved almost entirely, and along with it a great deal of the gothic too. Laura Palmer, it turned out, had been murdered by none other than her father, Leland Palmer, possessed by the evil demon BOB. With the purpose of identifying the murderer of Laura Palmer gone, the already sprawling postmodern bricolage of the second season spun further into soap opera, comedy, absurd theater, police procedural, noir, and more, while continuing to split into an ever-widening series of increasingly confusing subplots that were only marginally if at all linked to a greater story line. Compared to season 3, however, season 2 nevertheless looks positively clear and purposeful. As the one-armed man asks early on in season 3, mirroring the viewer's sense of dislocation and disconnection as we try to orient ourselves in a universe that has become unmoored from the woods and mountains of the show's beginnings, "Is it future? Or is it past?" We are never quite sure.

The sense of the weird, the dark, and the outright freakish was of course always part of *Twin Peaks*. Yet even at their most obtuse, seasons 1 and 2 still teased toward the potential of narrative closure. As Catherine Spooner has argued in a reading of the recurrent motif of curtains and veils in the two first seasons, what interested Lynch about the original murder of Laura Palmer was "not the solution of the mystery but the process of unveiling."[3] Nevertheless, in seasons 1 and 2 at least we are as viewers presented with precisely such a process of unveiling, even if this process mostly tends to lead to yet another set of velvet curtains, another set of veils.

Season 3 seems intent on thwarting such expectations entirely. While there are plenty of murders and mysterious disappearances, we are not offered the sense of clarity of purpose Laura Palmer's murder served in season 1, let alone the potential for the resolution of such. Similarly, while season 2 was arguably disjointed and in the end did not offer any clear resolution, the many subplots were nevertheless tied together by a general sense of agency and culpability of a central cast of human or demonic characters (BOB, Leo, Leland, Jacques Renault, Windom Earle). In season 3, any such pretense of pinning down individual culpability is long since gone. Not only is there no errant father possessed by evil demons but there is no singular victim either. Rather, we are offered a grander tapestry of a world in which human agency seems to have dissipated entirely, neatly summed up by the fact that the ingenious and reasoned mind of seasons 1 and 2, Dale Cooper, has been reduced to an idiot savant whose sole purpose in life seems to be the pursuit of, tellingly, a cup of coffee.

Given that Lynch is, generally speaking, committed to "frustrating viewers who seek closure and rational explanation,"[4] attempts at unraveling or fully explaining any Lynchian production are usually doomed to fail. Still, we will be arguing that a gothic reading of *Twin Peaks* season 3 seen in the light (and the darkness) of the Anthropocene can perhaps also explain earlier intimations of anthropogenic change caused by unbridled energy consumption not yet fully formed in the earlier body of work. Always an intuitive rather than a rational artist, Lynch has to some extent proven highly sensitive to what was to come, even as he has always looked to the past with a mostly kind, petro-nostalgic, and patriarchal gaze.

Gothic Auto-geddon

The car and the motorized vehicle are at the heart of Lynch's artistic vision. As an artist often "charged with having an unhealthy obsession with the United States of his own adolescence,"[5] Lynch's work invariably includes direct or indirect references to an age of innocence in which "the charisma of energy, as an American idea and a force,"[6] could be cherished without disconcerting thoughts of global warming and rising seas. Industrial wastelands, suburban streets, and the motif of the diner aside, the automobile and the road are recurrent features of most, if not all, of Lynch's central body of cinematic work set in contemporary times. From the crazy antics of the road movie *Wild at Heart* (1990) to the frenetic opening of a car blazing down a blacktop in *Lost Highway* (1997) set to David Bowie's track "I'm Deranged," from the mysterious and intimidating nighttime rides of *Blue Velvet* (1987) and *Mulholland Drive* (2001), even to the uncharacteristically sedate plot of *The Straight Story* (1999), Lynch's movies inevitably revolve around a fetishistic, nostalgic, and sometimes manic fascination with gas, machinery, and mobility. This was certainly also the case in the first two seasons of *Twin Peaks,* in which we view Cooper in his sedan speaking into a Dictaphone as he fondly observes the passing firs, the power of Leo's menacing (albeit often immobile) truck, the confused and almost always unspent potency of James's motorbike, on to the giddy energy of Bobby's rides.

If "to be modern is to be mobile as never before," and if "the automobile has been imbricated as a normal and necessary tool for personal independence and the successful management of a nuclear family,"[7] Lynch has from his debut with *Eraserhead* to the release of *Twin Peaks* season 3 consistently seemed queasy about the latter but rarely the former. Insofar as one can discern a plot in *Eraserhead,* for instance, it seems primarily to be about the estrangement, alienation, and struggle of upholding the integrity of the nuclear family in the face of the modern world. As the protagonist attempts and fails first to keep his wife and then ensure the survival of his child, Lynch paints a clear and horrifying picture of the nuclear family, a warning that continues throughout Lynch's career, from the rot, death, and decay at the foot of the white picket fence in the opening of *Blue Velvet* on to, of course, *Twin Peaks* and the murder of Laura Palmer. A similar consistent sense of dread cannot be said to pertain to the automobile and the open road as such. For while they can be menacing and ominous, they are as often expressions of a wild, erotic, and exultant freedom, as when Lula and Sailor of *Wild at Heart* escape the strictures of, precisely, suburbia and the life of the nuclear family to express their freedom and the wildness of their hearts on the open road. In comparison, *Twin Peaks* season 3 seems more willing to commit to a critique of the pursuit of limitless energy, albeit of course in a distinctly Lynchian and ambiguous manner in that he never commits to an outright critique of petro-culture. Indeed, as we shall be arguing, season 3 seems to gesture toward the White Sands nuclear explosion as the serpent in the garden, the moment in which American innocence was ripped apart by a mushroom cloud.

Reflecting on her first encounter with *Twin Peaks* a quarter of a century after it first premiered, Linnie Blake remarks that "*Twin Peaks* was first broadcast . . . in a world in which the certainties of state and nation, society and self, were being changed utterly by the radical energies of neoliberalism. This is the world we inhabit today."[8] While Blake is more concerned with "the twin energies of neoliberal economics . . . and postmodern philosophy"[9] rather than with "energy" as such, her critical assessment of the original two seasons, delivered in 2016 just one year prior to the release of season 3, foreshadows some of the concerns on energy addressed by Lynch in the latter season. While season 3 contains its fair share of Lynch staples in terms of automobile pleasures, a sense of foreboding linked to energy as such runs through the entire season. This is at its most explicit in episode 8, "Got a Light?," in which imagery of coal, gas, and nuclear intermix explosively, literally as well as figuratively.

Starting out with the typical Lynchian setting of two people racing in a car to escape the law, the episode shifts gear radically once we move from the intimate space of the interior of a car and, later, the equally intimate interior of the club the Roadhouse to a setting and a perspective where the human cannot be. As the camera tracks the first atomic explosion in New Mexico in 1945, we at first witness the explosion from afar only to then dive into the explosion itself in a phantasmagoric five-minute sequence of a continuous explosion going all the way down to the level of the atom. Eventually, however, as the perspective draws back from the molecular level, once again to settle at a level perceptible and familiar to the human eye, the camera rests—tellingly—at a lonely desert road as well as a gas station. The atomic explosion ushering in a new and terrifying energy regime has released a demonic force into the world never before seen in history, and yet it manifests in both location and form in versions of energy consumption that now belong to the past. The so-called Woodsman, called into being by the Promethean effort of humans playing with the fire of the sun, stands as a conduit and reminder of energies traditional, modern, and mythic.

Dressed in a plaid shirt, sporting a full and unkempt beard, and wearing a padded hat with ear flaps, the Woodsman seems the stereotype of a logger of a kind populating the backwoods of the logging town in which the original series was set. And while the appearance of the Woodsman in the desert of White Sands, New Mexico (rather than in the woods of Twin Peaks), is at first incongruent in the treeless expanse of the desert, the incongruity is of course also to some extent the point. The malevolent force called into being by humanity's decision to invoke nuclear fission—the most powerful of energy's demons known to date—in fact alludes to almost all of civilization's main sources of unclean energy.

Evoked by nuclear fission (atomic energy), but dressed like a logger (wood), the Woodsman also resembles a miner, smeared from top to toe in soot and dark dust (coal), yet his first interaction with humans is—significantly—through a car window (oil). Fast-forwarding eleven years after the atomic blast in White Sands in 1945 and the initial advent of this new dark force at the gas station, the Woodsman makes his presence known to humankind in 1956. Stepping out of the desert late at night, the Woodsman flags down an older couple to ask if they have "got a light?" Driving off in a panic, the older couple flees the scene, leaving the genie unleashed by the light of the atomic blast by the roadside. This is no Frankensteinian monster, though. For unlike Shelley's forlorn creature, there are no redeeming qualities about this Promethean being. The fire has indeed been lit. But it gives off neither light nor warmth.

Drink Full, and Descend

Intersecting with human lives primarily in settings that involve oil in some form or other (cars, gas stations, roads), the appearance of the Woodsman in episode 8 clearly portends the appearance of evil in an otherwise harmonious world. Once again, Lynch may seem to express petro-nostalgia, for it is telling that it is again the 1950s that stand as the time both of innocence and also, of course, of the fall. Having failed to get a light from the older couple in the car, the Woodsman walks to a local radio station, kills off the receptionist and the DJ, takes over the broadcast, and repeatedly chants, "This is the water, and this is the well. Drink full, and descend." Nuclear power and thus immeasurable energy unleashed, humanity will have its fill but fall from grace as a result.

Yet to read the dark currents of energy coursing through *Twin Peaks: The Return* solely and literally as a mediation on the gradual loss of innocence due to increasingly reckless use of energy would be to do both Lynch and the series a disservice. Indeed, the very form of the third series is about the amplification of energy of all kinds. Furthermore, each strand of the series—Cooper's charismatic "idiotic" serendipity, the search for reasons why the Black Lodge exists, the drug deals over the border—are separated, amplified, and intertwined in a glorious spiral of what in Greek rhetoric is called *enargeia*. The intention, perhaps, is to subvert entropy, in that the third series makes an endless loop of the previous series, feeding off itself and its own energy in, precisely, the constant "returns" of the third season's title, but (perhaps?) also generating a return of energy invested.

The original *Twin Peaks* was a deeply mediated fantasy meditation on fantasy meditations about being American. It laughed at soap opera and cherished it at the same time, a love letter to the format even as it ridiculed it over and over and over again. In contrast, *Twin Peaks: The Return* refuses to do any such thing. This is seen most clearly, or perhaps obliquely, in Lynch's refusal to live up to fans' expectation of the "return" of Dale Cooper to the realm of humankind. With season 2 infamously ending with the entrapment of Cooper in the Black Lodge, the source and sanctum of dark energy on an alternate plane, season 3 frustratingly continues to defer this return. With Lynch teasing the original show's fans for almost the entirety of the third season with a Cooper that is the exact opposite of the original Cooper (smart and full of energy vs. Dougie's idiotic lethargy), the seeming satisfactory release of energy unleashed by episodes 16 and 17 once we *finally* get Cooper back is frustrated once again in episode 18. It is as if episode 18 of season 3 is the tulpa[10] of the "good" episodes 16 and 17, an uncanny double that (like the episodes prior to episode 16 stupidly goes on and on [like that road] or Dougie before Cooper becomes him). Whatever release may have momentarily been released by watching Cooper munch sandwiches and finally make critical decisions is doubly deflated by the intrinsically unsatisfying conclusion, a seemingly endless shot from what seems to be Cooper's dream. It's your worst nightmare of an ending, worse than a nightmare one.

Still, at least Laura gets to remain herself. So is she redeemed? And how? The tulpa of Laura has already appeared. She has appeared as part of the horrifying world of murder-incest that objectifies her, as a hallucination from which Laura suffers—not unlike what is perhaps the golden tulpa of that image, scary-crying Laura in Donna's doorway that Cole hallucinates. And so, in the interior scene with Harold, BOB-Laura appears as a Kali-like blue demonic being with tongue hanging out, enjoying power. Presumably that is what BOB thinks he can become once he has messed with Sarah and totally fused with Laura. The basic energy of having sex and producing a baby has nothing to do with the teleological narrative of it. But one can't *actually* "become death, destroyer of worlds," as Oppenheimer famously didn't say during the White Sands test. Nothing can become that.

Here are the demonic thoughts of dark energy released: thinking that one can be God, and an idea that God can see everything and is all powerful—or all good, or all evil. The energy in the atom is not intrinsically dangerous. It is one's idea of what that power makes of you. The essence of Wyndham Earle of season 2 is therefore also here in a distributed way, the inverse of the collected droplet, the bindu that is Laura, that contains the enlightened essence. And who is responsible for this energy? The White Lodge, if the black-and-white format of the "Got a Light" episode is anything to go by.

Yet the trouble with light is that it oscillates, shuddering like the inside of the White Lodge basement to which Cooper descends in season 2. With the hindsight of episode 8 of *Twin Peaks: The Return*, we can now speculate that the White Lodge appears to be installed during the first millisecond of the atom bomb test, when foolish people who opened their eyes beheld a gorgeous violet light, symbolized by the rippling ocean (of ultraviolet and gamma) energy around the lodge into which Cooper falls. A kind of supercollider supersymmetry seems to operate in which black and white, real and tulpa/fake, particle and antiparticle, zoom out of the 1945 explosion that inaugurates for geological science the Anthropocene in its fullest, most demonic and patriarchal aspect.[11]

This is exemplified by the entity Jowday/Joudy/Judy and the manner in which she (?) symbolizes the development of the series as a whole, as of the expectations of the fans to see Cooper redeemed from the demonic transformation in which season 2 culminates. An ancient mythological being known to take female form, Judy is (negative) energy, here separated from matter by the bomb. Judy is, like energy, in several places at once. Demonic Judy is the tulpa, the zombie-like husk, the manufactured one, just a body without a face, that releases the demon of energy when the Gadget detonates. Later, we are introduced to Smile Judy, the one inside of Sarah who eats the neck of the rapist at the bar in episode 14, the mature form of the creature that at the end of episode 8 crawls down her throat in an obvious nasty and misogynistic sinthome image of fellatio of an utterly passive woman. Watching the first two series of *Twin Peaks*, in which righteous men like Cooper work to save the girls from themselves, *Twin Peaks: The Return* offers something a monster of a third series that is the TV equivalent of the larval demon that comes out of the egg. We want stories to be incestuous, but we do not want to *know* that—this horrible, twisted, sick thing happening to our beloved series in which we can depend on the reasoned, and reasonable, logic of the male detective to save the day. It's like Lynch ripped the series' skull off, a horrible desecration of that *Twin Peaks* Umwelt where the top lawyer in town can rape and murder his daughter in front of everybody, where what looks like mammal behavior is actually insect behavior (insect, incest).

As a theme, Lynch has of course gestured toward this before, so perhaps this should not come as such a surprise. Take the opening scene of *Blue Velvet*, for instance, where the camera gradually tracks from the supposed harmony of white picket fence America only to descend to the creeping and crawling insect life of rot and decay but also teeming insect life just below the surface of a neatly manicured lawn. Later, through the incestuous howl of Dennis Hopper's Frank screaming "Mommy. Mommy. Mommy. Mommy. Baby wants to fuck!," a young Kyle MacLachlan plays the part of amateur detective Jeffrey, who voyeuristically witnesses the Oedipal display partly in horror, partly aroused. Significantly, Frank also instructs Dorothy/Mommy, but in effect also Jeffrey, and by extension us as viewers, "Don't you fucking look at me!"[12]

Judging from the outraged responses of fans and critics alike, we do not, in fact, want to look at it, or at least not too closely. The cozy nostalgia of the earlier seasons that seemed to somehow still promise, incestuous rape or not, that everything will be fine is not allowed any foothold in *Twin Peaks: The Return*. While Good Cooper is finally restored in episode 16, this seeming reestablishment of patriarchal reason and righteousness is in fact a ruse. As we move to smiling Laura at the end of the season in episode 18, we are shown a transition from the fantasy image of the sexually powerful and politically empowered woman as demonically enjoying (just a grin without a mind) to the knowing noir smile of an actual woman who actually saves the whole thing, even when someone like Cooper is ready to shoot another guy in the balls through a table (and by the way, what a scene that is). And looked at another way, even the misogynist fantasy can be used as a stepping-stone to achieve this result; otherwise, that doesn't work either. For the series deals with the ways in which assuming one can violate a woman's body as a condition of being a certain kind of person are expressed in all kinds of ways in all kinds of forms, conjured in that misogynist image of a smile that will eat you like a spider, with the implication (because of what the man is saying) that this could be after sex—the vagina dentata. The threat of sexual display, which in the end is the threat of appearance as such.

Logs of Ignorance

We long for the good old days, when we knew what Lynch (and everything else) was all about. Just remember the pre–World War II magic of the silver screen. The magic of cinema. The magic of making people feel things. The weird music. The weird living room warmth. The weird electrical stuff making weird noises. It looks weird, like an old black-and-white film of itself. It's almost as if we have tried to get to the end of *Twin Peaks* only to find ourselves back not just with *Blue Velvet* but with that Lynchian Ur-text *Eraserhead*, albeit now with the terrifying and inescapable totality of the Anthropocene that was only then beginning to take shape when the film came out in 1977, four years after the oil crisis of 1973.

Remember, there can be magic. Things can be different. In the end, you can split atoms because you know quantum theory, and you know quantum theory because at a basic level, things aren't static lumps, they are quivering alive, yet not—they are dead, yet they live. That's what a magic world feels like. It can be a bit spooky. Or a bit lame, like a 1980s video effect, of which season 3 is so full. But often in a good way, like the White Lodge, which exists in the femtosecond during which the atom begins to split, where the light is way off the edge of the spectrum and hence can only be represented to humans, as a deep violet ocean of energy in which is floating a lodge/electrical device of yore/Jack Rabbit's palace, a place where you can visualize things.

As a conclusion, we must turn to the expenditure of energy, in all its forms, of the ecology of a twenty-first-century *Twin Peaks* set against a late twentieth-century *Twin Peaks*. For if in the latter it was still possible to be nostalgic for a 1950s America ruled by petrol and patriarchy, this position seems untenable, to say the least, today, in which the *oeikeios* of the Anthropocene has so radically upset the cozy petro-nostalgia of an earlier Lynch. If "the protagonists in film noir appear cursed by an inability to dwell anywhere" even as "nostalgia and longing for older urban forms combined with a fear of new alienating urban realities pervade film noir,"[13] this sense of unease seems to have been doubled down on in the Anthropocene. "Insecurity, estrangement and lack of orientation and balance are sometimes so acute in Lynchland that the question becomes one of whether it is possible to ever feel 'at home,'"[14] Chris Rodley remarks in *Lynch on Lynch—Revised Edition* (2005) a decade and a half ago, and certainly Lynchland has become ever more so in *Twin Peaks: The Return*.

Here we must return to the Woodsman once again, a creature of the atom bomb that looks, incongruously, like Abraham Lincoln.[15] Supposedly born in a log cabin and often portrayed as being somewhat wooden, Lincoln is of course America, and the American home, epitomized. Yet the trouble with *Twin Peaks*'s Lincoln is that he's a *burned* log. He's an idea. He's an old bad idea that thinks of matter as fuel. It's the stripping of things to stuff you can measure (such as $e = mc^2$ squared) that can do a lot of damage, so be careful what you think. In contrast, the Log Lady is the in-between figure: her log is surely not dead. But is it alive? For while she dies, her log is turning gold. And so, looking back on all three seasons in light of the latest, we must ask ourselves, *Was* this story about the bunny going down the hole? Or about the bunny girls? Was this the story of the little girl who lived down the lane? Ultimately, we find ourselves no further forward. The uncomprehending stupidity of the obviously central Lucy and Andy is what we all are, how we even in our knowing come close to knowing as the sound our most dumb idea of a thing makes. The energy of knowing, which, as a meditator, Lynch knows is in the end awesome.

Hyle, the Greek for what the Log Lady is holding, is used figuratively, by stripping it of its woodiness (to produce a bland manipulable substance, a.k.a. the anthropocentric idea of fuel) to mean *matter.* Despite how many think art is this demonic force from another dimension that needs to be tamed, you need to kind of sort of get on its side. That's because the problem really is in the appearance dimension, including your basic default idea of appearance as an ineffective surface. Everything is fuel for this predictable human-scaled future which is actually the past eating the future—your bastard demon going round and round and round.

Dancing: Coda

To attempt to offer any conclusive reading to a Lynchian text is, as remarked earlier, a futile gesture. Still, while Lynch seems as averse to politics as he is to narrative resolution (if not revolution), it is significant for the purposes of this volume that the characteristic sense of Lynchian unease seems to have shifted in recent years. That staple of the gothic, the uncanny, is as prevalent as ever in *Twin Peaks: The Return.* Yet, rather than manifesting locally—in the woods outside of Twin Peaks, in the living room of the Lelands, in the ballroom of the Great Northern—there is a sense in season 3 that it is the world as such that is broken, uncanny, not to be put together again. "Fuck Gene Kelly, you motherfucker," the always belligerent Albert Rosenfield utters when caught in a rain shower in New York City in episode 6 of season 3. For Albert, as for David and all the rest of us, there is no more dancing in the rain, no more pretending not to be aware that the fossil fuel dream was in fact a nightmare.

NOTES

1. Stephanie LeMenager, *Living Oil: Petroleum Culture in the American Century* (Oxford: Oxford University Press, 2014).
2. Reza Negarastani, *Cyclonopedia: Complicity with Anonymous Materials* (New York: Re.Press, 2008).
3. Catherine Spooner, "'Wrapped in Plastic': David Lynch's Material Girls," in *Return to Twin Peaks: New Approaches to Materiality, Theory and Genre on Television,* ed. Jeffrey Andrew Weinstock (Houndmills, U.K.: Palgrave Macmillan, 2016), 119.
4. Jeffrey Andrew Weinstock, "'It's a Strange World: David Lynch," in *The Routledge Companion to Cult Cinema,* ed. Ernest Mathijs and Jamie Sexton (London: Routledge, 2020), 348.
5. Linnie Blake, "Trapped in the Hysterical Sublime; *Twin Peaks,* Postmodernism, and the Neoliberal Now," in Weinstock, *Return to Twin Peaks,* 234.
6. LeMenager, *Living Oil,* 4.
7. Sheena Wilson, Adam Carlson, and Imre Szeman, "On Petrocultures; or, Why We Need to Understand Oil to Understand Everything Else," in *Petrocultures: Oil, Politics, Culture,* ed. Sheena Wilson, Adam Carlson, and Imre Szeman (Montreal: McGill-Queen's University Press, 2017), 9.
8. Blake, "Sublime," 231.
9. Blake, 230.
10. A being or object that is created through spiritual or mental powers, hence essentially a being created solely out the energy of mind.
11. Jan Zalasiewicz, Colin N. Waters, Mark Williams, Anthony D. Barnosky, Alejandro Cearreta, Paul Crutzen, Erle Ellis et al., "When Did the Anthropocene Begin? A Mid-Twentieth Century Boundary Level Is Stratigraphically Optimal," *Quaternary International* 383, no. 5 (2015): 196–203.
12. David Lynch, dir., *Blue Velvet* (Wilmington, N.C.: De Laurentiis Entertainment Group, 1986).
13. Edward Dimendberg, *Film Noir and the Spaces of Modernity* (Cambridge, Mass.: Harvard University Press, 2004), 7.
14. Chris Rodley, ed., Introduction to *Lynch on Lynch,* rev. ed. (London: Faber and Faber, 2005), x–xi.
15. The actor Robert Broski, who plays the Woodsman, was prior to his appearance in *Twin Peaks: The Return* primarily known for playing Lincoln both on television and in film.

Part IV

CHTHULUCENE

Anthropocene, Plantationocene, and Capitalocene, and related concepts, such as Gynocene, are designed to identify the figure or process causing current and future (climate) upheaval. Thus they are all, as T. J. Demos has observed, "names of resistance."[1] Donna Haraway's contribution to this list—Chthulucene—is certainly also a concept that encourages resistance, but it does so in different ways. In *Staying with the Trouble: Making Kin in the Chthulucene* (2016), Haraway notes with Anna Tsing that the Anthropocene is importantly different from previous eras by the obliteration of refuges where a multitude of interconnected species can find shelter, recuperate, transform, die, and come to life again. Humanity is ultimately just another creature in this network of interdependent beings. The naming of this period or state as the Chthulucene is an effort to direct attention to the ways in which these always-connected forms of life enable each other and how they are affected by the detrimental effects of the Anthropocene as assemblages and systems rather than as individuals. Chthulucene is thus a concept that fosters what Tsing has termed the "art of noticing,"[2] where what is noticed is precisely the reality of the forces that tie them/us together and the existence of these vital interconnections. Moreover, Chthulucene is conceived not simply as a descriptor but as an agentive concept that, in Haraway's characteristic prose, "entangles myriad temporalities and spatialities and myriad intra-active entities-in-assemblages—including the more-than-human, other-than-human, inhuman, and human-as-humus."[3] In this way, Chthulucene identifies not primarily the reasons why the planet is experiencing a climate crisis but the complex, tentacular nature of the damaged planet all species inhabit. At the same time, the concept actively decenters the human as species and, in so doing, seeks to collapse Anthropocentrism as logic and practice.

For a student of gothic and horror, it is tempting to assume that the concept has been inspired by H. P. Lovecraft's Cthulhu mythos. There are certainly similarities between the tentacular, underground, and horrific universe that Lovecraft imagined and the understanding of ecological relations that informs Haraway's Chthulucene. However, as Haraway observes, whereas the chaotic and monstrous are abject in Lovecraft's misogynist and racist mythos, they are familiar and intimate in Haraway's description. The bodies of the plants and animals that inhabit this planet are hosts to literally trillions of other microbial beings in an infinitely complex network of connections. The horror of the Chthulucene is thus not, as in Lovecraft, the tentacular nature of life on the planet but the failure by the Anthropos to recognize and embrace the planet's multispecies nature. Such neglect will eventually also leave humans without refuge—a process already occurring within precarious communities across the planet.

Because the Chthulucene is not coined to identify detrimental processes or human agency, it offers a kind of systemic hope. The slogan of Haraway's Chthulucene is "make kin not babies."[4] This is a call that encourages two related processes: a considerable reduction of humans on an overpopulated planet and, just as important, a nurturing of the intimate relations that exist between the Anthropos and nonhuman life, and between nonhuman forms to which humanity is marginal. Learning to love across species borders, to value kinship even with the microbes that have coevolved with and now nurture the (human) body, is a step toward hope for a planetary survival that may, or may not, include the human. Thus critics like Eben Kirksey have used the Chthulucene to consider futures where the human has become extinct but where love and desire are still distinct possibilities.[5]

The chapters of this part all demonstrate a keen awareness of the material processes and the thinking that have brought about the planetary emergency. Thus they do not in any way resist the notions that capitalism is the driving force of effects like global warming and the current depletion of biodiversity, or that humans in the Global North have been the agents of capitalism. At the same time, these chapters are also concerned with connections beyond those that exist between the human, capitalism, and climate change. In explorations of multispecies border crossings, death, and the threat of extinction, they move into, but do not necessarily confirm, the conceptual territory that Haraway has helped outline.

In the first chapter of the part, "The Anthropocene Within: Love and Extinction in M. R. Carey's *The Girl with All the Gifts* and *The Boy on the Bridge*," Johan Höglund explores two novels by M. R. Carey that envision a future where a fungal plague has transformed the better part of humanity into braindead and voracious "hungries." Unlike the standard zombie narrative, these novels do not revolve only around (violent and futile) human resistance to the corporeal invasion and decay that the plague entails. Instead, Höglund argues that these novels consider the positive transformative potential of multispecies becoming. The solution that these novels propose is thus not the fortification of the epistemological and ontological borders that set the human apart from, and above, other forms of life but rather the embrace of a multispecies becoming that enables being beyond the confines of the human.

Laura R. Kremmel's chapter "Rot and Recycle: Gothic Eco-burial" explores how the notion of the sanitized human corpse emerged in burial rituals in the Global North and how new eco-friendly burial systems as well as gothic are problematizing these rituals and the human exceptionalism out of which they grew. The chapter accounts for the historical emergence and proliferation of the notion that the human corpse is a pollutant rather than an ecosystem undergoing transformation. Firmly rooted in Haraway's and Tsing's rethinking of the notion of human death and relations between humans and other forms of life, Kremmel then shows how gothic, from its earliest beginnings to the present, has interrogated this notion via images of lively decay and by recognizing the hybrid, multispecies nature of the human corpse.

In the chapter "Erotics and Annihilation: Caitlín R. Kiernan, Queering the Weird, and Challenges to the 'Anthropocene,'" Sara Wasson investigates how Keirnan's new weird writing complicates not only the notion of the Anthropocene but also Haraway's alternative concept Chthulucene. The chapter's comprehensive reading of Kiernan's work reveals an oeuvre that clearly understands the long history of life on this planet as fundamentally queer, multi-species, and more-than-human but that eschews Haraway's often exultant hope for a symmetrical and liberating meeting between life-forms. Instead, Wasson identifies in Kiernan's work a dark and foreboding awareness of the fragility of *Homo sapiens* as it encounters and merges with other forms of life. The strange and often violent erotics that such meetings entail does not promise to revitalize the human but rather forms part of a planetary renewal to which the Anthropos is utterly marginal.

In the collection's final chapter, "Monstrocene," Fred Botting explores the limits of the many attempts to name the dark era that the human being has engineered and is currently living through and trying to understand. Working through and critiquing some of the concepts that have been used to grasp the ongoing damage done to the planet, Botting observes how much of the conceptual territory still serves to resurrect and make comfortable the very notion of the human in ecology. In an attempt to deviate not simply from these concepts but from the very process of meaning making, Botting offers the "undark" as a condition that exists beyond the epistemological limits of humanist evocations of nature and proposes the "monstrocene" not as an alternative concept but as a collective notion capable of disturbing the apparent rationality and objectivity of much of the existing nomenclature. "Monstrocene" thus challenges the reader to precisely read, reread, and rethink (ecological) relationships in an era of climate disruption, this in an effort to avoid solidifying and compartmentalizing these connections. Such an undertaking, Botting suggests with Anna Tsing, may take its cue from the entangled, ongoing, resistant, and restorative image of the mycelium and the potential of the mushroom, not to resist precarity and unpredictability, but to shape lives out of these conditions.

NOTES

1. T. J. Demos, *Against the Anthropocene: Visual Culture and Environment Today* (Berlin: Sternberg Press, 2017), 85.
2. Anna Tsing, *The Mushroom at the End of the World: On the Possibility of Life in Capitalist Ruins* (Princeton, N.J.: Princeton University Press, 2015), 17.
3. Donna Haraway, *Staying with the Trouble: Making Kin in the Chthulucene* (Durham, N.C.: Duke University Press, 2016), 101.
4. Haraway, 102.
5. Eben Kirksey, "Queer Love, Gender Bending Bacteria, and Life after the Anthropocene," *Theory, Culture, and Society* 36, no. 6 (2018–19): 197–219.

The Anthropocene Within

Love and Extinction in M. R. Carey's The Girl with
All the Gifts *and* The Boy on the Bridge

JOHAN HÖGLUND

In "Queer Love, Gender Bending Bacteria, and Life after the An-thropocene" (2018), Eben Kirksey considers what a truly postapoca-lyptic future might look like. In this future, anthropogenic climate change has made the world uninhabitable to humans, and also to most advanced forms of life. Interestingly, Kirksey's essay is partly motivated by a perceived need to interrogate the notion that such a development must be thought of as tragic:

> If the Anthropocene/Capitalocene/Chthulucene comes to an un-timely end, this could mean extinction for many life forms that we love. But if we kill ourselves, and those we love, a multitude of unloved others will continue with their own affairs. . . . Many kinds of life are involved in their own interspecies love stories. Humans are not exceptional in our capacity to experience en-tangled empathy—many other creatures have an awareness of others' interests and a motivation to satisfy those interests.[1]

The notion that Kirksey puts forward is provocative, first because it forces the reader to face the possibility of a complete man-made extinction. Kirksey envisions a future devoid of humans, and of the Nature that once emerged out of Enlightenment epistemolo-gies. However, the real challenge of Kirksey's proposition is the notion that such extinction is not the end of everything, that an ecology will persist, meaning that humans are disposable to the planet, to agency, to history, even to love itself. This love is not the anthropogenic, heteronormative emotional bonding celebrated in mainstream culture but a complex and interspecies queer erotics that constantly remakes the world.[2]

This rethinking of love and who can practice it allows Kirksey to speculate on the entangled empathy that can build between microscopic organisms, and perhaps also between the human animal and the multitude of organisms that inhabit this species. Such empathy is possible because, as new microbiology is increasingly revealing, and as will be described in more detail herein, the human body is in itself an ecosystem. Rather than existing as a discrete being, it is host to trillions of other forms of life that nurture the human body but also deny it the homogeneity and sacredness that have so often been attributed to it by members of its own species. The failure to love and cherish connections to these life-forms is destroying the health of the human body, just like the failure to love and cherish the infinitely complex system that constitutes ecology is eroding the biodiversity of the planet.[3]

Culture has only recently begun to acknowledge and explore these strange relationships and what they mean in a time of climate crisis. As discussed in the Introduction, Amitav Ghosh argues in *The Great Derangement: Climate Change and the Unthinkable* (2016) that the realist paradigm that accompanied the emergence of Nature as a category separate from humanity during the Enlightenment elides the catastrophic and uncanny. In a time of climate crisis, which is also a time when human science has begun to understand the weird and complex connections that exist between the human body and microbial worlds, normative realism bars humans from comprehending the complexity of life and how the climate crisis is destroying it. Unfettered by the representational paradigm of realism, gothic is better able to accommodate the strange and catastrophic events that accompany the climate crisis.[4] Its departure from conventional realism also makes gothic singularly capable of exploring the invisible, uncanny multispecies world that the human body constitutes. Now that the already strange and uncanny multispecies ecology that inhabits (human) animal bodies is growing increasingly uncanny as it deteriorates due to various environmental factors, gothic is one of the few cultural modes capable of making both the climate crisis and the weird nature of the human body comprehensible to a human reader.[5]

This chapter explores gothic in the Anthropocene by focusing on new gothic narratives that recognize that the body is a multispecies ecology and that this ecology is as deeply affected by the climate crisis as the biosphere. The focus of the chapter is M. R. Carey's postapocalyptic novels *The Girl with All the Gifts* (2014) and *The Boy on the Bridge* (2017), two texts that narrate multispecies being and becoming in an age of profound climate emergency. I argue that these novels convey dark stories of ecological and social upheaval and of *human* interiority suffering from anthropogenically engineered deterioration. However, rather than seeking ways of salvaging conventional modes of humanity and restoring the imagined hegemony of man, these texts imagine how interspecies empathy and love can rise to the surface also in an age of extinction. The chapter first discusses the revolutionary new research in microbiology that has revised the role that microbes have played in evolution and that they perform for all life. Drawing from a wide range of science texts, the chapter notes that the human being is a multispecies ecosystem and not simply an individual bounded by a certain genome and set of experiences. Via Donna Haraway's consideration of this new science, the chapter then turns to the two novels that constitute its primary material.

The Anthropocene, New Microbiology, and Staying with the Trouble

In the conventional imagery of the Darwinian evolution of *Homo sapiens*, a swarthy, crumpled primate grows more erect and pale the farther right (into the future) the eye travels, until a tall white male with a spear in his hand emerges. This figure walks into an empty void that represents a future that does not require or even allow for further evolutionary change. Normative evolutionary history thus tells a story about the becoming of a being that is not simply white and male but also bounded by the limits of his own white body. The spear symbolizes both his ability to create and manipulate tools and the fact that he has reached this ultimate evolutionary stage through struggle with all other species, rising above and beyond them. Although still dressed in animal skins, he is discernible as an individual with a clear gender and racial identity.

What new microbiological research argues is that the human should not be depicted as this bounded biological and psychological entity. The human body, as this research shows, is an assemblage of thousands of species the members of which outnumber

the cells of the human body. According to the most recent estimates, the human body is made up of roughly 3–3.7 trillion human
cells but it is also inhabited by 3–4 trillion bacterial cells belonging to five hundred to one thousand different species.[6] Together
with archea,[7] viruses, and fungi, these bacteria make up the interconnected microbiome of the human body.[8] While the shape and
function of the human body are determined by its roughly twenty
thousand genes, it is also provided essential aid by some of the at
least two million genes that the microbiome contains.[9] In this way,
the microbe is not, as it has frequently been described, an atavistic
pathogen that parasitizes the (human) animal body but a part of a
versatile system that serves its own needs, the needs of the host,
and, through the cycle of life, death, and decomposition, the planetary ecosystem.[10]

In place of the white male walking purposefully into the future,
new microbiology thus places a multispecies assemblage whose
"anatomical, physiological, immunological, and developmental
functions evolved in shared relationships of different species," as
argued by Scott Gilbert et al.[11] In other words, the human has not
evolved as a discrete individual but as "integrated communities of
species."[12] Thus the human cannot be considered an individual "in
any sense of classical biology: anatomical, developmental, physiological, immunological, genetic, or evolutionary."[13] Viewed in this
way, the human being appears more like a complex wilderness than
the bounded characters readers encounter in the realist novel.

The human ecosystem is also like the planetary ecosystem in
the sense that it is adversely affected by sudden anthropogenic
changes to environments that have evolved during millennia. The
most easily discernible symptom of this in the human animal is the
appearance of a number of what have been referred to as twenty-
first-century illnesses or modern plagues. Illnesses that have become exponentially more common during the late twentieth and
early twenty-first centuries include acne, allergies, autism, cancer,
eczema, diabetes, and obesity.[14] These illnesses are, unlike viral epidemics, so-called noncommunicable diseases, and they have now
"surpassed infectious diseases as the principal cause of sickness
and death, worldwide."[15] The increasing prevalence of these illnesses can be related to what has been termed *dysbiosis,* or microbial imbalance in the body. Dysbiosis can be related to a number
of factors, including, as claimed by Martin Blaser, the overuse of

antibiotics both in human health care and in animal farming[16] but also the release of chemicals and microplastics into the environment,[17] as well as new, so-called Western diets that are low in essential nutrients and fiber but high in meat, sugars, and saturated trans fats.[18]

These examples bring out similarities in how the human microbiome is depleted and damaged and the ways in which damage is done to the planetary ecosystem. Global warming is harming the planet and causing the sixth mass extinction of species on the planet in ways that are similar to how misuse of antibiotics and poor diets are causing a reduction in essential microbes in the (human) animal. However—and this is not surprising when the human is viewed as an ecosystem folded into other ecosystems rather than as a discrete individual separated from ecology—the connection between the destruction of planetary biodiversity and dysbiosis goes beyond the simile. Many of the pollutants that are harmful to planetary ecosystems also cause damage to the microbiome to which the human body is host. Heavy metals like mercury, plutonium, and lead released into the environment by human activity are harmful to all living systems and cause both dysbiosis and ecosystem decline.[19] In this way, dysbiosis triggered by Western diets, by oversubscribed antibiotics, or by pollutants introduced into the environment by humans can be considered as a kind of Anthropocene taking place within the human body.

This realization encourages us to rethink our own relationship to the world we inhabit. Donna Haraway has urged humans not simply to pay attention to microbes but to see human existence as intimately intertwined with that of other macroscopic and microscopic species. While accepting the need for descriptors like Anthropocene and Capitalocene, Haraway has proposed the Chthulucene as a concept that does not primarily serve to categorize the species and processes that are damaging the planet but that rather identifies the "ongoing symchthonic forces and powers of which people are a part."[20] In this way, she proposes the Chthulucene as an era that "entangles myriad temporalities and spatialities and myriad intra-active entities-in-assemblages—including the more-than-human, other-than-human, inhuman, and human-as-humus."[21] This is an understanding of life on the planet that resists the normative evolutionary paradigm and the centrality of the individual to instead acknowledge the prevalence and long dominance of "rich multispecies assemblages that include people" on Earth.[22] Such a nonanthropocentric understanding of the planet, and of evolution, leads to the realization that earthly survival is only possible if the needs of these assemblages, and the entangled needs of the planet in its entirety, are considered.

Haraway asks the reader to "stay with the trouble," which is a way of encouraging the reader to recognize the need of a paradigm shift that acknowledges this interconnectedness of the various beings that inhabit the world and to commit to the difficult work that this paradigm shift entails. A way to stay with the trouble is to help narrate stories that problematize anthropocentric perspectives and enable an understanding of the planet and the human being as multispecies worlds. In Haraway's words, "stories for living in the Anthropocene demand a certain suspension of ontologies and epistemologies, holding them lightly, in favor of a more venturesome, experimental natural history."[23] In her own work, Haraway has turned her attention most often to science fiction and what can be called art activism—modes and media that encourage such adventurous and experimental histories. However, Haraway's call for stories for living in the Anthropocene also creates a space for gothic and for gothic studies. This mode has always suspended the ontologies and epistemologies that literary, realist fiction laid down. In many ways, that is a definition of gothic.

The experimental nature of gothic, its built-in ability to challenge conventional natural histories, aids it in the exploration first of the fact that the body is a symbiotic ecosystem and then of the notion that this ecosystem is suffering due to anthropogenic interference. This does not mean, of course, that gothic automatically produces stories for the Anthropocene that promote an understanding of the interconnectedness of species. In her writing, Haraway clearly separates her concept of the Chthulucene from gothic horror writer "H. P. Lovecraft's misogynist racial nightmare monster Cthulhu."[24] If Haraway's Chthulucene is a tribute to the uncanny, tentacular, multispecies nature of all life, Lovecraft's Cthulhu mythos summons images of uncanny, tentacular, uncontrollable, nonanthropocentric life only so that the reader can despise and fear it. In this way, conventional ontologies and epistemologies both inform and haunt gothic. Indeed, in some narratives, multispecies life is introduced only so that it can be destroyed by the vast arsenal of modernity—by rational scientists;

by discourses of racial, sexual, and evolutionary purity; and by military violence. In this way, and as will be argued in my analysis, there is gothic that recognizes that anthropogenic manipulation of the microbiome is damaging the multispecies (human) animal body, but the resolution the mode offers is not necessarily an embrace of Haraway's Chthulucene. In the imperial, military gothic that has achieved a certain hegemony, in particular in U.S. Hollywood cinema, entangled and multispecies worlds are still being fought by machine gun–wielding special forces soldiers. But there is also gothic that meanders away from this fantasy of how the agents of modernity salvage the future through hypermasculine, technological violence to instead imagine the formation of new forms of being and new types of emotional connections that extend beyond the human.

Gothic and the Anthropocene Within

M. R. Cary's novels *The Girl with All the Gifts* and *The Boy on the Bridge* are two recent gothic texts that do in fact recognize the entangled and tentacular nature of microbial and (human) animal worlds and that explore these connections against an Anthropocene backdrop. The two novels take place in the same postapocalyptic world; *The Boy on the Bridge,* published a few months after the film version of *The Girl with All the Gifts* premiered, functions as a prequel. In the following discussion, I devote attention primarily to the first novel and use the second to clarify certain details. The two novels draw from a very long tradition of gothic and horror writing. In particular, they traverse some of the same intellectual territory first laid out by Richard Matheson's *I Am Legend* (1954) and then further explored by George Romero in a number of zombie films.

The protagonist of *The Girl with All the Gifts* is a ten-year-old, extremely intelligent, imaginative, blonde girl by the name of Melanie. Every morning, Melanie is strapped into a wheelchair and driven into an underground classroom that is part of a complex of military bunkers where she has spent all of her conscious life. Melanie has a fraught relationship with the soldiers who transport her between her cell and the classroom and with the physician, Dr. Caldwell, who visits the bunker from time to time. However, she loves her teacher Miss Justineau, who tells her and the class stories from time to time. Some of these are Greek myths, and, listening to them, Melanie decides that she would prefer to be called Pandora, a name that is said to mean precisely "the girl with all the gifts." Melanie is indeed supremely intellectually gifted, and it is easy to assume that the name suits her for this reason. However, it actually means "gift giver," and anyone familiar with Greek mythology knows that the gift that Pandora finally gives is a dark one.

Melanie is generally aware of the fact that she inhabits a post-apocalyptic world where so-called hungries roam. The hungries are the better part of humanity that has now succumbed to a microscopic fungus named Ophiocordyceps. This fungus is a fictional version of an actual fungus that exists outside of this fiction: *Ophiocordyceps unilateralis*. It can be found in tropical climates and adheres to the bellies of foraging ants. When the fungus reaches the ant, it breaks through its exoskeleton and infects the circulatory system and the brain. Once it has accessed the brain, the fungus can manipulate the behavior of the ant. The infected ant will climb up the stem of a plant that matches certain conditions in temperature and humidity and then bite through the main vein of the plant with unusual force. When the ant has become locked into the plant in this way, the fungus will paralyze the ant and kill it. The fungus then matures inside the ant, growing out of its body. Eventually, fungal spores will erupt through the head of the dead ant, releasing into the environment to begin the cycle anew.

In the novel, Ophiocordyceps has now mutated and entered into a parasitic relationship with the Anthropos. The physician Dr. Caldwell is able to discern the exact nature of this relationship through a microscope:

> Gross and fine structures are rendered in pin-sharp detail, like an illustration in a textbook. . . . She shifts the slide minutely under the turret, [and sees] foreign matter—dust motes, human hair and bacterial cells as well as the expected fungal mycelia—among the neurons. The nerve cells themselves are completely and thrillingly laid out to her gaze. . .
>
> She sees exactly how the cuckoo Ophiocordyceps builds its nests in the thickets of the brain—how its mycelia wrap themselves, thread-thin, around neuronal dendrites, like ivy around an oak. Except that ivy doesn't whisper siren songs to the oak and steal it from itself. . . . The massively parallel structures of

the human brain have regrouped, forlorn and outnumbered, around and between the fungus-choked nerve cells. Some uninfected clusters of neurons have actually grown denser, although the newer cells are bloated and threadbare, ruptured from within by jagged sheets of amyloid plaque.[25]

In this passage, the text moves far into the world of microbes and visualizes connections that can only be perceived in the microscopic realm. It is clear from this, and other descriptions in the novel, that the fungus has a distinct agency of its own and that the human has become a vehicle for the parasite. The passage depicts a type of tentacular, Chthulucene love affair, perhaps, but in this passage, it is clearly an unrequited love that consumes the (human) host.

Whereas *The Girl with All the Gifts* never states what led to the evolution of the Ophiocordyceps variant that infects humans, *The Boy on the Bridge* makes it clear that anthropogenic manipulation of the fungus was the probable cause: "There's a prevailing theory that these medicinal uses of the fungus were the precursors to the hungry plague—the doorway through which *Cordyceps* infected human populations."[26] In other words, the eruption of the parasite inside the human body is an example of the Anthropocene within. Just as man-made antibiotics or pollutants are eroding the inside of the (human) animal body in the present, the man-made fungus variant is damaging the insides of the humans of the novel. All advanced brain function disappears. In the place of rational thought is an imminent need to bite and feed on uninfected animal life, and thus also to spread the fungus.

At the beginning of the novel, Melanie has not yet figured out what the reader soon understands: that she is also a "hungry" of sorts. However, for some obscure reason, she retains her intellectual faculties. In other words, Melanie is neither human nor fungal hungry but a multispecies hybrid whose actions are fueled by the needs of both her human and her fungal natures.

To the scientists on the base, such hybridity is unacceptable and unthinkable. Melanie has been brought to the base along with similarly infected children not to save them from the postapocalyptic world but so that Dr. Caldwell can understand how Melanie and the other children are able to resist the detrimental effect of the fungus. The children believe that they attend a school of some sort, and they are indeed stimulated through regular teaching and stories. However, at certain intervals, Dr. Caldwell will bring a child into the laboratory, kill it, remove its brain, and analyze it. In the early part of the book, Dr. Caldwell has operated on one of the children (cruelly, without the use of now priceless anesthetics). The boy both dies and does not die as the top of his head is opened up and his brain lifted out:

> Subject number twenty-two, whose name is Liam if you accept the idea of giving these things a name, continues to stare at her, his eyes tracking her movements. It doesn't mean he's alive. Dr Caldwell takes the view that the moment of death is the moment when the pathogen crosses the blood-brain barrier. What's left, though its heart may beat (some ten or twelve times per minute), and though it speaks and can even be christened with a boy's name or a girl's name, is not the host. It's the parasite.[27]

Dr. Caldwell's assistant is deeply uncomfortable with the procedure, but Dr. Caldwell insists that "the subject presents as a child but is actually a fungal colony animating a child's body. There's no place for sentiment here."[28] Dr. Caldwell's one mission is to save *Homo sapiens* from the extinction that seems imminent, and she refuses to recognize an in-between, multispecies state of being. When colleagues object to the treatment the children receive, she states bluntly, "If I make a vaccine, it might cure people like Melanie, who already have a partial immunity to *Ophiocordyceps*. It would certainly prevent thousands upon thousands of other children from ending up the way she has. Which weighs the most, Helen? Which will do the most good in the end? Your compassion, or my commitment to my work?"[29]

The question Dr. Caldwell asks is important. If humanity is, as anthropocentric models of being have long insisted, a bounded individual and a species apart, exercising compassion with fungal colonies seems absurd. From this perspective, the fungus is clearly a freakish parasite, a microbe selfishly feeding off the sacred, rational mind of the human. While Dr. Caldwell sounds callous, there is a sense that she may turn out to be the heroine of the story, the one who miraculously invents the cure and reinstates the hegemony of humankind. There is a long tradition of such closures in gothic fiction, where the heroic scientist finds the cure and things return to the status quo of modernity.[30]

However, before Dr. Caldwell has the opportunity to dissect Melanie, the base is overrun by a group of survivalists known as "junkers," who inhabit the lands outside the base. Dr. Caldwell, a couple of soldiers, Miss Justineau, and Melanie manage to escape in an army vehicle, and in the process, Melanie bites some of the junkers, saving Miss Justineau's life but also discovering that she is indeed host to the fungus, that she has an innate desire to feed off living bodies. For Melanie, this experience and the realization it brings trigger an identity crisis. How can she both love Miss Justineau and want to eat her? Is she truly a human being? If not, to what species does she belong?

These questions become increasingly central as the small group makes its way through what remains of England. The destination is a base called Beacon, the only remaining walled-in colony of humans left in the nation. During the slow and hazardous journey, they encounter more of the infected children. Because these children have never been in the company of uninfected human adults, they lack a functioning language and survive by hunting animals and the occasional stray *Homo sapiens*. The group also runs into what amounts to a dense forest of fungi growing out of the decomposing bodies of fully dead hungries. Seeing the forest, Dr. Caldwell theorizes that the fungus has developed a new strategy. These enormous fungal growths mimic the fungi growing out of the heads of parasitized ants; they contain seed pods full of spores and await some kind of environmental trigger that will set them free, turning the contagion airborne. If this occurs, all human beings, including those hiding in Beacon, will become infected.

Close to this forest, the group discovers an abandoned but advanced and still functional research vehicle equipped with a precise electron microscope, a tool that Dr. Caldwell has previously lacked. Dr. Caldwell manages to lure one of the feral children into a trap, decapitates him, and examines his brain with her new equipment. This allows her to see the difference between the brains of a first-generation and a second-generation hungry.[31] She explains to Melanie:

> The fungus utterly wrecks the brain of a first-generation
> hungry. . . . In the second generation . . . the fungus is spread

evenly throughout the brain. It's thoroughly interwoven with the dendrites of the host's neurons. In some places it actually replaces them. But it doesn't *feed* on the brain. It gets its nourishment only when the host eats. It's become a true symbiote rather than a parasite.[32]

This is an answer to the questions that Melanie has been asking herself. She realizes that she is neither human nor fungus but a multispecies, symbiotic hybrid. This explains the instinctual, protective love she feels both for the hungries and for the hybrids she comes across. This leads on to another realization: her true identity as Pandora, the giver of gifts. Melanie supplies the environmental trigger that the fungal growths are waiting for by setting them on fire, effectively obliterating the entire human species. She explains her actions to one of the soldiers:

> If you keep shooting them [the hungries] and cutting them into pieces and throwing them into pits, nobody will be left to make a new world. Your people and the junker people will keep killing each other, and you'll both kill the hungries wherever you find them, and in the end the world will be empty. This way is better. Everybody turns into a hungry all at once, and that means they'll all die, which is really sad. But then the children will grow up, and they won't be the old kind of people but they won't be hungries either. They'll be different. Like me and the rest of the kids in the class.[33]

The only human to survive this apocalypse is Miss Justineau, who finds shelter in the protective environment of the research vehicle.[34] In a supremely ironic reversal of fates, she will live out her days encased by the vehicle or a biohazard suit, continuing to teach the new hybrid children reading, arithmetic, and classical literature.

Posthuman Presents in Gothic

The Girl with All the Gifts clearly outlines a very different intellectual and corporeal territory than most other zombie narratives, where the typical resolution to the zombie plague is constant machine gun fire and the antidote produced by the scientists sheltered by this fire. In *The Girl with All the Gifts*, capitalist technoscience was what brought on the catastrophe in the first place. Thus the scientists, guns, and soldiers that constitute the only conceivable antidote to the zombie plague in other narratives are not allowed to grasp sudden triumph out of a dissection of Melanie's infected body. A different way of thinking, a thinking beyond the Anthropos, even beyond the notion of "saving," is necessary to realize the postapocalyptic future.

In this way, the extinction of the Anthropos is not necessarily tragic in *The Girl with All the Gifts*—certainly not as tragic as the alternative future of constant killing and destruction that Melanie envisages. Prospects for the planet may still be bleak, but something is gained by making room for tentacular multispecies being and becoming. In this way, *The Girl with All the Gifts* imagines a future in which mankind has indeed gone extinct but where love is still a possibility. The novel makes it possible to envisage the hybrid children forming communities very different from current human society. The new microbiome has made the second-generation hungries much more resilient and effective. They will have no need to develop a fossil fuel economy, enabling also love between them and the planet. Thus, the novel enables a love not simply between human–fungal hybrids but also between the hybrids and the fungus itself and between these entangled entities and the planet into which they are folded. As Kirksey has proposed, symbiotic entanglement is perhaps best described as a form of love. Melanie's decision to let humanity die out is, in fact, imagined not as an act of anger but as one of love.

This does not mean that Kirksey or Carey is promoting the extinction of the Anthropos. Rather, Kirksey's observation—and that of many other scholars who can be tentatively labeled as posthumanist—that to push "beyond anthropocentric concerns, into the world of this microbe, also offers an opportunity to imagine the possibilities of life without us"[35] and his contention that even if the "Anthropos destroys itself, and other creatures we love, perhaps it is possible to embrace post-human futures"[36] are not calls for collective human self-extermination. Rather, "learning how to love and care for invertebrates, and their microbial companions, in an era of extinction could open up lively post-human possibilities."[37] Carey's novel should perhaps be read in the same way: not as a request to give up on humankind as a species but as a gothic call to embrace tentacular, multispecies life in the Chthu-lucene, to "make kin" as Haraway proposes.[38] Such a call is not a death knell but a request to form emotional attachments across the species barriers erected by Enlightenment anthropocentrism. Such attachments can be the foundation of a new ethics in the time of the Anthropocene.

NOTES

1. Eben Kirksey, "Queer Love, Gender Bending Bacteria, and Life after the Anthropocene," *Theory, Culture, and Society* 36, no. 6 (2018–19): 199.

2. See Sarah Wasson's chapter "Erotics and Annihilation: Caitlín R. Kiernan, Queering the Weird, and Challenges to the 'Anthropocene'" in this collection for another discussion of the queer erotics of non-human and more-than-human life-forms.

3. The notion that we should cherish the life of microbes may seem counterintuitive in a world that has experienced the Covid-19 pandemic, but this pandemic only further emphasizes the need to consider the wants and natures of microbes. Viruses are a hazard to human life and to societies, but viral "phages" also cooperate with bacteria to keep both the human immune system and the ecosystem well balanced. See Karin Moelling, "What Contemporary Viruses Tell Us about Evolution: A Personal View," *Archives of Virology* 158, no. 9 (2013): 1833–48.

4. Amitav Ghosh, *The Great Derangement: Climate Change and the Unknowable* (Chicago: University of Chicago Press, 2016), 24.

5. While this chapter uses "Chthulucene" rather than "Capitalocene" as proposed by Jason W. Moore and Andreas Malm, I recognize, as proposed by Moore, that the climate crisis that is currently unfolding has not been caused by the Anthropos as a species but by a capitalism rooted in, fueled by, and fueling colonialism.

6. For the number of bacterial cells that live inside and on the human body, see Ron Sender, Shai Fuchs, and Ron Milo, "Revised Estimates for the Number of Human and Bacteria Cells in the Body," *PLoS Biology* 14, no. 8 (2016): e1002533. For the number of bacterial species that inhabit the human body, see Jack Gilbert, Martin Blaser, Gregory Caporaso, Janet Jansson, Susan V. Lynch, and Rob Knight, "Current Understanding of the Human Microbiome," *Nature Medicine* 24, no. 4 (2018): 392–400.

7. Archea are unicellular organisms like bacteria and were long classified as such. No authoritative estimation of the number of viruses, archea, or fungi that make up the microbiome exists, but viruses are believed to outnumber human cells by 100:1. See John L. Mokili, Forest Rohwer, and Bas E. Dutilh, "Metagenomics and Future Perspec-

tives in Virus Discovery," *Current Opinion in Virology* 2, no. 1 (2012): 63–77, suggesting that there are vastly more archea, bacteria, fungal cells, and viral particles than human cells in the human body.

8. The bacteriome, archaeome, virome, and mycobiome collectively make up the microbiome, and it is as such that I will refer to it in this chapter. However, it should be observed that this term is often used in literature synonymously with *bacteriome*.

9. See Gilbert et al., "Current Understanding."

10. Bacteria perform a number of essential functions in (animal) bodies. As an example, the digestive system of a cow cannot digest the cellulose that binds the nutrients in the grass it eats. This job is outsourced to bacteria that have coevolved with the cow. As Lynn Margulis puts it in *The Symbiotic Planet: A New Look at Evolution* (London: Weidenfeld and Nicolson, 1998), "the cellulose-degrading microbes, in a very real sense are the cow" (122).

11. Scott F. Gilbert, Jan Sapp, and Alfred I. Tauber, "A Symbiotic View of Life: We Have Never Been Individuals," *Quarterly Review of Biology* 87, no. 4 (2012): 334.

12. Gilbert et al.

13. Gilbert et al.

14. For general discussions of the connection between a damaged human microbiome and various forms of illness, see Martin Blaser, *Missing Microbes: How Killing Bacteria Creates Modern Plagues* (New York: Henry Holt, 2014); Alanna Collen, *10% Human: How Your Body's Microbes Hold the Key to Health and Happiness* (London: William Collins, 2015); and Ed Yong, *I Contain Multitudes: The Microbes within Us and a Grander View of Life* (New York: HarperCollins, 2016), 103–43.

15. See Walter H. Moos, Douglas V. Faller, David N. Harpp, Iphigenia Kanara, Julie Pernokas, Whitney R. Powers, and Kosta Steliou, "Microbiota and Neurological Disorders: A Gut Feeling," *BioResearch Open Access* 5, no. 1 (2016): 138.

16. See Blaser, *Missing Microbes*.

17. See Clémence Defois, Jérémy Ratel, Ghislain Garrait, Sylvain Denis, Olivier Le Goff, Jérémie Talvas, Pascale Mosoni, Erwan Engel, and Pierre Peyret, "Food Chemicals Disrupt Human Gut Microbiota Activity and Impact Intestinal Homeostasis as Revealed by *In Vitro* Systems," *Scientific Reports* 8, no. 11006 (2018), and Liang Lu, Ting Luo, Yao Zhao, Chunhui Cai, Zhengwei Fu, and Yuanxiang Jin, "Interaction between Microplastics and Microorganism as Well as Gut Microbiota: A Consideration on Environmental Animal and Human Health," *Science of the Total Environment* 667, no. 1 (2019): 94–100.

18. See, e.g., Kristina B. Martinez, Vanessa Leone, and Eugene B. Chang, "Western Diets, Gut Dysbiosis, and Metabolic Diseases: Are They Linked?," *Gut Microbes* 8, no. 2 (2017): 130–42.

19. The identification of heavy metals released into soil by human activity is considered one of the "golden spikes" or markers of the beginning of the Anthropocene age. See Yadvinder Malhi, "The Concept of the Anthropocene," *Annual Review of Environment and Resources* 43, no. 77–104 (2017): 77–104, and Jerôme Breton, Sébastien Massart, Peter Vandamme, Evie De Brandt, Bruno Pot, and Benoît Foligné, "Ecotoxicology inside the Gut: Impact of Heavy Metals on the Mouse Microbiome," *BMC Pharmacology and Toxicology* 14, no. 62 (2013), for information on how heavy metals cause dysbiosis.

20. Donna Haraway, *Staying with the Trouble: Making Kin in the Chthulucene* (Durham, N.C.: Duke University Press, 2016), 101.

21. Haraway.

22. Haraway.

23. Donna Haraway, "Symbogenesis, Sympoiesis, and Art Science Activisms for Staying with the Trouble," in *Arts of Living on a Damaged Planet: Ghosts and Monsters of the Anthropocene*, ed. Anna Lowenhaupt Tsing, Heather Anne Swanson, Elaine Gan, and Nils Bubandt (Minneapolis: University of Minnesota Press, 2017), M45.

24. Haraway, *Staying*, 101.

25. M. R. Carey, *The Girl with All the Gifts* (London: Orbit, 2014), 387–88.

26. M. R. Carey, *The Boy on the Bridge* (London: Orbit, 2017), 171.

27. Carey, 44–45.

28. Carey, 112.

29. Carey, 357.

30. See, e.g., the film version of *World War Z* (2013), in which a combination of special forces military violence and medical research saves the day for the Anthropos.

31. In *The Boy on the Bridge*, the relationship between fungi and human brain is described in more detail: "he [Greaves] finds himself staring at a dense mat of fungal mycelia. The brain is one vast spider web of threads, woven about and through the regular neurons all the way from the outer cortex to the thalamus and transverse fissure. By volume, this brain is half human and half fungus. But where is the damage? The human cerebral matter ought to have been hollowed out, devoured by the fungal invader. There ought to be a 55–80 per cent reduction in actual brain mass and a visible degeneration of whatever tissue still remains. A crust of microglial cells overlaying the damaged cortical areas. Myelin sheaths stripped away leaving bare neurons firing fitfully and futilely into synaptic gaps that have become mud wallows of necrotic juices. None of that is present. If this brain has been invaded, it is mounting a robust defence." Carey, *Boy on the Bridge*, 172.

32. Carey, *The Girl*, 431–32.

33. Carey, 456.

34. *The Boy on the Bridge* actually salvages a slice of the Anthropos. Having discovered that the fungus does not thrive at high altitudes, a group from Beacon have relocated to the Cairngorms in Scotland. In the final pages of this book, this small and starving community is discovered by a now grown Melanie, who is escorting Miss Justineau, driving the research vehicle. This salvaging of both humanity and Miss Justineau reduces some of the intellectual impact of *The Girl with All the Gifts*. Yet, even in this novel, humanity will be forever confined to this elevated region as the rest of the Earth is contaminated by the airborne fungus.

35. Kirksey, "Queer Love," 5.

36. Kirksey.

37. Kirksey.

38. Haraway, *Staying*, 102.

« 14 »

Rot and Recycle

Gothic Eco-burial

LAURA R. KREMMEL

The gothic arose out of eighteenth-century graveyard poetry's obsession with mortality and decay. When poet Robert Blair vows "to paint the gloomy horrors of the tomb" in one of these early examples, "The Grave" (1743), he reaches for "low-brow'd misty vaults / Furr'd round with mouldy damps and ropey slime," and "thy trusty yew, / Cheerless, unsocial plant! That loves to dwell / 'Midst sculls and coffins, epitaphs and worms."[1] A more well-known text that inherits such macabre fascination might be Mary Shelley's *Frankenstein* (1818), in which Frankenstein remarks, "To examine the causes of life, we must first have recourse to death."[2] His goal may be to defeat human death, following a growing attitude of his age that humans should be exempt from mortality, but he does not disregard the influence of human decay: "bodies deprived of life, which, from being the seat of beauty and strength, had become food for the worm."[3] From his study of reciprocity between corpse and surrounding environment, "how the worm inherited the wonders of the eye and brain," he identifies the corpse's valuable contribution to the living ecology of the grave, just as Blair notes the intermingling of animal and plant matter in graveyards.[4] Mary Shelley was no stranger to cemeteries herself. Scenes of Frankenstein scavenging in charnel houses while grieving the loss of his mother call to mind stories of Shelley lingering around her own mother's grave in St. Pancras Old Churchyard.[5] Of course, by her own death in 1851, St. Pancras was considered one of the most toxic of the London cemeteries, and Shelley's parents were exhumed to be buried with her elsewhere.[6] Spaces where the dead are laid exhibit human convergence with the nonhuman and the anxieties, dangers, and possibilities of a network of decay.

Both Blair and Shelley use the imagery of the grave to evoke horror, shock, and disgust, associations that remain strong for much of the Western world. Despite missions like the Order of the Good Death[7] to remove fear from funerary rituals, social norms maintain a repulsion toward mortality, tied to concerns that human decay leads to loss of human exceptionalism through fearful integration into the ecology of the grave. As a result, modern funerary rituals are designed to sustain the human recognizability of the deceased, holding back this multispecies union. As ecofeminist Val Plumwood puts it, "Human Exceptionalism positions us as the eaters of others who are never themselves eaten and has profoundly shaped dominant practices of self, commodity, materiality, and death— especially death."[8] The attitude that hybridity—allowing the corpse to join a network of decay with living nonhuman entities— destroys human exceptionalism is based not on the fact that the body becomes less human (because the process of decay is very human) but rather on the anthropocentric idea that the human should be elevated above the rest of the planet. As anthropologist Anna Tsing writes, "entanglement bursts categories and upends identities," which causes discomfort, particularly during times of loss.[9] The shift from Anthropocene to the "myriad temporalities and spatialities and myriad intra-active entities-in-assemblages" that Donna Haraway calls the Chthulucene clashes with limited ideas about honoring the dead.[10]

Modern traditions of Western death care are in part motivated by defenses and defensiveness, exhibited by avoiding discussion of death and attempting to preserve and isolate the body. Yet, Haraway stresses the impossibility of these practices through terms like *sympoiesis*, "making-with," and *ongoingness*, "nurturing, or inventing, or discovering, or somehow cobbling together ways for living and dying well with each other in the tissues of an earth whose very habitability is threatened," all widely applicable to the multispecies network of decay in the grave.[11] To some, this convergence, this "making-with" (which Haraway carefully says is "not a synonym for mutually-beneficial"), is an afront to the memory of the human and a source of horror.[12] These attitudes motivate destructive treatment of human remains, impacting the surrounding ecosystem of which they become a part. In the eighteenth and nineteenth centuries, this means overcrowding churchyards so that the dead can remain part of the family parish and community. Starting in the late nineteenth century, this also means using wasteful, dangerous materials to protect the human form from hybridity. Gothic language and images are used to emphasize the destruction of both.

Death care treatments force the body into continued participation in the Anthropocene by contaminating soil and groundwater, wasting materials, and creating pollutants in service to an artificial idea of human wholeness. As I argue in this chapter, the gothic imagination unsettles the notion of the sanitized, isolated corpse at the core of human exceptionalism, acting as an agent of ecocriticism by actively promoting transformation and hybridity through human decomposition. While the idolization of nature in Romantic gothic literature dramatizes the decay and nonhuman hybrid networks of the grave, the hyperactive gore of the twenty-first-century gothic in examples like NBC's adaptation of *Hannibal* (2013–15) similarly illustrates the power of decomposition to dismantle sustained anthropocentrism of the dead. Though locating the corpse within the context of horror appears to do little to alleviate anxieties about it, the gothic importantly acknowledges and emphasizes decomposition by obsessively making it visible. Jesse Oak Taylor, for these reasons, posits that the gothic can offer literature of the Anthropocene its genre conventions as reliable tools that "[imbue] pollution and toxicity with the bodies of ghosts, doppelgangers, and demons," revealing that nature "is not merely diminished or domesticated but also resurgent, uncanny, often terrifying."[13] In other words, with gothic elements come agency and power.

The gothic will always be a space where fear is expected and explored, providing useful contexts to discuss mortality and decay, which are already connected to fear. Even when those discussions begin outside this generic space, the anxiety and horror associated with the existential loss of human exceptionalism in the grave trigger an impulse to reach for gothic frameworks. I argue, then, that the gothic, in championing abject hybridity throughout its literary tradition, also provides a discursive framework to confront anthropocentric ideas about death. In this way, it serves a vital role in disrupting avoidance of death processes by making those processes

Figure 14.1. Cemeteries were overcrowded, causing health concerns. St. Pancras Old Church, Pancras Road, London, looking west. Etching by G. Cooke, 1827. Wellcome Collection. Attribution 4.0 International (CC BY 4.0).

visible, undeniable, and accessible. Unlike other contexts, such as religion and science, the language of the gothic can facilitate discussions about innovative and transgressive eco-burial techniques that are accompanied by extremes in disgust and disturbance. Crucially, the rhetoric of terror and horror exposes the natural processes of death that, as Kristeva famously says, "we thrust aside in order to live" and forces an engagement with their cultural and environmental impact, highlighting the power of biological and ecological processes to be frightening but also commonplace.[14] In doing so, it expands the possibilities of "making-with" and "ongoingness" within death care, shifting human relationships with the nonhuman networks of the grave's ecology and expanding the possibilities of these "entities-in-assemblages."

In the eighteenth century, the corpse was an object of fear, not just as a shocking prop in gothic tales or a daunting reminder of mortality, but also as a dangerous source of threatening nonhuman entities: miasma, toxins, and disease. In fact, most continue to view a corpse as medically dangerous today, despite evidence to the contrary.[15] As Suzanne Kelly puts it, "embalming accompanied by a new order of funerary practices, redrew the lines of dirty and clean, remaking the decay of the dead body into a pollutant," while introducing the actual pollution of formaldehyde and other chemicals into the body and where it is buried.[16] In short, discussions of death have been fraught with concerns about the contamination of the corpse and its need for sanitation and containment through methods that do threaten the environment and public health. The gothic disrupts these notions of sanitation by valuing networks of decay.

The Nineteenth-Century Cemetery: Keeping the Dead Around

As one of the most quintessential gothic locales, the cemetery is in no way a dead space. Its occupants grow into various states that feed and nourish a complex ecosystem that Sarah Bezan calls "necro-ecology," the "vitalism of decomposition," which integrates a body into a larger, nonhuman network.[17] Her use of the word *vitalism* is particularly meaningful within a Romantic-era medical context, in which the vital element gave the body a mysterious life power. In drawing attention to the morbid vitality of the grave, the gothic encourages that same awe. Dead matter in the necro-ecology is remarkably hyperactive, joining a complex nonhuman network of organisms and microorganisms. Thus, when I refer to "dead/death" in this chapter, I refer only to the annihilation of the human as an individual, not to the end of the human body's necro-ecological life.

In the nineteenth century, while gothic writers like Shelley were raising the dead, the dead were causing their own trouble. The Industrial Revolution brought a visible influx of bodies to urban areas, bodies that would eventually need to be buried. As a result, this period saw an increased anxiety about cemeteries for two related reasons: overcrowding and pollution. Urban churchyards, subject to the "packing system," suffered an excessive volume of bodily remains in their small, central locations: the same plot became subject to multiple burials, multiple coffins stacked on top of one another. If the first body was not deep enough to allow for this, it was dug up and reburied farther into the earth. As a result, the bodies at the top were often close enough to the surface to be easily exposed and the living exposed to them.[18] A health inspector in Huddersfield estimated in 1850 that one churchyard held 38,298 bodies, "nine bodies per square yard distributed in what he

estimated to be twenty-one layers."[19] The same overcrowding was
reported in early American cemeteries in the first half of the nineteenth century, particularly in Boston and New York.[20] Calls for
burial and cemetery reform in Britain began as early as the 1720s
and culminated in the 1850s, a timeline that also includes the
birth and rise of the gothic and its preoccupation with dangerous
corpses and life after death.[21]

Both burial reform literature and the gothic situated the living
as victims of the dead but also the dead as victims of a system in
need of change. One emphatic reformer, Francis Seymour Haden[22]
of the Royal College of Physicians, Edinburgh, describes of the early
nineteenth century, "The soil of the old city graveyard had become
so saturated and super-saturated with animal matter that it could
no longer properly be called soil."[23] According to medical theory, it
was not the bodies themselves that were the problem but rather
the air that they infected and the odors they caused, the amount
of soil insufficient to subsume the concentrations of decay. Before
germ theory, bad smells were thought to carry miasma or effluvia,
spreading illnesses that could be fatal. Both Haden and an earlier
outspoken surgeon, George Alfred Walker, go to great lengths to
describe the various conditions under which the most dangerous
miasmas were produced. Walker's 1839 *Gatherings from Graveyards*
claims that cemeteries in their current overcrowded state were a
danger to public health, equating the dead to a supernatural curse
or phantom infiltrating spaces and seeking revenge for their im-
proper care. The packing system and the buildup of miasma are
worsened, reformers argue, by human attempts to preserve the
body. Sealing the coffin protects it from soil, moisture, and worm-
life for a short time, Walker argues, but it also causes effluvia to
amass, becoming more dangerous when it eventually breaks free.[24]

Cemetery reformers were not shy or formal when it came to
describing the damage miasma could cause,[25] and Walker is particularly known for deliberately borrowing the popular dramatic
language and tropes of tales of terror that would have been recognizable to nineteenth-century audiences. He calls cemeteries a "national evil—the harbingers, if not the originators of pestilence,"
claiming that the "injurious and destructive agencies" they contain
are "constantly in operation, and armed with invisible and irresist-
ible powers" and "pestiferous exhalations."[26] Granting an agency to
the corpse that is startlingly akin to the gothic tradition's graphic

Laura R. Kremmel

Figure 14.2. Walker warned that cemeteries should not be used for social events while the problem of overcrowding existed. G. A. Walker, *Lectures on the Metropolitan Grave-yards.* Wellcome Collection. Attribution 4.0 International (CC BY 4.0).

depictions, he condemns "the tremendous risk incurred by the mutilations of the resistless dead . . . thus made the instrument of punishment to the living."[27] Of cemeteries and the bodies within them, he claims, "their insatiable appetite, yet unglutted, is constantly devouring fresh victims."[28] Haden uses similar language, referring to burial practices causing "a vilification of the dead."[29] In fact, every gothic scene of a ghost or a skeleton attacking or wooing the living to join it in death is a demonstration of what these reformers claimed could happen in overcrowded, miasma-filled cemeteries. The gothic, then, provides characters, language, and images to portray the severity of anthropocentric damage.

The cure to these systemic burial ills was reciprocity between necro-ecology and the body—the nonhuman network and the human—which was not just appropriate but *the right* of the dead. Haden, in particular, claimed to stand for the right to proper burial, including full access to conditions that promote decomposition: soil, oxygen, hydration, and the vermin that aid in those processes, the worms and maggots used by gothic writers to accent graphic scenes of human mortality. The infamously graphic author Matthew Lewis provides ample representative use of such necro-ecological concepts within the early gothic tradition. His depiction in *The Monk* (1796) of the imprisoned Agnes in her living grave, cradling her dead child while maggots and worms rove both their bodies, refuses to exceptionalize the human by saving it from nonhuman assemblages. In his 1801 poem "Alonzo the Brave and the Fair Imogine," a dead knight returns to enact vengeance on his unfaithful lover. When he lifts his visor, "the worms they crept in, and the worms they crept out, and sported his eyes and his temples about," flaunting the vitality of decomposition's multispecies networks.[30] Such vivid descriptions acknowledge the power of this ecology below or beyond human observation, a power of the natural that rivals the supernatural. These texts confront that power by making it frightening.

Gothic elements, then, depict decomposition as an active process that appears threatening, but less so than the anthropocentric avoidance of decay described by reformers. At the same time that Walker and Haden characterize the buildup of decomposing bodies as human-made villains, the gothic's use of the supernatural turns this villainy into an agent of ecocriticism: had these bodies been provided conditions that promote decomposition, they would not have overwhelmed this necro-ecology. Gothic justice and revenge, promoting ecological processes for a narrative purpose, illustrate the human body in the act of hybridity. John Keats features such gruesome examples of necro-ecological revenge in the poem "Isabella; or, The Pot of Basil" (1818). When Lorenzo is murdered, his animal matter begins to fully participate in a nonhuman network when his lover Isabella brings his head home and plants it in a pot of basil, which "drew / nurture besides, and life, from human fears, / from the fast mouldering head there shut from view."[31] The head, no longer just human, appears as part of the basil and its soil, tormenting the killers and driving them into exile. Natural burial in this literature may seem to be dangerous, but only in the form of Lorenzo's revenge, a specifically gothic postmortem threat driven by the murderers' neglected value of life and power of death.

Modern Remains: Purifying and Polluting the Dead

Anxieties and misconceptions about unsanitary overcrowded cemeteries in the nineteenth century differ little in the twenty-first century. Cemeteries may not be as overcrowded as those using the London packing system, but they are quickly reaching full capacity in urban areas. These concerns, combined with the cost of funerary services, are slowly pushing some to consider eco-burial options. The rhetoric of the rights of the dead to decay and of the avoidance of burial pollution are surprisingly similar to rhetoric used in the ages of Walker and Haden. Haden, who claimed "that the natural destination of all organized bodies that have lived, and that die on the earth's surface, is the earth" encouraged burying bodies soon after death and "in coffins (if we must have coffins) of such a construction as will not prevent their resolution. No coffin at all would, of course be best."[32] A current advocate for green burial, Suzanne Kelly likewise claims that burial in crypts and cremation "[distance] the dead body from its own decomposition and [eradicate] the ecological value of its reintegration into the cycles of nature. In sum, the drive to distance the dead body from its own decay . . . [creates] a prohibition on returning the dead body to the elements."[33] As outspoken mortician and founder of the Order of the Good Death Caitlin Doughty adds, "The soil teems with life, as does the dead body. . . . Microscopic sorcery takes place when a body is placed just a few feet deep in the soil."[34] Attempts to seal the body within caskets and crypts interfere with the body's right to engage in the aforementioned "myriad intra-active entities-in-assemblages" that Haraway describes as a crucial turning away from anthropocentric practices.

Natural burial, an option in some areas, involves no lasting materials that would interfere with the necro-ecology by polluting or hindering hybridity: everything buried is biodegradable, rejecting caskets treated with sealants, adorned with varnish and metal, and placed within cement vaults that enable landscaping. Rather than an elaborate headstone, a simple rock found within the area or a native plant is used to mark the grave, particularly for the more extensive green burials, which occur in designated green cemeteries.[35] Twenty-first-century ecocritical concerns focus on the materials[36] employed by the funeral industry to prepare and bury the body: rather than an excess of gore overwhelming an ecosystem, there is a chemical/material lack of gore. Beginning in the mid-nineteenth century, Western death care not only preserves the body by encasing it away from the necro-ecology but also delays composition by filling the body with toxins. Embalming grew out the medical field's need to preserve bodies for dissection or display, until it became a popular way to preserve and transport

Figure 14.3. Caitlin Doughty demonstrates a natural burial in an episode on her YouTube channel, "Ask a Mortician." "ECO-DEATH TAKEOVER: Changing the Funeral Industry, Dec. 15, 2017," https://youtu.be/pWo2-LHwGMM.

bodies killed during the American Civil War and to augment British Victorian death culture in the 1890s.[37] Though the Civil War standard—arsenic—is no longer used, embalming chemicals, such as formaldehyde and methanol, can have harsh effects on soil and water quality, not to mention those who prepare them.[38]

Altering the timeline of decomposition can also add to ecocritical concerns. Katrina Spade, the innovator behind the decomposition company Recompose, explains, "In the weeks and months following a conventional burial, [embalmed] bodies slowly decompose anaerobically, and this lack of oxygen creates methane, a particularly powerful greenhouse gas."[39] As Tsing helpfully explains, "until quite recently . . . the most important interspecies interactions, in this worldview, were predator-prey relations in which interaction meant wiping each other out."[40] Allowing the body to decompose leaves it exposed to interactions that are seen as predatorial (i.e., food for worms), and embalming is thought incorrectly to prevent that. The gothic exposure that the Chthulucenic notion of "multispecies assemblages" is more complicated stands to shift these assumptions.[41]

The popular option of cremation may avoid these specific threats, but it also creates dangerous pollution through the release of mercury and other toxins into the atmosphere, as well as consuming large amounts of energy.[42] Nonetheless, cremation is mistaken by many to be an eco-friendly alternative: fire is considered to be "clean." New options, such as alkaline hydrolysis or water crema-tion, get stalled in production for the simple fact that they are seen as disturbing, uncivilized, and downright gothic by producing an easily disposable sludge along with bone ash. A 2008 bill attempt-ing to legalize alkaline hydrolysis in New York (where it is still not legal, except for medical remains) was nicknamed "Hannibal Lecter's Bill" for the fear that the residue would make its way into water and food matter, relocating a practical and environmentally conscious method of body disposal to dramatic and fearful gothic contexts.[43]

Though Hannibal is undoubtedly best known for his lavish feasts of human flesh, the hyperstylized NBC adaptation also features inventive and less-discussed examples of eco-burial. The first epi-sode, "Apéritif," sets the tone as special agent Will Graham and his psychiatrist Hannibal help the FBI track down the serial killer the Minnesota Shrike, a hunter who "honors every part" of his prey. In fact, in good eco-conscious fashion, the Minnesota Shrike case is classified as an abduction case: no bodies, body parts, or bodily debris is left behind. Only when you waste the body does it become murder, the killer explains, a philosophy shared by many of the murderers in the show. This perspective is predicated on an en-during relationship between the dead and the surrounding world: what is created from the corpse adds beauty, performs a function, or alleviates pain. Thus the body takes on new life beyond the an-thropocentric limits of conventional death care, transforming and hybridizing with a necro-ecology that exceeds even the boundaries of Bezan's definition. Recycling or repurposing the dead by losing its humanness occurs so frequently throughout the series that any of a number of examples could have been chosen for discussion, including the killer who turns bodies into musical instruments, since recycling the body into decorative or functional objects has precedent in today's funeral economy.[44] There's also the killer who plants a human–tree hybrid in a parking lot, a take on current ef-forts to combine conservation efforts with green cemeteries, as well as technology that theoretically allows you to "become a tree" when you die.[45] There is also the killer who lobotomizes patients in pain and turns them into beehives, though this so far has no equivalent in the present death industry. Because it speaks directly to some of the controversial innovations in eco-burial today, the

Figure 14.4. Screenshot of the mushroom garden in NBC's *Hannibal,* season 1, episode 2, "Amuse-Bouche" (2013).

remainder of this chapter will focus on the killer who plants his own mushroom garden.

Exemplifying the astounding symbiotic force belowground, mushrooms and other fungi also elicit cultural reactions of revulsion and "grossness" to which the contemporary gothic aspires. Episode 2, "Amuse-Bouche," centers around a forest patch of corpses, planted with their arms sticking out of the ground to intravenously feed them and facilitate the growth of mushrooms. Aesthetically exposing and augmenting the biological processes that occur in decomposition, the scene triggers the abject where animal meets fungal matter. Remove the serial killer, however, and this method is not far from a controversial technique that has captured the cultural imagination for its environmental involvement and disturbing embrace of hybridity. Since 2008, Jae Rhim Lee and her company, Coeio, have been working on an alternative burial option that initiates decomposition with fungal spores. The Mushroom Suit, renamed the Infinity Burial Suit, is a biodegradable burial garment with "biomix" mushroom mycelium sewn into it. According to the company, whose name means "coming together," the goals are to "aid in decomposition, work to neutralize toxins found in the body, and transfer nutrients to plant life." They claim that the Mushroom Suit boosts biological and ecological processes, removing pollutants in the body[46] through mycoremediation (the process by which mushrooms neutralize toxins) and protecting the

Figure 14.5. Jae Rhim Lee models an early version of the Infinity Burial Suit in her 2011 TEDGlobaltalk, "My Mushroom Burial Suit." https://www.ted.com/talks/jae_rhim_lee_my_mushroom_burial_suit.

body's right to nourish the earth by decomposing.[47] As anti-gothic as this sounds, the FAQ section of the website implies that this method is also burdened with disturbing associations: questions such as "Will the mushrooms eat me while I'm alive?" (the answer is no). Though, perhaps, they were right to ask. During experiments, Lee fed "shiitake and oyster mushrooms with [her] own body tissues and excretions—her skin, hair, nails, blood, bone, fat, tears, urine, feces, and sweat."[48]

Though there is debate about whether the suit actually works and convincing criticism of its insinuation that green burial is toxic and unsafe,[49] the concept behind it has become popular for its green claims.[50] In 2019, the Mushroom Suit became a topic of social media conversation when the late actor Luke Perry was buried in one. Though the volume of positive and curious responses shows a growing acceptance of eco-burial options that embrace transformation and hybridity, many cannot help but move this conversation to the gothic, reacting in disgust and leaving comments like "No! Makes me ill. I'm never eating another mushroom" and "Wow, that's a really terrible thought."[51] News of Perry's burial broke just weeks after Washington became the first state to legalize human composting, led by Spade. When still experimenting with composting techniques, Spade was aware of her project's gothic undertones. In an informal interview, she said, "Wait, let's not call them 'experiments,' that makes it sound like I'm a mad scientist. . . . We're here setting up *the mounds*. No, that's equally creepy."[52] News of human composting promoted similar, more heated social media debates, including the exchange "It's respect for the Earth," "You respect dirt. I'll respect men," and the comment "Oh my god *can you imagine the smell?*"[53] These commenters buy in to the funeral industry's "promise of preserving and protecting the body from the elements that surround it" and the "promise to protect the dead body from its own decomposition back into the earth."[54] Resistance to human transformation into nonhuman networks is still based on the notion that the body must be sterilized and the environment, already "dirty," pollutes it. At the same time, the preceding comments suggest that the corpse also threatens a misconceived idea of the earth as pure. The mushroom exists in the space between these conflicting ideas. As conflicting, negative perceptions of eco-burial options show, the gothic and horror are where these conversations can exist, at least for now.

The killers in *Hannibal* do not share these aversions to decay, combining the productive abject of both the mushroom and the gothic. As one character notes, the mushroom killer "enthusiastically [encourages] decomposition," and the graphic and repeated display of such decomposition throughout the episode is a primary source of horror, beautiful and grotesque in its attention to the details of the necro-ecology of which Will is clearly in awe.[55] Both the episode and current burial innovations echo those nineteenth-century conversations about a corpse's integration into the environment. Walker, Haden, Lee, and Spade see "encouraging decomposition" as a solution to types of pollution caused by mismanagement of body disposal and, again, as *the right* of the deceased. The mushroom gardener in *Hannibal* revels in the decay that leads to expansive network growth, honoring it as an achievement beyond the human, beyond the Anthropocene.

The killer's regard for hybridity goes even further than natural burial, however, as he harvests necro-ecological energy and applies it to what he sees as a problem with humans in isolation: the inability to connect. In the killer's words, "if you walk through a field of mycelium, they know you are there. . . . The spores reach for you as you walk by."[56] By planting bodies for the purpose of growing mushrooms that make connections, the killer draws attention to the powerful reciprocity of elements above- and belowground,

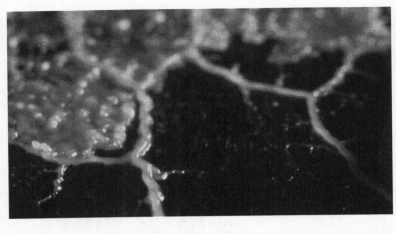

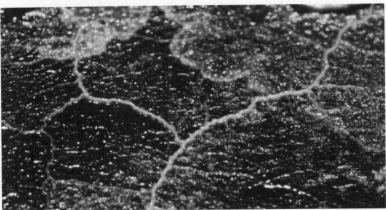

Figure 14.6. Screenshots demonstrating the movement and communication of multi-species networks in NBC's *Hannibal,* season 1, episode 2, "Amuse-Bouche" (2013).

hybridizing humans and fungi into one necro-ecological network stronger than any human community. Tsing corroborates the wonder of the mushroom's capacity to connect, referring to its atmosphere as an active city and the fungi within it as web builders joining other organisms together for feeding as well as sharing nutrients. "Follow fungi into that underground city, and you will find the strange and varied pleasures of interspecies life," she writes, an intimate assemblage similar to what the mushroom killer describes.[57] Like Haraway's notion of Chthulucene, she seeks alternatives to the Anthropocene, finding that mushrooms represent a mingling of human and nonhuman: "the very stuff of collaborative survival."[58] The celebrated visuals of *Hannibal* demonstrate how this works in close-up, slow motion of the incredible growth within nonhuman death networks. As Tsing says, "making worlds is not limited to humans."[59]

The gothic flaunts the unsettling but undeniable power of these decomposition processes; it amplifies, acknowledges, and participates in the concerns of eco-burial reformers, while also presenting a creative—if sinister—platform for discussion and images on which to draw. As innovative eco-burial options expose anxieties and misconceptions about bodily remains and burial practices by instigating a turn toward gothic contexts, opportunities to disrupt the urge to sanitize and isolate human remains also arise. At the same time that reform texts in the past and today draw on gothic to illustrate and instigate change, the gothic graphically demonstrates the macabre and disturbing value of alternative burial practices that disrupt anthropocentric attachments and promote the nonhuman network of the grave. Opportunities for conversations about mortality, decomposition, and necro-ecology within the context of stylized gothic fear encourage a reevaluation of death-related fears outside the text, making fear an important part of ecocritical conversations that challenge the boundaries and exceptionalism of the human.

NOTES

1. Robert Blair, "The Grave," in *The New Oxford Book of Eighteenth-Century Verse*, ed. Roger Lonsdale (Oxford: Oxford University Press, 2009), 368.
2. Mary Shelley, *Frankenstein: Annotated for Scientists, Engineers, and Creators of All Kinds*, ed. David H. Guston, Ed Finn, and Jason Scott Robert (Cambridge, Mass.: MIT Press, 2017), 33.
3. Shelley.
4. Shelley.
5. According to legend, tracing the name on her mother's grave taught young Mary to read, and she would have secret meetings with Percy Bysshe Shelly at the same location.
6. Samantha Matthews, *Poetical Remains: Poets' Graves, Bodies, and Books in the Nineteenth Century* (Oxford: Oxford University Press, 2004), 144. In the 1860s, overcrowding and the new railway line would cause

exhumation of thousands of graves, which author Thomas Hardy took charge of managing.

7. A death positive movement begun by mortician Caitlin Doughty and primarily run by women working in various areas within and around the death industry.

8. Val Plumwood, *The Eye of the Crocodile*, ed. Lorraine Shannon (Canberra: Australian National University, 2012), 91.

9. Anna Lowenhaupt Tsing, *The Mushroom at the End of the World: On the Possibility of Life in Capitalist Ruins* (Princeton, N.J.: Princeton University Press, 2015), 137.

10. Donna Haraway, "Anthropocene, Capitalocene, Plantationocene, Chthulucene: Making Kin," *Environmental Humanities* 6 (2015): 160.

11. Donna Haraway, *Staying with the Trouble: Making Kin in the Chthulucene* (Durham, N.C.: Duke University Press, 2016), 58, 130.

12. Haraway, 60.

13. Jesse Oak Taylor, *The Sky of Our Manufacture: The London Fog in British Fiction from Dickens to Woolf* (Charlottesville: University of Virginia Press, 2016), 100.

14. Julia Kristeva, *Powers of Horror: An Essay on Abjection* (New York: Columbia University Press, 1982), 3.

15. According to the Centers for Disease Control and Prevention, "the sight and smell [of remains] are unpleasant, but they do not create a public health hazard." "Interim Health Recommendations for Workers Who Handle Human Remains after a Disaster," Centers for Disease Control and Prevention, September 15, 2008, https://www.cdc.gov/disasters/handleremains.html. Thomas W. Laqueur adds in *The Work of the Dead: A Cultural History of Mortal Remains* (Princeton, N.J.: Princeton University Press, 2015) that "twenty-first-century doctors who ought to know better still act as if corpses are a threat to health. . . . There is no medical foundation for this policy. . . . Rotting flesh may be disgusting, but it is not a good vector of disease" (231–32).

16. Suzanne Kelly, "Dead Bodies That Matter: Toward a New Ecology of Human Death," *Journal of American Culture* 35, no. 1 (2012): 43.

17. Susan Bezan, "Necro-Eco: The Ecology of Death in Jim Crace's *Being Dead*," *Mosaic: A Journal for the Interdisciplinary Study of Literature* 48, no. 3 (2015): 192–95.

18. Lisa Murray, "'Modern Innovations?' Ideal vs Reality in Colonial Cemeteries of Nineteenth-Century New South Wales," *Mortality* 8, no. 2 (2003): 136.

19. Laqueur, *Work of the Dead*, 225.

20. Tanya D. Marsh, "A Brief History of the American Cemetery," in *Changing Landscapes: Exploring the Growth of Ethical, Compassionate, and Environmentally Sustainable Green Funeral Service*, ed. Lee Webster (2016), 15–16.

21. Karen Sánchesz-Eppler, "Decomposing: Wordsworth's Poetry of Epitaph and English Burial Reform," *Nineteenth-Century Literature* 42, no. 4 (1988): 416.

22. Sometimes spelled "Hayden."

23. Francis Seymour Haden, *Earth to Earth: A Plea for a Change of System in Our Burial of the Dead* (London: Macmillan, 1875), 54.

24. Haden, 96.

25. And scholars such as Thomas W. Laqueur claim that even they knew what they said wasn't true, that the dead were less dangerous than the living (229–30).

26. George Alfred Walker, *Gatherings from Graveyards: Particularly Those in London* (London: Longman, 1839), iii, v, vii. Similar to the "noxious exhalations [that] may arise from dead bodies," as described by Dr. Samuel Ackerly of the New York Board of Health in 1822. Marsh, "A Brief History," 17.

27. Walker, *Gatherings,* 10.

28. Walker, 5–6.

29. Haden, *Earth,* 5.

30. Matthew G. Lewis, "Alonzo the Brave and the Fair Imogine," in *Tales of Wonder,* ed. Douglass H. Thomson (Peterborough, U.K.: Broadview Editions, 2010), 64.

31. John Keats, "Isabella; or, The Pot of Basil," in *The Longman Anthology of Gothic Verse,* ed. Caroline Franklin (Harlow, U.K.: Longman, 2011), 476.

32. Haden, *Earth,* 7, 16.

33. Kelly, "Dead Bodies That Matter," 47.

34. Caitlin Doughty, *From Here to Eternity: Traveling the World to Find the Good Death* (New York: W. W. Norton, 2017), 108.

35. "What Are Natural Burials and Green Funerals?," The Good Funeral Guide, https://www.goodfuneralguide.co.uk/what-is-a-green-funeral/. If green burial seems anti-gothic, the Good Funeral Guide's web page includes the comment "the best look is probably the there's-nobody-here look," which fits well within particularly contemporary gothic tropes.

36. According to the Green Burial Council and Mary Woodsen's often-cited statistics, every year, the United States buries 4.3 million gallons of embalming fluid, containing 827,060 gallons of toxins like formaldehyde; 1.6 million tons of concrete; 20–30 million feet of hardwood; and 64,500 tons of steel. Caskets and vaults are treated with a host of chemicals that can leak into the ground. See Webster, ed., *Changing Landscapes.*

37. As Jani Scandura points out, this trend coincides with the publication of Bram Stoker's *Dracula.* Scandura, "Deadly Professions: 'Dracula,' Undertakers, and the Embalmed Corpse," *Victorian Studies* 40, no. 1

(1996): 1–30. She writes, "Dracula, the truly consummate undertaker, does not just beautify corpses; he preserves them eternally. Indeed, he seems to embalm them" (9).

38. Norman L. Cantor, *After We Die: The Life and Times of the Human Cadaver* (Washington, D.C.: Georgetown University Press, 2010), 83–84.

39. Katrina Spade, "How Your Death Affects Climate Change," in Webster, *Changing Landscapes*, 97.

40. Tsing, *Mushroom at the End of the World*, 139.

41. Haraway, "Anthropocene, Capitalocene, Plantationocene, Chthulucene," 160.

42. Doughty, *From Here*, 135.

43. Philip R. Olsen, "Flush and Bone: Funeralizing Alkaline Hydrolysis in the United States," *Science, Technology, and Human Values* 39, no. 5 (2014): 681.

44. For example, the company LifeGem will turn ashes into a diamond, Andvinyly will press ashes into a vinyl record, and Art from Ashes will incorporate ashes into glass baubles.

45. Bio Urn and Capsula Mundi are two examples that involve burying ashes with seeds or young trees. However, ashes do not themselves add any organic or nutritional content that promotes plant growth. Doughty, *From Here*, 148. In fact, many claim that ashes *prevent* root growth. Marketing them as a green alternative is part of what those in the field call "greenwashing."

46. According to Coeio's website, "the Centers for Disease Control in the US says we have 219 toxic chemicals in our body. These include tobacco residues, dry cleaning chemicals, pesticides, fungicides, flame retardants, heavy metals, preservatives, etc. The CDC reports that the chemical Bisphenol-A (BPA), a synthetic estrogen and plastic hardener which causes reproductive and neurological damage, is found in 93% of adults age 6 and older." Józef Żychowski and Tomasz Bryndal's study of cemetery groundwater contamination, "Impact of Cemeteries on Groundwater Contamination by Bacteria and Viruses—a Review," *Journal of Water and Health* 13, no. 2 (2015): 285–301, identifies potential pollutants in "chemical substances applied in chemotherapy" (285) as well as other cosmetic and medical items. However, how threatening these chemicals are is a subject of debate.

47. Jae Rhim Lee, "Coeio: The Infinity Burial Suit," http://coeio.com/.

48. Linda Weintraub, *To Life! Eco Art in Pursuit of a Sustainable Planet* (Berkeley: University of California Press, 2012): 228.

49. As Sarah and Tim Crews argue in "Decomposition Is Free, So What's Up with the Infinity Burial Suit?," in Webster, *Changing Landscapes*, the mushroom suit as an art project admirably represented transformation. When it transitioned to a functional, selling object, it became

dangerous greenwashing that, they claim, ignores the science of decomposition (187–89).

50. Joe Sehee, "Is There Hope for the Planet in a 'Post Truth' World?," in Webster, *Changing Landscapes*, 207–8.

51. See Janet Haneberg (@JanetHaneberg), "No! Makes me ill. I'll never eat another mushroom," Twitter, May 6, 2019, https://twitter .com/JanetHaneberg/status/1125519379993714689, and Dena Lee (@Denalee907), "Wow :/ that's a terrible thought. Just cremate me and spread my ashes down in SW Florida in the Gulf of Mexico, set my spirit free o:)," Twitter, May 5, 2019, https://twitter.com/Denalee907/ status/1125239741937541121. These are, of course, alongside countless jokes about him being a "fun guy."

52. Doughty, *From Here,* 110.

53. Fowlthing, comment on Hallie Golden, "Could 'Human Composting' Mean a Better, Greener Death?," *CityLab,* January 14, 2019, https://www.citylab.com/environment/2019/01/human-composting -washington-katrina-spade-burial-death/580015/; Carl Jacobs, comment on Hallie Golden, "Could 'Human Composting' Mean a Better, Greener Death?," *CityLab,* January 14, 2019, https://www.citylab .com/environment/2019/01/human-composting-washington-katrina -spade-burial-death/580015/; Urbandetail, comment on Hallie Golden, "Human Composting May Soon Be Legal in Washington State," *Boing-BoingNet,* April 22, 2019, https://boingboing.net/2019/04/22/human -composting-may-soon-be-l.html.

54. Suzanne Kelly, "Dead Bodies That Matter: Toward a New Ecology of Human Death," *Journal of American Culture* 35, no. 1 (2012): 45.

55. "Amuse-Bouche," *Hannibal: The Complete First Season,* season 1, episode 2, dir. Michael Rymer, NBC, 2013.

56. "Amuse-Bouche."

57. Tsing, *Mushroom at the End of the World,* 137.

58. Tsing, 23.

59. Tsing, 24.

« 15 »

Erotics and Annihilation

Caitlín R. Kiernan, Queering the Weird, and Challenges to the "Anthropocene"

SARA WASSON

"Weird" writing's preoccupations with geological spans of "deep time," the inadequacy of human reason, and the mutual entanglements of material organic and inorganic all mesh well with the goal of decentering Anthropos. This chapter examines Caitlín R. Kiernan's stories of ancient stone, abyssal sea, and sexualized violation to illustrate how a weird poetics may simultaneously limit and enrich nonanthropocentric "arts of noticing," while remaining wary of elevating all weird to an ideal response.[1] Kiernan's imagining of the more-than-human encounter evokes Donna Haraway's Chthulucene in certain ways, a vision of the way "critters—human and not—become-with each other, compose and decompose each other, in every scale and register of time."[2] While Haraway here recognizes "every scale and register," her writing mostly emphasizes mutual, intricate, often joyful intermeshing—"speaking resurgence to despair" (71). Kiernan's writing, by contrast, features a very different register and dynamic: *asymmetrical* relationships in which the human may become annihilated substratum. While much of Haraway's language evokes playfulness and mutuality, Kiernan's emphasizes solemnity, awe, and the numinous. Kiernan's weird involves not only defeat of human reason or disgust at contamination but also desire for such boundary crossing, abasement, terror, and violation. Although Kiernan is very different from Haraway in this way, at moments she offers what I suggest calling the Chthulucene in a minor key: her hallucinatory tableaux of desire and torment meld ancient past and strangely beautiful futurities—albeit ones that are no longer, except in a haunted sense, human.[3]

I use the term *more-than-human* rather than *nonhuman* because, as Susan Leigh Star observes, "nonhuman is like non-white. It implies a lack of something."[4] The term *more-than-human* reminds us that "the non-human world not only exists but has causal powers and capacities of its own" and "highlight[s] the absolute dependence of humans on a vast and complex array of nonhuman entities, only some of which are subject to human control."[5] The term usefully chastens arrogance about human agency and offers a fitting humility to our encounters with other creatures, plants, and inorganic material—stone, for example, moves, has force and generative capacities, and—arguably—even forms of agency and desire. As Jeffrey Cohen notes, for example, stone comprises "boisterous landscapes. Full of relation, teeming with narrative, stone is seldom inert,"[6] even if our own perceptions and fleeting timescales are inadequate to the task of fully perceiving this lithic vitality.

As described in the Introduction to this collection, "weird" writing is typically defined in terms of defeat of human reason and a profound affective response.[7] China Miéville describes weird as fundamentally about a vulnerable encounter with absolute otherness: the sense that "through the little tears, from behind the ragged / edges/ things are looking at us."[8] Although H. P. Lovecraft and writers of the periodical *Weird Tales* are the best known early practitioners, the twenty-first century has seen weird flourish into arcane new blooms.[9] Caitlín R. Kiernan (1964–) is a celebrated contemporary writer of weird, hailed as "perhaps the best weird writer of her generation."[10] Author of more than 240 short stories, ten novels, and a monthly magazine of "weird erotica," she is also a vertebrate paleontologist. Her fiction is informed by her interest in deep time and monstrous forms.[11] Her oeuvre resists genre classification: while much is horrifying, she resists the label of genre horror on the grounds that her affective reach is more broad.[12]

To date, academic commentary on Kiernan has often focused on her representation of social exclusion or her development within a Lovecraftian tradition.[13] Kiernan is transgender, a woman and a lesbian, and the experience of multiple marginalizations has influenced her work. James Goho argues, for example, that Kiernan's writing "pushes upon readers our biological self in all of its fragility, despair and hurt . . . to illustrate the destructive force of socially constructed norms and standards that marginalize individuals."[14] While conceding that some of her work grapples with marginalization, however, Kiernan herself has said that "I don't feel like I write many 'message' stories, not in a political sense."[15] As I will show, Kiernan's melancholy tableaux of sexualized violation also do something else: they invite us to consider an imaginative relationship to the more-than-human that is transformative, devastating, and beautiful, even if it does not include our own survival. These stories are not only about bewilderment and disgust but about something else: a craving *for* that transformation. In the process, her writing resists some pervasive critical oversimplifications about what "weird" can offer to deanthropocentric "arts of noticing," as well as showing, by contrast, how weird tropes and conventions may unexpectedly risk exacerbating a text's anthropocentricism.

Weird fantasies of surrender to the more-than-human are not new. Lovecraft's short story "The Shadow over Innsmouth" (1936), for example, concludes with the narrator imagining descending through the sea, "through black abysses to Cyclopean and many-columned Y'hanthlei, and in that lair of the Deep Ones we shall dwell amid wonder and glory for ever."[16] Yet, as S. T. Joshi notes, Kiernan's writing has "a plangency that his narratives lack . . . teas[ing] out the emotive ramifications of . . . the bizarre, terrifying, at times ineffable scenes."[17] Central to this plangency is a longing for connection with or submission to more-than-human entities, while not denying the pain and grief that ensue from such violation. Jeff VanderMeer observes:

> The people in these stories don't really survive their encounter with the supernatural. . . . The supernatural isn't something terrifying in Kiernan's view—it can be, but that's not the true point. . . . [It] is also something beautiful and unknowable in intent, and often wedded to the natural world. . . . In almost all of these stories . . . the characters seem to encounter the supernatural as part of a need for connection, even if the thing they connect with is Other and will be the death of them.[18]

Kiernan's scenarios trouble conventional sanctities of corporeal boundary and use rhythmic, image-rich prose to emphasize the human participant's dread and desire. Joshi observes that "even in those passages whose subject-matter is perfectly chaste, her prose beckons us with a lapidary manipulation of rhythm."[19] Her sensuous writing presents human animals enmeshed with more-than-human forces in mysterious and profoundly asymmetrical ways.

Her work abounds in tableaux of corporeal and mental suffering. Among other things, it shows human bodies violated and transformed in abject ways by themselves or by others[20] or characters fascinated by the aftermath of another's violation.[21] Goho describes some of her corporeal reconfigurations of the human as "anthro-technological bodies," such as a violin made of bones, blood, and guts or a chandelier made from a surgically altered woman.[22] With regard to the "arts of noticing," Kiernan's tableaux of specifically more-than-human violation offer entry points for readers' affective engagement with both human fragility—usually feared and avoided—and also the potential of transformation, to be feared, yes, and even potentially ending in annihilation, yet also offering awe-full nonanthropocentric futures for which human bodies may serve as a literal substrate.

The Work of Weird: Challenging or Reinforcing Anthropocentrism?

As many critics have argued, weird writing may fruitfully disrupt anthropocentrism by showing the defeat of human rational comprehension and geological scales of time and evoking revulsion, unease, and awe. I will briefly address this reading but then proceed to challenge and nuance this accepted perspective within gothic studies.

Core to much writing against anthropocentrism is the need to respect the recalcitrance and opacity of the more-than-human. The object-oriented ontology strand of speculative realism is particularly emphatic about this message, as in Timothy Morton's concept of "hyperobjects," discussed in the Introduction to this collection.[23] A humility toward the unknowability of the more-than-human, and indeed a troubling of the sanctity of "the human" altogether, is also important for critics working in the very different philosophical framework of Gilles Deleuze and Félix Guattari's conception of entities as "assemblage," a "hodgepodge" of elements and forces, dynamic and subject to change.[24] Deleuze and Guattari offer a range of concepts to describe the emergence, ambiguities, and fractures of assemblages and the "lines of flight" of their becomings and transformations.[25] There are important differences between object-oriented ontologists and new materialists, but both emphasize agency in forces and entities other than the human.[26] Challenging anthropocentrism requires new "arts of noticing." As Anatoli Ignatov says, we need art that "increase[s] awareness of our embeddedness within a larger system of forces, energies and flows . . . the coexistence of multiple animal and plant worlds, governed by different temporal modes."[27] Thinking through ecological crisis requires thinking in numerous timescales, from the paleoecological to the momentary to the future horror and silence of the outcomes of our ongoing sixth mass extinction event.[28]

The challenge for "arts of noticing" is not only conceptual but affective, and the weird's evocation of unease and disgust is also useful in challenging anthropocentric assumptions. Crucially, however, this constellation of troubled affects is not synonymous with "ecophobia," as Simon Estok defines it, a contemptuous fear rooted in the delusion of human supremacy.[29] Claire Quigley suggests that the weird disrupts a "taken-for-granted anthropocentric worldview" through grotesqueries that "instil a fear of contamination within the human protagonists," but that statement does not quite capture the affective disturbance attendant on the weird.[30] Desire, awe, and terrified fascination are also part of the potential affective repertoire evoked by, for example, Kiernan's permutations of weird, and these responses, too, can center the more-than-human in potentially useful ways. Writers draw on a language of the eerie, spooky, and numinous to describe the radical unknowability of ecological processes and more-than-human agencies. Elaine Gan, Nils Bubandt, Anna Tsing, and Heather Anne Swanson speak of "the spookiness of the past in the present";[31] Morton describes hyperobjects as having a "menacing shadow," "like faces pressed against a window, they leer at me menacingly";[32] and Eugene Thacker suggests that unease at evacuation of the human is a useful sensibility to foster in response to the ecological catastrophe to which human violence has been so central, even if our meager reason can never fully understand the complex workings of that disaster.[33] Since Thomas Friedman coined the term *global weirding* in 2010, the term has increasingly gained connotations of a blend of epistemological defeat and affective unease in the fate of ecological catastrophe.[34]

Nonetheless, "weird" fictions of encounters with ancient horrors are not inevitably helpful for nonanthropocentric "arts of noticing," and some deployments may reinforce certain long-established erasures of the more-than-human. I will identify four potential risks and address how Kiernan's work partly resists them.

First, the weird's tendency to ceremonially estrange the more-than-human as devastatingly other may implicitly reinforce the difference between human and more-than-human that characterizes anthropocentric thinking. Yet here, too, weird is weirder than it may seem, because one of the crucial characteristics of weird is that the encounter with the more-than-human is intradiegetically *real*. Core to its shock is that it has always been here: the characters' failure to realize its entanglement with their bodies and worlds is a perceptual failure rather than a fantasy. As Fisher says, "what we might call ordinary naturalism—the standard, empirical world of common sense and Euclidean geometries—will be shredded by the end of each tale, it is replaced by a hypernaturalism—an expanded sense of what the material cosmos contains."[35] Kiernan's bacterial erotics, as I will show, are a particularly vivid exemplar of this move. The more-than-human is not separate from, distant from, the human—the human *is* the more-than-human, in the most practical sense, always transcorporeal, as Stacy Alaimo puts it: "the human is ultimately inseparable from 'the environment.' . . . 'Nature' is always as close as one's own skin—perhaps even closer."[36]

Second, fantasies of monstrous violation may risk reinstating human significance, if a single human is singled out as meriting the weird entity's attention due to some quality in that individual. Some of Kiernan's work does present figures chosen for particular torment (e.g., Angevine of the short story "Houses under the Sea" [2003] or the narrator of "Far from Any Shore" [2014]), but these figures are not chosen for intrinsic qualities but due to ill luck; the ensuing violations are opportunistic.[37] All Kiernan's writing emphasizes human insignificance amid deep time and cosmic vastness; as she says, "our smallness and insignificance in the universe at large. In all *possible* universes. Within the concept of infinity. No one and nothing cares for us. No one's watching out for us."[38] Her work unremittingly shows us humans as just . . . not that special.

Third, representations of encounters with ancient horror as singular, astonishing events may distract from the way that multiple timescales always operate in the present and, relatedly, may obscure the fact that the Anthropocene is also a Capitalocene, an era of ecological crisis accelerated by the transformations of industry and political economy.[39] The workings of capital hinge on such time scales, in, for example, petroculture extraction: the energy-hungry machine of world capital running on "a Tellurian entity [formed] under unimaginable pressure and heat in the absence of oxygen and between the strata."[40] Jason W. Moore encourages us to "see human organization as something more-than-human and less-than-social" and to ask, "how do specific combinations of human and extra-human activity work—or *limit*—the endless accumulation of capital?"[41] In this regard, Kiernan's characters' encounters with the more-than-human happen, not in a vacuum, but in contexts shaped by capitalism and human activity, such as mines shaped through extraction capitalism in the previous century, a municipal water feature in a public park, a deep-sea space traversed by submarines funded for deepwater research, and military space exploration. In the short story "In the Water Works (Birmingham, Alabama 1888)" (2003), the rocks of the Appalachias underpin industries and socialities: "limestone is overlain by . . . reddish sandstone . . . lifeblood of the city locked away in those strata, clot-thick [sic] veins of hematite for the coke ovens and blast furnaces dotting the valley below."[42] The anthropomorphism of this passage has the paradoxical consequence of showing the human community as inevitably also more-than-human. The human community's "lifeblood" is geological, from "clotthick veins of hematite."

A fourth potential risk of weird is that it may singularize the more-than-human and erase its networks. Weird fiction is not the only discourse that tends to singularize the strange: "factual" descriptions of abyssal sea zones, for example, have a long lineage of problematic representation in this regard. Alaimo observes that deep-sea zones are often represented in our cultural imaginary as empty spaces, to be crossed or reached through or under, and Philip Steinberg argues that part of the failure to recognize the diversity and teeming life of the deep ocean stems from the way mercantile capitalism has tended to see oceans as things to cross; and of course, extractive petrocultures configure the rock beneath the ocean as resource.[43] The vitality in the depth of oceans has often been effaced, with widespread and inaccurate assumptions that all life on earth relies ultimately on plant photosynthesis of the sun's energy. In fact, in ocean zones beyond sunlight, chemosynthesis supports food chains of abundant life and many times more species than are found on land. Representations of such life, however, are often impoverished in a particular way. The convention in cataloging is for vivid, single creatures hanging suspended in deep black.[44] Photographers describe the work taken to edit the image to make it uniformly black, and Alaimo warns that in such representations, "the substance, agencies, and significance of the seas disappear. . . . The backdrop belies not only the vast expanse of the oceans but the intra-acting material agencies of oceanic ecologies and human entanglements."[45] The weird's tendency to concentrate on opaque, single entities meshes well with the object-oriented ontology strand of speculative realism, which emphasizes the opacity and self-containment of any entity (including ourselves) but fits less easily with vital materialism, focused as it is on networks and intermeshed assemblage.

Kiernan's story "Houses under the Sea" resists some of those erasures. Scientific dredging is presented as disrupting marine ecologies and the complexity of the water recognized. When the narrator watches the recording of the deep-sea spaces two kilometers below the surface, he does not see undifferentiated black.

Figure 15.1. *Jellyfish.* Pixabay, Creative Commons, 2016. https://jooinn.com/white -sea-creature.html/.

The steady fall of marine snow becomes so heavy that it's difficult to see much of anything through the light reflecting off the
whitish particles of sinking detritus. . . .
    "It's a little bit of everything," [he imagines Angevine say-
ing]. . . . "Silt, phytoplankton and zooplankton, soot, mucus,
diatoms, pellets, dust, grains of sand and clay, radioactive fallout, pollen, sewage. Some of it's even interplanetary dust particles. Some of it fell from the stars."[46]

Similarly, in the short story "Bridle" (2006), when a female kelpie kisses a human woman, the latter tastes "silt and algae, fish
shit and . . . fine particulate filth."[47] At moments such as these,
Kiernan's weird does not wholly reduce strangeness and grotesquerie to a conveniently single entity but broadens her attention
to the blurry edges that characterize all entities, including ourselves. More than that, her work invites us to imagine a state of
being compelled and appalled by the more-than-human, yearning
for transformation—even annihilation—under its force. Like the
cult members of "Houses under the Sea" (2003), her characters are
"dazed, terrified, enraptured, lost."[48]

Queering Delight and/or Annihilation in the Chthulucene

As the Introduction to this book notes, multiple -cenes have been
theorized to rectify the anthropocentricism of the concept of the
Anthropocene. One such coinage in particular is especially useful in counteracting the risks to weird representation, risks that
I identified in the foregoing discussion. Haraway's concept of the
"Chthulucene" recognizes all life and inorganic material as enmeshed, located and combined in intricate assemblage, emphasizing mutual enfleshment and corporeal entanglement, the mutual
constitutiveness of beings.[49] Her term Chthulucene is not homage
to Lovecraft's version of the monster but emphasizes chthonic en-
meshing between human animal and more-than-human.[50]
    Haraway's description of the Chthulucene is emotionally com-
plex and includes grief, for any response "must include mourning
irreversible losses."[51] Yet, the abiding quality emerging in Haraway's
descriptions is horizontal connection, mutuality, and playful, de-
lighted intimacy. Haraway's framework for the Chthulucene is capacious and absolutely has room for abjection and suffering, but

that slant is not emphasized in her prose. Kiernan's approach, by contrast—equally entangled, equally monstrous—is shot through with a blend of abjection and awe, a sense of an annihilating sublime. Like Haraway, her writing explores bodies entangled, but this entanglement occurs in registers of suffering and forbidden desire. In some ways, solemnity, awe, and a sense of the numinous may also have value in decentering the Anthropos. Eileen Crist warns that anthropocentric history has

> unfolded by silencing nonhuman others, who do not [get recognized as entities that can] speak, possess meanings, experience perspectives, or have a vested interest in their own identities. These others have been *de facto* silenced because if they once spoke to us in other registers—primitive, symbolic, sacred, totemic, sensual, or poetic—they have receded so much they no longer convey such numinous turns of speech.[52]

Kiernan's fleshly and monstrous entanglements are distinctly less friendly and democratic than better-known instantiations of the Chthulucene yet may also be useful in their disturbance and asymmetry.

Corporeal and psychological agony have been a preoccupation of gothic ever since it emerged as a literary form in the late eighteenth century and, later, became a mode inhabiting other genres, including the weird tale.[53] Gothic offers "an image language for bodies and their terrors," says David Punter, and evokes, in Steven Bruhm's words, "the body's repressed fragility and vulnerability."[54] Yet the paradox of gothic has always been that pleasure attends this suffering, pleasure for the reader and sometimes also pleasure for characters indulging forbidden longings.[55] Pain and counter-hegemonic pleasure are also inextricably entangled in Kiernan's descriptions of more-than-human encounter, as in the way her protagonists desire erotic destruction[56] or in the way her work's futurities do not echo heteronormative reproductive notions of futurity,[57] or in the way her work enacts an ethics of recognizing other life-forms as profoundly other but in intense relation with us.[58] Without disputing the value in those approaches—queering hardly happens in one way, after all—the term *queering*, laden as it is with the connotations of "strange" and "wrong," can also suggest other kinds of sensual transgression. In Kiernan's writing, desire

is often transgressive and taboo, self-destructive, even annihilatory, yielding not domesticated security but radical uncertainty,
pain, and change. Put that way, this kind of queering reminds us
of Lee Edelman's critique of reproductive futurity, in which the
structuring trope of a society is the imagined future of a child
who serves as "the perpetual horizon of every acknowledged politics, the fantasmatic beneficiary of every political intervention."[59]
Edelman suggests "queerness" may strategically refuse such futurity, "nam[ing] the side of those not 'fighting for the children' . . .
outside the consensus by which all politics confirms the absolute
value of reproductive futurism"; "the queer must insist on disturbing, on queering, social organization as such. . . . For queerness can
never define an identity; it can only ever disturb one."[60]

Kiernan's work certainly troubles futurities imagined for the
idealized child, yet her work exceeds an interpretation derived
from Edelman's work. First, like Haraway's, her writing is less concerned with human society and more concerned with connections
with the more-than-human. Haraway and Edelman are answering
very different questions and in very different emotional registers,
yet both are rightly suspicious of the way futurities tend to function to limit awareness. Haraway defines the "Chthulucene" as "a
kind of timeplace for learning to stay with the trouble of living and
dying in response-ability on a damaged earth"; her focus is "tales of
the ongoing."[61] Edelman embraces the defiant subversive possibility of negating a future orientation as part of resistance to conventional heteronormativity; Haraway embraces a gleeful, intimate
framework of entangled monstrosity to help readers imagine other
modes of sociality and being, across species lines. Edelman urges
us to resist the seductive idealization of the (white, privileged)
child, and Haraway urges us to "make kin, not babies!"—in other
words, to connect cross-species with other entities in the present,
rather than being oriented to a longitudinal scale of future human
reproduction.[62]

Kiernan's writing both echoes and offers a twist to each of these
approaches. Her dominant affective registers are desire and dread,
and she challenges any human-centric reproductive futurity, but
does it in a very particular way. Much of her writing is actually
preoccupied with generation, but with human bodies functioning
as partial *substrate* for such reproduction and consumed in the
process. Several of her stories imagine strangely generative bodies

transforming in the act and the more-than-human futurities they evoke. To put it glibly, the bodies of such characters help to make kin and (some version of) babies, but in the service of a future generation that lacks anything recognizable of the human—yet is haunted by it. I will explore how Kiernan's work presents such change and close by suggesting that visions of such futurity hold hope without anthropocentrism.

"Ancient Bacterial Gods" and Stone with Agency: Humans as Substrate for More-than-Human Change

The defeat of reason is central to Kiernan's approach to the weird. She describes her own writing as "almost always" weird in that "it departs from what most people view as the reality. Consensus reality."[63] Human animals are not knowing, and the unknown remains mysterious: she increasingly resists the "reveal" of the supernatural or monstrous elements. "What is weird fiction but a journey into the unknown, and if you make the unknown known, why bother?"[64] Her narrators—often paleontologists, geologists, journalists, authors, or other adept readers of signs—fail to make sense of what they encounter. In "Houses under the Sea," the cult members of the Open Door of Night record their cult leader's terrible knowledge in floor paintings. The narrator recalls:

> The intricate interweave of lines, the lines that she believed would form a bridge, a *conduit*. . . . Everyone's seen photographs of that floor, although I've yet to see any that do it justice. A *yantra*. A labyrinth. A writhing, tangled mass of sea creatures straining for a distant black sun. Hindi and Mayan and Chinook symbols. The precise contour lines of a topographic map of Monterey Canyon. Each of these things and *all* of these things, simultaneously.[65]

An anthropologist is analyzing the map, but neither she nor the first-person journalist narrator can uncover quite what happened. Similarly, in "Far from Any Shore," the paleontologist narrator and her colleagues cling to rationality: "We laughed because we're scientists, and our enlightened, educated minds don't project superstitious nonsense onto oddly shaped rocks. . . . The wind snatched at our laughter and dragged it off into the night to haunt the ears of mule deer, jackrabbits, and pronghorn antelope."[66] As the final image implies, their forced merriment proves unfounded; two die and one becomes a possessed murderer. At the end of the story, the scientist narrator laments, "Ah, God, how I wanted to make sense here at the end. How I wanted linear narrative and compositional coherence, here at the end."[67] Rationality, science, and even logic are defeated within these stories.

Yet, beyond the defeat of reason, Kiernan's characters also have a range of intense affective responses to the more-than-human. She often writes from the perspective of a human animal submitting to sexualized degradation by something more-than-human, ancient and strange. Being kissed and forced to swallow silt and waste—so does a human woman describe encountering a kelpie in a decaying urban park.[68] The transformations are numerous but almost always painful, such as the lesbian geologist who is tormented by a mystical cold creature in "The Cryomancer's Daughter" (2006): "I might as well be stone now. She has made of me the very thing I've spent my life researching and cataloguing, for what is ice but water assuming a solid mineral form? I am made her petrifaction."[69]

Some of Kiernan's protagonists feel satisfaction in their irrevocable change, as does the supplicant of "The Hole with the Girl in Its Heart" (2005–7), who is swallowed by a star and feels deep gratitude.[70] Yet, with a few exceptions, the transformations presented in Kiernan's fictions are not as much a matter of fellowship as those implied in Haraway's vision. Kiernan's encounters are typically violent and annihilatory. In "Houses under the Sea," for example, cult leader Jacova Angevine tells her followers that a sea goddess "will prepare halls from coral and glass and the bones of whales. . . . Down there, you will know nothing but peace, in her mansions, in the endless night of her coils."[71] In fact, however, Angevine lives in terror of the force beneath the waves, which marked her when she drowned as a child, leaving sucker scars all over her body, ultimately drawing her down for permanent torment.[72]

The characters yearning to be changed do not usually articulate their reasons, the prose offering only a sense of the numinous as an explanatory force: awe, a longing for annihilation, despair, wonder. The journalist narrator of "Houses under the Sea" pines for his lost lover, Angevine, the leader of the suicide cult, and he's simultaneously revolted by and drawn to what the cult venerates. When he sees the statue at their altar, he is nauseated by "that corrupt and bloated Madonna of the abyss, its tentacles and anemone tendrils and black, bulging squid eyes, the tubeworm proboscis snaking from one of the holes where its face should have been."[73] Yet, at the same time, he does crave another monstrous, marine-changed body: Angevine's, scarred by countless suckers and ultimately transformed to resemble a deep-sea creature. On a videotape recorded by a submersible, the narrator sees

> Jacova Angevine, her face at the bottom of the sea, turned up towards the surface, towards the sky and Heaven beyond the weight of all that black, black water. . . .
>
> She opens her eyes and they are *not* her eyes, but the eyes of some marine creature adapted to that perpetual night . . . eyes like matching pools of ink, and something darts from her parted lips.[74]

He dreams of Angevine and yearns to join her. "[She] takes me down, down, down, like the lifeless body of a child caught in an undertow. And I'd go with her, like a flash I'd go."[75]

Faced with stone, sea, and the strange organisms within them, Kiernan's characters are baffled and disgusted but also compelled, unable to look away or leave, and in some cases unable to resist surrendering to transformation offered by the more-than-human. Indeed, Fisher suggests that this is the core quality that differentiates weird from horror: "the weird cannot only repel, it must also compel our attention."[76] In Kiernan's "The Water Works," for example, the geologist is shown a coiling, chitinous organism discovered deep in rock strata:

> "Ugly little bastard, ain't he?" the foreman says, and spits again. "But you *ain't* never seen nothing like it before, have you?" And Henry shakes his head, no, never, and now he wants to look away, doesn't like the way the thing in the bottle is making him feel, but it's stretched itself out again and he can see tiny fibers like hairs or minute spines protruding from between the segments.[77]

The insectile thing revolts him but also calls to him—he wants to look away, "*but* it's stretched itself out again and he can see the

tiny fibers." His intention to refuse, to look away, to not feel, is
thwarted by the thing moving, stretching, in ways that compel
him. Another creature found in stone elicits a similar response in
the sequel novel *Threshold* (2001), which explores this same site
generations later. Chance Matthews is a student paleontologist,
trained by her grandmother, and is confident in her ability to read
the signs of "lost and ancient seas . . . as plainly as the books on the
library's shelves."[78] She tries to classify and date a trilobite fossil
she finds among her grandmother's possessions but realizes it is
unclassified, "tens of millions of years" older than any other record of such a creature.[79] "'What are you?' she asks the rock, as if it
might answer."[80] The fossil is not only mysterious but aggressively
uncanny:

> *Unpleasant light,* Chance thinks. *An unclean, slippery sort of light,*
> and she scolds herself for letting all the weirdness get to her. . . .
> But then the rock seems to wink at her again, briefest flash of
> greasy light, and there's something else, the realization that it's
> difficult to look directly at the septahedral plate for very long,
> that it seems to force her eyes away after only a few seconds.[81]

The stone simultaneously resists her scrutiny, evokes an intense
visceral response, and compels her.

Kiernan's work consistently presents stone as an agent: alive,
deliberate, and acting on human animals. "The Water Works," for
example, opens by describing the Red Mountain, "weathered tip
end of Appalachia's long and scabby spine," the "limestone and
iron ore bones" whittled away and exposed, and rain "turn[ing] the
ground to sea slime again, primordial more the color of a butch-
ery."[82] The animalistic description implies that the stone is alive
and flayed (although, to be sure, the life of stone can also certainly
be described in nonanimal ways). Even more important, stones *affect* people, and choose to do so. In her poem "Marrow" (1981), Ursula Le Guin describes how, when she stops trying to masterfully
pry meaning from a stone, the stone speaks to her: "and the marrow of my bones / heard, and replied."[83] Stones in Kiernan's writing
are even more assertive, acting on human bodies and minds. The
first-person narrator of "Far from Any Shore" is a female paleontologist suffering a breakdown after an experience at an excava-
tion. She unearths a stone that causes "an icy, thrumming tingle

that resonates through the flesh and bones of my hand and then moves gradually up my arm."[84] The stone is "a contagion—organic, mnemonic, visual, tactile, older even than the strata of blue-grey shale and yellow chalky limestone . . . something infinitely communicable that has slept since the stone that entombed the beautiful petrified skeletons of our *Selmasaurus* and *Pteranodon* was only carbonaceous grit and clayey slime."[85] The infection takes her two colleagues and torments them until their bodies are "gnawed and twisted and refashioned," and the narrator describes hearing the soft, wet, hungry sounds of something developing in the hotel bathroom, born and enabled through the changes of her colleagues' bodies: "the soft body of something without a spine or even any definite form."[86]

The vector for these changes is bacterial infection. Bacteria are ancient forces that predate and will outlast us, inhabiting all time scales, including the lithic. For this reason, Cohen suggests that bacteria are maybe "visible" to the lithic in a way that fleeting individual human bodies are not: "life can hold perdurability only if the bacterial and the human are one: then you are nearer to stone's speed, then stone can see you."[87] The scale of bacterial temporalities is reflected in further coinages of -cene, such as the "cyanocene" extending from 2.4 billion years ago to the present day, inaugurated by cyanobacteria that could photosynthesize, producing the oxygen that caused the first mass extinction event, and the "Wolbachiacene," a term playfully coined by Eben Kirksey to convey the longevity and influence of Wolbachia bacteria in invertebrates for the past 150 million years.[88] Similarly, there is no clear boundary between the human and the bacterial: "the" human *is* partly bacterial, depending on a bacterial microbiome for everything from digestion to neurological function to immune defenses.[89] "The" human is an assemblage including the microbiome. Kiernan's writing regularly explores a bacterial erotics of transformation, treating human tissue and biomes as material for change.

The short story "Metamorphosis A" (2006) describes a society devastated by a contagion unleashed by rock extraction, "gold mines in South Africa and Siberia, the biology of extremophiles, endoliths and cryptoendoliths, contaminated core samples, virulence, infectivity."[90] Infected people are stung, their flesh turning necrotic, then become a quivering, faceless mass. Yet some people actively seek out the contagion. The narrator's female companion,

among others, chooses to descend below the city to become infected, and he thinks of her "offering . . . furtive prayers . . . to
ancient bacterial gods for the grace of this change . . . to shed your
unwanted and unyielding humanity."[91] The narrator is appalled at
her change after she makes that choice, her face destroyed, but
thinks, "At least I do not have to look into your blue eyes and see
whatever might have been there at the end, whatever pain or loss
or regret, whatever confusion or terror. Worse yet, what ecstasy or
relief."[92] He cannot bear to watch the process as it occurs but sits
beside her bed and listens to the painful change of slow degeneration (in his view) or blessed transformation (in hers).[93]

Such scenes can be analyzed in terms of a single human's desire for annihilation, or as masochistic fantasy along the lines of
Deleuze's "Coldness and Cruelty," and indeed several elements of
the scene underline that reading (ceremony, suspense, and submission to a powerful force).[94] Here, however, I wish to focus on
the story's preoccupation with more-than-human reproductivity.
When the narrator of "Metamorphosis A" musters the courage to
look at his partner's transformation, he sees

> a chrysalis. . . . Spines sprout from that more substantial mess
> curled fetal on the bed and sunk partway into the sheets and
> mattress. It pulsates faintly, gently, because of course you still
> need air. . . . There's an iridescent, peacock-blue cleft where your
> vagina used to be. . . . Your face is gone, obliterated by these
> relentless alterations.[95]

His partner has chosen to become a generative substratum for incomprehensible, ravenous microbial change, "countless generations . . .
born and nurtured deep within the hive of you."[96] In reality, bacteria
in the vaginal microbiome are transmitted through passage through
the birth canal, and studies indicate that this microbiome benefits
infant gut bioflora.[97] In this short story, that vaginal bacterial substratum has become a particularly distinctive component of a devastating, triumphant bacterial flourishing.

A similar transformation occurs in the short story "Galapagos"
(2009). Set in 2037, the story is a written record by a first-person
woman narrator, Merrick, sent to ascertain what happened on a
spaceship after the commander broadcast a message implying
a collective intention to commit suicide. Merrick's lesbian lover

Amery was on board, and when Merrick reaches the ship, Amery addresses her across the comms system. Merrick walks through the corridors as Amery commands, noticing the walls thick hung with indescribable organic masses, while Amery speaks across the comms with "soft elation," saying, "We have ten million children. Soon, we will have ten million more."[98] Merrick turns the corner and

> I see her, then. All that's left of her, or all that she's become. The rough outline of her body, squatting near one of the lower bunks. Her damp skin shimmers . . . pocked with countless oozing pores or lesions. . . . . . There is constant, eager movement from inside her distended breasts and belly. And where the cleft of her sex once was, I don't have the language to describe what I saw there. But she bleeds life from that impossible wound.[99]

Merrick realizes that Amery chose to be unrecognizably changed in the process of becoming a substratum for alien bacterial life. The title of the story, evoking Darwin's writing, implies the emergence of new species.

At first glance, such stories by Kiernan might seem to describe the erasure of human in the service of something other, but of course the bacterial microbiome and human tissue that enable these changes *are* "the" human—despite the deceptive definite article, "the" human is always an assemblage. Angevine's body becomes substrate for marine changes, the academic of the "Cryomancer's Daughter" becomes petrified, the academics in "Far from Any Shore" become revelatory new life-forms, and the women of "Galapagos" and "Metamorphosis A" become hives of bacterial transformation: all these bodies become the start of something new, but that new thing has human tissue and microbiome as part of its origin. Haraway insists that nothing about the Chthulucene has to be about "wiping out what has come before"; rather, it can be "full of inheritances, of remembering, and full of comings, of nurturing what might still be."[100] Kiernan's Chthulucene in a minor key offers a variation on this: a future of traces, remnants, and hauntings.

In what sense can such encounters be seen as hopeful? I will suggest several answers. Degradation is central to both the beauty and the horror of Kiernan's transformations. The bodies of these human animals become less human, their corporeal integrity, dignity, even recognizability, changed into something both more appalling and more fruitful.[101] To refer back to the Deleuzian concept of assemblage, the transformed bodies ensuing from such encounters can be understood as transformed assemblages, and these transformations can be understood in terms of "lines of flight" and new "ways of becoming." Whitney Bauman, for example, says, "Taking a cue from queer theory . . . I want to listen to the 'abjections' (or left-overs, remainders) that have built up around the planet in response to attempts at mastery and control. It is in listening to these abjections that new possibilities for planetary becoming might emerge."[102] These disintegrations imagine new becomings, equivocal and contingent positions that rightly undermine human illusions of authority and corporeal integrity.

While Kiernan's work is in somber, incantatory, and sublime register, it nonetheless overlaps in several ways with the postapocalyptic bacterial bacchanalia imagined and celebrated by Kirksey. He describes how Wolbachia bacteria affect their hosts, changing their gender, sterilizing, or selectively killing embryos, and even causing new species to emerge, and Kirksey suggests that they offer a way to imagine nonanthropocentric futurity: "rather than continue to bemoan the loss of critical functions (as emergent ecological communities flourish around us), it is time to more fully appreciate the possibilities of love in the Wolbachiacene."[103] Kirksey's discourse is exuberant, while Kiernan's is awe-full, but both make us notice a generativity that exceeds us.

Kiernan's work dramatizes how the weird is not only about uncertainty, disorientation, and disgust but also about desire and a yearning to be altered—perhaps annihilated, certainly changed. Kiernan's work engages longing for such change without sanitizing it as either apotheosis or horizontal fellowship and mutuality: annihilation and violation are also part of the necessary story. She pushes us to find language for a complex mesh of affects that can augment our sense of weird challenges to anthropocentrism, beyond defeat of reason or disgust at grotesquerie. Other kinds of desire and hunger are at play in the field of more-than-human encounter, other weirds to add to our repertoire of arts of noticing, even for a Chthulucene in a minor key. Shudder, slither, and strangeness are not always salvation. They are more interesting than that.

NOTES

1. For "arts of noticing," see Anna Lowenhaupt Tsing, *The Mushroom at the End of the World: On the Possibility of Life in Capitalist Ruins* (Princeton, N.J.: Princeton University Press, 2015).
2. Donna Haraway, *Staying with the Trouble: Making Kin in the Chthulucene* (Durham, N.C.: Duke University Press, 2016), 2. Subsequent references in parentheses.
3. I discuss the analogy of the "minor key" in more detail in Sara Wasson, "Spectrality, Strangeness and Stigmaphilia: Gothic and Critical Disability Studies," in *The Routledge Companion to Literature and Disability,* ed. Alice Hall, 70–81 (London: Routledge, 2020).
4. Susan Leigh Star, personal communication, cited in Eben Kirksey, Craig Schuetze, and Stefan Helmreich, "Introduction: Tactics of Multispecies Ethnography," in *The Multispecies Salon,* ed. Eben Kirksey (Durham, N.C.: Duke University Press, 2014), 3.
5. Alisdair Rogers, Noel Castree, and Rob Kitchin, *A Dictionary of Human Geography* (Oxford: Oxford University Press, 2013), s.v. "more-than-human."
6. Jeffrey Jerome Cohen, *Stone* (Minneapolis: University of Minnesota Press, 2015), 21–22.
7. Ann VanderMeer and Jeff VanderMeer, eds., Introduction to *The Weird* (London: Corvus, 2011), xv; Mark Fisher, *The Weird and the Eerie* (London: Repeater, 2016), Kindle edition.
8. China Miéville, "AfterWeird," in VanderMeer and VanderMeer, *The Weird,* 1115.
9. VanderMeer and VanderMeer, Introduction, xv–xx.
10. VanderMeer and VanderMeer, xix.
11. Kiernan's paleontological writing includes C. R. Kiernan and D. R. Schwimmer, "First Record of a Velociraptorine Theropod (Tetanurae, Dromaeosauridae) from the Eastern Gulf Coastal United States," *The Mosasaur* 7 (2004): 89–93; Caitlín R. Kiernan, "Stratigraphic Distribution and Habitat Segregation of Mosasaurs in the Upper Cretaceous of Western and Central Alabama," *Journal of Vertebrate Paleontology* 22, no. 1 (2002): 91–103; D. R. Schwimmer and Caitlín R. Kiernan, "Eastern Late Cretaceous Theropods in North America and the Crossing of the Interior Seaway," *Journal of Vertebrate Paleontology* 21, no. 3 (2001): 99A; Caitlín R. Kiernan, "Clidastes Cope, 1868 (Reptilia, Sauria)," *Bulletin of Zoological Nomenclature* 49 (1992): 137–39.
12. Jeff VanderMeer, "Interview: Caitlín R. Kiernan on Weird Fiction," March 12, 2012, http://weirdfictionreview.com/2012/03/interview-Caitlín-r-kiernan-on-weird-fiction, para. 10.
13. James Goho, "The Figure of the Gothic Body in the Fiction of Caitlín R. Kiernan," *Studies in the Fantastic* 5 (2017): 78–98; Timothy Jarvis, "The

Weird, the Posthuman, and the Abjected World-in-Itself," *Textual Practice* 31, no. 6 (2017): 1133–48.

14. Goho, "Figure," 81.

15. Erin Stocks, "Author Spotlight: Caitlín R. Kiernan," *Lightspeed,* November 6, 2010, http://www.lightspeedmagazine.com/nonfiction/author-spotlight-Caitlín-r-kiernan/, para. 6.

16. H. Lovecraft, "The Shadow over Innsmouth" (1936), http://www.hplovecraft.com/writings/texts/fiction/soi.aspx, para. 247.

17. S. T. Joshi, Introduction to Caitlín R. Kiernan, *Beneath an Oil-Dark Sea* (Burton, Mich.: Subterranean Press, 2015), 13, 15.

18. Jeff VanderMeer, "Making Her Own Light," in Caitlín R. Kiernan, *The Ammonite Violin* (Hornsea, U.K.: PS, 2018), vii–x.

19. Joshi, Introduction, 14.

20. Caitlín R. Kiernan, "The Beginning of the Year without a Summer," in *The Dinosaur Tourist,* 9–24 (Burton, Mich.: Subterranean Press, 2018); Kiernan, "The Voyeur in the House of Glass," in *Ammonite Violin,* 149–64.

21. Caitlín R. Kiernan, "The Mermaid of the Concrete Ocean," in *Beneath an Oil-Dark Sea,* 285–98.

22. Goho, "Figure," 92; Caitlín R. Kiernan, "The Ammonite Violin," in *Ammonite Violin,* 85–104; Kiernan, "A Season of Broken Dolls," in *Beneath an Oil-Dark Sea,* 111–26.

23. Timothy Morton, *Hyperobjects* (Minneapolis: University of Minnesota Press, 2013), 1; Morton, "An Object-Oriented Defense of Poetry," *New Literary History* 43, no. 2 (2012): 208.

24. Gillés Deleuze and D. Lapoujade, *Two Regimes of Madness* (New York: Semiotext(e), 2007), 177.

25. Gilles Deleuze and Félix Guattari, *A Thousand Plateaus* (New York: Continuum, 1987), 4.

26. Geoffrey Harman, "A Well Wrought Broken Hammer," *New Literary History* 43, no. 2 (2012): 191; Morton, *Hyperobjects,* 20; Jane Bennett, "Systems and Things," in *The Nonhuman Turn,* ed. Richard Grusin (Minneapolis: University of Minnesota Press, 2015), 229; Catherine Keller and Mary-Jane Rubenstein, "Tangled Matters," in *Entangled Worlds,* ed. Catherine Keller and Mary-Jane Rubenstein, 1–18 (New York: Fordham University Press, 2017).

27. Anatoli Ignatov, "Practices of Eco-Sensation," *Theory and Event* 14, no. 2 (2011), https://muse-jhu-edu.ezproxy.lancs.ac.uk/article/440480, para. 8.

28. G. Ceballos, P. R. Ehrlich, A. D. Barnosky, A. García, R. M. Pringle, and T. M. Palmer, "Accelerated Modern Human-Induced Species Losses: Entering the Sixth Mass Extinction," *Science Advances* 1, no. 5 (2015): 1–5.

29. Simon Estok, "Theorizing in a Space of Ambivalent Openness," *Interdisciplinary Studies in Literature and Environment* 16, no. 2 (2009): 203–25.

30. Claire Quigley, "The Weird in Fantastika," *Fantastika* 1, no. 1 (2017): 4–5.

31. Elaine Gan, Nils Bubandt, Anna Lowenhaupt Tsing, and Heather Anne Swanson, "Haunted Landscapes of the Anthropocene," in *Arts of Living on a Damaged Planet: Ghosts and Monsters of the Anthropocene*, ed. Anna Lowenhaupt Tsing, Heather Anne Swanson, Elaine Gan, and Nils Bubandt (Minneapolis: University of Minnesota Press, 2017), G3.

32. Timothy Morton, *Dark Ecology* (New York: Columbia University Press, 2016), 20–27.

33. Eugene Thacker, *In the Dust of This Planet* (New York: Zero, 2011).

34. Thomas Friedman, "Global Weirding Is Here," *New York Times*, February 17, 2010, https://www.nytimes.com/2010/02/17/opinion/17friedman.html; Gerry Canavan and Andrew Hageman, "Array," *Paradoxa* 28 (2016), http://paradoxa.com/volumes/28/introduction; Morton, *Dark Ecology*.

35. Fisher, *Weird*.

36. Stacy Alaimo, *Bodily Natures* (Bloomington: Indiana University Press, 2010), 2.

37. Caitlín R. Kiernan, "Houses under the Sea," 2003, *Nightmare Magazine*, May 8, 2013, http://www.nightmare-magazine.com/fiction/houses-under-the-sea/; Kiernan, "Far from Any Shore," in *Dinosaur Tourist*, 25–40. Subsequent references are in parentheses.

38. VanderMeer, "Interview," para. 14, emphasis in original.

39. Jason W. Moore, ed., *Anthropocene or Capitalocene? Nature, History, and the Crisis of Capitalism* (Oakland, Calif.: PM Press, 2016), 1–12.

40. Reza Negarestani, *Cyclonopedia* (Melbourne: Re.press, 2008), 17.

41. Moore, "Anthropocene or Capitalocene?," 5.

42. Caitlín R. Kiernan, "In the Water Works (Birmingham, Alabama 1888)," in *Trilobite* (Burton, Mich.: Subterranean Press, 2003), 69. Subsequent references are in parentheses.

43. Philip Steinberg, *The Social Construction of the Ocean* (Cambridge: Cambridge University Press, 2001), 23, 113.

44. Census of Marine Life, http://www.coml.org/; Claire Nouvian, *The Deep* (Chicago: University of Chicago Press, 2007); Stacy Alaimo, "Violet-Black," in *Prismatic Ecology*, ed. Jeffrey Jerome Cohen, 233–51 (Minneapolis: University of Minnesota Press, 2014).

45. Alaimo, "Violet-Black," 241.

46. Kiernan, "Houses under the Sea," paras. 77, 79.

47. Caitlín R. Kiernan, "Bridle," in *Ammonite Violin*, 26.

48. Kiernan, "Houses under the Sea," para. 8.

49. Swanson et al., "Bodies," M1–M2.
50. Donna Haraway, "Symbiogenesis, Sympoesis, and Art Science Activisms for Staying with the Trouble," in Tsing et al., *Arts of Living,* M33.
51. Haraway, *Staying,* 101.
52. Eileen Crist, "On the Poverty of Our Nomenclature," in Moore, *Anthropocene or Capitalocene?,* 18.
53. Fred Botting, *Gothic,* 1st ed. (London: Routledge, 1996), 12; VanderMeer and VanderMeer, Introduction, xviii.
54. David Punter, *Gothic Pathologies* (Basingstoke, U.K.: Palgrave Macmillan, 1998), 14; Steven Bruhm, *Gothic Bodies* (Philadelphia: University of Pennsylvania Press, 1994), xv.
55. Catherine Spooner, *Postmillennial Gothic* (London: Bloomsbury, 2017); Tim Jones, *The Gothic and the Carnivalesque in American Culture* (Cardiff: University of Wales Press, 2015).
56. Catriona Mortimer-Sandilands and Bruce Erickson, "A Genealogy of Queer Ecologies," in *Queer Ecologies,* ed. Catriona Mortimer-Sandilands and Bruce Erickson, 1–47 (Bloomington: Indiana University Press, 2010).
57. Lee Edelman, *No Future* (Durham, N.C.: Duke University Press, 2004).
58. Timothy Morton, "Queer Ecology," *PMLA* 125, no. 2 (2010): 277.
59. Edelman, *No Future,* 8–9, 2–3.
60. Edelman, 8, 17.
61. Haraway, *Staying,* 2, 76.
62. Haraway, 102.
63. VanderMeer, "Interview," para. 10.
64. VanderMeer, para. 22.
65. Kiernan, "Houses under the Sea," para. 145.
66. Kiernan, "Far from Any Shore," 26–27.
67. Kiernan, 37–38.
68. Kiernan, "Bridle," 26.
69. Caitlín R. Kiernan, "The Cryomancer's Daughter," in *Ammonite Violin,* 61.
70. Caitlín R. Kiernan, "The Hole with the Girl in Its Heart" (2005–7), in *Ammonite Violin,* 183–90.
71. Kiernan, "Houses under the Sea," para. 16.
72. Kiernan, para. 167.
73. Kiernan, para. 164.
74. Kiernan, paras. 185, 189.
75. Kiernan, para. 229, emphasis in original.
76. Fisher, *Weird.*
77. Kiernan, "Water Works," 66.
78. Caitlín R. Kiernan, *Threshold* (New York: Penguin, 2007), loc. 476, Kindle edition.
79. Kiernan, loc. 2345.

80. Kiernan, loc. 2356.
81. Kiernan, loc. 2774–76.
82. Kiernan, "Water Works," 61.
83. Ursula Le Guin, "The Marrow," in Tsing et al., *Arts of Living*, M17.
84. Kiernan, "Far from Any Shore," 25.
85. Kiernan, 37.
86. Kiernan, 38–39.
87. Cohen, *Stone*, 30.
88. Dorion Sagan, "Coda. Beautiful Monsters: Terra in the Cyanocene," in Tsing et al., *Arts of Living*, M169–74 (p. 169); Eben Kirksey, "Queer Love, Gender Bending Bacteria, and Life after the Anthropocene," *Theory, Culture, and Society* 36, no. 6 (2019): 203.
89. Scott Gilbert, Jan Sapp, and Alfred Tauber, "A Symbiotic View of Life: We Have Never Been Individuals," *Quarterly Review of Biology* 8, no. 4 (2012): 325–41; Scott Gilbert, "Holobiont by Birth," in Tsing et al., *Arts of Living*, M73–M90.
90. Caitlín R. Kiernan, "Metamorphosis A," in *Ammonite Violin*, 128.
91. Kiernan, 133.
92. Kiernan, 132–33.
93. Kiernan, 131.
94. Deleuze argues that masochism involves a tableau of two frozen figures, straining toward each other with consummation relentlessly deferred: "Waiting and suspense are essential characteristics of the masochistic experience. . . . Formally speaking, masochism is a state of waiting." Gilles Deleuze, "Coldness and Cruelty," in *Masochism* (1967; repr., New York: Zone, 1991), 33, 71.
95. Kiernan, "Metamorphosis A," 132–33.
96. Kiernan, 131.
97. Josef Neu, "Developmental Aspects of Maternal-Fetal, and Infant Gut Microbiota and Implications for Long-Term Health," *Maternal Health, Neonatology, and Perinatology* 1 (2015): 6.
98. Caitlín R. Kiernan, "Galapagos," in *Beneath an Oil-Dark Sea*, 226–27, 236–37.
99. Kiernan, 237.
100. Haraway, *Staying*, 2, 76.
101. Matthew Calarco, "Identity, Difference, Indistinction," *New Centennial Review* 11, no. 2 (2011): 56.
102. Whitney Bauman, "Climate Weirding and Queering Nature," *Religions* 6, no. 2 (2015): 748; James Morgart, "Deleuzions of Ecohorror," *Horror Studies* 8, no. 1 (2017): 115–30.
103. Kirksey, "Queer Love," 213.

« 16 »

Monstrocene

FRED BOTTING

For Jacques Lacan, "Freud's unconscious is not at all the romantic unconscious of imaginative creation. It is not the locus of the divinities of the night."[1] In other words, the Freudian unconscious is not contained by a familiar, universal duality of daylight and darkness, nor does it readily deliver itself to human consciousness or understanding, remaining as impediment, failure, lacuna, and cut.[2] As scene, locus, or milieu, it is neither an object nor composed of objects and exhibits an an-anthropocentric agency antipathetic toward humanism. The refusal of the poles of Romantic enlightening and nocturnal divination situates the negating *un-* of the "unconscious" in a crepuscular gap (producing and disturbing relations between levels, times, places, agencies, objects): not primordial, nor instinctual, something of the unconscious remains "preontological."[3] Where the popular unconscious of imaginative light and nocturnal divinity marks the contours of the monstrocene, the Freudian unconscious lies in relation to undarkness. "Undark" comes by way of another cut, another negation, another *un*—a darkness that is not (not darkness, not light). The Freudian unconscious emerges as a negation of so many lesser unconsciouses:

the unconscious prior to Freud, *is not* purely and simply. This is because it names nothing that counts any more as an object— nor warrants being granted any more existence—than what would be defined by situating it in the "un-black" [*l'in-noir*].

The unconscious before Freud has no more consistency than this un-black—namely, the set of what could be classified according to the various meanings of the word "black," by dint of its refusal of the attribute (or virtue) of blackness (whether physical or moral).[4]

Before Freud, it "is not." With psychoanalytic discourse, the unconscious appears as the fissure resulting from the incision of the signifier in the real, a scission rearranging all prior relationships. "Un-black" is the position from which the unconscious is made to count, the set of all non-Freudian unconsciouses; it re-marks the constitutive gap and structural exceptionality that allows the Freudian unconscious to emerge in the first place. "Un-black" also closes off and opens up an uncounted time and unlit loci of no-space and no-things: undermining formations sustaining light and darkness in a monstrocene framing humanity and its others, Un-black as "undark" discloses a nondarkness preceding night and light, a nonillumination before dark and day.

It may seem inappropriate to invoke psychoanalysis—too human, too linguistic, too phallogocentric—at a time when planetary-scale crises (of ecosystems, climate, species) demand considerations outside or beyond human concerns, but the Anthropocene is too human, too rife with fantasies, anxieties, horrors: it is "our epoch and our condition"; its "shock" is not the impact of an external, alien force but an effect of "our own model of development, our own industrial modernity, which, having claimed to free itself from the limits of the planet, is striking Earth like a boomerang."[5] Unbearably intimate, it is also beyond the grasp of humans. Fact and fantasy, the Anthropocene is "fabulously textual," to use Jacques Derrida's account of nuclear apocalypse's imminence and deferral: its facts derive from the mineral and chemical traces that will have registered, at a geological level, the cumulative effect of human activity on planetary systems, and they fuel the fantasies circulating amid multiple extrapolations, warnings, denials, and speculations of and on the significance and implications of those marks.[6] In the Anthropocene, some modes of textuality resurface in efforts to read complex lines of causal interrelation and action, in imaginings of a planet without humans, in rethinking milieux of thought beyond humanist frames and in reimagining worlds of interconnected lives, agencies, bodies, and ecologies. All this, as Donna Haraway notes, requires "webs of speculative fabulation."[7] Unlike nuclear catastrophe (its imminence checked in a mutual assurance of destruction), the Anthropocene has already happened and is still to come: the marks of irreversible human planetary impact lie at a geological level—deeper, that is, than human history—but have yet to reveal their full effects or significance to and on so many members of the species responsible.

Paul Crutzen's and Eugene Stoermer's observations that the effects of centuries of human activity—agricultural, industrial, technological, and social—had combined to leave a lasting impact on the planet itself posed new and urgent questions of humanity, its history, its damaging relationship to other forms of life, and their—and its own—milieu: humans have become a "major geological force" or, as Dipesh Chakrabarty puts it, "a force of nature in a geological sense."[8] Distinguished by shifting, interdependent, and multiscalar relations and effects, the "epoch" is difficult to construe in older modern and humanist terms because the very conditions and milieux that were previously and necessarily overlooked or naturalized as "nature" in the heavy march of human progress come to the fore in unpredictable, active, and extensive ways: "the human species' damaging of its own milieu is not an accident that we might otherwise have avoided, precisely because climate—as *our* milieu—is something that our very dependence upon will preclude us from ever really seeing."[9] What was unseen, unthought, or unrecognized now tests the limits and thresholds of visibility, thinking, and knowing: "man cannot *appear* to himself as a geological force, because being a geological force is a mode of disappearance."[10]

In becoming a "major geological force," humans are not only confronted with their own destructive planetary impact but find human subjectivity, knowledge, and thinking, and their sense of other beings, things, space, and time, transformed. It is now hard to speak of objectivity and facts because the "objective fact" of climate change shifts relations between subjects and objects to disclose the way that humans are intrinsic to global patterns of cause and effect: "the very notion of objectivity has been totally subverted by the practices of humans in the phenomena to be described."[11] Agency, too, alters and divides: while the Earth "has taken back all the characteristics of a full-fledged *actor*" in complex global processes, its status remains vulnerable, "an active, local, limited, sensitive, fragile, quaking, and easily tickled envelope."[12] For humans, too, the Anthropocene becomes a "sign of our power, but also of our impotence."[13] Interdependencies and intertwined powers and vulnerabilities hold humans and their world in an increasingly delicate balance, a "precarious attachment to a fragile planet."[14]

Being *in* the Anthropocene, being a subject of or to climate change, undoes a humanist imaginary based on distance, mastery, and vision and undermines distinctions of inside and outside. It refuses a single (authoritative) perspective on—and over—things in a redistribution of agencies, effects, levels, and scales, revealing "multiple and incongruent systems for which we do not have a point of view."[15] In the many acts of consumption that are the daily habit of millions in the West, there are few directly visible consequences that allow consumers to see or take responsibility for the huge effects that the sum of little acts entails at the level of habitats, species, or ecosystems: human agency appears thoroughly nonhuman when it is perceived in terms of different scales.[16] Historically, too, the ramifications of climate change are significant: when natural or geological and human histories start to overlap, lines of continuity and difference are disrupted in a "collapse of the age-old humanist distinction between natural history and human history."[17] The scale and uncertain temporalities of the Anthropocene signal narrative unravelings of present, past, and future: "we have to insert ourselves into a future 'without us' to be able to visualize it." Such a fantastic and ahistorical projection, losing the thread of a narrative teleology in casting it impossibly toward an inexistent human subject, indicates the extent to which historical practice and understanding have been "thrown into deep contradiction and confusion."[18]

If the scale, speed, distance, and proximity of the Anthropocene test the limits and confound the capacities of human action, thought, and history, they also challenge language. Climate change and environmental crisis, as Rob Nixon notes, "present formidable representational obstacles": the gradual and barely perceptible effects of what he calls "slow violence" require the production and circulation of new, more strategically effective images, narratives, and representations.[19] Stories and metaphors matter: "it matters which figures figure figures, which systems systematize systems." Names, too: the current planetary situation means "a big new name is warranted." For Haraway, "diverse earth-wide tentacular forces" touch on and turn from the weird horror of Cthtulu toward a "Chtulucene" embracing a legion of mythic names ("Naga," "Gaia," "Tangaroa," etc.) to imagine different interanimations of promise and possibility among living figures, "entangling myriad temporalities and spatialities and myriad intra-active entities-in-assemblages."[20] Stories, names, and figures matter in the process of giving form to the life of things, relations, and notions as yet out of reach.

But names and narrations are also part of the problem, short-circuiting invention, circumlocuting change, curtailing conceptual capacities and considerations, names and narrations promoting denial, occlusion, deception, deferral, and distraction. In respect of climate change, it has never been as simple as publicizing the scientific facts and receiving a global mandate to introduce remedial measures. The "story of awakening is a fable": there is no moment at which a simple statement of truth separates a "blind past" from a "clear-sighted present"; instead, "it means deconstructing the official account in its managerial and non-conflictual variants, and forging new narratives for the anthropocene and thus new imaginaries."[21] Stories matter in the making of new imaginaries, but media, management, and administrations tell tales too. Engaging with what Michel Serres calls a "second pollution" is also required: along with "material, technological, and industrial pollution," a "second pollution" remains "invisible" and places "time in danger" in what amounts to "cultural pollution" inflicted on the "long-term thoughts" serving, in the shape of science (truth), bureaucracy (continuity), and media (sensation), as "guardians of the Earth, of humanity, and of things themselves."[22] Unbalanced by short-term interests and pressures for immediate satisfaction, secondary pollution contaminates the planning, respect, and harmony necessary to Serres's "natural contract."

"At stake is the Earth in its totality, and humanity collectively."[23] With the global threat comes a new collective human agent: the name of an epoch identifying an obscure object also introduces a new subject. The threat named as "Anthropocene" brings a new "we" into being, a subject coterminous with the epoch identifying its end: this new collective entity distinguishes no enlightened, universal European humanity or manifestation of some enduring progressive spirit but a figure born in the face of its own demise, a species "we" "generated from destruction."[24] At the point of danger and naming, a planetary subject-species dissipates among

a range of new names. These names deflect blame; specify different global and class interests; extend, deflect, or condense forces
and periods of historical origins: "capitalocene," "corporatocence,"
"plantationocene," "thermocene," "thanatocene," "cthulucene,"
"entropocene," "neganthropocene."[25] A second pollution persists
even as the scale and complexity of the first pollution emerge as an
obscure, palpable, multilayered agglomeration of interconnected
forces and effects: naming, while bringing an issue into focus, may,
as it dissipates and dissonates, engender only further factions
and distractions, polarizations and deflections, placing different
frames around crises and conjuring different threats. Or worse,
this new, bewildering, terrifying, barely comprehensible scene
might be painted as a monster that only serves to horrify and paralyze all thought, all imagination, all response—another dark Thing
prowling the monstrocene.

Dark Things

Mary Shelley writes, "Life and death appeared to me ideal bounds
that I should first break through and pour a torrent of light onto
our dark world."[26] Darkness may not simply be the other side to
light, nor the figure for the operations of an unknown, passive,
or inert nature that challenges human knowledge to even greater
efforts of understanding (and appropriation). Things may be more
active, autonomous, and inimical to humanity; they may even be
malign. Where objects are ordered and subordinated to human
observation and production, other things seem to escape a realm
of solid and inert objectivity regulated by a predictable physics of
mass, energy, gravitation, and light. Things do things, on their own
and to others, suggesting powers in part furnished with qualities
normally associated with subjectivity, such as agency, will, or intention. Inexplicable, they are attributed to malignant, if not demonic, determinations. The speculative ghost story "The Malice
of Inanimate Objects" (1933) by M. R. James suggests as much
when its conversational narrative posits an agency of and inter-
course between everyday objects existing outside human super-
vision. The human world of family and friendships, the life related
in realism, is upset by a "world of things" that has no respect for
human conversations, commerce, or work: insignificant and everyday objects—collar studs, inkstands, fires, razors, and extra stair

steps—manage to "pass word around" and set traps for those moving blithely through a world assumed to accord with human expectations.[27] The organized activities of small things can even be fatal, as the story attests.

At the end, narrative speculation balks at the notion of a separate world of things able to act in concert and outside human determination. Inimical and malignant as things are, they remain tied negatively and in opposition to the human world against which they conspire. A different malignancy is, somewhat indefinitely, supposed, "something not inanimate behind the Malice of inanimate objects."[28] Some self-moving, if not living, agent, it seems, directs the machinations of things. Designated as "not inanimate," this subject-thing is not identified as being human nor, directly, as being animate. Nor is it named as a divine or demonic power: the double negative neither allows nor refuses a definite binary polarization as, refusing dialectical resolution, it withdraws agency from the commerce of things without positing any identifiable figure or force—spiritual, supernatural, physical, or human—as definitive cause. Only a shadowy "something" is suggested, animating things as if at a double remove (the gesture of "not in-" negating the negation of animation without synthesis). While defusing the idea that any agency is possessed by things themselves, it prompts a return to, and quasi-ethical reflection on, the world of human behavior: the story closes with the lesson that humans "should examine and if possible rectify any obliquities in our recent conduct" (otherwise, the malignancy of things will visit retribution on us for our sins).[29] The story's moral—at the limits of a human world threatened by a conspiracy of objects and an uncertain agency—arises, as it were, "in a thing, darkly."

Things are also active in the familiar and strange darknesses of object-oriented ontology (OOO) and object-oriented—or "dark"—ecology (OOE). For Timothy Morton, the objects that conspire and interconnect in the multiscaled spatiotemporalities of the Anthropocene become "hyperobjects" undermining—to "uncanny effect"—"normative ideas of what an 'object' is in the first place" and disclosing an agency that appears "more than a little demonic."[30] The strangeness of the Anthropocene is "weirdly weird" in the manner of speculative realism's relation to reality.[31] Its work of darkness goes beyond conventional frames of horror and gothic monstrosity. Graham Harman's account, inspired by a curious fellowship with H. P. Lovecraft's fictions, comments that, "rather than inventing a monster with an arbitrary number of tentacles and dangerous sucker-mouths and telepathic brains, we must recognise that no such list of arbitrary weird properties is enough to do the trick. There must be some deeper and more malevolent principle at work in our monsters that escapes all such definition."[32] Words fail, monsters too: Lovecraft's style leaves "real objects" "locked in impossible tension with the crippled descriptive powers of language."[33] Which is why reality remains weird: it is "incommensurable with any attempt to represent or measure it."[34] Though "no *direct* contact" with real objects can be achieved, there may be "*indirect* access to things-in-themselves" through a process of "allusion" that indicates a thing without making it present: concealed from representation, a thing may nonetheless "deform the sensual world."[35] While experience testifies to a direct link between real and sensual things, the reality of objects remains out of reach because they have no direct relation to each other: they connect only in a "vicarious" manner.[36] Connection takes place in darkness and amid spectral powers: "vicarious causation" calls up a world composed not of isolated and mindless atoms but "packed full of ghostly real objects signalling to each other from inscrutable depths."[37] Withdrawn, a real object lies in "obscure, cavernous underworlds," leaving reality composed of "weird substances with a taste of the uncanny about them."[38] Some kind of "allure" arises when things assume "ghostly power" beyond their evident properties, a power of deep internal animation that seems to be "demonic."[39]

Dark ecology, in a similar vein, tracks the way in which reality finds itself possessed by a "withdrawn yet vivid spectrality of things," a world in which previously solid and fixed forms "become misty, shifty, nebulous, uncanny," where a "spectral strangeness" shadows all being from discrete life-forms to ecosystems and biospheres.[40] Like the weirdness evinced in the speculative realist understanding of objects, the Anthropocene discloses how reality "is becoming more vivid and unreal," "more spectral," and demands that "ecological existence" be considered in terms of relations "with ghosts, strangers, and specters."[41] Wider unrealities pertaining to matters of complexity, space, scale, and nature also evoke monstrosity: hyperobjects intimate "monstrously gigantic" temporal scales, preontological "ghosts" haunting social and psychic space and turning smooth and locatable space into places of "truly monstrous and uncanny dimensions."[42] The sense and scale of hyperobjectal haunting register a significant disturbance in—even collapse of—conventional scaffoldings of humanist thinking and, importantly, dispense with any grounding in an all-too-human, Romantic, and maternal idea of "nature." An "impediment to proper relationships with the earth and its life-forms," a notion of ecology without a "*concept* of nature" opens onto a "thinking of the interconnectedness" of living things.[43]

Yet here, too, be monsters. As the Anthropocene discloses nature "in its truly toxic and nightmare form,"[44] glimpses of an open, interconnected living ecology begin to be occluded by the figures thrown up to protect human borders and systems of thinking. The spectral reality of the Anthropocene comes to dominate all existence and every horizon, sucking all darkness into the consuming dark-depressions, dark-uncannies, and sickly dark-sweetnesses of dark ecology.[45] Rather than evincing a "dark side" to the "thinking of interconnectedness" required of ecology, the image of a "goth" sensibility—of staying with "a dying world"[46]—curtails the appeal to and pursuit of other modes of thought: it becomes too (darkly) enamored of a disturbed and dejected situation, too much in love with dis-easeful dying and too absorbed by figures of abjection and horror. Frankenstein's creature offers an image of human abjection.[47] Though appearing in a novel that "questions the very idea of nature," he enunciates (like the voice of "a poisoned rainforest") a demand "to love the disgusting, inert, and meaningless," the very conditions of humanity and its idea of nature that ecology sets out to dismantle.[48] Almost a hyperobject, the human species is reduced (again and like the world it has defiled) to a mirrored monstrosity absorbed in specular revulsion: "we," as human individuals addressed collectively, are said to be "in the vicelike death grip of a gigantic entity," and that entity is nothing other than "ourselves as the human species."[49] The formulation eloquently entertains coincident divisions of scale perceptible in the misrecognitions engendered by an Anthropocenic embrace of individual and species responsibility. But it also articulates a liberal and guilty abjection and self-loathing evoked in acknowledgments of an unthinking complicity in planetary destruction.

A familiar image from horror fiction reinforces, quite neatly and with weirder effect, the intimacy and self-loathing of human–

nonhuman recognition, a zombie species requiring a new form of subjective–collective recognition: "I am a component of a zombie." It occurs, however, in a familiar space of monstrosity, a "dark mirror" reflecting a human "I" as nothing more than "a cone in one of its eyes."[50] Richly revolting and appropriately weirding in terms of proximity, scale, and point of view, any outside cedes to an other side collapsing on a negative image of sameness: a reversed perspective still preserves (humanized) structures of opposition and difference (dark–light, other–self, monster–human). It follows the lines of polarized differences enunciated as the basis of humanstrosity in *Frankenstein*'s monstrous Romantic reiteration of *Paradise Lost*. But the monstrous observations on the identity-in-opposition of man's perplexing and intractable combination of baseness and nobility moves to another (undead) extremity, a conflation of the monstrocenic doubling of a human first-person plural as the untouchable sacredness of our selves mired in the shit (our feces, our effluent—but not compost) that we are.

In an ecology without nature and a world alien to humanity, there is much of (gothic) darkness and familiar strangeness produced, circulated, and recited in modernity to delineate and sustain inversely a rational and human order of things, as if to affirm negatively—and reassuringly blinkered—that we live, already and again, in gothic times. The loss of nature and the humanized, comforting world that dark ecology proposes imagines only the horrors of inversion, collapse, uncanniness, and abjection. In the process, it finds itself prepossessed by the negative dimensions of its dispatch of human and natural worlds: its avocation of goth sensibility reproduces the darker figures that seem to be as much impediments to the necessity of interconnected ecological thought as nature. We remain on "charnel ground":

> Without a world, there is no Nature. Without a world there is no life. What exists outside the charmed circles of Nature and life is a *charnel ground,* a place of life and death, of death-in-life and life-in-death, an undead place of zombies, viroids, junk DNA, ghosts, silicates, cyanide, radiation, demonic forces, pollution.[51]

Being without world or nature—for ecological thought—constitutes a necessary precondition, a sacrifice of the comfort and illusions of Nature's maternal charms to a realization of our everyday life/death in the fluorescently overlit "emergency room of ecological existence."[52] The new gothic times of this new dark age are indeed riven with familiar horrors, forms, and figures. But while they provide a disgusting and abject description of (humanized) nature and world as toxic and nightmarish, they remain recognizable from popular postapocalyptic fictions: their familiarity returns to human norms (like all good monsters) or closes off—in horrified recoil and paralysis—any glimpse of a future beyond human screens (remaining at the limits of monstrocene).

Dark ecology—rather than engaging with the complex and entangled realm of things—lurks at the edges of an uncanny or nebulous realm that assumes the limit function of "Thing" (*das Ding*) in object-oriented ontology.[53] Fantastic humanist imaginings meet their limit in the Thing without really troubling the phantasmatic-ideological milieu of human existence: "we are losing a fantasy—the fantasy of being immersed in a natural or benevolent Mother Nature."[54] While that loss makes for a "very dangerous person," it only discloses a vanishing maternal illusion, dissolving the light side of Romantic nature but not crossing the limits of the darkness that holds it place.[55]

The hauntology and monstrosity prepossessing dark ecology employ a particular version of Derrida's undoing of ontology without engaging the way in which spectrality acknowledges a more pervasive embrace of (inhuman/monstrous/vampiric) systems of exploitation, occultation, and exchange in which the "fantastic" or "phantasmagoric" form of the commodity defines all relations in a commerce of and among things. From this perspective, the Anthropocene has always been a "phantasmagorocene" in which doubled Derridean monstrosity plays a part:

> The future is necessarily monstrous: the figure of the future, that is, that which can only be surprising, that for which we are not prepared, you see, is heralded by species of monsters. A future that would not be monstrous would not be a future; it would already be predictable, calculable, and programmable tomorrow. All experience open to the future is prepared or prepares itself to welcome the monstrous *arrivant*.[56]

Unpredictable, unprogrammed, unrecognizable in any terms the present may project, future monstrosity (altogether different from anything a humanized world can imagine) would, by definition, exceed the representational capacities of fiction. As a dark ecological refrain, Derrida's "arrivant"—transposed as "strange stranger"—applies to life-forms, reconceives existents ("life is monstrosity"), and redefines species-difference, with the help of Darwin, as a collapse of standard scientific assumptions of "species, variation, monstrosity."[57] "Strange strangeness" also demonstrates an ethical openness to alterity at the heart of any encounter with other beings and an intimacy with hyperobjects as ("strange strangers") and preserves an open and surprising (if nearly extinguished) future—a "future future."[58]

Tautology accompanies invocations of the "arrivant" and strangeness, tacitly acknowledging another, more problematic aspect of Derrida's monstrous conception of futurity: raising issues of representation, naming, imagining; acknowledging a monstrous capacity of resistance; yet disturbing the ground and frames of figuration to disclose and close off a formless reality or unknown future. Tautology's repetition of and insistence on representation, however, register both representation's failure and some elusive, unnameable pressure on representation as it entangles and turns back on itself. Here the circulation of strange or monstrous figures is diverted from the monstrosity they tried to welcome, so that, in repetition, strangeness dissipates and the otherness of any encounter leaks away: "the strange stranger is not only strange but strangely so."[59] A strangely strange stranger is not a familiarly strange stranger, nor a strangely familiar stranger, nor a familiarly familiar stranger, nor even, maybe, a stranger at all. Hanging on to a future future that remains open and unpredictable also, in the repetition of terms announcing its reinvocation, involves (quite literally-rhetorically in the re-citation of the same term) closing it off, an excess tautology that returns to and restores the surfaces and limits of familiar (human) signification (repetition-difference becomes repetition-same).

"As soon as one perceives a monster in a monster, one begins to domesticate it."[60] That is, strangeness is assimilated and disarmed in a process rendering monsters homely and familiar. Surprise is curtailed, along with any sense of alterity and unpredictability. As difference becomes eclipsed, another effort is required to sustain the monstrosity of an "arrivant": "normal monstrosities"—domesticated, figured, familiarized—are distinguished from more disturbing and unpredictable types, "monstrous monstrosities." Differentiation, once framed by the urgency and difficulty of sustaining a position open and able to "welcome" monstrosity and futurity, tends toward a new caution against closing off the future and assimilating otherness: "one cannot say: 'here are our monsters,' without turning the monsters into pets."[61] Dark ecology's strangers are in danger, it seems, not so much of alerting or opening Anthropos to the precariousness and unpredictability of a future that is and is not its own but of remaining amid a familiar gloom, its monstrous, undead, spectral, and replicated avatars less promises of difference and possibility to come than banal, abject figures of barely altered sameness, "anthropets" of an ecology of darkness.

Sublime/Excrescence

Mary Shelley notes that "futurity, like the dark image in a phantasmagoria, came nearer and more near till it clasped the whole earth in its shadow."[62] The capacity to imagine self where it cannot be, beyond the limits of individual or species finitude, and thus, curiously, to enjoy the comforts of terror, traces an apocalyptic path through the Anthropocence: Chakrabarty, commenting on Alan Weisman's The World without Us (which details how a planet reshapes itself after the demise of humans), defines its impossible historico-narrative flight as an imaginative insertion of "us" into a future where we cannot be in order to comprehend current crises in a mode that privileges imagination over existence.[63] As Frances Ferguson puts it, "to think the sublime would be to think the unthinkable and exist in one's own non-existence."[64] Weisman's position compares with postnuclear imaginings of a world without humans.

Jonathan Schell's The Fate of the Earth tracked the devastation attendant on accidental nuclear catastrophe and depicted the few—nonhuman—beings capable of living on. Characterized as a "nuclear sublime," it retained eighteenth- and nineteenth-century aesthetic modes in that, maintaining distance, it did not immerse itself in a future of "total annihilation" but diverted into "calculations of exactly how horrible daily life would be," thereby deploying the "trick" of the sublime—living "to tell the tale of our encounter with it."[65] Evoking a dynamic of imagined loss and recovery, the sublime breaches continuities of sense, reason, imagination, subjectivity, and objectivity, then, in the gap that is thrown up; it invigorates a movement of restoration, the institution of an idea or activation of instincts of self-preservation, that renews consciousness and frees subjectivity from the feeling of "being bound by the world of circumstances" beyond control. In the same movement, it "returns us to the world of circumstances with a certain benevolence towards them."[66] The encounter, however, is always missed; the imagined threat and sense of power are "mislocated."[67]

Sublimity does not always proffer freedom, imaginative release, or even a return to self, species, and nature. Mary Shelley's *The Last Man* tells of the recovery and editing of fragments of a tale of the future found in the Sibyl's cave in 1818. The story, the writings of the last man on earth that are left for nonexistent readers of a future past, details the effects of a great pestilence wiping out humanity in the late twenty-first century. Amid its political and Romantic ruminations and melancholy—a melancholy engaging the losses of person, others, world, and future—a different sense of humanity and nature accompanies a revised mode of sublimity. The plague is not the only sign of an elemental disorder of things: great winds ravage the earth for months and intimate the incomprehensible presence of a "hostile agency at work around us." Its effects are physical and psychological, prompting thoughts not of sublime powers but of individual and species vanity, frailty, and finitude: in the proximity to powers beyond humanity, a proximity in which death is close by and random, individual and species insignificance and vulnerability come to the fore: "What are we, the inhabitants of this globe, least among the many that people infinite space? Our minds embrace infinity; the visible mechanism of our being is subject to the merest accident." Linked to a juxtaposition of individual frailty and mankind's immortality, the thought of infinity or species survival is no consolation. Instead, vain, arrogant assumptions about being "lords of creation, wielders of the elements, masters of life and death," are shaken by the scale of elemental disruption: "losing our identity, that of which we are chiefly conscious, we glory in the continuity of our species, and learn to regard death without terror. But when any whole nation becomes the victim of the destructive powers of exterior agents then indeed man shrinks into insignificance, he feels his tenure of life insecure, his inheritance on earth cut off."[68] Minor, meaningless, insecure, and divested of the illusion of the earth as his property and the ground of his future, Mankind loses access to the sublimity conjoining self and species. Only its negativity remains, without elevation or restoration: "a feeling of awe, a breathless sentiment of wonder, a painful sense of the degradation of humanity."[69] This erasure of sublimity discloses a more monstrous face and force. The negativity, moreover, assumes the place of Nature, transformed: no longer "our mother, our friend," it turns on humans with a "brow of menace"; previously passive, gentle, and benevolent, she becomes admonitory and powerful, evincing a cosmic capacity outside human illusions of control to "take our globe, fringed with mountains, girded by the atmosphere, containing the condition of our being, and all that man's mind could invent or force achieve; she could take the ball in her hand and cast it into space, where life would be drunk up, and man and all his efforts for ever annihilated."[70] Man is nothing, less than nothing: the last man recognizes himself and "all human powers and features" as "a monstrous excrescence of nature."[71]

An image of darkly destructive nature, feminine, absolutely indifferent, and capable of reducing humanity to nothing more than monstrous excrescence, also appears in Sadean philosophy, where nature manifests an implacable, relentless, and rational imperative evacuating and annihilating all the trappings sustaining humanity—virtue, goodness, morality, law, religion—except the violence come of pleasure in destruction. No more than "froth," excrescences cast by an indifferent nature intent on perpetual destruction, humans—in contrast to the vulnerabilities exposed in *The Last Man*—are enjoined to aspire to and replicate an imperative of violent destruction that can never be satisfied since it imagines—beyond any natural cycles—a "perpetual metempsychosis, a perpetual variation, a perpetual permutation embracing all things in perpetual movement."[72] Nature is divided between a "secondary nature" of cycles of light and dark, death and life, creation and destruction, and a nature of pure negation overriding "all laws" and lying beyond "all foundations."[73] A "pure negation," undark perhaps, remains beyond the horizon and limit of humanized constructions of nature. While the a-sublimity of Shelley's nature and the perpetual destruction of Sade's inversely glimpse its negative powers in violence and the degradation of humanity, the undoing of human illusions of mastery devolves to images of an absolute difference–indifference and another power and malevolence that mirrors the secondary negativity of human projections: rendered subordinate, appendages, excrescences, and froth, and, in Shelley's case, more open to the vulnerability of self, others, and species, humanity's status can at least take curious comfort in the fact that the planet is powerful enough to remain as impervious to human actions as it is indifferent to human life. A dark, active, and destructive nature at least remains stable in its malevolence and thereby absolves responsibility and occludes any sense of a precariously balanced and vulnerably interwoven system of relations.

Checked, the sublime stumbles: while imaginative powers of terror, wonder, or awe are turned into glimpses of pure negation, the possibility of renewal or recuperation just about remains. Discounting Burkean and Kantian models—the former for its submission at a distance and the latter for its "lack of speculation"—Morton advocates a "*speculative* sublime that actually tries to become intimate with the other."[74] To do so involves a disavowal of terror and awe: intimacy requires an encounter based on horror.

Here, it seems, the argument tacitly entangles various threads of horror and alterity: from the ethical "there is . . ." of Emmanuel Levinas ("there is . . . horror") to the abhorrence arising from crossings of supposedly inviolable corpo-symbolic borders in abjection, to the unbearable intimacy of "horrorism" in which any dignity-and-singularity-in-vulnerability between self and other is quite literally blown apart in a bloody, fatal inmixture. For all the horror it finds exuding from being, ethical respect sits oddly with other forms: abjection's intimacy engenders repulsion as well as establishing a point for the re-erection of symbolic and sacred values, and, drawing on Ann Radcliffe's polarization of terror and horror (in which the latter is numbing), horrorism admits only the paralysis of meaning, distinction, and sense that comes of a dissolution of human dignity and singularity.[75] Speculative or otherwise, the sublime offers little purchase on the Anthropocene. Neither terror nor horror will do.

The last man is only a figure of "ecocidal totalization."[76] It is difficult, then, to think of the Anthropocene in terms of a "recuperable sublime."[77] Though the "we" of the Anthropocene is born in relation to a projection of destruction and self-destruction, the rapidly succeeding dissipation of its multiscalar objectivity amid different names, times, and blames collapses distances and proximities, agencies and responsibilities, ideas and objects.

Anthropocene "erases all sublimity,"[78] except perhaps an "ecocidal sublime."[79] In contrast, postapocalyptic imaginings and narratives reenact a mode of sublime recuperation in which a future populated by monstrous humans from vampires to zombies stages a war of and within humanity in which an attempt is made to separate out its own "inhuman fragment."[80] These allegories for "humanity gone awry" employ monstrous figures to embody a "bad humanity" in the future so that good humans can imagine their redemption in the present. Sublime apocalyptic fictions thus exorcise "tendencies that have marked the species to date," turning current human failings into external and futural threats. Dividing good and bad, diverting humanity from itself, expunging inhumanity and projecting a bad present into a monstrous future, postapocalyptic fictions depart from and return to the present with a purged view of humanity and an all-too-rosy occlusion of its appalling conditions and divisions.[81] Projecting terrors and horrors into the future refuses to recognize the extent to which postapocalyptic scenarios are already playing themselves out, though not necessarily amid a "blessed" liberal world of abundant goods, freedoms, or leisure time.[82] Given that "the mansion of modern freedoms stands an ever-expanding base of fossil fuel use," and abundance for some is depletion for others, the horror of climate catastrophe is a horror for the "us" of the first world.[83] For many, those projected postapocalyptic conditions of precarity, violence, and scarcity are barely different to "what life already is, and necessarily has been, outside the luxuries of first world anxieties about the future of 'humanity.'"[84] Postapocalyptic narratives also close off horizons for thought, action, and different relations of being. Whether in the form of a renascent cosmopolitan humanity (as in *Arrival*) or a return to primitive humanism (as in *Mad Max*), future fictions serve to "occlude all the silenced, fugitive, submerged, unlived but imagined futures that are not those of man and world."[85]

Fictions, in delineating the losses of current Western lifestyles, give form to a future totality of destruction as nothing but horror. In doing so, they not only prompt anxious recoil, paralysis, or defensive reaction but display a huge failure of imagination: closing off, in horror, any consideration of a future different from the projection of one's own present displays the "incapacity to imagine what is other than itself as non-catastrophic."[86] Horror stakes a limit in darkness and destruction—and recoils; terror engenders an imagining of evil and a return to good, surviving, newly re-humanized, beyond the darkness. Yet while apocalyptic futures collapse on the present, save it, fantastically, from itself, divert its gaze from itself, or simply let it look away, neither terror nor horror challenges the terms of representation or moves away from polarizations of light and dark in which perceptions are framed. "Against this," Colebrook suggests, "we might think less of forces in strife or operating by way of good and evil, or light and dark, and more by way of twilight—discernible distinctions but always amid a potentially overwhelming indifference."[87] Indifference signals both a lack of pathological investment pertaining to particular vested interests and a significant reduction, if not rupturing, of the value and dominance given to the binary oppositions sustaining single yet partial perspectives. A crepuscular approach refuses polarities of light and dark with the aim of admitting greater diversity, fluidity, and openness to thinking—an admission, of course, that requires disenchantment and evacuation of prevailing assumptions (otherwise as-yet-but-how-to-be-imagined futures are all too hastily given form and shading).[88]

Indifference also characterizes a hard and implacable kernel integral to the dynamic of the sublime. Reading de Man reading Kant, Colebrook identifies an aspect of materiality that refuses to give itself to or support human imagination and cognition, a form of sublime whose materiality "has not been humanized" and discloses itself as "inhuman, purely intense, devoid of homely sense and affect."[89] As a mode engendering "privation" and "defacement," it refuses projections of sense, affect, or image. It is a "sublime without an idea"[90] and, by implication, without self or self-preservation. A site of nonrecuperation, nontranscendence, pure negation, an indifferent and in-different (dis)articulation of self and other, idea and thing, the material sublime enables the abandonment of other sublimities (as they institute ideas and preserve selves) and allows the rethinking of nature: "not nature as some absent sacred beyond" but "as a composed interconnected, and dynamic unity that is constituted as a series of modes of existence."[91] Such a dynamic unity is not, however, to be conceived as "Thing," as yet another limit for human imagination, fantasy, or reason to throw up, but as "some interconnected whole that refuses any noumenal presence."[92] There is no either–or here, no light or dark, but both and more: different relations, other possibilities.

Meshwork

Jacques Lacan: "everything that blossoms in the unconscious spreads like a mycelium."[93] Considering the Anthropocene need not be a matter of (catastrophes of) light or dark, thing or Thing, human or monster. The milieu of planetary existence is beyond the grasp of a humanized, polarized perspective, a matter of living, animate, and inert relations, interconnections, interdependencies; of vulnerabilities and risks within interrelated systems of alterity, rather than hierarchies of power and control; a matter of "precarious attachment to a fragile planet" which—though all-embracing—cannot be subsumed into a visible totality because it is difficult to view one's own milieu, difficult to establish "a point of view" for "multiple and incongruent systems."[94] The life emerging in this milieu, though "fragile," "is not especially human"[95] but is a multiplicity of temporal and spatial "non-overlapping incompossible lines of life and time,"[96] forms of ongoing existences outside and across a merely human perspective, and requires a thinking of it "as the milieu for our ongoing life, *and* as the fragile surface that holds us all together in one web of risked life, even if we cannot practically grasp or manage the dynamics of this totality."[97] As "one web of risked life," this milieu links "all bodies (organic and otherwise) into a single complex, multiply determined and dynamic whole."[98] It bears similarity to the "mesh" of entities "interconnected in an interobjective system" that is "infinite and beyond concept" and in which we still find ourselves "hopelessly entangled" while remaining "fully responsible."[99] But the web of risked life is not necessarily monstrous or inhabited by strange strangers. Nor is its totality so infinite and conceptual as not be whole. Nor does it necessarily engender extremes of hopelessness and responsibility for humans. It involves at least and in part a greater awareness of mutual vulnerabilities and shared precariousness as well as an intimacy of otherness that embraces rather than opposes human life, whatever that might become.

Perhaps some relation to this web of risked life can be explored in the unformed form of a mycelium, a meshwork if not a mesh, a planetary milieu or unconscious, as it were. When Lacan opens the unconscious to undarkness, he also cites a metaphor by which Freud characterizes its multiplicity and interconnectedness: "mycelium." The image of an extensive, interlinked complex of living fungal structures offers, for Freud, a sense of the "intricate network of our world of thought," a "meshwork" beyond consciousness, subjectivity, and interpretation to articulate the emergence of a dream wish through the "tangle of dream thoughts"; it appears "like a mushroom out of its mycelium."[100] A fecund metaphor for the unconscious, it suggests further entanglements of self, other, subject, enunciation, scene, and milieu. The meshwork concentrates meaning at particular nodal points or buttons (as dream wish) and disperses identity across the multitude of relations, connections, separations, gaps, and holes, whole in excess of finality, totality, or mastery. Marking a distribution and multiplication of sites of being amid conditions of intimate alterity, the meshwork challenges reductive operations of representation and manifests its own generative capacities: in this scene of figuration, whatever presses and condenses across various points of particular entanglement produces diverse effects and images, unformed shapings and shadings offering instances of (metaphorical–metonymic–material) invention and movement. "Mushroom" becomes the dream's "navel"; biological interconnections extend from ecology to living bodies: the knot and scar of every human birth marks the necessary and insurmountable relation between beings.

Mycelium offers a different image of planetary ecology as a "living network," a network that displays the possible sentience of, interdependence of, and communication between ecological systems: it is a network, moreover, that might help "save the planet," given the capacity of fungi to repair habitats, forests in particular; filter polluted water; recycle debris; and remove toxins.[101] For Anna Tsing, fungi tell different tales. Her ethno-ecological account examines the matsutake mushroom's place in and effect on various environmental, social, cultural, commercial, and global histories. It starts from the present as a precarious site of ruins and salvage. Questioning any idea of nature outside human relations, her discussion elaborates "interspecies entanglements" in a manner that refuses to separate ecological relations from capitalist transformations. Instead, she asks "what manages to live despite capitalism."[102] Moving away from *Anthropo-* requires attending to what may be left, to "patchy landscapes," "multiple temporalities," shifting scales, and "shifting assemblages of humans and non-humans."[103] Here mushrooms offer hints of survival—not in saving the world or redeeming our human selves but in "precarity," in living on and living with indeterminacy, vulnerability, unpredictability. Mushrooms, though living in the shadows amid decay, remain indifferent to the monstrocene, more open, perhaps, to tales of undarkness.

NOTES

1. Jacques Lacan, *Four Fundamental Concepts of Psychoanalysis*, trans. Alan Sheridan (Harmondsworth, U.K.: Penguin, 1977), 24.
2. Lacan, 25, 153.
3. Lacan, 29.
4. Jacques Lacan, "Position of the Unconscious," in *Ecrits*, trans. Bruce Fink (New York: W. W. Norton, 2006), 704.
5. Christophe Bonneuil and Jean-Baptiste Fressoz, *The Shock of the Anthropocene*, trans. David Fernbach (London: Verso, 2016), 11, 22.
6. Jacques Derrida, "No Apocalypse, Not Now (Seven Missiles, Seven Missives)," *diacritics* 14, no. 2 (1984): 23.
7. Donna Haraway, *Staying with the Trouble: Making Kin in the Chthulucene* (Durham, N.C.: Duke University Press, 2016), 101.
8. See Paul J. Crutzen and Eugene F. Stoermer, "The 'Anthropocene,'" *IGBPNewsletter* 41 (2000): 18, and Dipesh Chakrabarty, "The Climate of History: Four Theses," *Critical Inquiry* 35 (2009): 208.
9. Claire Colebrook, *Death of the PostHuman: Essays in Extinction* (Ann Arbor, Mich.: Open Humanities Press, 2014), 1:21.
10. Catherine Malabou, "The Brain of History; or, The Mentality of the Anthropocene," *South Atlantic Quarterly* 116, no. 1 (2017): 41.
11. Bruno Latour, "Agency at the Time of the Anthropocene," *New Literary History* 45, no. 1 (2014): 2.
12. Latour, 3.
13. Bonneuil and Fressoz, *Shock*, 11.
14. Anna Tsing, *The Mushroom at the End of the World: On the Possibility of Life in Capitalist Ruins* (Princeton, N.J.: Princeton University Press, 2015), 2, and Colebrook, *Death of the PostHuman*, 11.
15. Colebrook, *Death of the PostHuman*, 11.
16. Timothy Clark, "Derangements of Scale," in *Telemorphosis*, ed. Tom Cohen (Ann Arbor, Mich.: Open Humanities Press, 2012), 150–51.
17. Chakrabarty, "Climate," 201.
18. Chakrabarty, 197–98.
19. Rob Nixon, *Slow Violence and the Environmentalism of the Poor* (Cambridge, Mass.: Harvard University Press, 2011), 2, 14.
20. Haraway, *Staying*, 101.
21. Bonneuil and Fressoz, *Shock*, 12.
22. Michel Serres, *The Natural Contract*, trans. Elizabeth MacArthur and William Paulson (Ann Arbor: University of Michigan Press, 1995), 30.

23. Serres, 4.

24. Tom Cohen, Claire Colebrook, and J. Hillis Miller, *Twilight of the Anthropocene Idols* (Ann Arbor, Mich.: Open Humanities Press, 2016), 8.

25. Cohen et al., 7; Bonneuil and Fressoz, *Shock*, 13; Haraway, *Staying*; Bernard Stiegler, *The Neganthropocene,* trans. William Ross (London: Open Humanities Press, 2018), 39.

26. Mary Shelley, *Frankenstein* (Oxford: Oxford University Press, 1969), 54.

27. M. R. James, "The Malice of Inanimate Objects," in *Casting the Runes and Other Stories,* ed. Michael Cox (Oxford: Oxford University Press, 1987), 288–92.

28. James, 292.

29. James.

30. Timothy Morton, *Hyperobjects* (Minneapolis: University of Minnesota Press, 2013), 139, 29.

31. Timothy Morton, *Dark Ecology* (New York: Columbia University Press, 2016), 8.

32. Graham Harman, *Weird Realism* (Winchester, U.K.: Zero Books, 2012), 22.

33. Harman, 27.

34. Harman, 51.

35. Harman, 238.

36. Harman, 256.

37. Graham Harman, "On Vicarious Causation," *Collapse* II (2007): 187.

38. Harman, 195; Graham Harman and Keith Tilford, "On the Horror of Phenomenology," *Collapse* IV (2008): 348.

39. Graham Harman, *Towards Speculative Realism* (Winchester, U.K.: Zero Books, 2010), 137.

40. Morton, *Dark Ecology,* 74.

41. Morton, *Hyperobjects,* 194; Morton, *Dark Ecology,* 198.

42. Morton, *Dark Ecology,* 25; Morton, *Hyperobjects,* 181; Morton, *Dark Ecology,* 20, 8.

43. Morton, *Ecology without Nature,* 2, 24, 184.

44. Morton, *Dark Ecology,* 59.

45. Morton, 5, 17, 160.

46. Morton, *Ecology without Nature,* 184.

47. Timothy Morton, "*Frankenstein* and Ecocriticism," in *The Cambridge Companion to Mary Shelley,* ed. Andrew Smith (Cambridge: Cambridge University Press, 2016), 148.

48. Morton, *Ecology without Nature,* 194.

49. Morton, *Dark Ecology,* 25.

50. Morton, 25, 35, 42.

51. Morton, *Hyperobjects,* 120.

52. Morton, 120.

53. Peter Wolfendale, *Object-Oriented Philosophy: The Noumenon's New Clothes* (Falmouth, U.K.: Urbanomic, 2014).

54. Morton, *Hyperobjects*, 196.

55. Morton, 196.

56. Jacques Derrida, "Passages—from Traumatism to Promise," in *Points*, ed. Elisabeth Weber, trans. Peggy Kamuf et al. (Stanford, Calif.: Stanford University Press, 1992), 386.

57. See Morton, *Dark Ecology*, 18; Morton, "*Frankenstein* and Ecocriticism," 153; and Timothy Morton, "Thinking Ecology: The Mesh, the Strange Stranger, and the Beautiful Soul," *Collapse* VI (2010): 271.

58. See Morton, "Thinking Ecology," 274; Morton, *Dark Ecology*, 67.

59. Morton, "Thinking Ecology," 274.

60. Derrida, "Passages," 386.

61. Jacques Derrida, "Some Statements and Truisms about Neologisms, Newisms, Postisms, Parasitisms, and Other Small Seismisms," in *States of Theory*, ed. David Carroll (Stanford, Calif.: Stanford University Press, 1990), 80.

62. Mary Shelley, *The Last Man*, ed. Morton Paley (Oxford: Oxford University Press, 1994), 257.

63. Chakrabarty, "Climate," 197–98.

64. Frances Ferguson, "The Nuclear Sublime," *diacritics* 14, no. 2 (1984): 6.

65. Ferguson, 6–7.

66. Ferguson, 7.

67. Ferguson.

68. Shelley, *Last Man*, 230.

69. Shelley, 232.

70. Shelley.

71. Shelley, 467.

72. D. A. F. Sade, *Juliette*, trans. Austryn Wainhouse (New York: Grove Press, 1968), 765–67, 769.

73. Gilles Deleuze, *Coldness and Cruelty* (New York: Zone, 1991), 27.

74. Morton, *Realist Magic: Objects, Ontology, Causality* (Ann Arbor, Mich.: Open Humanities Press, 2013), 128.

75. See Emmanuel Levinas, *There Is: Existence without Existents*, trans. Sean Hand (Oxford: Blackwell, 1989), 29; Julia Kristeva, *Powers of Horror*, trans. Leon S. Roudiez (New York: Columbia University Press, 1982), 17; Adriana Cavarero, *Horrorism*, trans. William McCuaig (New York: Columbia University Press, 2009), 23; Ann Radcliffe, "On the Supernatural in Poetry," *New Monthly Magazine* 16 (1826): 150.

76. Cohen, *Telemorphosis*, 71.

77. Colebrook, *Death of the PostHuman*, 105.

78. Colebrook, 81.

79. Colebrook, 27.

80. Colebrook, 84.

81. Colebrook, 206.
82. Claire Colebrook, *Sex after Life: Essays in Extinction* (Ann Arbor, Mich.: Open Humanities Press, 2014), 2:17; Claire Colebrook, "Anti-catastrophic Time," *New Formations* 92 (2017): 103.
83. Chakrabarty, "Climate," 208.
84. Colebrook, "Anti-catastrophic Time," 103.
85. Colebrook, 108.
86. Colebrook, 103.
87. Cohen et al., *Twilight of the Anthropocene Idols,* 84.
88. Colebrook, *Death of the PostHuman,* 55.
89. Cohen et al., *Twilight of the Anthropocene Idols,* 123, 113.
90. Cohen et al., 120.
91. Cohen et al., 118.
92. Cohen et al., 120.
93. Jacques Lacan, *Four Fundamental Concepts of Psychoanalysis,* trans. Alan Sheridan (Harmondsworth, U.K.: Penguin, 1977), 26.
94. Colebrook, *Death of the PostHuman,* 11, 21, 11.
95. Colebrook, *Sex after Life,* 148.
96. Colebrook, "Anti-catastrophic Time," 112.
97. Colebrook, *Death of the PostHuman,* 10.
98. Colebrook, 10.
99. Morton, *Hyperobjects,* 83; Morton, "Thinking Ecology," 268, 277.
100. Sigmund Freud, *The Interpretation of Dreams,* trans. James Strachey (Harmondsworth, U.K.: Penguin, 1976), 671–72.
101. Paul Stamets, *Mycelium Running: How Mushrooms Can Save the World* (Berkeley, Calif.: Ten Speed Press, 2005), 55, 58, 69.
102. Tsing, *Mushroom,* vii.
103. Tsing, 19–20.

Contributors

Fred Botting is professor of English at Kingston University. He has written extensively on gothic fiction and literary theory and published the monographs *Gothic, Limits of Horror: Technology, Bodies, Gothic,* and *Gothic Romanced: Consumption, Gender, and Technology in Contemporary Fictions.*

Timothy Clark is professor emeritus of English at the University of Durham. His most recent books are *Ecocriticism on the Edge: The Anthropocene as a Threshold Concept* and *The Value of Ecocriticism.*

Rebecca Duncan is research fellow at the Linnaeus University Centre for Concurrences in Colonial and Postcolonial Studies and coordinator of the research cluster Aesthetics of Empire. She is author of *South African Gothic: Anxiety and Creative Dissent in the Post-apartheid Imagination and Beyond* and coeditor of *Patrick McGrath and His Worlds: Madness and the Transnational Gothic.*

Justin D. Edwards is professor of English and chair in gothic studies at the University of Stirling. He is coauthor of *Mobility at Large: Globalization, Textuality, and Innovative Travel Writing* and *Grotesque*; editor of *Technologies of the Gothic in Literature and Culture: Technogothics*; and coeditor of *Tropical Gothic in Literature and Culture: The Americas* and *B-Movie Gothic: International Perspectives.*

Michael Fuchs is postdoctoral fellow at the University of Oldenburg in Germany. He is coeditor of six books, most recently *Fantastic Cities: American Urban Spaces in Science Fiction, Fantasy, and Horror.*

Rune Graulund is associate professor in American literature and culture at the Center for American Studies and director of the research cluster Anthropocene Aesthetics at the University of Southern Denmark. He is coauthor of *Grotesque* and *Mobility at Large: Globalization, Textuality, and Innovative Travel Writing*.

Johan Höglund is professor of English at Linnaeus University. He is author of *The American Imperial Gothic: Popular Culture, Empire, Violence* and coeditor of *Animal Horror Cinema: Genre, History, and Criticism*; *B-Movie Gothic: International Perspectives*; and *Nordic Gothic*.

Esthie Hugo is associate lecturer in English at the University of the Witwatersrand.

Dawn Keetley is professor of English and film at Lehigh University. She is author of *Making a Monster: Jesse Pomeroy, the Boy Murderer of 1870s Boston* and editor of *Jordan Peele's Get Out: Political Horror*. She has edited and coedited collections on *The Walking Dead* and is also coeditor of *Plant Horror: Approaches to the Monstrous Vegetal in Fiction and Film* and *Ecogothic in Nineteenth-Century American Literature*.

Laura R. Kremmel is assistant professor of English at South Dakota School of Mines and Technology. She is coeditor of *The Palgrave Handbook to Horror Literature* and author of *Romantic Medicine and the Gothic Imagination: Morbid Anatomies*.

Timothy Morton is Rita Shea Guffey Chair in English at Rice University. They are author of *All Art Is Ecological, Spacecraft,* and *Hyperobjects* (Minnesota, 2013) and coauthor of *Hyposubjects: On Becoming Human*.

Barry Murnane is associate professor of German studies at the University of Oxford and fellow in German at St. John's College. He is author of *"Verkehr mit Gespenstern": Gothic und Moderne bei Franz Kafka* and coeditor of collections on German gothic, including *Populäre Erscheinungen: Der deutsche Schauerroman um 1800* and *Popular Revenants: The German Gothic and Its International Reception, 1800–2000*.

Jennifer Schell is professor of English at the University of Alaska Fairbanks. She is author of *"A Bold and Hardy Race of Men": The Lives and Literature of American Whalemen*.

Lisa M. Vetere is associate professor of English at Monmouth University. Her writing was published in the collection *The Ecogothic in Nineteenth-Century American Literature*.

Sara Wasson is reader in gothic studies at Lancaster University. She is author of *Transplantation Gothic: Tissue Transfer in Literature, Film, and Medicine* and *Urban Gothic of the Second World War: Dark London*.

Jeffrey Andrew Weinstock is professor of English at Central Michigan University and associate editor for *Journal of the Fantastic in the Arts*. His books include *Giving the Devil His Due: Satan and Cinema, The Monster Theory Reader* (Minnesota, 2019), and *The Age of Lovecraft* (Minnesota, 2016).

Index